Management for Professionals

More information about this series at http://www.springer.com/series/10101

B. Rajesh Kumar

Wealth Creation in the World's Largest Mergers and Acquisitions

Integrated Case Studies

Springer

B. Rajesh Kumar
Institute of Management Technology
Dubai, United Arab Emirates

ISSN 2192-8096 ISSN 2192-810X (electronic)
Management for Professionals
ISBN 978-3-030-02362-1 ISBN 978-3-030-02363-8 (eBook)
https://doi.org/10.1007/978-3-030-02363-8

Library of Congress Control Number: 2018959863

This Springer imprint is published by the registered company Springer Nature Switzerland AG
The registered company address is: Gewerbestrasse 11, 6330 Cham, Switzerland

Preface

Mergers and acquisitions (M&As) represent a major force in modern financial and economic environment. Whether in times of boom or bust, M&As have emerged as a compelling strategy for growth. The modern day biggest companies have all taken its form today on account of a series of restructuring activities like multiple mergers. Acquisitions continue to remain as the quickest route companies take to operate in new markets and to add new capabilities and resources. The value of M&A deal rose from $200 billion in 1992 to about $4.74 trillion by 2017. The deal volume during the historic M&A wave during the period 1995–2000 totaled more than $12 trillion. This casebook clinically analyzes the wealth created in the world's largest mergers and acquisitions in terms of deal value. This casebook focuses on integrative approach to examine all aspects of mergers and acquisition processes.

The first chapter introduces the concept of mergers and acquisitions, processes involved, and strategic perspectives on mergers and acquisition. The chapter also aims for cross-fertilization in theory building and applied research by examining the linkage between mergers, acquisitions, and wealth creation. The following chapters discuss the largest mergers and acquisitions in terms of deal value and examine the wealth created by the merging firms. Another objective is to examine whether corporate performance has improved after merger or acquisition.

The acquisition of Mannesmann by Vodafone was aimed to consolidate Vodafone AirTouch's position in Europe. With the union, Vodafone and Mannesmann had controlling stakes in ten European markets, thereby giving the merged entity the most extensive European coverage for any wireless carrier. The merger between AOL and Time Warner created the world's largest vertically integrated media and entertainment company. The merger was considered as one of the biggest failed mergers as the expected synergies between AOL and Time Warner never actually materialized. The acquisition of Verizon Wireless by Verizon Communications elevated Verizon's position with leadership position in network performance, profitability, and cash flow. The combination of highly complementary portfolios of Dow and DuPont was intended to create leadership position for the combined company in the industry. In one of the largest transatlantic deals ever, Belgian-based InBev acquired Anheuser-Busch in a deal valued at $52 billion. The Kraft–Heinz merger resulted in the creation of the third largest food and beverage company in North America and fifth largest food and beverage company in the world.

Pfizer has grown by megamergers and acquisitions. In the year 2000, Pfizer acquired Warner–Lambert for $111.8 billion. In the year 2003, Pfizer and Pharmacia merged to become a leading research-based pharmaceutical company in the world. During December 1998, Exxon and Mobil merged to become the third largest oil company in the world at the time of the deal. Citicorp and Travelers Group merged to create the world's largest financial services company with banking, insurance, and investment operations in 100 countries. AT&T acquired Time Warner to become the premier integrated communications company in the world.

In 2007, ABN AMRO was acquired by a consortium of banks known as RFS Holdings BV. This acquisition was aimed to create stronger businesses with enhanced market presence and growth prospects. The merger between Glaxo Wellcome and SmithKline created the world's largest pharmaceutical company. Royal Dutch Shell acquired BG Group for US$70 billion. This acquisition catapulted Shell as the world's second largest non-state oil company after ExxonMobil in terms of market capitalization. AT&T and BellSouth Corporation merged to emerge as an integrated provider in the wireless, broadband, video, voice, and data markets. In 2001, Comcast took over AT&T broadband unit for $72 billion. This deal created the biggest cable company in the United States with 22.3 million subscribers. JPMorgan Chase had grown through mergers and acquisitions over a period of time. In the year 2000, the Chase Manhattan Corporation acquired JPMorgan & Company in an all-stock deal valued at $30.9 billion. Charter Communications' acquisition of Time Warner Cable and Bright House Networks created the second largest broadband provider and third largest pay-TV provider in the United States. In 2015, Actavis completed the acquisition of Allergan Inc. in a cash and share transaction valued at $70.5 billion. In one of the largest ever acquisition in the technology sector, Dell acquired EMC in a cash and stock deal valued at $74 billion. Altria Group had spun off Philip Morris International tobacco arm. In 1999, Vodafone Group Plc and AirTouch Communications Inc. merged to create one of the world's leading mobile telecommunications group.

Verizon Communications was formed by the merger of Bell Atlantic and GTE Corp. in one of the largest mergers in US history. British Petroleum merged with Amoco in a deal valued at $48.2 billion. US West had merged with Qwest. Qwest later merged with CenturyLink. WorldCom and MCI had merged in a deal valued at $37 billion. In the year 2016, Microsoft Corp. had acquired LinkedIn for $196 per share in an all-cash transaction valued at $26.2 billion.

In one of the biggest acquisition, P&G had acquired Gillette in a deal valued at $57 billion. In one of the biggest hostile acquisition, Oracle took over PeopleSoft to become the world's second largest seller of business applications software behind SAP. The Bank of America had undertaken a series of acquisitions as a part of its growth strategy.

Gaz de France (GDF) was acquired by ENGIE SA in a reverse merger deal valued at €70 billion. In the year 2004, after a bitter takeover battle, France's largest drug maker, Aventis, was acquired by a smaller rival company Sanofi-Synthelabo SA in a deal valued for € 55.2 billion. Bayer acquired Monsanto for

US$128 per share in an all-cash transaction. In 2009, Roche had acquired Genentech for $46.8 billion. The acquisition of Orange was a major step of France Telecom toward the strategy of internationalization to become European leader and global player. Merck and Schering-Plough Corp. merged in a deal valued at $41.1 billion. Zeneca and Astra had merged to form a new company called AstraZeneca in a deal valued at $67 billion. HP and Compaq had merged in a deal valued at $25 billion. WhatsApp was acquired by Facebook in a deal valued at $19 billion. The JDS Uniphase–SDL merger was valued at $41 billion. KKR acquired First Data Corp. in a deal valued at $29 billion. Lucent Technologies Inc., the top maker of phone equipment, bought Ascend Communications Inc. for $20.3 billion in stock for expansion into the fast-growing internet equipment industry. France-based Vivendi and its television subsidiary Canal+ had acquired Canada-based Seagram in a stock deal valued at $33.7 billion. In one of the biggest transatlantic mergers, German automaker Daimler-Benz purchased Chrysler for $38 billion. This merger turned out to be a colossal failure. In 2006, Mittal Steel announced a hostile bid for Arcelor. After a bitter struggle, the two companies merged to become the world's largest steel company.

Dubai, United Arab Emirates B. Rajesh Kumar

Acknowledgment

I would like to thank the production and editorial staff at Springer who guided this book through the publishing process. I wish to acknowledge the valuable guidance and support of Matthew Amboy, Senior Editor at Springer. My thanks go to Su Faith, Assistant Editor, and her team for all the cooperation and support for the publication of this book. I also acknowledge the content of various websites and sources of information to which I referred.

Contents

Mergers and Acquisitions 1

Introduction

Corporate restructuring like mergers and acquisitions (M&A) has become worldwide phenomena for firms to achieve their strategic objectives. In an ever-changing business environment, mergers and acquisitions have become one of the quickest routes for companies to operate in new markets and add resources to existing resources. In an environment of globalization and rapid technological changes, mergers and acquisitions have become a compelling strategy for growth for companies. M&A is a common strategic technique adopted by companies in both boom and bust times. M&A have also great significance in the modern political environment. The corporate battle between Mittal Steel and its unsolicited bid on Arcelor had stirred up passions in Europe. All modern-day corporations have undertaken restructuring activity like M&A in different periods of time. M&A are processes of importance not only to companies but also to all other stakeholders like employees, competitors, communities, and the economy.

M&A is a century-old activity which happened in waves. The value of M&A deal rose from $200 billion in 1992 to about $4.74 trillion by 2017. The deal volume during the historic M&A wave during the period 1995–2000 totaled more than $12 trillion. During the period 1996–2001, American companies were involved in 74,000 acquisitions and 57,000 alliances (Dyer et al., 2004). It was said that during that period of 6 years, CEOs signed roughly an acquisition and a partnership every hour each day.

The first merger wave happened during 1890–1905 period. During this period approximately 1800 firms disappeared as a result of consolidation. Major companies like General Electric, Eastman Kodak, American Tobacco, and DuPont were formed during this merger wave. The second merger wave was during the 1920s. This period was characterized by market crash during 1903–1904 and World War I. During this wave, approximately 12,000 firms got disintegrated. The third wave

B. R. Kumar, *Wealth Creation in the World's Largest Mergers and Acquisitions*, Management for Professionals, https://doi.org/10.1007/978-3-030-02363-8_1

Table 1.1 Value of M&A deals during 2012–2017

Year	Amount in billion dollars
2012	3329.56
2013	3698.86
2014	4811.91
2015	5871.02
2016	4892.97
2017	4740.97

Source: Statista (2018)

of 1960s was also known as the period of conglomerate merger movement. This merger movement was classified as the period of unrelated mergers where companies choose the path of diversification into new product markets. The fourth wave of merger wave was during the 1980s. This wave was characterized by the hostile takeover activity. This period also witnessed the rapid growth and decline of the leveraged buyout movement. The fifth wave of mergers that occurred in the 1990s was known as strategic mergers. The fifth wave was characterized by the advancement of new technologies and globalization of products, services, and capital markets. The fifth wave focused on core competencies as source of competitive advantage (Table 1.1).

Strategic Drivers for M&A in Different Industry Sectors

Globalization of products and service goods has facilitated the trend of convergence of consumer needs, preferences, and tastes which have led to the creation of demand and supply of goods and services in different countries. Technological advancement has led to massive investment in R&D, design, marketing, and distribution. Companies have to adapt globalization through mergers and acquisitions to achieve economies of scale and recover cost. Financial innovation and easy accessibility of capital to finance acquisitions were factors which contributed for the development of M&A. Companies need to offer services across geographies to compete effectively. The process of acquiring is much faster than that of organic growth strategy. The success of large companies can be attributed to its acquiring skills. Using M&A strategy, Siemens was able to expand quickly into major electronic market like in the United States. Siemens has integrated these acquisitions into a solid strategic platform. Cisco Systems has a well-articulated strategy of expanding its product range through acquisition of small niche companies. General Electric has made over 791 acquisitions over a period of time. The reasons to acquire or merge a firm may range from industry consolidation, customer acquisition, forward or backward integration, or synergy with existing businesses.

During the period 1985–2007, 51 large pharmaceutical companies got consolidated into 10 organizations. M&A activity peaked during the 1980s and 1990s. Most of the leading firms in pharmaceutical sectors are the product of one or more horizontal mergers. For example, GlaxoWellcome–SmithKline Beecham is the product of combination of GlaxoWellcome, SmithKline, and Beecham. Aventis has resulted from the consolidation of Hoechst, Rhone-Poulenc, Rorer, Marion, Merrill, and Dow. Pfizer is the product of the combination of Pfizer, Warner–Lambert, Pharmacia, Upjohn, and Wyeth. The major factors for mergers and acquisitions in pharmaceutical sector had been the desire for greater scale, market share, improved geographical expansion, and enhanced technological competencies. Major pharmaceutical companies involve in M&A activity for building up their drug pipelines. The increasing cost of the cycle of development of new chemical entity compels pharma firms to choose options like mergers and acquisitions. The merger of pharma giants like GlaxoWellcome and SmithKline Beecham PLC reflects the importance of research as a critical factor for the survival of pharma companies. The 1990s was known as the era of horizontal mergers in pharmaceutical industry. Pharma companies such as American Home Products (AHP), American Cyanamid, Glaxo and Wellcome, Hoechst and MMD, Upjohn, and Pharmacia undertook horizontal mergers in the 1990s. M&A in the pharma sector lead to synergy in scale and operations. The late 1980s and early 1990s saw the genesis of megamergers. It was stated that after the merger of Ciba and Sandoz to form Novartis in the year 1996, the cost savings amounted to CHF 1.5 billion in the first year alone of the merger. Companies find it critical to merge or acquire when there is shortfall in their R&D pipeline. For example, Glaxo acquired Wellcome in the year 1995 when its bestselling drug Zantac was becoming off patent. The acquisition of Wellcome renewed its pipeline overnight which included drugs like Seroxat. The major challenge faced by pharmaceutical firms is the aftereffects of patent expiration of large number of blockbuster drugs. In the year 2013, nearly $137 billion worth of branded drugs lost their market exclusivity. Pfizer's revenues from major drugs like Zoloft and Zithromax were reduced by 70% since the patent expiry on these drugs which happened in the year 2005 and 2006. The biggest blockbuster drug of Pfizer – Lipitor – became off patent in the year 2011. One of the major reasons for Pfizer's acquisition of Wyeth Pharma had been to acquire Wyeth's lineup of vaccines and biotechnology medicines. The costs of research process are increasing significantly. In the United States, the average time from discovery to Food and Drug Administration (FDA) approval is approximately 15 years. The odds of a compound making it through this process are around 1 in 10,000, while the cost of development is around $200 million. Consolidation like mergers and acquisitions is transforming the pharma sector in the context of changing environmental conditions.

Telecommunication sector is facing the challenges of growth, convergence, business transformation, technological change, and regulatory pressures. The industry has witnessed the removal of many barriers of entry on account of factors like lower prices, higher quality, and higher degree of innovation. The aftereffects had been that now telecom firms are perusing the strategy of M&A or alliance with firms which already have a presence in that market. Costly investments in the sector are another driving force behind M&A activity in the sector. Consolidation is a by-product of fall in mobile telephony revenues. The consolidation in the telecom sector can be categorized into three forms: cross-market consolidation, in-market consolidation, and consolidation of ownership for control. In cross-market form of consolidation, major telecom operator groups acquire controlling stakes in other groups which have a presence in multiple markets. "In-market" consolidation consists of merging operations within the same market. The last form involves ownership consolidation for greater control of operations. The biggest M&A deals in this sector consisted of Vodafone AirTouch–Mannesmann merger, SBC–Ameritech deal, and AT&T/Bell South deal.

M&A in technology sector is basically meant to acquire new products and technologies. In the information technology sector, acquisition of knowledge is the major value driver for M&A activity. Convergence in the industry sector is another trend observed. There has been growing demand for one-stop shopping. The modern trend is that IT services companies offer all services from integrated computer systems to IT consulting to overseeing back-office processes. The primary driver for deals in this sector had been the demand for strategic technologies in support of convergence of the industry sector. Convergence has emerged as a major theme for facilitating M&A in the global technology sector (Kumar, 2012). In the technology market, there had been blurring of the boundary between the software and hardware sectors. The major technology deals in the sector include JDS Uniphase deal, HP–Compaq merger, KKR's first deal, Lucent Technologies–Ascend Communications merger, etc.

The merger waves in entertainment and media sector had been in response to deregulation and technology development. The changing nature of the industry with strategic shift toward digital media acted as a catalyst for deal activity in the sector. The M&A wave in the E&M sector happened as old media companies reoriented themselves to emerge as online media companies. Some of the biggest deals in the sector included Time Warner merger, Time Warner's acquisition of Turner Broadcasting, Time Warner AOL deal, Disney's acquisition of ABC, Viacom's acquisition of CBS, and the Vivendi CBS deal. In 1989, Time Inc. and Warner Communications merged to create a world power in the field of media and entertainment. During the year 2000, Time Warner was taken over by American Online at a 71% premium to its share price on the announcement date. This merger created the world's largest vertically integrated media and entertainment company. But this merger proved to be one of the world's most disastrous merger in the history of M&A.

In the energy sector, M&A in the 1980s and 1990s were concentrated in the North American region. The decade of 1990s was the period of mega mergers in energy sector which witnessed mergers like Exxon merger with Mobil, BP's acquisition of Amoco, and Chevron's merger with Texaco. During the boom period, the high commodity prices boosted the cash flows of major oil companies which led to the increase in M&A activity.

The primary motives for mergers and acquisition in finance sector are costs savings and revenue enhancement. M&A in financial sector also aimed to achieve economies of scale. Economies of scope in the financial sector M&A arise from cross selling of products. The synergies for financial sector M&A can be attributed to client-driven linkages, geographic linkages, and product-driven linkages. M&A

deals in financial sector would benefit from the diversification of income from multiple products, client groups, and geographies. The major strategic drivers for M&A activity in financial sector are advances in information technology, financial deregulation, and globalization of financial and real markets. The technological developments have also facilitated financial service firms to offer a wide array of products and services to a large number of clients across different geographic areas. The removal of legal and regulatory barriers has led to financial industry consolidation through cross-border merger and acquisition activity. Over 10,000 financial firms were acquired in the industrialized nations during the period 1990–2001. Some of the biggest deals in the sector include Royal Bank of Scotland's acquisition of ABN AMRO Holding, Citicorp–Travelers Group merger, and NationsBank acquisition by Bank of America.

The steel industry has witnessed mergers, concentration of resources, and streamlining of operations between steel mills, raw material suppliers, iron and steel manufacturers, equipment manufacturers, and traders particularly in Europe and the United States. M&A activity in steel industry aims to achieve economies of scale, to increase negotiating power with customers and vendors, and to enter into new geographic areas. The biggest merger in the sector had been the ArcelorMittal deal. The strategic drivers in the auto sector had been economies of scale and augmentation of product ranges. The biggest deal in auto sector was the Daimler–Chrysler deal.

The companies in the consumer goods sector use M&A to expand globally, enter new markets, and focus on core brands. The major deals in the sector include Procter & Gamble's acquisition of Gillette, InBev's acquisition of Anheuser-Busch, and KKR's acquisition of RJR Nabisco.

Different M&A Strategies[1]

M&A strategy can be classified as the overcapacity M&A, geographic roll-up M&A, and product or market extension M&A. Mergers and acquisitions can become a solution to deal with overcapacity in mature industry. It can also become an alternate option to roll-up competitions in geographically fragmented industries. M&A also can be used to extend new products or markets. It can become a substitute for R&D and "exploit eroding industry boundaries by inventing an industry." In overcapacity M&A, the strategic objective of the acquirer would be to eliminate excess capacity, gain market share, and create operationally efficient environment. The acquisition of Chrysler Corporation by Daimler-Benz and Manufacturers Hanover by Chemical Bank are examples of the overcapacity M&A. The geographical roll-up M&A is characterized by successful companies expanding geographically but at the same time remaining operationally local. For example, the acquisition of local banks by Bank One. In product or market extension acquisition,

[1] Joseph L Bower, Not All M&A are alike, and that matters, *Harvard Business Review*, March 2001, Page 93–101.

acquisitions are used to extend a firm's product line or its international coverage. An example for product or market extension acquisition is the buyout of Snapple by Quaker Oats. Acquisitions are used to acquire R&D skills. The successes of Microsoft and Cisco can be attributed to the substitute acquisitions for R&D. For example, Cisco acquired approximately 62 companies to gain R&D expertise. Industry convergence M&A occurs when firms observe that there is scope for the emergence of new industry and adopt a strategy to position itself in the new industry by culling resources from existing industries which are in decline stage. The buyout of Paramount and Blockbuster by Viacom and purchase of NCR, McCaw, and TCI by AT&T are examples for this type of mergers.

Motivation for Mergers and Acquisitions

Bidding firms acquire target firms for many reasons. Acquisition of management talent and capabilities could be a source of potential gain in M&A activity. The acquired management talent possesses firm-specific or industry-specific knowledge which would be of immense value to the acquirer firm in target's industry sector. The human resources team of the target company may have strong relationships with other stakeholders such as suppliers and customers.

Mature industries are characterized by low growth rates. There exists heightened competition in mature industries with fixed-cost structures. Hence for survival, companies engage in M&A activity. The strategic driver for overcapacity M&As is to eliminate overcapacity in mature industry. The geographical roll-up merger is signified by geographic expansion in fragmented industry. Diversification and globalization are strategic drivers of product and market extension mergers. Technology changes are the strategic driver for R&D induced mergers (Krug, n.d). The establishment of a competitive position in an emerging industry is the strategy for industry convergence. Acquisitions are a means of faster growth than internal development. The value addition in horizontal merger is economies of scale, market share improvement, and expansion into new markets. Diversification mergers are important for acquiring technological knowledge and management talent. The value created by the merger of firms may result from more efficient management, economies of scale, improved production techniques, combination of complementary resources, redeployment of assets to more profitable uses, exploitation of market power, or any number of value-creating activities that falls under the rubric of corporate synergy.[2] Motivations for mergers and acquisitions include increase in efficiency by creating economies of scale, or disciplining inefficient managers; exploitation of asymmetric information between acquiring firm managers and acquiring, or target, firm shareholders; solution to agency problems associated with the firm's free cash flow; and increase in market power and utilization of tax credits.

[2] Fred Weston, Kwang S Chung, Susan E Hoag, *Mergers, Restructuring, and Corporate Control*, PHI 2006.

Types of M&As

A merger involves combination of two companies into a larger company. In a merger, the acquiring company takes over the assets and liabilities of the merged company. In a merger, all the combining companies are dissolved, and only the new company exists. Acquisition is a more general term which encompasses in itself a range of acquisition transactions. It could be acquisition of tangible and intangible assets, rights, or other obligations. An acquisition is also known as takeover. An acquisition is the buying of one company called the target by the acquirer. Acquisition can be friendly or hostile. In a friendly takeover, the process is through negotiation between the acquirer and target boards. In a hostile takeover, the target board tries to prevent the takeover. Acquisitions usually refer to a small company being acquired by a large company. Reverse acquisition involves the acquisition of a large company by a smaller company. Acquisition of a company by its own management or by a group of investors is known as management buyouts. Asset acquisition involves buying the assets of another company.

Horizontal merger involves the merger of two companies that sell the same product in the same geographic market, for example, ArcelorMittal merger in steel industry sector. The merger of Daimler-Benz and Chrysler is another classical example of horizontal merger. The basic objective of horizontal merger is to increase market share and create economies of scale. Economies of scale are achieved by spreading fixed costs across a larger revenue stream. Redundant resources and assets are also eliminated in the process. Anti-competitive concerns are the disadvantages of a horizontal merger. Market extension merger and product extension merger are the two basic types of mergers. Market extension mergers are aimed to increase and to expand the firms' existing products and services into the new markets. In other words, firms produce the same products in different geographic markets. Through market extension merger, the merging firms can get access to a bigger market and client base. An example of market extension merger would be the acquisition of Eagle Bancshares Inc. by the RBC Centura. RBC diversified its operations by entering into the financial market of Atlanta. Product extension merger involves the merging of firms which produce similar products and services but are not in direct competition with each other. The acquisition of Mobilink Telecom Inc. by Broadcom is an example of product extension merger. Broadcom manufactures Bluetooth personal area network hardware systems and chips for IEEE 802.11b wireless LAN. Mobilink Telecom Inc. manufactures handsets that are equipped with the global system for mobile communications technology.

Vertical mergers are mergers between firms which have a buyer–seller relationship. Vertical mergers occur between firms which operate in different segments within an industry's supply chain. These firms produce different goods or services which are all related to one specific finished product. Examples for vertical merger include Time Warner acquisition of Turner Corporation and AOL–Time Warner. Vertical mergers lead to increased synergies. Vertical merger firms are characterized by operations in different stages of value chain or operate in different stages of value chain. Hence these firms have very different sets of resources and capabilities. Vertical mergers are meant to reduce dependence on supplies and buyers. This type of mergers reduces supplier's risk and improve efficiencies. Pepsi's acquisition of Pizza Hut, Taco Bell, and KFC can be considered as an example of vertical merger.

Conglomerate mergers are mergers between two companies having totally unrelated business activities. The merger between The Walt Disney Company and American Broadcasting Company is an example of a conglomerate merger. Conglomerate mergers utilize the financial strength of acquirer firm. Philip Morris the tobacco company acquired General Foods in the year 1985 for $5.6 billion. The basic motive of conglomerate merger is financial synergy. A pure conglomerate merger occurs in a scenario wherein a firm in the industry with low demand growth relative to the economy acquires a firm operating in an industry with high expected demand growth. The acquirer firm can use its internal funds to finance investment opportunities in the target firm thereby lowering the cost of capital. If the cash flow streams of the two firms are not perfectly correlated, then the bankruptcy probabilities can be lowered. Lender's risk can be decreased, and debt capacity can be increased.

Congeneric merger occurs when two merging firms are in the same general industry but have no mutual buyer–supplier relationship such as a bank and leasing company. Example is Prudential's acquisition of Bache & Company. Concentric mergers expand product lines and markets. Reverse merger involves the acquisition of a bigger company by a weaker or smaller company. Reverse merger also involves the merger of a parent company into its subsidiary or the acquisition of a profit-making company by a loss-making company. A reverse merger also occurs when a private company becomes a public company by acquiring control of the public company. The merger of Armand Hammer into Occidental Petroleum and Ted Turner's merger with Rice Broadcasting to form Turner Broadcasting are examples of reverse merger.

Synergies in Mergers

Synergy concept aims to maximize the wealth creation for the merged entity. In the context of synergy, the value of the combined firm must be greater than the sum of the values of bidding and target firms operating independently. Cost-based synergy is realized through cost reduction as a result of combination of similar assets in the merged businesses. Cost synergy leads to economies of scale specifically for sales and marketing, administrative, operating, and/or research and development costs. The focus of revenue-based synergy is to enhance capabilities and revenues. Revenue-based synergies also combine complementary competencies. Revenue synergy can be achieved if the merged business develops new competencies which would facilitate them to command a higher price through product innovations. Revenue synergy can be achieved through product cross selling, higher prices due to less competition, or achieving higher market shares. M&A can also create three kinds of synergies through combination and customization of resources differently. Modular synergies are created when firms manage operations independently and pool the results for greater profit. For example, both an airline and hotel chain gain from their collaboration when they club their consumer choices. Hotel guests earn frequent flyer miles through the association with airline companies. Sequential synergies result when one company completes its operations and forwards the result to another partner to do its share of work. The collaboration between a biotech and pharma company would lead to sequential synergies. Reciprocal synergies can be realized through horizontal mergers in which firms execute projects through an iterative knowledge sharing process.

Operating synergies facilitate firms to increase their operating income or growth rate. Operating synergy results from economies of scale which allows firms to become more cost efficient and profitable. The sources of operating synergy can be attributed to greater pricing power, reduced competition, and higher market share. These competitive advantages can lead to higher margins. The combination of functional strength can also lead into operating synergy. Operating synergy can be achieved when a firm with good product line is acquired by a firm with good marketing skills. Sources of operating synergy arise when companies acquire target firms in high-growth markets like emerging markets. Increase in sales can contribute toward sources of operating synergy when target firms are acquired with an established distribution network and brand names.

The impact of merger or acquisition on the cost of capital of the combined company is called the concept of financial synergy. In financial synergy, the cost of internal financing will be lowered. Financial synergy can be hypothesized in the context of investment opportunities and internal cash flows. A firm in declining industry has fewer investment opportunities but has cash cow characteristics with large cash flows. A growth industry firm has good potential growth opportunities but limited cash flow. When firms with such characteristics merge, the cost of capital will be lowered due to lower cost of internal funds, as well as possible risk reduction, savings in floatation costs, and improvement in capital allocation. The debt capacity of the combined firm would be greater than the sum of the two firms' capacities before merger. Lewellen (1971) observes that merged firms increase their financial leverage without increasing the premerger level of risk propensity on account of an increase in the debt capacity as a result of merger. On account of the advantages related to tax deductibility of interest payments on corporate debt, increases in financial leverage may prove to be beneficial to the shareholders of merging firms. The conglomerate merger of two firms with imperfectly correlated cash flow streams would increase the total debt capacity of the merged entity. In summary, a combination of a firm with excess cash and limited investment opportunities and another firm with high return investment opportunities but limited cash can create higher value for the combined firm. Myers and Majluf (1984) observe that value will be created in mergers when firms rich in financial slack acquire slack-poor firms.

Value Creation in Mergers

Market power and revenue growth are the two major sources of value creation in horizontal mergers. In a scenario of constant price elasticity of products, the market share increase would contribute toward revenue enhancement as a result of horizontal merger. Revenue enhancement in horizontal merger also results from network externality. The combination of functional areas like production, marketing, sales and distribution, and R&D functions in horizontal mergers would lead to cost savings. The same activities can be carried out at a lower cost than either firm's individual cost. The production and fixed costs can be reduced. In horizontal mergers, cost savings can also result from economies of scale in production, marketing, sales and distribution, logistics, branding, and R&D. Cost savings in horizontal mergers result from economies of scope in branding, marketing, distribution, production, and logistics. Scope economies are achieved when costs are spread over an increased range of output of different products.

Vertical mergers increase the vertical integration of a firm by taking over a customer or supplier. Vertical consolidation leads to reduction in market uncertainties thereby lowering transaction costs. These transaction cost savings include search and information costs to gather price and product characteristics of suppliers, cost for contract conclusion, quality control cost, and administrative costs. Revenue enhancement is possible as vertical mergers increase the scope to provide package of services and products rather than only few products. Vertical mergers have blurred the boundary walls which separate the banking, insurance, and asset management industries. Bancassurance is based on the backward integration of banks to source insurance industry products and forward integration of insurance companies to acquire distribution channels. Travelers Group brought the brokerage firm Smith Barney to diversify from insurance business into securities business. Later Travelers Group; Salomon Brothers, the investment bank and security trading firm; and the commercial bank Citibank consolidated into a full-fledged financial institution called Citigroup. In telecom industry, the trend is toward industry convergence where the scope of consolidation of different media platforms within a single company is observed. The speed of vertical and horizontal mergers will accelerate as the computing, communications, and broadcasting industries are coming closer.

In conglomerate or unrelated acquisitions, the value creation exists due to coinsurance effect. The major value effect in a conglomerate merger is based on specific risk reduction which lowers the cost of capital. Lewellen (1971) suggested that the combination of two unrelated businesses whose cash flows are imperfectly correlated can reduce the risk of default of the enterprise.

Due Diligence in Mergers and Acquisitions

Due diligence is the process of examining all aspects of a company which include manufacturing, financial, legal, tax, information technology systems, labor, regulatory, and intellectual property issues. Due diligence is done to evaluate a potential target company for acquisition. The process of due diligence helps in negotiating deals for acquisition and for valuation of the company. A major critical part of due diligence is to analyze the firm's financial resources. Due diligence includes examination of organizational structure, management style, operational aspects which include production technology, processes and systems, human resources, legal aspects, and information systems. The basic aim of due diligence is to assess the benefits and liabilities of the proposed acquisition. Cultural due diligence is also a critical part of the due diligence process. Cultural due diligence examines how two firms with different cultural aspects like corporate policies, rules, compensation plans, leadership styles, communication, and work environment will adapt to the differences and how post-merger integration would be successful. The process of cultural due diligence aims to maximize the value of human capital resources which include retention of existing employees and incentive plans.

Methods of Payment in M&A

The method of payment in M&A involves cash, exchange of shares, or hybrid. In a cash deal, the payment is by cash. Cash deals are basically for acquisitions where the acquirer takes control of the target firm as its shareholders are paid out. In exchange of shares, the acquirer's stock is offered as a consideration. Hybrid acquisition involves the combination of cash and debt or a combination of cash and stock of the purchasing entity. Stock offers could send a signal that acquirer's shares are overvalued. There are two ways to structure an offer for exchange of shares. Companies can either issue a fixed number of shares or they can issue a fixed value of shares. In fixed shares offer, the number of shares to be issued is fixed, but the value of the deal may fluctuate between the announcement of the offer and the closing date, depending on the bidder's price. In fixed value offer, the acquirer issues a fixed value of shares. In this deal, the number of shares issued is not fixed until the closing date and depends on the prevailing price. Research studies covering more than 1200 major deals have shown that shareholders of acquiring firms fare worse in stock transactions than in cash transactions. Myers and Majluf (1984) have found that differential stock returns of bidders in mergers may be due to the method of acquisition financing. The Myers and Majluf (1984) study suggests that managers will prefer cash offer if they believe that their firm is undervalued, while stock exchange would be the medium of exchange if the acquirer stocks are overvalued.

Post-merger Integration

The process of combining the organizational systems of two merged firms is known as post-merger integration. Integration involves integration of systems, processes, procedures, strategy, and reporting system. Integration planning is one of the most difficult tasks of successful merger or acquisition. General Electric Capital Services has a streamlined integration process called pathfinder model. Basically, an acquirer integrates five core functions such as information technology, research and development, procurement, production and networks, and sales and marketing. The essential steps in implementation of takeovers involve rationalization of core functions like manufacturing and sales/distribution activities, integration of support functions of the target into the acquirer, and removal of overheads related to business. The major challenges to integration are resistance to change and cultural incompatibility.

Review of Research Studies on Mergers and Acquisitions

Research have extensively documented on the impact of stock market reaction to the announcement of mergers and acquisitions. There are basically two approaches which deal with mergers and acquisition profitability. The first method called event studies examines the abnormal returns to shareholders in the period surrounding the announcement of a merger or acquisition. The abnormal or excess return is the raw return less a benchmark of what investors required that day, which typically would be the return on a large market index or the benchmark return specified by the capital asset pricing model. The analysis involving the difference between return on stock and return on market index is known as market return method. In the market model method, the expected rate of return on security is found out using the market model. The model parameters are estimated by regressing daily stock returns on market index over the estimation period. Residual analysis basically tests if the return to the common stock of firms or group of firms is greater than or less than that predicted by the general market relationships between return and risk. Event studies highlight insights about market-based returns to target firm shareholders, buyers, and the combined entity. The findings of 25 empirical studies show that target firm shareholders earn significant positive returns irrespective of the duration of time period, type of deal, and observation period. Studies of market-based returns to the buyer's shareholders give mixed results. Approximately 40% of 50 empirical studies show negative announcement returns for the acquirer firms, while 60% show positive returns. Empirical studies have also examined the abnormal returns to buyer and target firms, combined by forming a portfolio of the buyer and target firms, and examined their weighted average returns or absolute dollar value of returns. Out of 24 such studies, 14 report positive gains. Mandelker (1974) examined the market for acquisitions and the impact of mergers on the return to stockholders of the constituent firms. The study proved that the market for acquisitions is perfectly competitive. The study by Asquith et al. (1983) examined the effect of mergers on the wealth of bidding firm's shareholders. Bidding firms gain significantly during the 21 days leading to the announcement of each of their first four merger bids. Selden and Geoffrey (2003) suggest that approximately 80% of acquisitions fail since they create no wealth for the shareholders of the acquiring firm. Jensen and Ruback (1983) suggest that corporate takeovers generate positive gains for target shareholders and the bidding firms' shareholders' gains are neutral. Moeller et al. (2004) examined the announcement return of 12,023 acquisitions by public firms during the period 1980–2001 and find that equally weighted abnormal returns were approximately 1.1%. Their study also observes that acquiring firm shareholders lose $25.2 million on average upon announcement. Studies covering more than 1200 major deals find that shareholders of acquiring companies fare worse in stock transactions than in cash transactions. Travlos (1987) provides direct confirmation of a differential return relationship across different methods of payment for bidding firms announcing takeover bids. This study highlights the fact that stockholders of pure stock exchange bidding firms experience significant losses at the announcement of the takeover, while the stockholders of cash-financing bidding firms earn normal returns.

The studies of M&A on financial performance basically examine the reported financial results of acquirers before and after the acquisition to see how the financial performance changes. These studies are structured as matched sample comparisons in which acquirers' performance is set against that of non-acquirers of similar size that operate in the same industry. The results of 15 studies on performance measures like profit margins, growth rates, return on assets, capital, and equity suggest mixed results. Two of these studies reported significantly negative post-acquisition performance, four reported significantly positive performance, and the rest showed insignificant results. A collection of studies based on M&A profitability in seven countries reported modest effects on firm profitability in 3–5 years after the merger. Healy et al. (1992) examined the post-merger cash flow performance of acquiring and target firms and explored the sources of merger-induced changes in cash flow performance based on 50 largest US mergers between 1979 and mid-1984. The study found out that merged firms showed significant improvements in asset productivity relative to their industries leading to higher operating cash flow returns. Cornett and Tehranian (1992) found that the post-acquisition performance of banks improved in terms of asset productivity and employee productivity. Switzer (1996) examined the change in operating performance of merged firms using a sample of 324 mergers which happened between 1967 and 1987. The study found that the performance of the merged companies improved after merger. The study also documented positive association between the abnormal revaluation of the firms involved around the merger and changes in operating performance. Healy et al. (1997) observed that strategic takeovers which are generally friendly transactions involving stock and firms in overlapping businesses are more profitable than financial deals which are usually hostile transactions involving cash and firms in unrelated business. Alok Ghosh (2001) compares the post- and pre-acquisition performance of merging firms relative to matched firms to determine if operating cash flow performance improves after merger. The above study finds no evidence of improvement of operating cash flow performance following acquisitions. Rovit and Lemire (2003) examine the performance of 742 large US companies which made 7475 acquisitions between 1986 and 2001 and find that acquirers carrying out more than 20 deals in 15 years outperformed firms which made 1–4 deals by a factor of 1.7 and non-buyers by a factor of 2.

Researchers have also attempted to build predictive model for mergers and acquisitions. Studies during the period 1950–1960 suggest that acquired firms tend to be relatively unprofitable, overly liquid, and generally sluggish (Hayes et al., 1967). Monroe and Simowitz (1971) find that acquired firms relative to non-acquired firms are smaller and have lower price earnings ratios, lower dividend payout, and lower growth in equity. Stevens (1973) using discriminant analysis finds that acquired firms tend to have more liquidity and use less debt as compared to non-acquired firms. Harris et al. (1982) study based on fixed coefficient probit specification finds that size and financial variables have statistical significance, while product market variables like industry concentration and advertising intensity have very little explanatory power. Wansley (1984) based on a sample of target firms during the period 1975–1976 finds that target firms used less leverage. Palepu (1986) using logit analysis examines the usefulness of six acquisition hypotheses in predicting takeover target and documents evidence for size hypothesis. Ambrose and Megginson (1992) find that the probability of takeover bid is positively related to tangible assets and negatively related to firm size and net change in institutional holdings. Owen (1995) uses logit regression to analyze the characteristics of both acquired and acquirer firms and finds evidence for the fact that acquired companies are young companies. Liquidity, leverage, growth, and profitability are major identifiers for target companies (Severiens, 1991; Robert, 2004).

References

Ambrose B, Megginson W (1992) The role of asset structure, ownership structure and takeover defenses in determining acquisition likelihood. J Financ Quant Anal 27:575–588

Asquith P, Robert B, David M Jr (1983) The gains to bidding firms from merger. J Financ Econ 11:121–139

Cornett M, Tehranian H (1992) Changes in corporate performance associated with Bank acquisitions. J Financ Econ 31:211–234

Dyer JH, Kale P, Harbir S (2004) When to ally & when to acquire. Harv Bus Rev 82(7/8):109–115

Ghosh A (2001) Does corporate performance really improve following acquisitions. J Corp Finan 7:151–178

Harris R, Stewart J, Guikley DK, Carleton W (1982) Characteristics of acquired firms: fixed and random coefficients probit analyses. South Econ J 49:164–184

Hayes III, Samuel L, Taussig R (1967) Tactics of cash takeover bids. Harv Bus Rev 45:135–148

Healy P, Palepu K, Ruback R (1992) Does corporate performance improve after mergers. J Financ Econ 31:135–175

Healy P, Palepu K, Ruback R (1997) Which takeovers are profitable? Strategic or financial? Sloan Manag Rev 38:45–47

Jensen, Ruback (1983) The market for corporate control. J Financ Econ 11:5–50

Krug JA Before the merger: merger motivations and objectives, from mergers and acquisitions: turmoil in top management teams, digital chapters Harvard Business Publishing BEP036

Kumar R (2012) Mega mergers and acquisitions, case studies from key industries. In: Palgrave Macmillan, United Kingdom

Lewellen J (1971) A pure financial rationale for the conglomerate merger. J Financ 26:521–537

Mandelker G (1974) Risk and return: the case of merging firms. J Financ Econ 1:303–335

Moeller S, Frederik S, Rene S (2004) Firm size and the gains from acquisitions. J Financ Econ 73:201–228

Monroe R, Simowitz M (1971) Investment characteristics of conglomerate targets: a discriminant analysis. Southern Journal of Business 15:1–16

Myers S, Majluf N (1984) Corporate financing and investment decisions when firms have information that investors do not have. J Financ Econ 13:187–221
Owen S (1995) The characteristics of firms involved in UK acquisitions. Working Paper. Department of Economics and Finance. Brunel University. Uxbridge, Middle Sex, UK
Palepu KG (1986) Predicting takeover targets. J Account Econ 8:3–35
Robert B (2004) Where M&A pays and where it strays: a survey of the research. J Appl Corp Financ 16:63–76
Rovit S, Lemire C (2003) Your best M&A strategy: smart deal makers methodically acquire through good times and bad. Harv Bus Rev 81(3):16–17
Selden L, Geoffrey C (2003) M&A needn't be a loser's game. Harv Bus Rev 81(6):5–12
Severiens JT (1991) Creating value through mergers and acquisitions: some motivations. Manag Financ 17:55–80
Statista, Value of M&A transactions globally 2013–2018, https://www.statista.com/statistics/267369/volume-ofmergers-and-acquisitions-worldwide/
Stevens D (1973) Financial characteristics of merged firms: a multivariate analysis. J Financ Quant Anal 8:149–158
Switzer J (1996) Evidence on real gains in corporate acquisitions. J Econ Bus 48:443–460
Travlos N (1987) Corporate takeover bids, methods of payment and bidding firms' stock returns. J Financ XLII:943–963
Wansley JA (1984) Discriminant analysis and merger theory. Rev Financ Econ 20:77–85
http://www.economywatch.com/mergers-acquisitions/type/extension-merger-product-extension.html

Vodafone Acquisition of Mannesmann 2

Introduction

Vodafone was established as the telecom subsidiary of Racal Electronics in the year 1984. In the year 1988, approximately 20% of the stock of Racal Telecom was sold to public on the London and New York Stock Exchanges. In 1991, Racal Telecom was fully divested from Racal Electronics and renamed Vodafone Group. Vodafone had undertaken a series of alliances and mergers and acquisitions (M&A) activity as a strategic pursuit for growth. During the mid-1999, Vodafone merged with AirTouch Communications Inc. of the United States to create Vodafone AirTouch. This $60 billion acquisition of US-based AirTouch Communications by Vodafone was focused on becoming the global leader in wireless communication. Vodafone AirTouch pursued a strategy in which customers in certain market segment were offered a package of integrated wireless and wired services. Vodafone was well known for its focused strategy of technological innovation and pioneering new product development. By 1999, Vodafone AirTouch PLC had a customer base of 31 million worldwide and business interests in 24 countries across 5 continents. The operations of Vodafone AirTouch extended to Europe, Africa, and Middle East. Vodafone was the largest UK operator for a very long time period. Vodafone AirTouch had a 45% stake in a planned joint venture with Bell Atlantic which covered more than 90% of the US population. Bell Atlantic was the largest wireless operator in the United States. This venture resulted in the creation of Verizon Wireless during April 2000. This joint venture had 23 million customers which included 3.5 million paging customers. This joint venture covered 49 out of top 50 US markets. During the late 1999, Vodafone AirTouch had a market capitalization of approximately £90 billion and was the second largest company in the FTSE 100 and third in the Euro Top 300. Earlier AirTouch had a number of tie-ups with Mannesmann in Europe.

Mannesmann was an engineering company headquartered in Germany and established in the year 1890. After World War II, the company transformed itself

B. R. Kumar, *Wealth Creation in the World's Largest Mergers and Acquisitions*, Management for Professionals, https://doi.org/10.1007/978-3-030-02363-8_2

from steel and coal manufacturer into a diversified conglomerate with business interests in automotive components, information technology, and plastics. The major businesses included the telecommunications, engineering, and automotive markets. During the 1990s, Mannesmann emerged as the largest mobile phone operator in Europe.

In 1991, Mannesmann launched Mobilfunk with technical support from AirTouch. In 1996, Mannesmann formed the business named Mannesmann Arcor by acquiring the fixed-line subsidiary of Deutsche Bahn in partnership with Deutsche Bank and AT&T. Mannesmann had also acquired interests in Cegetel in France and Tele. Ring in Austria. In 1999, Mannesmann acquired majority stakes in Italian operators Omnitel and Infostrada. During the period October 1999, Mannesmann paid Hutchison Whampoa £20 billion for 44.82% stake in Orange. With this acquisition Mannesmann became Europe's largest mobile network operator.

The Merger Story

There had been a long history of collaboration between Vodafone and Mannesmann. But the overnight bid on October 20, 1999, for Orange by Klaus Esser, the chairman of Mannesmann, was taken seriously by Chris Gent, Vodafone's CEO, who considered this move as a strategic initiative to compete with Vodafone. On November 13, 1999, the UK-based Vodafone AirTouch, the world's largest mobile phone group, announced a takeover bid for the German telecommunications and engineering group Mannesmann AG on the basis of an exchange of shares between the two companies. The Mannesmann management and supervisory board consistently opposed the deal. This offer was the largest unsolicited takeover bid at that time. On the basis of Vodafone's closing price of £2.85 on November 18, 1999, each Mannesmann share was valued at €240 and the Mannesmann group at €124 billion (£78 billion). This offer was a significant premium to Mannesmann's closing price of €143 preceding 1 month. The initial merger talks which were on friendly terms soon turned out to be hostile with Chris Gent, the Vodafone CEO, and Klaus Esser, the Mannesmann CEO, at loggerheads. On November 19, 1999, the Mannesmann supervisory board officially rejected the Vodafone offer. Vodafone came forward with a new improved proposal which appealed directly to the Mannesmann shareholders to exchange their shares in the ratio of 53.7 Vodafone AirTouch shares for one Mannesmann share. Mannesmann management stated that Vodafone is not strategic fit to their business since both companies have very different structures and economic growth prospects. Vodafone focuses on mainly mobile phones, while Mannesmann is much more diversified with businesses in engineering, automotive, telecommunications, and tubes.

Mannesmann management argued that the company had valued itself over €350 per share which represented a significant increase of €157.8 when it had bid for Orange. During November and December of the year 1999, Vodafone AirTouch organized a major shareholder campaign in different parts like continental Europe, the United States, and United Kingdom to convince Mannesmann shareholders the rationale for the deal. On December 23, Vodafone directly approached Mannesmann shareholders with a tender offer. Mannesmann attempt to get an injunction restraining Goldman Sachs to act on behalf of Vodafone also proved futile. During the second week of January 2000, Vodafone announced that it would propose to increase the offer price if Mannesmann CEO agreed for a friendly takeover. On January 30, 1999, Vodafone and Vivendi announced a joint mobile/Internet portal. As a part of the deal, Vodafone offered Vivendi half of Mannesmann's 15% share of the French fixed-line firm Cegetel. This deal announcement surprised the board of Mannesmann. The Mannesmann management changed its tactics when it realized that Vodafone's hostile takeover might succeed. On February 3, 2000, Mannesmann board of directors accepted Vodafone's offer. Each Mannesmann shareholder received 58.964 Vodafone shares which gave them 49.5% stake in the new company. Vodafone AirTouch offer of €353 per share valued Mannesmann approximately $180 billion. This represented an increase of almost 75% from Vodafone's first offer. The new combined entity had a market capitalization of $350 billion. The combined entity became the fourth largest company in the world in terms of market value after Microsoft, GE, and Cisco at the time of the deal.

Earlier Vodafone had stated that the company is interested only in its telecommunication operations and intended to sell its engineering and automotive businesses. These businesses accounted for 80% of Mannesmann's total workforce. This merger could also be discussed within the cultural perspective. Hostile takeovers of German firms by foreign firms were rarely observed. It was initially portrayed that the Vodafone AirTouch's acquisition will result in huge job losses. Politicians, labor unions, and press of Germany joined together to protest against the hostile deal.

Different political outfits also raised voices of concern and sought government protection against the hostile takeover. The relatively unanimous reactions of German politicians had provoked strong counterreactions in British press which called the German debate "nationalistic and hypocritical."

According to German laws, 75% of outstanding shares needs to be tendered for transfer of control. Chris Gent Vodafone CEO assured German labor unions and government about no job cuts. Mannesmann employees and German public had voiced strong reservations about the takeover bid. Vodafone initiated a campaign to project a more socially acceptable and employment-friendly image. On November 24, 1999, the president of Vodafone, Christ Gent, issued an open letter to all the employees of Mannesmann in all leading German daily newspapers assuring that the rights of the employees, trade unions, and work councilors would be fully safeguarded and there would be no additional job losses. It was assured that Mannesmann would continue to have a co-determined supervisory board with employee representatives. The employment perspectives in telecommunication would be improved in favor of the Dusseldorf region. The fixed-line division of Mannesmann telecommunication would become an independent company under the merged entity.

Vodafone also gave assurances of adoption of Mannesmann corporate culture which included activities like employee representation on supervisory board. On the basis of these assurances, unions decided in favor of the merger. When it became clear that the hostile takeover attempt would succeed, Mannesmann management changed its approach and negotiated for a friendly takeover. Concrete plans were chalked out for the integration process. The new company was called Vodafone AirTouch although the Mannesmann name was retained in Germany. Dusseldorf became one of the European headquarters for the merged company. This headquarter served the existing continental European mobile and fixed-line telephone business. Initially Vodafone was reluctant to offer more than 50% of the shareholding to Mannesmann shareholders during the hostile takeover attempt. Finally, Mannesmann shareholders managed to get approximately 50% of the shareholdings although they contributed only 35% to operating earnings. On April 12, 2000, the European Commission gave phase I clearance for its acquisition of Mannesmann AG. As a part of its ruling, European Union ruled that Vodafone must divest its stake in Orange and open its networks to competitors for 3 years. After the announcement by European Union, Vodafone's share rose 2.8% to 322 pence with market capitalization of £200 billion. Vodafone thus became the largest European company by market capitalization by that time. As part of the regulatory requirement, Mannesmann entered into an agreement with Siemens AG and Robert Bosch to dispose of 50% stake in ATECS. The transaction was valued at approximately € 9.6 billion. In 2000, Mannesmann sold Orange to France Telecom in a deal worth around £31 billion, thus creating Europe's second largest mobile phone group. Vodafone also topped the bidding for the five UK third-generation mobile phone operating licenses.

Thus after a 3-month battle, Germany's Mannesmann AG agreed to be taken over by Britain's Vodafone AirTouch PLC in a friendly $180.95(£224) billion all-share deal. On February 3, 2000, Mannesmann board agreed to the Vodafone offer.

Merger Highlights

The public bid announcement of the takeover was on December 20, 1999. The formal offer was accepted by 98.62% of Mannesmann's shareholders at the closing date on March 27, 2000. The transaction was effected by an all-share offer of Vodafone AirTouch shares in exchange for Mannesmann shares.

Under the terms of the revised deal valued at £224 billion, Mannesmann shareholders got 49.5% of the merged company with 58.96 shares of Vodafone AirTouch for each Mannesmann share. The revised deal valued Mannesmann shares at 350.5 euros each. The key terms of the merger were as follows:

1. (de Donald, 2009) A revised offer of 58.9646 Vodafone AirTouch shares for each Mannesmann share.
2. (Higson, n.d.) The revised offer valued each Mannesmann share at € 350.5 and Mannesmann's share capital at € 181.4 billion, based on Vodafone AirTouch's closing price of 368.5 pence on February 3, 2000.
3. (Streamingmedia, 2000) Dr. Klaus Esser joined the Vodafone AirTouch Board as an executive director. Four members of Mannesmann's supervisory board joined the Board of Vodafone AirTouch.

Goldman Sachs was the principle advisor for Vodafone AirTouch, while Morgan Stanley and Merrill Lynch were advisors for Mannesmann.

Regulatory Issues

The European Commission approved the merger on the condition that all shareholdings in Orange need to be divested. The commission also stipulated that the entire share capital of any subsidiary or future holding company of Mannesmann or the divestor through which such participations are also required to be divested. As a result of the merger, Mannesmann was delisted from Frankfurt's Xetra Dax share index.

Strategic Perspective of the Merger

From the opportunity perspective, during the early 2000, the mobile phone market was one of the fastest-growing segments in the telecommunications industry. During the period 1997–1999, the mobile market grew from 203 million customers to 475 million customers. Vodafone did not have high market shares in European Union in spite of the fact that the European Union was consolidating into a single market. Vodafone had a low cost structure and focused on research and development for the delivery of innovative solutions. Vodafone' s strongest resources were human resources, innovation, and knowledge. By the year 2000, Vodafone was the largest telecom company in Europe which was twice the size of its nearest competitors. Its technological resources were strong as it developed a next-generation wireless standard, UMTS, which allowed for voice and data on the same wireless network. Vodafone positioned itself as a cost leader whereby it was able to operate with margins greater than its competitors (Byles, 2006).

The takeover created the world's largest mobile phone operator with 42.3 million customers in Britain, the United States, Germany, Italy, France, and other markets. The deal was one of the world's largest corporate takeovers. It was envisaged that the cost savings from combining the two companies would amount to £500 million. It was one of the biggest horizontal mergers in telecommunication history. The chief executive of Vodafone AirTouch, Chris Gent, said that the intention of the takeover was to create "a Microsoft of mobile phones."

Vodafone's aim was to consolidate its position in the European market with the acquisition of Mannesmann. Germany had the lowest penetration rate in Europe and the potential revenue per customer as well above the European average. As a result of the merger, Vodafone and Mannesmann had controlling stakes in ten European markets. The acquisition gave the merged entity the most extensive wireless coverage in the European market (Ivan, 2013). Both Vodafone AirTouch and Mannesmann benefitted from their respective geographical coverage. The merger was intended to create a superior platform for development of mobile data and Internet services.

The telecom mobile industry was witnessing transformational change during the late 1990s. The third-generation (3G) rollout was expected in Japan in 2002 and in Europe and United States by the year 2003. As a result, the telecom industry would witness a new generation of Internet applications and bandwidth services. The convergence of the mobile telecoms, multimedia, and Internet sectors has become the trend. Both Vodafone and Mannesmann realized the importance for control of the strategic assets for becoming the dominant players in the multimedia world. The enormous cost of 3G licenses also forced companies to look for economies of scale. It was viewed by some analysts that Vodafone would be required to pay €30 billion to €40 billion for licenses to cover their existing territories in the scenario of 3G rollout. The high cost of 3G licenses would put enormous pressure on network operators to look for economies of scale with the focus on emerging data services. In the context of these changes, telecom companies were looking for global acquisition targets. Even in spite of strong mobile growth, many regions were becoming competitive and increasingly saturated with penetration over 75% in many developed markets. Telecom companies were focusing on enhancing customer retention and average revenue per user as a means to protect margins. The merger was aimed at realizing significant purchasing economies for infrastructure, IT and handset procurement, and savings network. Vodafone and Mannesmann had a unique bargaining power against handset manufacturers to negotiate design functionalities which were unavailable to competing operators.

The merger was expected to generate savings of more than £ 1 billion by the year 2004. The merger was expected to create company with mobile phone interests in 15 European countries with 30 million customers. Globally it was expected to have 42 million customers.

During the time of merger, Vodafone AirTouch had stakes in 24 countries worldwide. The company was listed on the London and New York Stock Exchanges. Vodafone AirTouch had interests in mobile telecommunication companies in ten EU member states. Out of these, Vodafone AirTouch had majority stakes in telecommunication companies in the United Kingdom, the Netherlands, Sweden, Portugal, and Greece and minority stakes in telecommunication companies in Belgium, France, Italy, and Spain (Mannesmann: the mother of all takeovers, 2010).

The merged entity's market share of European mobile telephony subscribers was estimated to be more than 30%. The second and third operators, Telecom Italia and Deutsche Telekom, had a market share of approximately 15% and 10%. British Telecom and France Telecom had market share of approximately 8%.

The acquisition of Mannesmann was aimed to consolidate Vodafone AirTouch's position in Europe. With the union, Vodafone and Mannesmann had controlling stakes in ten European markets thereby giving the merged entity the most extensive European coverage for any wireless carrier. It was mutually beneficial as Vodafone AirTouch was expected to benefit from the additional coverage provided by Mannesmann in Europe, whereas Mannesmann's operation would benefit from Vodafone's widespread coverage in the United States. Through buying a competitor, Vodafone expected to gain their entire market share and eliminate the risks associated with competition between the two companies. Gaining the fixed-line capabilities was a source of diversification for Vodafone.

From a legal perspective, European regulation favored convergence wherein mobile phone operators could offer the same voice and data services as fixed-line operators. The convergence of fixed-line telephony and wireless telephony was expected to favor the mobile phone market as it was growing fast and fixed-line customers had the potential to switch to mobile operators since the same services were available. The mobile phone industry capital requirements were low compared to the capital requirements of the telecommunications industry as a whole. But within the mobile phone industry, capital requirements presented a significant barrier to entry. Since the spectrum licenses went up for auction, the most financially fit and liquid mobile phone operators could cross the barrier entry. The major competitors of Vodafone AirTouch in Europe were Deutsche Telekom, France Telecom, Telefonica, British Telecom, and Telecom Italia. Unlike its competitors, Vodafone focused exclusively on the mobile telephony market. The management of Vodafone believed that Vodafone would continue to operate as a pure wireless company since voice, data, and Internet would all move wireless in the future. Vodafone's exclusive focus on mobile was a part of its competitive strategy. Vodafone focused on acquisitions to gain cost advantages through economies of scale. The aim was to achieve technological leadership in the mobile telephony industry.

Vodafone had merged with AirTouch to become the largest mobile phone operator in the world. The merger gave Vodafone an easy entry into North American market since AirTouch was already the leader in that market. Thereafter Vodafone pursued the strategy of penetration of mobile phone services to the largest possible number of customers and largest possible markets. Vodafone also formed strategic alliance with Bell Atlantic. Vodafone aimed to block competitors through multipoint competition. In the context of Vodafone's low market share in continental Europe, Vodafone pursued a global international corporate-level strategy. Vodafone followed a strategy of entry into international markets initially through mergers and later through acquisitions and alliances. Vodafone had strategic alliances with its competitors in Europe like Mannesmann, Belgacom, BT, Cegetel, TDK, and TTW. Vodafone acquired 35% of D2 from Mannesmann. Vodafone again associated with Mannesmann to buy 21% of the Italian company Omnitel. Vodafone established alliances with government companies in Greece, Holland, Portugal, and Sweden. Through these partnerships in Europe, Vodafone increased its market share. Vodafone continued to dominate in market through joint ventures with TDC Mobile and France Telecom. Vodafone also acquired Eircell, Ireland's leading mobile company (Table 2.1).

Post-merger Integration

The integration of culture and skills of Mannesmann was one of Vodafone AirTouch's biggest challenges. Vodafone had committed to the principle of codetermination in Mannesmann's governance structure. An integration committee was established with representatives from both Vodafone AirTouch and Mannesmann. Mannesmann had 5 representatives (1 executive and 4 nonexecutives) out of a total of 19 on the new Vodafone AirTouch Board. Dr. Klaus Esser, the chief at Mannesmann, joined the Board of Vodafone AirTouch as an executive director and continued to be the CEO of Mannesmann. Klaus Esser had the additional responsibility of the separation of the industrial businesses. On the successful separation of the industrial businesses, Dr. Esser gave up his executive responsibilities at Mannesmann and became the nonexecutive deputy chairman of Vodafone AirTouch.

Table 2.1 Acquisitions by Vodafone AirTouch

Year	Acquisitions
1999–2000	Acquires Mannesmann
2000–2002	On November 3, 2000, Vodafone acquires 2.18% of China Mobile for 2.5 billion. By 2002, Vodafone increases stake in China Mobile by approximately 3.27%
2001–2003	By 2001, Vodafone had a 20% direct interest in SFR and 15% stake in Cegetel Groupe SA, the French telecommunications group. By 2003, the Group's stake in SFR increased to approximately 43.9%
2001–2003	In 2001, Vodafone acquired BT's 17.8% shareholding in Vodafone Spain. By 2001, Vodafone had 91.6% stake in Vodafone Spain. By 2002, Vodafone acquired further 2.2% interest in Vodafone Spain for 400 million pounds. By January 2003, the Vodafone Group acquired the remaining 6.2% interest in Vodafone Spain for approximately 1.4 billion pounds
2004–2005	Vodafone held 66.7% stake in Vodafone holdings K.K. and a 39.67% stake in Vodafone Japan by March 2004. On account of merger of Vodafone K.K. and Vodafone holdings K.K., the Group held 97.7% stake in the merged company Vodafone K.K. by October 2004
2014	Merger with Grupo Corporation ONO SA
2016	Liberty Global and Vodafone Dutch
2017	Merger of Vodafone India and Idea

Vodafone AirTouch continued to develop Mannesmann's wireless Internet business within the combined group. Another strategic objective of the combined group was to integrate and develop Mannesmann's tele-commerce activities. Vodafone AirTouch decided to retain all current ongoing existing facilities and activities in the Dusseldorf area. In addition, the emphasis was on expanding data products and services at Dusseldorf area. Vodafone AirTouch also focused on the repositioning of Mannesmann's tube businesses. Mannesmann agreed to remove the 5% voting restriction in its articles of association.

Merger Analysis

The period of merger was in the midst of dot.com euphoria and Internet hype. The strategic focus of Mannesmann had been for the reorientation of the company from industrial firm to service and telecommunication provider. On February 4, 2000, the Mannesmann supervisor board approved the takeover. The board also authorized millions of euros in bonuses for Mannesmann executives. The CEO of Mannesmann received 30 million euros which in fact triggered breach of trust allegations and years of legal wrangling which ended in multimillion euro settlement. The 2.5 months of corporate takeover battle saw Vodafone and Mannesmann spending half a billion euros on legal fees and publicity campaign alone. It is said that when all formalities were complete, Vodafone paid 190 billion euros for Mannesmann which made the deal the most expensive hostile takeover in the history of corporate world.

However, in reality Vodafone plunged into massive losses after one-off costs of more than £23.5 billion connected to the Mannesmann deal (Tables 2.2, 2.3, 2.4, and 2.5).

Table 2.2 Comparison of Mannesmann AG and Vodafone AirTouch PLC, March 2000

	Mannesmann	Vodafone
Turnover (million euros)	23,265	13,069
Employees	130,860	29,465
Return on sales (EBITDA/sales)	18.45%	40.25%
Market value (million euros)	119,572	149,400
Ratio of market value to turnover	5.14	11.40
Market value per employee (million euros)	0.91	5.07

Source: Annual Reports (1999, 2000a, b)

Table 2.3 Highlights for Mannesmann in 1999

	Sales in euro million	Employees in 000
Engineering	6602	229
Automotive	5482	216
Telecommunications	4654	982
Tubes	2338	26

The sales figures increased by 134% in the year 2000 to account for the merger. The sales increased by 91% and 52%, respectively, in the year 2000 and 2001, respectively. In 2002 the sales increased by 33% and by 10% in the year 2003. The stock return amounted to 52% in the year 2000. The stock returns declined by 44% and 32% in the year 2001 and 2002, respectively. The 5-year post-merger (2001–2005) average sales growth was 33%. The 5-year average growth rate in cash flow in the post-merger period (2001–2005) was approximately 39%.

During the period 1996–1999, Vodafone's gross, operating, and net margins, return on assets, and return on equity were higher than its competitors. During the period 1996–2000, Vodafone was less liquid on an average basis compared to its competitors. This was since they maintained lower inventory levels as a percentage of working capital. During the period 1997–2000, the debt ratios of Vodafone were above the industry averages. During the merger period, Vodafone was in a superior financial position compared to its competitors. After Mannesmann acquisition, Vodafone doubled in size.

Operating Performance Analysis (Table 2.6)

The values are given in million pounds. The above table compares the premerger financial highlights with that of the post-merger financial highlights of Vodafone. The year of merger is defined as "0"; the period before merger as −1, −2,−3 years, etc.; and the post-merger period as +1,+2, and +3. For the year-on-year comparison, the year of merger is avoided to account for merger effects. The average growth rate of sales in the premerger 4-year period 1997–1999 was 30.9%, while the average 5-year growth rate of sales in the post-merger period 2001–2005 was 37.5%. The average growth rate of assets in the above premerger period was 27.8%, while the average growth rate of assets in the post-merger period declined to register negative growth rate of −1.9%.

Table 2.4 Operating highlights of Vodafone (£million)

Year	1999	2000	2001	2002	2003	2004	2005	2006	2007	2008	2009
Sales	3360	7873	15,004	22,845	30,375	33,559	34,133	29,350	31,104	35,478	41,017
Gross profit	1551	3514	6302	9399	12,479	14,098	10,878	12,280	12,379	13,588	15,175
EBITDA	1326	3182	4331	8702	12,669	15,268	14,023	14,221	15,195	16,280	18,537
EPS	4.1	2	−16.1	−23.8	−14.4	−13.2	9.7	−35	−9.8	12.5	5.8
ROCE	42.3%	1.2%	−4.6%	−8.6%	−3.8%	−3.2%	6.3%	−12.4%	−1.7%	11.2%	5.2%
ROE	68.9%	0.3%	−6.7%	−11.5%	−7.4%	−7.3%	5.6%	−22%	−7.1%	9.3%	3.8%
Stock return		52%	−44.2%	−32%	−12.2%	16.5%	12.3%	−9.9%	18.1%	16.9%	−13.5%

Table 2.5 Financial highlights (£million)

Year	1999	2000	2001	2002	2003	2004	2005	2006	2007	2008	2009
Total assets	3643.6	150,851	172,362	162,867	163,239	147,129	133,906	124,195	109,617	127,270	152,699
Long-term debt	1137	6038	10,772	12,584	13,175	12,224	13,190	16,750	17,798	22,662	31,749
Year-end market capitalization	35,674	213,749	125,474	88,413	76,579	86,860	90,757	72,443	71,592	80,162	64,424

Table 2.6 Premerger and post-merger comparison of financial highlights

Year	1995	1996	1997	1998	1999	2000	2001	2002	2003	2004	2005
	−5	−4	−3	−2	−1	0	1	2	3	4	5
Sales	1152.6	1402.2	1749	2470.8	3360	7873	15,004	22,845	30,375	33,559	34,133
Operating profit	203.3	293.7	342.2	374.2	510.4	981	−6989	−11,834	−5451	−4230	−4111
Total assets	1409.5	1763.4	2421.8	2502.3	3643.6	150,851	172,362	162,867	163,239	147,129	133,906

Stock Wealth Analysis: Acquirer

Vodafone made the bid announcement on November 13, 1999. Vodafone is listed in NASDAQ. The 11-day average return analysis surrounding the period of announcement shows that returns were negative on the announcement day. The stock price fell by 2.27% on the announcement day and further by 8.54% one day after the merger announcement. The premerger announcement period witnessed positive returns for the Vodafone stock. The Board of Mannesmann rejected the offer initially on November 19, 1999. It is observed that the news had positive effect on Vodafone stock returns. For analysis purpose, "zero" is the announcement day. The stock price increased by 4.13% on November 19. The Board of Mannesmann finally accepted the offer on February 3, 2000. On February 2, 2000 Vodafone stock price increased by 6.7%. But the stock market reacted negatively to Mannesmann board's acceptance offer. The stock price fell by approximately 2% on the day of the announcement and further fell by 6.3% and 6.7% for the next 2 days (Table 2.7).

The analysis of cumulative returns for Vodafone stock surrounding the different time window for merger announcement reveals that the Vodafone stock lost wealth in the shorter time windows surrounding the merger announcement and the stock gained in the longer window period. The cumulative returns for the shortest time window of 3 days (−1 to +1) was −10.54% while for the 5-day window period (−2 to +2 days) was −15.99%. Vodafone stock gained by approximately 34% on cumulative return basis during the 83-day period (−10 days to +72 days) (Fig. 2.1; Tables 2.8 and 2.9).

Table 2.7 Daily returns surrounding merger announcement period for Acquirer: Vodafone

Days	Price	Returns (%)
−10	51.99	2.73
−9	55.48	6.72
−8	55.63	0.26
−7	54.61	−1.83
−6	56.87	4.13
−5	57.23	0.64
−4	59.20	3.44
−3	59.78	0.98
−2	60.58	1.34
−1	61.74	1.92
0	60.34	−2.27
1	55.19	−8.54
2	55.34	0.26
3	51.26	−7.37
4	52.57	2.56
5	53.66	2.08
6	54.75	2.04
7	51.48	−5.98
8	51.41	−0.14
9	52.42	1.98
10	56.79	8.33

Fig. 2.1 Cumulative returns for Vodafone

Table 2.8 Cumulative returns surrounding the merger announcement for Vodafone

Time window	Cumulative returns (%)
−1 to +1 days	−10.54
−2 to +2 days	−15.99
−5 to +5 days	−2.90
−10 to +10 days	8.03
−5 to +20 days	3.00
−5 to +30 days	1.76
−10 to +72 days	33.89

Table 2.9 Average stock returns surrounding the merger period

Year	1996	1997	1998	1999	2000	2001	2002	2003	2004	2005
	−4	−3	−2	−1	0	1	2	3	4	5
Stock returns	8.16%	6.16%	61.8%	87.9%	52%	−44.2%	−32%	−12.2%	16.5%	12.3%

The cumulative returns for Vodafone stock was fluctuating during the time window −10 days to +72 days. The preannouncement period witnessed increases in stock prices. The merger announcement period witnessed high fluctuations in stock price returns.

The stock returns for Vodafone were positive during the premerger period. The average yearly returns for Vodafone stock was approximately 88% in the year 1999. In the year of merger, the stock returns were 52%. For the next 3 years, returns were negative. In 2004 and 2005, the position improved and registered positive returns.

Wealth Analysis of Target Firm

Vodafone had initially offered 43.7 Vodafone shares for each Mannesmann share. Based on this offer, Mannesmann was valued at 203 euros ($209.50) a share which was a 9.4% premium to Mannesmann's share price as on November 11, 1999. Mannesmann share closed at 185.20 euros or $191. This offer price amounted to a 25% premium to the share price before the speculation about the deal. The offer valued the entire company of Mannesmann including its planned acquisition of the British mobile phone operator Orange at $106.4 billion. Later Vodafone offered 53.7% of its shares for each Mannesmann share which gave the deal a valuation of 240 euros, or $247.20 per share. This offer price represented an 18% increase on Vodafone's initial bid and a 54% premium over Mannesmann's share price as on October 18, 1999, before the takeover activity started. This was a pure stock swap acquisition. No cash was involved in the stock swap. Under the terms of the final deal, Mannesmann shareholders received 58.96 Vodafone shares for each Mannesmann share. This gave Mannesmann 49.5% stake in the new company despite the fact that it contributed only 31% of the year's earnings before interest, tax, depreciation, and amortization. The final bid valued Mannesmann shares at 350.50 euros per share.

Shareholder value at risk (SVAR) is the premium percentage paid for the acquisition multiplied by ratio of market value of the seller relative to the market value of the buyer. The greater the percentage of premium paid to the sellers and greater their market value relative to acquiring company, the higher the SVAR. SVAR was estimated as 14.40% for this merger.

References

Annual Report (1999, 2000a) Vodafone AirTouch

Annual Report (1999, 2000b) Mannesmann A G

Byles C (2006) Vodafone air touch: the acquisition of Mannesmann, case analysis, May 2006. Virginia Common Wealth University, United States of America

de Donald P (2009) Vodafone AirTouch acquires Mannesmann in a record setting deal, introduction to mergers and acquisitions, mergers, acquisitions and other restructuring, an integrated approach to process, tools, cases and solutions, 2nd edn. Academic Press, United States of America

Higson C Value creation at Vodafone, London Business School, CS 09–009

Ivan P (2013) https://prezi.com/vekeydq-afgy/vodafone-mannesmann-merger. Accessed 20 June 2017

Mannesmann: the mother of all takeovers (2010) http://www.dw.com/en/mannesmann-the-mother-of-all-takeovers/a-5206028. Accessed June 21 2017

Streamingmedia (2000) Vodafone Air touch and Mannesmann agreement on terms for a recommended merger. http://www.streamingmedia.com/Articles/News/Online-Video-News/Vodafone-Airtouch-And-Mannesmann-Agreement-On-Terms-For-A-Recommended-Merger-61825.aspx. Accessed 20 June 2017

https://www.eurofound.europa.eu/observatories/eurwork/articles/vodafones-hostile-takeover-bid-for-mannesmann-highlights-debate-on-the-german-capitalist-mode

American Online: Time Warner Merger and Other Restructuring

3

Introduction

Highlights of Time Warner

Time Warner Inc. is global leader in media and entertainment industry with business interests in television networks and film and TV entertainment. The three main segments of Time Warner are Turner, Home Box Office, and Warner Bros. Turner businesses consist of cable networks and digital media properties. Home Box Office segment consists of premium pay television and OTT services. Warner Bros consists of television, feature film, home video, and video game production and distribution. The company focuses on delivering high-quality content worldwide on a multi-platform basis. The company aims to strengthen its position within the traditional TV ecosystem and increase its content and services offered directly to consumers. Time Warner is a leader in innovation for more than 100 years. The operating divisions like Home Office Inc., Turner, and Warner Bros. have emerged as symbols of creativity and excellence. HBO along with its sister channel Cinemax have become the world's leading premium pay television and subscription video on demand (SVOD) service. Turner operates more than 180 channels globally. The major network brands of Turner include TNT, TBS, Adult Swim, truTV, Turner Classic Movies, Turner Sports, Cartoon Network, Boomerang, CNN, and HLN. Turner's digital properties include bleacherreport.com, NBA.com, NCAA.com, PGA.com, and the CNN digital network.

B. R. Kumar, *Wealth Creation in the World's Largest Mergers and Acquisitions*, Management for Professionals, https://doi.org/10.1007/978-3-030-02363-8_3

HBO offers original production which includes series, film documentaries, championship boxing, concerts, and family as well as Hollywood blockbusters. HBO is the most-watched pay service in the United States which provides hit Hollywood films to global consumers across a wide range of platforms and offerings. Cinemax services feature more than 1000 movie titles annually as well as new and exclusive prime-time high impact series. HBO and Cinemax Branded Services include HBO, HBO NOW, HBO GO, HBO on Demand, HBO2, HBO Signature, HBO Family, HBO Comedy, HBO Zone, HBO Latino, etc. CINEMAX includes Cinemax, MAX GO, Cinemax on Demand, More Max, Action Max, 5 Star Max, Max Latino, Outer Max, and Movie Max.

Warner Bros. is an entertainment industry leader with business focus in feature films, television, home entertainment, video games, and consumer products. The Warner Bros. Television Group spans the entire portfolio of Warner Bros. television businesses which include worldwide production, traditional and digital distribution, and broadcasting. Warner Bros. Entertainment includes Home Entertainment, Warner Home Video, Warner Bros. Advanced Digital Services, Warner Bros. Interactive Entertainment, Warner Bros. Technical Operations, and Warner Bros. Anti-Piracy Operations. Warner Bros. Studio facilities oversee the physical operations of Warner Bros. Time Warner focuses on using its industry leading operating scale and brands to create, package, and deliver high-quality content globally.

Corporate Restructuring by Time Warner (Table 3.1)

Table 3.1 Timeline of restructuring by Time Warner

Year	Events
1976	Warner Communications buys Atari Inc.
1986	Warner buys out American Express share of Warner – AMEX Cable for $400 million
1988	Warner acquires Lorimar Telepictures Corp.
1989	Time merges with Warner Communications
1996	Time Warner acquires Turner Broadcasting System. AOL have five million members
1998	AOL completes acquisition of CompuServe
1999	Time Warner establishes joint venture with AT&T to offer telephone service in 33 states. AOL completes its acquisition of Netscape Communication Corporation
2000	Time Warner and America Online announce $181 billion merger
2006	CBS Corporation and Time Warner create a new broadcast network, The CW
2009	Time Warner completed the spin-off of AOL Inc.; Time Warner Inc. announced the separation of Time Warner Cable Inc. through a tax-free spin-off
2010	Time Warner's Latin American division bought Chilean nationwide terrestrial television Chilevisi6n
2014	Time Warner Inc. completed the spin-off of Time Inc.
2015	AOL was acquired by Verizon Communications for $4.4 billion
2016	AT&T acquires Time Warner

Time Inc. Merges with Warner Communications

In 1990, Time Inc. merged with Warner Communications (WCI) to form Time Warner Inc. The merger was termed as merger of equals. The merger was valued at $18 billion. Time exchanged 12.5% of its shares for about 10% of Warner share. Each Warner share was exchanged tax free for 0.465 share of Time Inc. common stock with an indicated market value of $50.74 based on Time's closing stock price of $109.125 a share on the day before the announcement of deal. The combined company had $10.7 billion debt.

The WCI holders received 0.7188774 of a share of Time Warner Inc. Time Inc. and Warner Communications merged to create a world power in the field of media and entertainment. The merger created the largest media and entertainment conglomerate in the world. Time was a leading book and magazine publisher with extensive cable television holdings. Warner was a major producer of movies and records and has a large cable television operation. The merger made Time Warner as one among the few global media giants which were able to create and distribute information in virtually any medium (Harris and Richter, 1989). The merger positioned Time Warner to compete against major European and Asian companies. At the time of merger, the merged entity had a stock market value of $15.2 billion and revenue of $10 billion.

Time brought to the combination Time magazine and other publications such as Life, People, Money and Sports Illustrated. It also controlled the second largest cable system in the United States, American Television and Communications Corporation, and Home Box Office, the nation's largest cable programming service, which included HBO and Cinemax. Time also maintained a significant presence in book publishing with its Book of the Month Club, Time-Life Books, and Little.

Warner Communications was established in 1971 when Kinney National Company spun off its non-entertainment assets due to a financial scandal. It was the parent company for Warner Bros. Pictures and Warner Music Group during the 1970s and 1980s. It also owned DC Comics and Mad. In the 1970s, Warner formed joint venture with credit card company American Express named Warner-Amex Satellite Entertainment which held cable channels like MTV, Nickelodeon, and Showtime. Later in 1984, Warner bough American Express stake in the joint venture and sold it to Viacom which was renamed as MTV Networks. In 1982, Warner purchased Popular Library from CBS Publications. In 1983, Warner was a takeover target of the News Corporation which was thwarted by offering larger stake in Warner to Chris Craft. Warner Communications had also acquired Lorimar Telepictures Corp., a preeminent supplier of television programs such as Dallas and Falcon Crest. The new entity owned the United States' most lucrative recorded music and magazine publishing businesses, the largest television programming operation for both pay cable and prime-time network television. The merger elevated Time Warner as the biggest television company in the world. The merger provided the scale for Time Warner to position against Japanese conglomerates like

Sony and Matsushita. This merger was also significant as it underscored the network companies' vulnerability to competition. The network companies are not allowed to own cable television systems. The merger facilitated Time Warner to create television programming, distribute it over its own cable system, and syndicate it around the world. For the combined firm, half of its revenues came from television-related subsidiaries (Rothenberg, 1990). The other half came from movie making, owning and operating one of the top six major music labels and publishing string of magazines which included Time, Fortune, and Money. After the merger, Time had packaged advertisements for its newest magazine in Warner videotapes; Warner's Looney Tunes cartoon characters appeared in books published by Time. Synergy benefits were realized through Time Warner Direct which oversees the Book of the Month Club and the Quality Paperback Book Club as well as the television offers for parapsychology books that sell by mail or telephone. Access to Time Warner's database of 13 million direct marketing customers enabled Warner Brothers to promote their major movies. Warner also became the source of numerous new products promoted by Time's direct marketing operations which included videotape series featuring Warner Brother's properties as World War II movies, Clint Eastwood films, and Looney Tunes cartoons.

Time Warner–Turner Broadcasting Merger

In 1995, Time Warner merged with Turner Broadcasting. This merger boosted Time Warner's position as the world's largest entertainment and media conglomerate (Fabrikant, 1996). Under the merger agreement, Time Warner purchased 82% of Turner Broadcasting, in a deal worth an estimated $7.5 billion. The merger gave Time Warner access to the important brands of Ted Turner which included the Cable News Network (CNN), the Cartoon Network, the Atlanta Braves baseball team, and two movie studios. Ted Turner the chairman of Turner Foundation became a major shareholder and vice-chairman of Time Warner. The merger faced stiff competition from major shareholders of Turner like Comcast Corporation, Continental Cablevision Inc., and US West, the regional Bell telephone company. US West filed a lawsuit to block the merger. US West's investment in Time Warner consisted of a 25.5% stake in the Warner Brothers Studio, Time Warner Cable, and HBO. Turner wholly owned a number of cable networks including Cable News Network (CNN), Headline News, Turner Network Television (TNT), WTBS, Cartoon Network, and Turner Classic Movies. Under the terms of deal, the combined entity was expected to have annual revenues of about $18.5 billion, surpassing that of Walt Disney Company. The combined company accounted for about 40% of all cable programming in the United States at the time of merger. At the time of merger, Time Warner was the second largest cable distributor behind Telecommunications Inc. with 11.5 million cable subscribers representing 17% of all US cable television households. Under the terms of all stock deal, Turner Broadcasting's shareholders received three quarters of a Time Warner share for each Turner class A or B share.

American Online and Time Warner Merger

AOL originally known as America Online is a web portal and online service provider based in New York. Founded in 1985, AOL was a leader in providing interactive services, web brands, Internet technologies, and electronic commerce services. It is a brand marketed by Oath, a subsidiary of Verizon Communications. In the mid-1990s, AOL was the most recognized brand on the web in the United States and was one of the early pioneers of the Internet. Initially AOL provided a dial-up service to customers, web portal, email, and instant messages. AOL also acquired a web browser through the acquisition of Netscape. AOL was spun off from Time Warner in the year 2009. On June 23, 2015, AOL was acquired by Verizon Communications for $4.4 billion. On September 3, 2015, AOL agreed to buy Millennial Media for US $238 million.

America Online and Time Warner completed their historic merger on January 2001. Time Warner was taken over by American Online (AOL) at a 71% premium to its share price on the announcement date (Sutel, 2000). AOL had proposed the acquisition in October 1999. The deal valued at $164 billion became the largest merger on record up to that time. The merger was structured as a stock swap. Time Warner shareholders received 1.5 shares of the new company for every share of Time Warner stock they owned. AOL shareholders received one share of the new company for every AOL shares they held. The shareholders of AOL and Time Warner held 55% and 45% of the new company, respectively. The combined entity had a market capitalization of $350 billion. AOL had operated two subscription-based Internet technologies. During the merger announcement, AOL had 20 million subscribers plus another two million through CompuServe. At the time of merger, AOL had less than one fifth of the revenue and workforce of Time Warner but had almost twice the market value. Case became the chairman of the new company called AOL Time Warner. Time Warner chairman Gerald Levin became its chief executive. Ted Turner retained the title of vice-chairman. Time Warner initially provided about 70% of the company's profit stream. The deal took a year to be approved by regulators.

The major brands of AOL Time Warner included AOL, CompuServe, CNN, Time, Netscape, TBS, TNT, Cartoon Network, HBO, Warner Music Group, Fortune, Sports Illustrated, Entertainment Weekly, and Looney Tunes. The deal marked a major turning point in the media industry. The deal valued Time Warner at about $108, a share which was a high premium over its price of $64.75, a share before the announcement date. On the news of the announcement of deal, Time Warner shares soared 39% initially. AOL shares fell $1.75 to $72.

Strategic Perspective

The merger created the world's largest vertically integrated media and entertainment company. Basically there was little overlap between the two businesses. Time Warner was a media and entertainment company, whereas AOL was largely an

Internet service provider offering access to content and commerce. The combination of Time Warner's broadband systems, media contents, and subscriber base was expected to create significant synergies and strategic advantages with AOL's online brand and Internet infrastructure. AOL had the brand and credibility to capitalize upon the growth of broadband Internet but lacked the infrastructure. As the leading provider of cable television, Time Warner had the distribution capabilities AOL needed. For Warner, merging with AOL was a more effective way to distribute its contents via online channels as opposed to building its own capabilities. The new merged entity was expected to provide an important new broadband distribution platform for America Online's interactive services and drive subscriber growth through cross-marketing with Time Warner's preeminent brands. Through the acquisition, AOL got more direct path into broadband transmission as Time Warner Cable systems served 20% of US markets at the time of merger. The cable connection facilitated the introduction of AOL TV which was designed to deliver access to the Internet through the TV transmission. At the time of acquisition announcement, AOL had 22 million subscribers; Time Warner had 28 million magazine subscribers, 13 million cable subscribers, and 35 million HBO subscribers. Through the acquisition, AOL accessed Time Warner's media content as well as Time Warner's large network of cable TV lines which had a market share of 20% in US households. As a result of the AOL deal, Time Warner acquired an online platform of 22 million subscribers which included CompuServe customers. This merger completed the digital transformation of Time Warner.

Reasons for Merger Failure

The expected synergies between AOL and Time Warner never actually materialized. One of the reasons often cited was the slowdown of advertising and subscription revenues to AOL. Time Warner services were also affected negatively by the economic impact of September 2001. Executives and employees showed heavy resistance to implement the growth strategies of the combined firm. The most significant reason for the failure of merger was the creation of a negative financial synergy. During the dot-com Internet bubble of the 1990s, AOL's stock was significantly overvalued. AOL's stock price increased by approximately 1468% during the period 1996–2001 and had an inflated market capitalization of $226 billion at the time of the merger. The merger transaction was a stock for stock merger. Hence though Time Warner had higher annual turnover than AOL, it was smaller in terms of market capitalization. Though the deal was billed as the merger of equals, in reality it was an acquisition. On the merger announcement date, AOL and Time Warner had market values of $165 billion and $76 billion, respectively. By 2004 the combined market value of the firm fell to about $78 billion. Before the regulatory approval for the merger, Time Warner was witnessing fall in profits and reduction in share prices. By 2001, when the merger was completed, the dot-com bubble finally burst which led to a significant reduction in the value of AOL. AOL took a goodwill write-off of nearly $99 billion in the year 2002. When AOL was demerged in 2009, AOL's value was a mere $5.7 billion, and the total value of the two companies was a seventh of their premerger price. By May 2009, the combined firm had market capitalization of only $28 billion. AOL was the king of the dial-up Internet world, but the new trend was supplementation by always on much faster broadband.

There were huge boardroom and cultural differences between AOL and Time Warner. The integration was superficial at corporate level. The situation was further worsened as the management structure was very unstable. The feuds over top executive positions led to four individuals taking up the chief financial officer position in a span of 3 years. Gerald Levin, the CEO of Time Warner, resigned only a year after the merger following post-merger disputes.

The merger faced integration challenges as the culture at the two organizations was entirely different. A key part of the merger strategy was to position AOL as the major global provider of high-speed services. Time Warner's cable competitors were reluctant to open up their networks for AOL as they feared that AOL could deliver video over the Internet and take away their core television customers. The cable companies were competing with AOL's dial-up and high-speed services by offering a tiered pricing system giving subscribers more options than AOL. AOL Time Warner, though a global leader in digital revolution, failed to build the business model of Internet telephony or voice over IP (VoIP) which was the emerging trend (Deal Book, 2010). The combined entity was not able to promote their idea of a combined music platform. In 2003, Time Warner decided to drop AOL from its name. In 2009 AOL had about six million paying subscribers in the United States, down from 13 million at the end of 2006. AOL revenues were down to $4.2 billion in 2009 compared to $9.1 billion in 2002. In 2009, Time Warner completed the separation of AOL from Time Warner through a spin-off involving a pro rata dividend distribution of all of the AOL common stock held by Time Warner to Time Warner stockholders.

AOL's subscriber base and advertising revenues were growing exponentially until the dot-com crash of 2000. As a part of a put option contract with German media giant Bertelsmann, AOL had to borrow $600 million in order to buy AOL Europe. By 2002, the total debt of the combined company reached $28 billion. The total loss including write-down of goodwill for 2002 reached $100 billion. The downfall of this merger is symbolic for the burst of the Internet bubble. At the time of the merger, AOL's stocks were overvalued mainly due to the Internet bubble.

The deal was expected to create the twenty-first-century media powerhouse which provided everything from Internet access to making movies and running cable TV channels to publishing magazines. But the whole deal turned out to be a big disaster that Time Warner had to drop the "AOL" from its name in the year 2003 (Knowledge@Wharton, 2003). AOL rapidly declined thereafter due to the decline of dial up to broadband. AOL was eventually spun off from Time Warner in the year 2009. By this time, AOL had only 2.1 million remaining dial-up customers. By the year 2002, the merger resulted in a net loss of $99 billion and both firms failed to realize the expected synergies. Time Warner chief Jeff Bewkes described the merger as the "biggest mistake in corporate history." Time Warner had a great stable of old media brands but was struggling to adapt to the online world. But AOL proved to be fading route for AOL into digital homes (Table 3.2).

Table 3.2 Comparison in the year before merger

	AOL June 1999	Time Warner Dec 1998
Sales	$4.8 billion	$14.6 billion
Earnings	$168 million	$762 million
Employees	12,100	67,500
Key assets	AOL CompuServe	Warner Bros, Time Inc., CNN, HBO

Wealth Effects of Merger on Time Warner (Tables 3.3 and 3.4)

Time Warner was trading at $212.13 in NYSE on the day before the announcement of the deal. On the announcement day, the stock price fell to $208.89. The stock price fell for the next 10 days except for a brief gain of 9.05% 3 days after merger announcement. One day before announcement, the stock gained by 7.27%. On the announcement day, Time Warner stock price fell by 1.53% and approximately by 12% on the day after merger announcement.

The analysis of the Time Warner daily stock returns over a 1-year period surrounding the merger period (January 1, 2000, to January 1, 2001) reveals that stock price lost value by about 57% during the time window of 1-year period. The stock price which was trading at $218.20 on December 31, 1999, dropped by half to $100.09 on December 29, 2000. During the shorter time window period surrounding the merger announcement, the stock registered only negative returns (Fig. 3.1).

The cumulative return analysis for Time Warner for a period of 1 year surrounding the merger period reveals that Time Warner stock lost wealth on cumulative basis. The stock returns were in the negative zone throughout the period except during the period +50 to +52 days.

Operating Performance Analysis

The operating performance analysis is done to examine whether the corporate performance have improved after the merger. The premerger operating performance is compared with the post-merger operating performance of combined company. The 5-year premerger financial data during the period 1995–1999 is compared with the 5-year post-merger financial data for the period 2001–2005. The year of merger (2000) is excluded from the analysis. The analysis is based on the 5-yearly average values during the pre- and post-merger period (Table 3.5).

The average growth rate of revenues during the premerger period 1996–1999 was 38.5%. The average growth rate of revenues during the post-merger period 2001–2005 fell to 3.4%. The operating income was −39 billion in the year 2002. The average growth rate in operating income during the premerger period was 97.8% while the average growth rate of operating income declined to −85% in the post-merger period. Hence it can be concluded that the operating performance declined in the post-merger period. Thus both stock market performance and operating performance of Time Warner declined in the post-merger period. The borrowings of the company also increased by a huge amount in the year 2002.

Table 3.3 Stock return analysis of Time Warner during the merger announcement

Day	Price	Returns (%)
−5	238.73	9.39
−4	221.48	−7.23
−3	213.03	−3.81
−2	197.75	−7.17
−1	212.13	7.27
0	208.89	−1.53
1	184.08	−11.88
2	172.76	−6.15
3	188.40	9.05
4	181.93	−3.44
5	176.17	−3.16
6	186.60	5.92
7	184.26	−1.25
8	186.24	1.07
9	178.33	−4.25
10	176.17	−1.21

Table 3.4 Cumulative return analysis

Time window period	Cumulative returns (%)
5 days to +5 days	−18.65
3 days to 3 days	−14.22
5 days to 30 days	−20.66
5 days to 246 days	−57.38

Fig. 3.1 Cumulative returns surrounding 1-year period for Time Warner

Table 3.5 Operating performance analysis (values in millions of dollars)

Year	1995	1996	1997	1998	1999	2000	2001	2002	2003	2004	2005
Merger period	−5	−4	−3	−2	−1	0	1	2	3	4	5
Revenues	8067	10,064	13,294	14,582	27,333	7605	37,166	40,961	39,565	40,993	42,407
Operating income	697	966	1271	1496	6035	1766	118	−39,875	5365	5502	3984
Net income	−166	−191	246	168	1948	1121	−4934	−98,696	2639	3108	2671
Borrowing	2023	3431	5413	3743	4332	104	10,692	23,535	2492	1320	6

Other Acquisitions

In August 2015, Turner acquired a majority interest in StreamPlanet Co., LLC ("iStreamPlanet"), a provider of streaming and cloud-based video and technology services. This acquisition was aimed at improving Turner's digital streaming capabilities.

Spin-Offs

Spin-Off of AOL

In the year 2009, Time Warner completed the spin-off of AOL Inc. One share of AOL common stock was distributed for every 11 shares of Time Warner common stock as of record date of November 27, 2009. Stockholders received cash payment instead of fractional AOL shares. The AOL spin-off was structured as a tax-free dividend to Time Warner stockholders for US federal income tax purposes, except for the cash received in lieu of fractional shares. The spin-off of AOL was aimed to streamline Time Warner's portfolio of businesses by focusing on creating, packaging, and distributing branded content. The spin-off gave Time Warner and AOL greater strategic and operational flexibility. AOL Time Warner merger was termed as one of the most disastrous corporate mergers in history. AOL has steadily lost subscribers for its dial-up Internet access business. The spin-off was aimed to make AOL a stand-alone public company with the focus to strengthen its core businesses and develop innovative products and services.

Spin-Off of Time Warner Cable

On March 12, 2009, Time Warner Inc. announced the separation of Time Warner Cable Inc. through a tax-free spin-off. Warner effected a one for three reverse stock split. 0.083670 share of Time Warner Cable common stock was distributed for each share of Time Warner common stockholders. Time Warner Cable is the second largest cable provider in the United States after Comcast Corp. with 13.3 million video subscribers. After the spin-off, Time Warner wanted to focus on cable network, entertainment, and publishing operations. Time Warner had emerged more of a full-fledged telecommunication business with expansion into high-speed Internet access and digital phone service with different needs which didn't fit as well with Time Warner's traditional media businesses. Cable operators typically have a more highly leveraged capital structure than pure content companies like entertainment and media companies, since they usually have to invest heavily in infrastructure. Time Warner Cable paid special cash dividend to holders of its common stock which amounted to $10.27 a share or $9.25 billion. Time Warner held 80% of the Time Warner Cable.

Spin-Off of Time Inc.

On June 6, 2014, Time Warner Inc. completed the spin-off of Time Inc. Time Warner distributed all outstanding shares of Time Inc. common stock to Time Warner shareholders at a distribution ratio of one share of Time Inc. common stock for every eight shares of Time Warner common stock held on the May 23, 2014, record date. The spin-off was aimed to position Time Warner as the world's leading video company. *Time* which was the United States largest magazine publisher was once the crown jewel in terms of profit and stature for Time Warner. Though *Time* magazine was still profitable, other brands like *Fortune* and *Entertainment Weekly* are not making large contribution. The advertising revenues from titles like Time, People and Sports Illustrated have been declining over the period of time. Time Warner decided to spin off its entire Time Inc. magazine group after talks with Meredith Corp failed over the proposed merger of most of their titles. The spin-off took place in a scenario whereby there appeared a permanent decline in newsstand sales and protracted advertisement slump.

AT&T Acquires Time Warner

On October 22, 2016, Time Warner entered into an Agreement and Plan of Merger with AT&T to combine with AT&T in a stock and cash transaction. The merger agreement was unanimously approved by the board of directors of both companies. The Time Warner shareholders adopted the Merger Agreement at a special meeting of shareholders held on February 15, 2017. The deal was valued for $85.4 billion in cash and stock. AT&T paid $107.50 per share evenly split between cash and stock. Time Warner's shareholders received $53.75 in cash and a specified number of shares of AT&T stock as set forth in the merger agreement. The number of shares distributed was determined by reference to the average of the volume weighted averages of trading price of AT&T common stock on the New York Stock Exchange on each of the 15 consecutive NYSE trading days ending on and including the trading day that is three trading days prior to the closing of the merger. The stock portion of the per share consideration was subjected to a collar such that if the average stock price was between $37.411 and $41.349, Time Warner shareholders received shares of AT&T stock equal to $53.75 in value for each share of Time Warner common stock. If the average stock price was below $37.411, Time Warner's shareholders would receive 1.437 AT&T shares for each share of Time Warner common stock. If the average stock price is above $41.349, Time Warner shareholders would receive 1.300 AT&T shares for each share of Time Warner common stock. The merger was expected to close before year-end 2017. Time Warner agreed to pay a $1.7 billion breakup fee if another company outbids AT&T's offer. AT&T was expected to pay $500 million if the deal gets blocked. AT&T aimed to finance the deal with $40 billion in bridge loans with 25 billion dollars financed from JP Morgan Chase & Co and $ 15 billion from Bank of America Corp.

The merger would facilitate the combined business to pair AT&T's millions of wireless and pay television subscribers with Time Warner's media portfolio which includes networks such as CNN, TNT, HBO, and Warner Bros. film and TV studio. AT&T focuses on the strategic plan that television and video can drive growth into a stalled wireless market. Time Warner focuses on strengthening its position within the traditional TV ecosystem and increasing the content and services offered directly to consumers. The combined company aims to be the first US wireless company to compete nationwide with cable companies by providing an online video bundle similar to a traditional pay television package (Gryta et al., 2016). The core wireless business has become saturated. The deal would help AT&T to find new areas of growth. AT&T faces pressures in its traditional wireless business. The firm lost 268,000 mainstream wireless phone customers, and its video business lost a net 3000 customers in 2016. The company had almost 200,000 video customers since it bought satellite television provider DirecTV in the year 2015. The deal is expected to result in about one billion dollar in cost savings within 3 years.

References

Deal Book (2010) How the AOL Time Warner deal went wrong? https://dealbook.nytimes.com/2010/01/11/how-the-aol-time-warner-deal-went-wrong/. Accessed 29 June 2017

Fabrikant G (1996) Holders back Time Warner Turner merger. http://www.nytimes.com/1996/10/11/business/holders-back-time-warner-turner-merger.html. Accessed 23 June 2017

Gryta T, Hagey K, Amol D (2016) AT&T reaches deal to buy Time Warner for $85.4 billion. https://www.wsj.com/articles/at-t-reaches-deal-to-buy-time-warner-for-more-than-80-billion-1477157084. Accessed 1 July 2017

Harris K, Richter P (1989) Time Warner merger creates a world power. http://articles.latimes.com/1989-03-05/news/mn-471_1_time-warner. Accessed 25 June 2017

Knowledge@Wharton (2003) Giving up on AOL Time Warner. https://www.cnet.com/news/giving-up-on-aol-time-warner/. Accessed 24 June 2017

Rothenberg P (1990) The media business; Time Warner's merger payoff. http://www.nytimes.com/1990/12/31/business/the-media-business-time-warner-s-merger-payoff.html?pagewanted=all&src=pm. Accessed June 27 2017

Sutel S (2000) AOL buys Time Warner for $162 billion. http://abcnews.go.com/Business/Decade/aol-buys-time-warner-162-billion/story?id=9279138. Accessed 27 June 2017

http://archipelle.com/Business/AOLTimeWarner.pdf. Accessed 22 June 2017

Acquisitions by Verizon

4

Introduction

Verizon Communications Inc. is a global leader, which provides broadband and other wireless and wireline communications services to businesses, government, consumers, and wholesale customers. Verizon Wireless has the most reliable wireless network in America with approximately 103 million retail connections worldwide. Verizon provides converged communications, information, and entertainment services over advanced fiber-optic network. The company offers integrated business solutions to customers in more than 150 countries. Verizon is included in the Dow 30 index. Verizon Communications Inc. was formed on June 30, 2000, with the merger of Bell Atlantic Corp. and GTE Corp. Verizon stock is traded on the New York Stock Exchange and NASDAQ. GTE and Bell Atlantic have each evolved and grown through years of mergers, acquisitions, and divestitures. Before the merger, GTE was one of the world's largest telecommunication companies with revenues of more than $25 billion. GTE was a leading wireless operator in the United States with more than 7.1 million wireless customers. Bell Atlantic was larger than GTE and served 43 million access lines which included 22 million households and more than two million business customers. The deal was valued at approximately $52 billion. The merger was designed to join the Bell Atlantic's sophisticated network which served its data-intensive customer base in 13 states of the United States with GTE's national footprint, advanced data communications capabilities, and long-distance expertise. Verizon Communications was added to the Dow Jones Industrial Average in the year 2004. Verizon had more than 100 million Americans connected to Verizon network daily. By mid-2000, Verizon became the leading provider of advanced communications and information technology solutions to large business and government customers throughout the world. Verizon Communications generated nearly $132 billion in the year 2015. The company was

B. R. Kumar, *Wealth Creation in the World's Largest Mergers and Acquisitions*,
Management for Professionals, https://doi.org/10.1007/978-3-030-02363-8_4

ranked number 15 among the Fortune 500 companies. Verizon operates the most reliable wireless network with more than 112 million retail connections worldwide. Verizon facilitated communication and entertainment services through advanced fiber-optic network and provides integrated business solutions to customers in more than 140 countries.

Verizon Communications Acquisition of Verizon Wireless

Verizon Wireless was founded as a joint venture of Verizon and Vodafone in the year 2000. The company was formed when Vodafone merged its United States Operations with Bell Atlantic. The aim of the merger was to create a new wireless business with a national footprint, single brand, and common digital technology (Colton and Carew, 2013). The joint venture consisted of Bell Atlantic's and Vodafone's wireless assets like Bell Atlantic Mobile, AirTouch, Cellular, PrimeCo Personal Communications, and AirTouch Paging. GTE's wireless operations became part of Verizon Wireless. Verizon became the majority owner with 55% of Verizon Wireless with the management control of the joint venture. Over a period of time, Verizon Wireless became the largest cellphone operator in the United States. On September 3, 2013, Verizon Communications Inc. agreed to pay $130 billion for the acquisition of Vodafone Group Plc's 45% indirect interest in Verizon Wireless. Thus Verizon Communications bought out its longtime partner Vodafone's stake. The transaction was immediately accretive to Verizon's earnings per share by approximately 10%. The merger was completed in the year 2014. The deal saw the British group Vodafone returning 71% of the net proceeds of $84 billion including all of the stock to the shareholders. The deal was the third largest deal in the world after the Vodafone takeover of Germany's Mannesmann and AOL's acquisition of Time Warner in the year 2000. The deal also saw Verizon raising one of the largest ever financing packages valued at $67 billion. Moody's Investor Service downgraded its ratings on Verizon on account of this additional debt amount which saw Verizon's debt load increasing to $116 billion. Gaining control of its biggest business partner was vital for Verizon as during the time of deal, wireless services accounted for $20 billion of the approximately $30 billion in revenue. Verizon had important focused plans like bundling mobile broadband services with wired offerings like high-speed fiber-optic connections. The deal happened at a critical time for American telecommunications industry. The wireless business had been witnessing gradual slowdown in subscriber growth. The growth rate of American wireless market was a mere 2.2%.

Vodafone obtained the cash to reinvest in its own businesses and buy competitors in Europe and emerging markets. Vodafone had committed to spend about $10 billion over 3 years in high-speed cellphone and broadband services across its markets in Europe and the developing world. The company aimed to use another $20 billion from the sale of its Verizon Wireless stake to reduce its debt burden.

Financial Highlights of the Deal

As per the terms of the deal, Verizon agreed to pay \$58.9 billion in cash and additional \$60.2 billion worth of its shares to Vodafone. The deal was for acquisition of 45% of Verizon Wireless. The wireless unit was thus valued at approximately \$290 billion (Michael and Scott, 2013). As a part of deal, Verizon sold its minority stake in Vodafone's Italian business Omnitel venture for \$3.5 billion. This transaction was a part of a series of smaller transactions tied to the deal.

Under the stock purchase agreement, Verizon issued 1,274,764,121 common shares to shareholders of Vodafone as the stock portion of the consideration for Vodafone's 45% indirect interest in Verizon Wireless. Verizon used proceeds from capital market transactions occurring in September 2013 and February 2014, as well as \$6.6 billion borrowed on February 21, 2014, under its Term Loan Credit Agreement for the payment of the cash portion of the consideration to Vodafone and related fees and expenses. Guggenheim Securities LLC, JPMorgan Securities LLC, Morgan Stanley & Co. LLC, and Paul J. Taubman served as lead financial advisors to Verizon Communications. Barclays and BofA Merrill Lynch served as financial advisors to Vodafone.

Strategic Perspective of the Deal

The deal catapulted Verizon with full ownership of the US wireless industry and industry leadership position in network performance, profitability, and cash flow. Over the past one and half decades, Verizon Wireless emerged as the largest and most profitable wireless company in the United States.

The announcement of the acquisition was made on September 2, 2013.The stock price of Verizon Communications was highly fluctuating over the window period of announcement. The cumulative return analysis for the 82-day period surrounding the announcement day shows that stock prices were on a downfall immediately surrounding the acquisition announcement and then gained momentum during the period +7 to +12 days after merger announcement. The cumulative returns peaked during the time window +30 to +35 days. Thereafter the stock price was showing declining trend till +74 days after acquisition announcement (Fig. 4.1).

"0" refers to the day of announcement of the acquisition event. Verizon Communications was trading at \$47.38 on the day before the acquisition announcement. On the announcement date, the stock was trading at \$46.01 and the next day the stock price increased to 46.78. The stock of Verizon registered loss of −2.9% on the day of announcement. The stock gained 1.7% on the day after announcement of acquisition news (Table 4.1).

The cumulative returns for Verizon Communications have been negative in all the shorter window time period surrounding the acquisition announcement. The 3-day cumulative return (−1 to +1 day) for Verizon Communications was −2.13%. The cumulative returns for the 93-day period were 3.96% (Table 4.2).

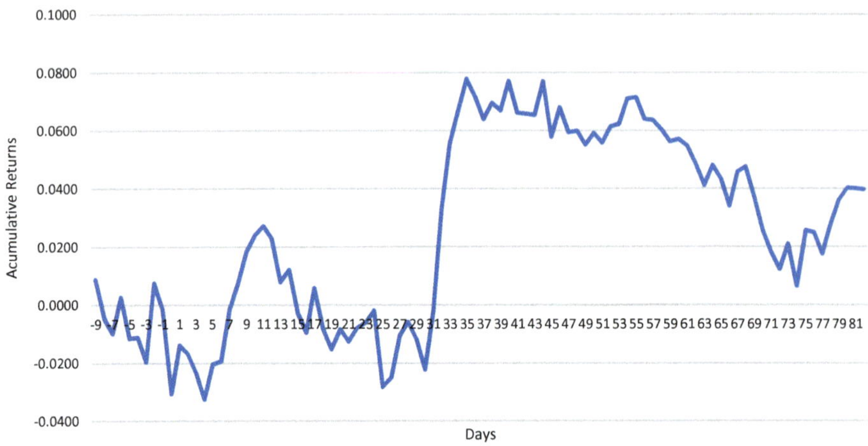

Fig. 4.1 Wealth effects of acquisition announcements for Verizon Communications

Table 4.1 Return analysis surrounding acquisition announcement for Verizon Communications

Day	Returns (%)
−5	−1.4
−4	0.0
−3	−0.8
−2	2.7
−1	−0.9
0	−2.9
1	1.7
2	−0.3
3	−0.6
4	−0.9
5	1.2
6	0.1
7	1.8
8	0.9
9	1.1
10	0.6

Table 4.2 Cumulative returns surrounding the acquisition announcement – Verizon Communications

Days	Cumulative returns (%)
−1 to +1 days	−2.13
5 to +5 days	−2.29
5 to +20 days	−1.10
1 to 30 days	−2.97
−9 to +82 days	3.96

The values are given in millions of dollars. The year of acquisition 0 is excluded from the analysis. The average growth rate of revenues in the pre-acquisition period was 4.3% which decreased to 1.6% in the post-acquisition period. The average growth rate in operating income which was negative (– 5% approximately) in the pre-acquisition period increased to 3.9% in the post-merger period. The average growth rate of free cash flow was negative in the premerger period (−17.9%) which further deteriorated to −36% in the post-merger period. The average growth rate of net income was negative (−34.6%) in the premerger period but increased to 14.3% in the post-merger period (Table 4.3).

Market capitalization, enterprise value, and total assets have been increasing over the 5-year period of analysis (Table 4.4).

The profitability analysis of the company was based on a 3-year comparison of profitability variables (average values) during the pre- and post-acquisition period. The average gross margin which was 59.08% in the pre-acquisition period slightly improved to 59.99% in the post-merger period. The average EBT margin increased from 9.96% to 16.71%. The average net margin of 1.77% in the premerger period increased to 10.52% in the post-merger period. The average ROA and ROE increased from 0.86% and 5.11% in the pre-acquisition period to 5.55% and 76.51% in the post-acquisition period on the basis of average values. The ROE was 124.48% in the post-acquisition period. The average ROI improved from 4.64% to 13.16%. The average ICR was 5.20 in the pre-acquisition period which slightly improved to 5.55 in the post-acquisition period (Table 4.5).

Table 4.3 Operating performance analysis surrounding acquisition period

Merger period	−3	−2	−1	0	1	2	3
Year	2010	2011	2012	2013	2014	2015	2016
Revenue	106,565	110,875	115,846	120,550	127,079	131,620	125,980
Operating income	14,645	12,880	13,160	31,968	19,599	33,060	27,059
Operating cash flow	33,363	29,780	31,486	38,818	30,631	38,930	22,715
Free cash flow	16,905	13,536	11,376	21,634	13,086	11,213	5122
Net income	2549	2404	875	11,497	9625	17,879	13,127

Data Source: Morning Star

Table 4.4 Financial highlights

Merger period	−1	0	1	2	3
Year	2012	2013	2014	2015	2016
Market capitalization	123,690	140,540	194,369	196,082	217613.2
Enterprise value	224,490	236,582	297,865	302,405	324,319
Total assets	225,222	274,098	232,708	244,640	244,180

Table 4.5 Profitability analysis

Merger period	−3	−2	−1	0	1	2	3
Year	2010	2011	2012	2013	2014	2015	2016
Gross margin in %	58.57	58.62	60.05	62.76	60.71	60.07	59.18
EBT margin in %	11.9	9.45	8.54	24.29	12.02	21.46	16.66
Net margin in %	2.39	2.17	0.76	9.54	7.57	13.58	10.42
ROA in %	1.14	1.07	0.38	4.61	3.8	7.49	5.37
ROE in %	6.36	6.45	2.53	31.94	37.65	124.48	67.4
ROI in %	4.62	5.65	3.66	12.54	10.38	16.72	12.38
Interest coverage	6.03	4.71	4.85	11.98	4.11	6.74	5.8

Verizon's Acquisition of AOL

On May 12, 2015, Verizon announced plans to acquire AOL. The deal was aimed to create unique and scaled digital media platforms for consumers, advertisers, and partners. Verizon's acquisition of AOL strengthened its growth strategy of LTE wireless video and OTT (over-the-top video) (Shields and Gryta, 2015).

During June 2015, Verizon completed its $4.4 billion acquisition of AOL from Time Warner (Rooney, 2015). AOL Time Warner merger was one of the world's largest failed mergers. The all-cash deal values AOL at $50 a share, a 23% premium over the company's 3-month volume-weighted average price. The new merger was worth a lot less than the failed $160 billion deal between Time Warner and AOL. At the time of the deal, Verizon's growth was largely driven by its wireless business which had approximately 108.6 million mobile connections. The company acquired AOL as a source for new cash cow for its businesses. With respect to consumer wireline business, Verizon was not realizing its expected gains. The company sold off its copper phone lines and DSL connections in smaller markets. Verizon's FiOS fiber business was making good gains through the attractive service bundle which included high-speed broadband, phone, and TV programming. The traditional avenues of voice, message, and data for revenue generation were reaching saturation point. In addition to dial-up services and content business, AOL had developed a sophisticated suite of advertising technologies for online and traditional media. AOL had a strong platform in video advertising which covered more than 50% of the US population. AOL's advertising unit had outpaced revenue growth among its content brand. AOL's successful digital platform was expected to facilitate the launch of Verizon's own Internet TV service. Verizon had acquired Intel's media assets in the year 2014 and video delivery network EdgeCast in year 2013. This deal was focused to create a major new player in the digital media business through the combination of one of the biggest mobile network providers with leading content producer. Verizon 's strategy was to offer all content from TV channels to publications by means of streaming over internet. The key assets of AOL included its subscription business; global content brands like The Huffington Post, TechCrunch, Engadget, MAKERS, and AOL.com, as well as its millennial-focused OTT, Emmy-nominated original video content; and its programmatic advertising platforms. On announcement of the acquisition, shares of AOL went up nearly by 19% in morning trade. The acquisition of AOL was aimed to contribute toward Verizon's "Internet of Things" technology platform which facilitated web-enabled devices which could communicate and coordinate with one another. AOL acquisition enabled Verizon to turn the data it generates to enable phone calls and deliver text messages into a viable new revenue stream since AOL provides ad tech infrastructure and marketer relationships which Verizon lacked. Verizon absorbed AOL's two million subscribers (Fitchard, 2015). Using AOL's digital platform, advertisers can go bid for advertisement slots. Through the deal, Verizon's mobile customers could personalize advertisements and contents. This deal may be termed as a kind of vertical merger. The deal advisors for Verizon were LionTree Advisors, Guggenheim Partners, and Weil, Gotshal & Manges. The advisors for AOL were Allen & Company LLC and Wachtell, Lipton, Rosen & Katz.

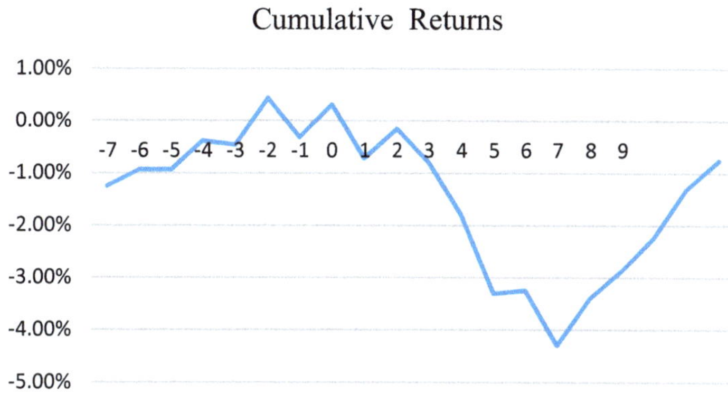

Fig. 4.2 Announcement effects on Verizon stock returns for AOL acquisition

Table 4.6 Announcement effect on stock returns of Verizon Communications

Day	Returns (%)
−7	−1.25
−6	0.32
−5	0.00
−4	0.55
−3	−0.08
−2	0.90
−1	−0.76
0	0.63
1	−1.03
2	0.57
3	−0.64
4	−1.00
5	−1.51
6	0.06
7	−1.05
8	0.90
9	0.54
10	0.62
11	0.92
12	0.55

The cumulative returns for the 20-day period surrounding the acquisition period were 0.55% for Verizon Communications stock. The 11-day cumulative returns (−5 to +5 day) were − 2.37%. The 3-day cumulative returns (−1 to +1 day) were − 1.16% (Fig. 4.2).

The public announcement of AOL acquisition was done on May 12, 2016.On the announcement day, Verizon stock gained 0.63%. The stock returns for 2 days after announcement was 0.57%. The maximum stock gain was 0.92% (on the 11th day) after the announcement (Table 4.6).

Acquisition of Yahoo by Verizon Communications

In July 2016, Verizon acquired Yahoo's core internet business for $4.8 billion. The aim of the acquisition was to use Yahoo's billion users to build an online advertising powerhouse to face the competition from Google and Facebook. In 2017, Verizon completed Yahoo acquisition and it planned to combine Yahoo and AOL assets into a subsidiary called Oath which covers some 50 media brands and one billion people globally (Baysinger, 2016). The deal heralded the end of the independent life of one of the oldest and most iconic internet brands. The sale of Yahoo signaled the continued massive consolidation which is witnessed by the online media and content industry which have adopted the strategy of bringing together multiple audiences to build economies of scale for stronger advertising businesses to face competition of companies like Google and Facebook. Oath Strategy is to position as one of the most significant platforms in the consumer brand space with access to over one billion consumers. Verizon had strengthened its brand portfolio with the additions of Yahoo, TechCrunch, Yahoo Mail, HuffPost, Tumblr, and Yahoo Finance. As a part of the finalized deal, Yahoo chief executive Marissa Mayer resigned with a "golden parachute" worth just over $23 million in cash, equity, and benefits. While Google and Facebook built their sprawling business empires, Yahoo has fallen in stature. Yahoo's internet properties strength of 200 million unique visitors was the major attraction to Verizon. Verizon aims to position Oath as a platform for advertisers to connect with large audiences and provide targeted information. The acquisition was in line with the trend in the telecom industry where companies joined for combining networking technology to exclusive content (Varettoni, 2014). Verizon had plans to reduce the employees at its Yahoo and AOL units by approximately 15%. In the previous year, Yahoo cut 15% of its workforce and AOL had cut 500 jobs. The non-acquired part of Yahoo was transferred to a holding company named Altaba. Altaba had a 15.5% stake in Alibaba and 35.5% holding in Yahoo Japan. As a result of the Verizon deal, two of the internet's earliest pioneers became corporate siblings. The merger combined Yahoo's one billion monthly active users which included 600 million on mobile with AOL's digital properties. Verizon aimed for extensive distribution opportunities. The Yahoo deal gave Verizon a boost for its go90 mobile platform.

The announcement of Yahoo acquisition was made on July 25, 2016. Figure 4.3 gives the stock returns for Yahoo surrounding the 21-day window period surrounding the acquisition period. The stock price fell steeply during the day of the announcement and recovered on the following day and rose steeply on +12 day onward. The cumulative returns for Yahoo stock for the 21-day window period were 12.59%.

On 1 day before announcement, the stock returns were 1.36%. On +1 day, the stock registered a gain of 1.15%. The stock returns were 1.38% on +8 day. The highest gain was registered on +13 day (3.36%) and + 14 day (4. 05%) (Table 4.7). The cumulative returns for the 11-day period (−5 to +5 day) of announcement were 2.91%. The 3-day (−1 to +1) cumulative return was −0.18% during the announcement period.

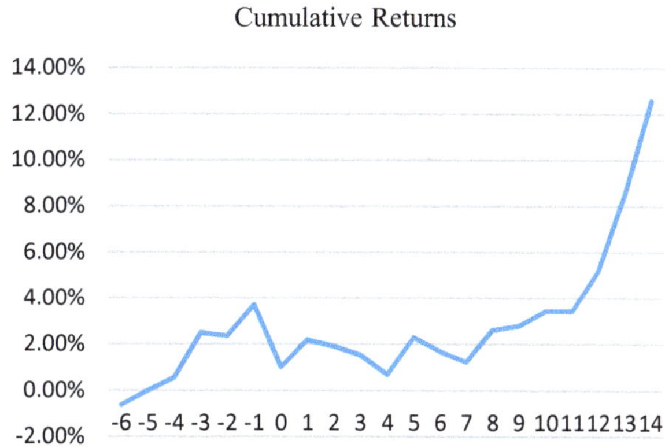

Fig. 4.3 Stock returns for Yahoo during the acquisition period

Table 4.7 Announcement effects for Yahoo stock

Day	Returns (%)
−6	−0.63
−5	0.61
−4	0.58
−3	1.91
−2	−0.13
−1	1.36
0	−2.69
1	1.15
2	−0.26
3	−0.36
4	−0.86
5	1.60
6	−0.59
7	−0.47
8	1.38
9	0.18
10	0.64
11	0.00
12	1.76
13	3.36
14	4.05

Figure 4.4 highlights the 23-day cumulative returns for Verizon Communications stock during the announcement of Yahoo acquisition. The cumulative returns for the 23-day window period were – 3.7%. The 11-day period (−5 to +5 day) cumulative return was 10%.

The returns of Verizon Communications were negative during the entire 23-day period surrounding the announcement period except on day −8 and – 1 day. The announcement day return for Verizon was −0.1% (Table 4.8).

In the year 2016, Frontier Communications completed its $10.54 billion acquisition of Verizon Communications' wireline operations, which provided services to residential, commercial, and wholesale customers in California, Texas, and Florida (Businesswire, 2016). The acquired businesses included approximately 3.3 million

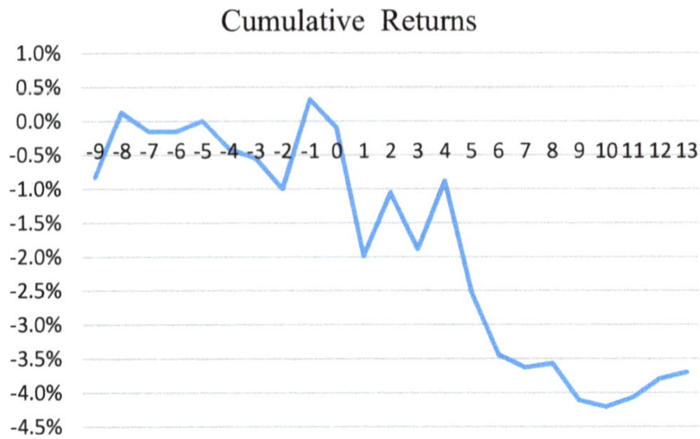

Fig. 4.4 Announcement effects for Verizon Communications during Yahoo acquisition

Table 4.8 Announcement returns for Verizon Communications

Day	Returns (%)
−9	−0.8
−8	0.1
−7	−0.2
−6	−0.2
−5	0.0
−4	−0.4
−3	−0.5
−2	−1.0
−1	0.3
0	−0.1
1	−2.0
2	−1.1
3	−1.9
4	−0.9
5	−2.5
6	−3.4
7	−3.6
8	−3.6
9	−4.1
10	−4.2
11	−4.1
12	−3.8
13	−3.7

voice connections, 2.1 million broadband connections, and 1.2 million FiOS video subscribers as well as the related incumbent local exchange carrier businesses. Frontier Communications Corporation is a Fortune 500 and S&P 500 company, which provides communication services to urban, suburban, and rural communities in 29 states. Yahoo changed its name to Altaba in June 2017.

Other Corporate Restructuring by Verizon

Through 2015, Verizon has made more than $110 billion in network investments in wireless. This is in addition to major spectrum purchases. In August 2008, Verizon Wireless expanded to many rural markets by completing its purchase of Rural Cellular Corp. for $2.7 billion in cash and assumed debt. In January 2009, Verizon Wireless completed its purchase of Alltel from Atlantis Holdings LLC, expanding the company's network coverage to nearly the entire US population. In December 2011, Verizon Wireless purchased Advanced Wireless Spectrum licenses from SpectrumCo which was the joint venture of Comcast, Time Warner Cable, and Bright House Networks and from Cox TMI Wireless (Tables 4.9 and 4.10).

Table 4.9 Acquisitions by Verizon

Year	Highlights of the deal
2005	Acquired MCI Communications Corp. in a merger deal valued at$8.5 billion
2007	Acquired CyberTrust a privately held provider of global information security services
2011	Acquired Terremark Worldwide Inc. which is a global provider of managed IT infrastructure and cloud services for total equity value of $1.4 billion
2011	Acquired CloudSwitch which is an innovative provider of cloud software technology
2012	Verizon acquired Hughes Telematics which specializes in the automotive and fleet telematics
2013	Acquired EdgeCast which was an industry leader in content delivery networks
2013	Acquired the assets and operations of upLynk a leading technology and television cloud company.
2014	Verizon and Intel Corp. purchased the assets of Intel Media which focuses on development of cloud TV products and services
2015	Verizon purchased AOL Inc. for an estimated total value of $4.4 billion

Table 4.10 Divestitures by Verizon

Year	Highlights of the deal
2002	Sold wireline access lines in Alabama, Missouri and Kentucky
2005	Sold wireline access in Hawaii
2006	Spun off US print and Internet yellow pages directories to new company called SuperMedia
2007	Spun off wireline businesses in Maine, New Hampshire, and Vermont to FairPoint Communications
2009	Spun off of wireline business in Arizona, Idaho, Illinois, Indiana, Michigan, Nevada, etc.
2015	Entered into an agreement with Frontier to sell Verizon's local exchange business and related landline activities for approximately $10.5 billion
2015	American Tower Corporation acquired the exclusive right to lease, acquire, and manage many of Verizon's wireless towers for up-front payment of $5.1 billion

References

Baysinger T (2016) http://www.adweek.com/digital/verizon-deal-yahoo-and-aol-are-finally-together-172658/. Accessed 6 July 2017

Businesswire (2016) http://www.businesswire.com/news/home/20160401005508/en/Frontier-Communications-Completes-Acquisition-Verizon-Wireline-Operations. Accessed 4 July 2017

Colton K, Carew S (2013) Verizon-Vodafone agree to $130 billion wireless deal. http://www.reuters.com/article/us-vodafone-verizon/verizon-vodafone-agree-to-130-billion-wireless-deal-idUSBRE97S08C20130903. Accessed 2 July 2017

Fitchard K (2015) The real reason why Verizon bought AOL. http://fortune.com/2015/06/24/verizon-gains-aol/. Accessed 6 July 2017

Michael J, Scott M (2013) Verizon seals long sought $130 billion deal to own wireless unit https://dealbook.nytimes.com/2013/09/02/verizon-reaches-130-billion-deal-to-buy-out-vodafones-wireless-stake/?mcubz=3. Accessed 3 July 2017

Rooney B (2015) Verizon buys AOL for $4.4 billion. http://money.cnn.com/2015/05/12/investing/verizon-buys-aol/index.html. Accessed 6 July 2017

Shields M and Gryta T (2015) https://www.wsj.com/articles/verizon-to-buy-aol-for-4-4-billion-1431428458. Accessed 5 July 2017

Varettoni B (2014) Verizon completes acquisition of Vodafone's 45 per cent indirect interest in Verizon wireless. http://www.verizon.com/about/news/verizon-completes-acquisition-vodafones-45-percent-indirect-interest-verizon-wireless/. Accessed 2 July 2017

5 DowDuPont Merger

Dow Chemical Company

The Dow Chemical Company was incorporated in 1947 under Delaware law. The market-driven integrated portfolio of Dow consisted of a broad range of technology-based products and solutions in high-growth sectors like packaging, infrastructure, transportation, consumer care, electronics, and agriculture. Dow Chemical employs approximately 56,000 people. The company has more than 7000 product families produced at 189 sites in 34 countries. In 2016, Dow had annual sales of $48 billion. The five operating segments of Dow included Agricultural Sciences, Consumer Solutions, Infrastructure Solutions, Performance Materials and Chemicals, and Performance Plastics. The Agricultural Sciences segment is a global leader in providing crop protection and seed/plant biotechnology products and technologies, urban pest management solutions, and healthy oils. The business invents, develops, manufactures, and markets products for use in agricultural, industrial, and commercial pest management. The Consumer Solutions segment had four global businesses, namely, Consumer Care, Dow Automotive Systems, Dow Electronic Materials, and Consumer Solutions – Silicones. The Infrastructure Solutions segment consists of portfolio of products such as architectural and industrial coatings, construction material ingredients, building insulation and materials, adhesives, microbial protection for oil and gas industry, telecommunications, and light and water technologies. The Performance Materials and Chemicals segment provides innovative technology and solutions: Chlor-Alkali and Vinyl, Industrial Solutions, and Polyurethanes. The Performance Plastics segment is the world's leading plastic franchise, and the portfolio is comprised of major global businesses: Dow Elastomers, Dow Electrical and Telecommunications, Dow Packaging and Specialty Plastics, and Dow Hydrocarbons and Energy. Dow Elastomers, Dow Electrical and Telecommunications, and Dow Packaging and Specialty Plastics serve high-growth, high-value sectors. The energy business of Dow is one of the world's largest industrial energy producers. The Union Carbide Corporation ("Union Carbide") is a wholly owned subsidiary of the company.

B. R. Kumar, *Wealth Creation in the World's Largest Mergers and Acquisitions*,
Management for Professionals, https://doi.org/10.1007/978-3-030-02363-8_5

Divestitures

During January 2015, Dow Chemicals sold its sodium borohydride (SBH) business to Vertellus Performance Chemicals LLC. SBH belonged to the Performance Materials and Chemical segment. During February 2015, Dow sold ANGUS Chemical Company which was again part of Performance Materials and Chemicals segment to Golden Gate Capital. The company sold its AgroFresh business to AgroFresh Solutions, Inc. ("AFSI") during July 31, 2015. In early 2017, the company announced an agreement to sell its global ethylene acrylic acid (EAA) copolymers and ionomers business to SK Global Chemical Co. as a part of the regulatory approval process for the merger transaction.

Restructuring Plan

During the second quarter of 2016, Dow's board of directors approved a restructuring plan which affected the ownership structure of Dow Corning. These activities resulted in a global workforce reduction of approximately 2500 employees. In 2013, the board of directors at Dow approved a share buyback program which authorized up to $1.5 billion to be spent on the repurchase of the company's common stock. Again in year 2014, the board expanded the buyback program with an additional amount of approximately $3 billion envisaged for repurchase of stocks over a period of time. In November 2014, the board of directors announced a new $5 billion tranche to its share buyback program. The total amount authorized for share buyback amounted to $9.5 billion.

Net sales, net income, long-term debt, and total assets are given in millions of dollars. The net sales of Dow Jones have been on decline trend over the 5-year period. The net income has been fluctuating over the 5-year period. The return on equity has been fluctuating over the 5-year period (Table 5.1).

DuPont

DuPont was founded in 1802 and was incorporated in Delaware in 1915.The company has operations in 90 countries worldwide, and 60% of consolidated net sales are accounted by regions outside the United States. The company consists of ten

Table 5.1 Financial highlights

Year	2012	2013	2014	2015	2016
Net sales	56786	57080	58167	48778	48158
Net income	1100	4816	3839	7783	4404
Long-term debt	19819	16732	18741	16215	20456
Total assets	69462	69380	68639	67938	79511
R&D as % of net sales	3	3.1	2.8	3.3	3.3
ROE %	5	19.4	18.6	34.4	15.3

businesses which are aggregated into six reportable segments. The company's reportable segments are Agriculture, Electronics and Communications, Industrial Biosciences, Nutrition and Health, Performance Materials, and Safety and Protection. Agriculture businesses, DuPont Pioneer and DuPont Crop Protection, focus on improving the quantity, quality, and safety of the global food supply and global production agricultural industry. Agriculture accounted for approximately 55% of the company's total research and development expense in the year 2015. Pioneer is a world leader in developing, producing, and marketing corn hybrids and soybean varieties. Crop Protection serves as the global production agriculture industry with crop protection products for field crops and specialty crops. Electronics and Communications (E&C) is a leading supplier of differentiated materials and systems for photovoltaics (PV), consumer electronics, displays, and advanced printing. Industrial Biosciences offers a broad portfolio of bio-based products across a range of markets such as animal nutrition, detergents, food manufacturing, ethanol production, and industrial applications. Nutrition and Health segment focuses on sustainable bio-based ingredients and advanced molecular diagnostic solutions by providing innovative solutions for specialty food ingredients, food nutrition, and health and safety. DuPont Performance Materials include DuPont Performance Polymers and DuPont Packaging and Industrial Polymers and provides innovative polymer science solutions.

Restructuring by DuPont

During November 2013, DuPont entered into a definitive agreement to sell Glass Laminating Solutions as a part of Packaging and Industrial Polymers to Kuraray Co. On July 1, 2015, DuPont completed the spin-off of its Performance Chemicals segment through the spin-off of all of the issued and outstanding stock of The Chemours Company. During December 2015, DuPont announced global cost savings and restructuring plan designed to reduce $730 million in costs. In January 2014, DuPont's board of directors announced a $5 billion share buyback plan. There is no required completion date for purchase under this plan. During the first quarter of 2015, DuPont announced buy back of shares of about $4 billion using the distribution proceeds received from Chemours. Approximately $ 2 billion were to be purchased and retired by December 31, 2015, and the remainder was to be purchased and retired by December 31, 2016. According to accelerated share repurchase (ASR) agreement which the company entered in August 2015, DuPont paid $2 billion to the financial institution and received and retired 35 million shares at an average price of $57.16 per share.

It was assumed that the value of DuPont common stock, the S&P 500 Stock Index, and Dow Jones Industrial Average (DJIA) was each $100 on December 31, 2010, and all dividends were reinvested (Table 5.2).

In the context of merger, it can be said that both DuPont and Dow's performance was showing declining trend during the merger period. The values are in millions of dollars (Table 5.3).

Table 5.2 Stock performance of DuPont

Year	31/12/2010	31/12/2011	31/12/2012	31/12/2013	31/12/2014	31/12/2015
DuPont	100	95	96	144	168	164
S&P500	100	102	118	157	178	181
DJIA	100	108	119	155	170	171

Table 5.3 Financial highlights

Year	2013	2014	2015
Total assets	52142	50490	41166
Net sales	28998	28406	25130
Net income	4862	3636	1959

DowDuPont

DowDuPont is the holding company, which comprises of the Dow Chemical Company and DuPont. The newly merged company focuses on forming strong independent publicly traded company in agriculture, materials science, and specialty products. The agricultural division is a global leader in production agriculture with presence in more than 130 countries. The product and service offerings of DowDuPont include seed germplasm, biotech traits, crop protection, seed-applied technologies, and digital agriculture. The division offers optimized global supply chains and customer-oriented sales, distribution, and channel networks. The crop protection solution includes cereal herbicides; corn and soybean herbicides; fungicides; insecticides; pasture and land management; rice, trees, and vines herbicides; seed-applied technologies; specialty crop herbicides; structural pest management; and turf and ornamental pest management. The materials science division offers packaging and specialty plastics, industrial intermediates and infrastructure, and performance materials and coatings. The industrial intermediates and infrastructure provide solutions, which enable unique properties in manufacturing processes, infrastructure markets, and downstream finished goods. The performance materials and coating division provide a broad range of technology platforms to create ingredients and solutions with exceptional performance and process enhancements for home and beauty care applications.

Merger Announcement

On December 11, 2015, Dow Chemicals and E. I. du Pont de Nemours and Company ("DuPont") announced that their boards of directors unanimously approved a definitive agreement under which the companies will combine in an all-stock merger of equal strategic combination. The combined company was named DowDuPont.

Merger Highlights

This merger was termed as a "merger of equals." Pursuant to the merger agreement, Dow shareholders received a fixed exchange ratio of 1.00 share of DowDuPont for each Dow share, and DuPont shareholders received a fixed exchange ratio of 1.282 shares of DowDuPont for each DuPont share. Each share of common stock, par value of $2.50 per share of Dow, was converted into the right to receive one share of common stock, par value $0.01 per share of DowDuPont. On December 30, 2016, four million issued and outstanding shares of Dow's cumulative convertible perpetual preferred stock series A (Dow Preferred Stock), par value $1 per share, were converted into 96.8 million shares of Dow common stock. Each share of common stock of DuPont with par value $0.30 per share issued and outstanding were converted into the right to receive 1.2820 shares of DowDuPont common stock. Each share of DuPont preferred stock, $4.50 series, and DuPont preferred stock, $3.50 series, which were issued and outstanding was unaffected by the mergers. On the basis of exchange ratio of 1.2820 set forth in the agreement, Dow shareholders owned 52%, and the remaining 48% were owned by DuPont shareholders Annual Reports DuPont Dow (n.d.). The Dow stock options and the DuPont stock options and other equity awards of the two companies were automatically converted into stock options and equity awards with respect to DowDuPont common stock based on same prior terms and conditions. The merger agreement restricted each of DuPont and Dow without the consent of the other party from making certain acquisitions and divestitures and entry into certain contracts. DuPont incurred $ten million in transaction-related costs in connection with the planned merger. Dow and DuPont shareholders each owned approximately 50% of the combined firm on a fully diluted basis excluding preferred shares.

The financial advisors of Dow for the deal were Lazard, Morgan Stanley & Co. LLC, and Klein and Company. The legal advisors for the deal were Weil, Gotshal & Manges LLP. DuPont's financial advisors were Evercore and Goldman Sachs & Co. Skadden, Arps, Slate, Meagher & Flom LLP were the legal advisors for DuPont.

Merger Completion

On September 01, 2017, DowDuPont announced the completion of the merger between the Dow Chemical Company (Dow) and E. I. du Pont de Nemours and Company ("DuPont") which was effective from August 31, 2017 (Alexander, 2017). The combined company would act as a holding company under the name "DowDuPont" with three divisions – agriculture, materials science and specialty products.

The shares of DuPont and Dow ceased trading at the close of the New York Stock Exchange (NYSE) on August 31, 2017. DowDuPont started trading on the New York Stock Exchange under the stock ticker symbol "DWDP" from September 1, 2017 (Mich and Del, 2017). The company replaced DuPont in the Dow Jones Industrial Average thereby continuing chemical industry representation in the stock index. The board of directors of DowDuPont comprised of 16 members – 8 directors who were formerly on the DuPont Board and 8 directors formerly on the Dow Board. After the merger announcement in December 2015, the firms expected to complete the deal by the second half of the year 2016, but the plan was delayed due to in-depth investigation by European Commission antitrust regulators. The Commission approved the deal after DuPont agreed to sell chunk of its pesticide business and most of its agricultural R&D to FMC (Reuters, 2017). The businesses being sold had generated about $1.4 billion in sales in the year 2016. In exchange, DowDuPont received $1.6 billion in cash and FMC's health and nutrition business.

Strategic Advantages

Through the merger, DowDuPont expects to maximize the value for all its stakeholders. The combination of highly complementary portfolios of Dow and DuPont was intended to create leadership position for the combined company. The merger was intended to create three industry powerhouses. The separation into three independent companies was aimed to realize substantial cost synergies as well as long-term growth and sustainable value. These strategic initiatives were expected to result in run-rate cost synergies of approximately $3 billion and the potential for approximately $1 billion in growth synergies. It was expected that the company would reach 100% run rate on the cost synergies within the first 2 years of merger closing. The combined company was expected to offer superior solutions and expanded product offerings. The merger eliminated the competition between Dow and DuPont for the development and sale of insecticides and herbicides. The merged company gained monopoly over ethylene derivatives which are used to manufacture food packaging and other products. DowDuPont became the world's largest chemical company by sales. By August 2017, DowDuPont had a market capitalization of approximately $150 billion by August 2017. After the restructuring, the largest of the firms was the materials science company with about $45 billion in sales. The division was composed mostly of Dow's petrochemical, plastics, and specialty chemical businesses. The division included DuPont's polymers business and Dow Corning silicone operations.

Integration Process

The new combined company was separated into three independent publicly traded companies through tax-free spin-offs.

The integration process of restructuring activity was meant to develop the future state operating models and organizational designs which would support the refined strategy of each intended company. Each division would have its own processes, people, assets, systems, and licenses in place to operate independently from the parent company. The intended separations were expected to be completed within 18 months of the merger completion.

The three independent companies formed as a result of the corporate restructuring were agriculture company, materials science company, and specialty products company. The agricultural company combined together the DuPont Pioneer, DuPont Crop Protection, and Dow AgroSciences. The materials science company combined the businesses of the Dow's operating segments like Performance Plastics, Performance Materials and Chemicals, Infrastructure Solutions, and Consumer Solutions along with DuPont's Performance Materials operating segment. The new materials science company offers the strongest and broadest portfolio of chemistry and polymer toolkit in the industry. The new company was in a competitive position with scale and competitive capabilities to offer differentiated solutions for customers in high-growth end markets which included packaging, transportation, infrastructure, and consumer care. The specialty products company consisted of businesses like DuPont Protection Solutions, Sustainable Solutions, Industrial Biosciences, and Nutrition and Health. The specialty products company focuses on emerging as a technology-driven innovation leader with highly differentiated products and solutions.

Regulatory Issues

On June 16, 2017, DuPont and Dow obtained US antitrust approval to merge on the condition that the companies would sell certain crop protection products and other assets. This merger was one of the biggest mergers of farm suppliers. The approval was quickly denounced by the head of the National Farmers Union which was of the opinion that farmers would face higher costs. On the basis of filings in US District Court of Columbia, the assets to be sold included DuPont's Finesse herbicide for winter wheat and Rynaxypyr insecticides. Dow will have to sell its US acid copolymers and ionomers business. DuPont received clearance to merger in the regions of Europe, China, and Brazil).

In the agriculture division, DuPont sales amounted to $ 8 billion, while Dow's share was $6 billion. In the specialty product division, DuPont's sales netted $11 billion, and Dow's sales share amounted to $2 billion before the restructuring. DuPont's share in the Performance Material sales was $5 billion, while that of Dow was $40 billion in net sales (Table 5.4).

Table 5.4 Restructured DowDuPont

Agriculture	Specialty products	Materials science
DuPont	DuPont	DuPont
Dow	Electronics and Communications	Performance Materials
	Nutrition and Health	Dow
	Industrial Biosciences	Performance Plastics
	Safety and Protection	Performance Materials and Chemicals
	Dow	Infrastructure Solutions
	Consumer Solutions	Consumer Solutions
	Dow Electronic Materials	Consumer Care
		Dow Automotive Systems

In industry in addition to Dow and DuPont merger deal, Bayer had a deal to buy Monsanto, and ChemChina had plans to buy Syngenta. PotashCorp and Agrium were planning merger.

Merger and Wealth Effects

Announcement Effects for DuPont

The public announcement of the merger was made on December 11, 2015. The below table gives the daily returns of DuPont stock surrounding the merger announcement during the 36-day time window period of −5 days to +30 days. It can be observed that the daily returns were highly fluctuating during the 36-day time window period. On −3 day of merger announcement, the stock price increased by 163%. On announcement day the stock price decreased by 62%. During +1 day after merger announcement, stock price increased by 174%. On +19 day after the announcement, the stock price increased by 189%. The daily cumulative returns for DuPont for the merger time window period of 448 days (−14 day to +433 day) were 3335% (Table 5.5).

The cumulative returns were increasing in the wider window period. The cumulative return for the 3-day period −1 to + day was 112%. The 11-day cumulative return for the period −5 to +5 day was 310% (Table 5.6, Fig. 5.1).

The cumulative monthly return for the 25-month time window (−1 month to +23 month) period after merger announcement was approximately 329% (Fig. 5.1).

Table 5.5 Returns for DuPont during the announcement window

Day	Returns	Day	Returns
-5	−0.65	13	−0.03
-4	0.06	14	0
-3	1.63	15	0
-2	0	16	0
-1	0	17	−0.64
0	−0.62	18	−0.04
1	1.74	19	1.89
2	−0.02	20	−0.11
3	−0.62	21	−0.03
4	1.61	22	−0.63
5	−0.03	23	1.56
6	0.01	24	0.21
7	0.03	25	−0.19
8	−0.63	26	0.24
9	1.67	27	0
10	−0.62	28	−0.69
11	1.66	29	1.63
12	0.03	30	−0.62

Table 5.6 Daily cumulative returns during merger announcement

Days	Cumulative returns (%)
−1 to +1	112
−5 to+5	310
−1 to +10	480
−5 to +200	1828

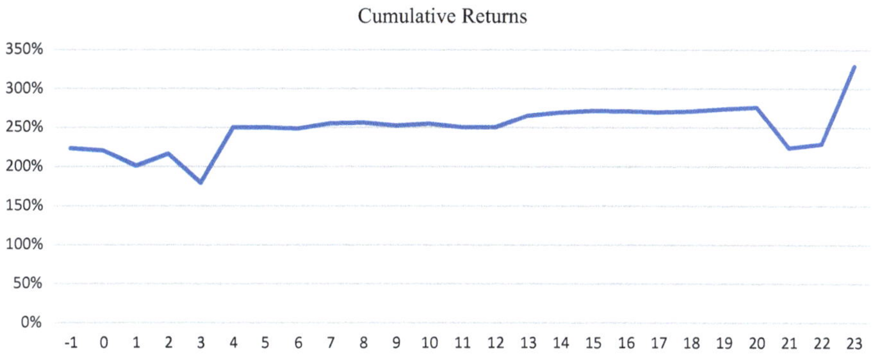

Fig. 5.1 Monthly cumulative return for 25-month period surrounding merger announcement for DuPont

Announcement Effects for Dow Chemical

The stock price declined during the merger announcement period. The announcement day period return for Dow Chemical was −3%. The stock returns on the 6th day after the announcement were 3%. The stock returns were negative in all most all days during the 36-day period surrounding the merger announcement (Table 5.8).

The cumulative daily returns for Dow Chemicals for 444-day merger period (−10 day to +433 day) were 29.1% (Fig. 5.2). The cumulative returns for the short time window period were negative. Only during the 11-day period (−10 day to +10 day), the stock registered positive cumulative returns during the short time window period (Table 5.9).

The cumulative monthly return for the 25-month time window (−1 month to +23 month) period after merger announcement was approximately 38%.

Table 5.7 gives the holding period yield for Dow Chemicals stock for different years.

Table 5.7 Holding period yield for Dow Chemical stock

Year	Holding period yield in %
2015	21.41
2016	14.6
2017	15.71

Table 5.8 Daily Returns for Dow Chemicals during merger announcement

Day	Return	Day	Return
-5	0.03	13	−0.003
-4	−0.02	14	−0.030
-3	−0.02	15	−0.008
-2	0.12	16	−0.022
−1	−0.04	17	−0.038
0	−0.03	18	−0.008
1	−0.04	19	−0.019
2	−0.01	20	−0.013
3	0.00	21	−0.026
4	−0.01	22	0.014
5	−0.01	23	−0.029
6	0.03	24	−0.021
7	0.01	25	−0.018
8	0.02	26	0.016
9	0.00	27	0.029
10	0.00	28	−0.024
11	0.01	29	0.007
12	−0.02	30	−0.025

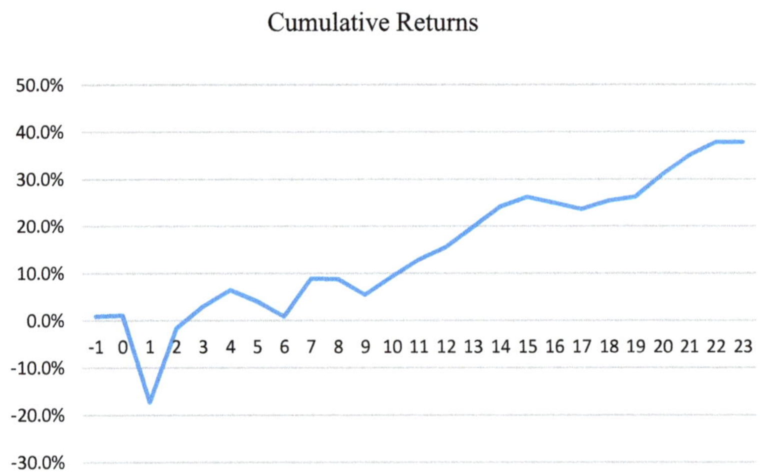

Fig. 5.2 Monthly cumulative return for 25-month period surrounding merger announcement – Dow Chemicals

Table 5.9 Cumulative returns surrounding the merger period

Day	Cumulative returns (%)
−1 to +1	−0.20
−5 to +5	−3.43
−10 to +10	1.67
−1 to +30	−31.18
−1 to +200	3.11

References

Alexander HT (2017) Drumroll Please….DowDuPont emerges, https://cen.acs.org/articles/95/i35/Historic-DowDuPont-merger-nears.html. Accessed 01 Sep 2017

Annual Reports DuPont Dow

Mich M, Del W (2017) DowDuPont merger successfully completed, http://www.dow.com/en-us/news/press-releases/dowdupont-merger-successfully-completed. Accessed 07 Dec 2017

Reuters (2017) Dow Chemical and Dupont have won US antitrust approval to merge. http://fortune.com/2017/06/16/dow-chemical-dupont-merger-antitrust-approval. Accessed 07 Dec 2017

6 Mergers and Acquisitions by Anheuser-Busch InBev

Anheuser-Busch InBev (AB InBev) is a Belgian-based transnational beverage and brewing company. The original company was formed through successive mergers of three international brewing companies. In 1987, Interbrew was formed by the merger of the two largest breweries in Belgium: Artois and Piedboeuf. Ambey was established in the year 1999 with the merger of the two biggest Brazilian brewers – Antarctica and Brahma. In the year 2004, Interbrew and Ambey merged to create the world's largest brewer InBey. The merger combined the world's third largest brewing company (Interbrew) with fifth largest brewing company (Ambey) to emerge as the world's number one beer maker. This deal resulted in the consolidation of top brands from Belgium, Canada, Germany, and Brazil. Anheuser-Busch was established in the year 1852. In 2008, the merger of InBev and Anheuser-Busch was completed. The combination resulted in the creation of one of the top five consumer product companies in the world. Under the terms of the merger agreement, all shares of Anheuser-Busch were acquired for 70 USD per share in cash for an aggregate of US$52 billion. During the year 2016, Anheuser-Busch InBev completed the acquisition of SABMiller for £69 billion (US $107 billion). By January 2017, the combined company had approximately 500 beer brands in 50 countries. The below table gives the timeline of different mergers and acquisitions (Table 6.1).

Anheuser-Busch was the largest brewing company in the United States. At the time of merger, it was also the world's largest brewing company based on revenues. The division had operated 12 breweries in the United States and 17 others overseas. The most well-known brands of Anheuser-Busch include the Budweiser, Busch, Michelob families, Natural Light, and Natural Ice. Anheuser-Busch also produces specialty beers, nonalcoholic brews, malt liquors like King Cobra and Hurricane family, and flavored malt beverages like Bacardi Silver family and Tequiza. In 2009, AB InBev announced the sale of its Busch Entertainment theme park division to the Blackstone Group for $2.7 billion. The company had been one of the largest theme park operators in the United States with ten parks throughout the United States.

B. R. Kumar, *Wealth Creation in the World's Largest Mergers and Acquisitions*,
Management for Professionals, https://doi.org/10.1007/978-3-030-02363-8_6

Table 6.1 Major mergers and acquisitions

Year	Deal
1947	SABMiller acquired South African Breweries
1988	Artois and Piedboeuf Brewery merged to form Interbrew
1995	Labatt Brewing Company acquired by Interbrew
1999	Brahma and Companhia Antarctica Paulista merged to form AmBev. Interbrew entered into a joint venture with Sun in Russia
2000	Interbrew acquired Bass and Whitbread in the United Kingdom
2001	Interbrew acquired Diebels of Germany. Later Interbrew acquired the Brauerei Beck & Co., the Glide Group, and the Spaten
2002	Interbrew strengthened its position in China by acquiring stakes in the K.K. Brewery and the Zhujiang Brewery
2004	Interbrew and AmBev merged to form InBev
2004	Anheuser bought Harbin Brewery
2005	Bavaria Brewery was acquired by SABMiller
2006	InBev acquires Cerveza Quilmes and Fujian Sedrin Brewery Co., Ltd, the maker of Sedrin beer
2007	InBev subsidiary Labatt Brewing Company acquires Lakeport Brewing Company
2008	Anheuser-Busch and InBev merged to form Anheuser-Busch InBev
2011	SABMiller acquires Foster's Group of Australia
2012	Cerveceria Nacional Dominicana and Grupo Modelo of Mexico are acquired by Anheuser-Busch InBev
2014	AB InBev reacquired Oriental Brewery which it had sold in the year 2009
2015	Meantime Brewing acquired by SABMiller
2016	Anheuser-Busch InBev (AB InBev) completes the acquisition of SABMiller

InBev was the second largest brewery company in the world. The company had strong presence in the soft drink market along with its core business of beer. Before the merger with AmBev, Interbrew was the third largest brewing company in the world by volume. InBev employed approximately 89,000 people and had operations in over 30 countries across the Americas, Europe, and Asia Pacific.

AB InBev based in Leuven, Belgium, is listed on Euronext with secondary listings on the Mexico and South Africa stock exchanges and with American depository receipts on the New York Stock Exchange. The diverse portfolio of AB InBev consists of over 500 beer brands which includes global brands like Budweiser, Corona, and Stella Artois and multicountry brands like Beck's Brewery, Castle Brewery, Castle Lite, Hoegaarden Brewery, and Leffe. The company employed approximately 200,000 employees in more than 50 countries worldwide. In the year 2016, AB InBev revenue was estimated as 45.5 billion US dollars.

InBev's Acquisition of Anheuser-Busch

In 2008, Belgian-based InBev acquired Anheuser-Busch in a deal valued $52 billion (Merced, 2008). This was one of the largest transatlantic deals. The all-cash deal for $70 a share created the world's largest brewer replacing the number one brewer SABMiller at the time of merger. The sweetened offer marked a 27% premium to Anheuser's record high stock price in the year 2002. The deal was the third largest ever foreign takeover of a US company.

The combined company had more than $36 billion in sales. The combined company was named as Anheuser-Busch InBev. Anheuser-Busch had well-known brands like Budweiser which were synonymous with the American beer. Anheuser's had huge advertising budget and strong distribution network. Many American beer giants had already been taken over by larger overseas rivals in the 1990s.The Miller Brewing Company was sold to South African Breweries in the year 1999. The Adolph Coors Company was bought by Molson of Canada in the year 2005. Initially Anheuser resisted the takeover efforts of InBev. Anheuser's stock which remained mostly constant earlier saw its stock price increasing on takeover announcement. InBev took a debt financing of $45 billion to finance the deal. The two companies had some alliances in the past. InBev distributed Budweiser brands of Anheuser in Canada. Anheuser imported InBev beers like Bass. In the year 2006, InBev sold its Rolling Rock brand to Anheuser-Busch for $82 million. The acquisition was expected to create benefits through revenue enhancement and cost savings. The combination was expected to result in cost synergies of at least $1.5 billion annually by 2011 in equally over a 3-year period. Anheuser earns about 85% of its profits from the United States. InBev had strong positions in Western Europe and Latin America and would be growing in Eastern Europe and Asia.

Merger of AB InBev with SABMiller

During the last two decades, beer industry witnessed trends of consolidation. Approximately ten brewers controlled half of the global beer market. By 2014, it had been shrunk to five: AB InBev, SABMiller, Heineken, Carlsberg Group, and China Resources. The merger between AB InBev and SABMiller reduced it to four.

The merger of AB InBev and SABMiller was completed on October 10, 2016. This merger happened approximately 8 years after InBev's acquisition of Anheuser-Busch. The merger resulted in the combined firm having operations in virtually all the major beer market and portfolio consisting of global, multicountry, and local brands. Through the merger with SABMiller, AB InBev was able to have a strong presence in key emerging markets like Africa and Latin America. The merger with SABMiller complemented AB InBev's strong presence in developed markets. Newbelco became the holding company for the combined firm. All the assets and liabilities of former AB InBev were transferred to Newbelco. Newbelco was renamed Anheuser-Busch InBev, and the former AB InBev was dissolved by operations of Belgian law. The shares in the former AB InBev were delisted from the Euronext Brussels, Bolsa Mexicana de Valores, and Johannesburg Stock Exchange. The new ordinary shares were admitted to listing and trading on these stock exchanges. The six geographic regions of AB InBev are North America, West Latin America, North Latin America, South Latin America, EMEA, and Asia Pacific. Six geographic regions of SABMiller were included in the existing six regions of AB InBev. SABMiller's operations were spread across 70 countries mostly in emerging countries. AB InBev operated in 26 countries with half of the sales accounted by two countries – Brazil and the United States. During the past decade, AB InBev had given total shareholder return of 492%, and SABMiller provided return of 508%.

The $100 billion merger between AB InBev and SABMiller was termed as the third largest acquisition in history and the largest ever in Britain. The new company started trading under the name Newbelco with annual sales of over $55 billion. The deal united the world's two largest beer makers which was the largest ever in the consumer industry. The deal combined AB InBev's Budweiser, Stella Artois, and Corona with SABMiller's Castle Lager and took the company into the fast-growing African and new Latin American markets. The merger resulted in an industry giant which accounted for 30% of the global beer sales. The combined group would sell one in four beers globally. At the time of the merger, Anheuser-Busch was already the world's largest brewer in the world. The combined group would account for 45% of the industry's profits. The acquisition is the most ambitious among a series of takeovers spearheaded by Jorge Paulo Lemann, the Brazilian billionaire who was AB InBev's single largest individual shareholder. Through a series of deals over the past 27 years, AB InBev had transformed itself into one of the world's largest brewer. AB InBev could look forward for SAB's presence in emerging markets to provide much needed growth opportunities. The joint portfolio of AB InBev and SABMiller consisted of more than 500 beers which included 7 of the top 10 global beer brands and 18 brands with retail sales of more than $ 1 billion. The combined company owned brands such as Corona, Beck's Brewery, Hoegaarden Brewery, Leffe, Shock Top, Landshark, Rolling Rock, and Foster's Group. AB InBev has purchased smaller craft breweries such as the Breckenridge Brewery in Colorado, Goose Island Brewery in Chicago, and 10 Barrel Brewing. As a part of the antitrust settlement, AB InBev assured to avoid engagement in practices that would restrict the distribution of smaller, rival brews such as providing rewards for distributors who sold more of AB InBev's brand than other brands. The megamerger resulted in new AB InBev controlling about 46% of the global beer profits and 27% of the world's beer production. The merger resulted in reduced reliance on the company's biggest US and Brazilian beer markets. African market which accounted for approximately 9% of the revenues became the new focus area of growth.

Transaction Highlights

The deal was valued at $104.3 billion. AB InBev had put forward two variations of its offer. The offer included a straight 45 pounds per share which was intended for the majority of investors and a cash and shares offer which was meant for SABMiller's two largest shareholders, Altria and the Santo Domingo family of Colombia who held 41% of SABMiller (Faust, 2016). Initially the value of AB InBev's offer declined when the pound depreciated in value as a result of Britain's decision to leave the European Union. This sequence of events compelled AB InBev to increase its offer to $104.3 billion. Altria had 27% ownership and voting stake in SABMiller. On merger completion the 27% ownership of Altria in SABMiller got converted into a 10.5% interest in the new company.

Under the terms of merger, each SABMiller shareholder was entitled to receive 45 pounds sterling in cash with respect to each SABMiller share. The merger agreement also stipulated a partial share alternative under which SABMiller shareholders can choose to receive 4.6588 pounds sterling in cash and 0.483969 restricted shares in respect of each SABMiller share in lieu of the full cash consideration to which they would otherwise be entitled under the combination (Report, 2016). The partial share alternative was limited to a maximum of 326,000,000 restricted shares and 3.1 billion pounds sterling in cash. During October 2016, Newbelco issued 163 276 737 100 ordinary shares ("Initial Newbelco Shares") to SABMiller shareholders through a capital increase of 85531 million euro equivalent to 75.4 billion pound sterling, as consideration for 1632767371 ordinary shares of SABMiller. The cash and share offer was worth more than the cash bid even though the new shares had to be held for 5 years. By splitting the vote, the deal would require backing from up to 85% of shares rather than 75% needed in a unified vote. The transaction was financed through a substantial portion of debt. On account of the merger, AB InBev's debt increased from $42.2 billion to $108 billion. The lead advisor of the deal for AB InBev was Lazard who received $135 million as banking and broking fees. The legal advisors Freshfields Bruckhaus Deringer received $185 million in legal fees. Atria received two seats on the new board of directors and approximately $3 billion in pretax cash.

Merger Synergy

The merger with SABMiller was expected to yield $1.4 billion annual savings for AB InBev in 4-year time at a one off cost of $900 million. This targeted savings would equal 13% of SABMiller's net sales after disposal of SABMiller's assets. As a part of deal, about 3% of the combined workforce was expected to be reduced (Reuter, 2016). AB InBev expected to get 30% of the cost savings from shutting overlapping offices and 25% cost savings from declined prices of raw materials and packaging. Synergies were also expected from higher brewing and distribution efficiencies and productivity improvements. By December 2016, AB InBev had cost savings of $2.80 billion. SABMiller had cost savings of $829 billion by the same period (Gerard, 2017).

Divestments due to the Merger Deal

AB InBev had plans to divest about $16.5 billion of SAB assets to secure approval from antitrust regulators in more than 20 countries. These included Peroni Brewery and Grolsch Brewery in Europe, Miller Lite in the United States, and Snow in China.

AB InBev has entered into a number of agreements to sell assets from the combined company to satisfy the regulators. As a result of merger, SABMiller divested its interest in the Peroni, Grolsch, and Meantime brand families and associated businesses (PGM businesses) in Italy, the Netherlands, the United Kingdom to Tokyo-based Asahi Group Holdings Ltd. The divestiture deal was valued at 2.5 billion euro on a debt-free/cash-free basis. During 2016, SABMiller's equity interest in China Resources Snow Breweries Limited (CR Snow) was divested to China Resources Beer (Holdings) Company Ltd for $1.6 billion dollar. China Resources had acquired SABMiller's 49% equity interest in the share capital of CR Snow (Bray, 2016). CR Snow became a wholly owned subsidiary of CRB. During October 2016, AB InBev had divested SABMiller's interest in MillerCoors which is a joint venture between the Molson Coors Brewing Company and SABMiller in the United States and Puerto Rico. The deal was valued at $12 billion. Under the terms of the joint venture agreement, the Molson Coors Brewing Company had acquired SABMiller's 50% voting interest and 58% economic interest in MillerCoors. Under European Commission's regulatory ruling for merger, AB InBev had to sell SABMiller's businesses in Poland, the Czech Republic, Slovakia, Hungary, and Romania (the CEE business) to Asahi for an enterprise value of 7.3 billion euros. During December 2016, AB InBev entered into a binding agreement to sell its entire indirect shareholding in the Distell Group Limited (Distell) to the Public Investment Corporation Ltd acting on behalf of the Government Employees Pension Fund (Distell Sale). During December 2016, the Coca Cola Company had an agreement with AB InBev to acquire 54.5% equity stake in Coca-Cola Beverages Africa ("CCBA") for $3.15 billion. The CCBA included the Coca Cola bottling operations in South Africa, Namibia, Kenya, Uganda, Tanzania, Ethiopia, Mozambique, Ghana, Mayotte, and Comoros.

Other Acquisitions of AB InBev

During the year 2016, AB InBev completed the acquisition of the Canadian rights to a range of primarily spirit-based beers and ciders from the Mark Anthony Group Inc. During the year 2015, AB InBev purchased all outstanding Grupo Model's shares held by third parties for a total consideration of $483 million dollars. As a result of the tender offer, Modelo became the wholly owned subsidiary of AB InBev, and Modelo was delisted.

Merger Announcement Effect on Acquirer AB InBev's Stock Price (Table 6.2)

Anheuser-Busch InBev (ABI.BR) is traded on the Brussels stock market. The merger announcement was made on November 11, 2015. On announcement day, the stock price gained 2.2%. On day 1 after the announcement, the stock price fell by −1.1%. On day +3 and day +4, the stock price gained by 1.6% and 3.4%, respectively. The maximum gain of 3.4% was registered on the 4th day after merger announcement (Table 6.2).

Table 6.2 Daily returns surrounding merger announcement

Day	Returns	Day	Return
−5	0.009	13	−0.009
−4	0.006	14	0.005
−3	0.015	15	−0.036
−2	−0.008	16	−0.006
−1	0.002	17	0.021
0	0.022	18	−0.014
1	−0.011	19	−0.008
2	−0.001	20	−0.003
3	0.016	21	−0.031
4	0.034	22	−0.018
5	−0.001	23	0.018
6	−0.012	24	0.006
7	0.015	25	0.027
8	0.016	26	−0.012
9	0.014	27	−0.015
10	0.013	28	−0.004
11	−0.005	29	0.022
12	−0.006	30	0.000

Table 6.3 Cumulative Returns for ABInBev surrounding the merger announcement

Day relative	Cumulative returns in %
−1 to +1	1.3
−5 to 5	8.25
−5 to10	12.8
−5 to 50	4.8
−5 to 200	−4.79
−5 to 504	−11.8

The cumulative returns during the immediate time period surrounding the merger announcement period were positive. The cumulative returns during the 3-day period −1 to +1 day were 1.3% (Table 6.3). The cumulative returns were negative in the larger window interval period. The cumulative returns during the 510-day window period −5 to +504 day were 11.8% (Fig. 6.1).

The cumulative returns were positive till +241 days and thereafter turned negative during the rest of the period of analysis (Fig. 6.1).

The above figure shows the stock price trend during the period 2013–2016. SABMiller was delisted from the London Stock Exchange on October 6, 2016 (Fig. 6.2)

Table 6.4 gives the holding period yield for Dow Chemicals stock for different years.

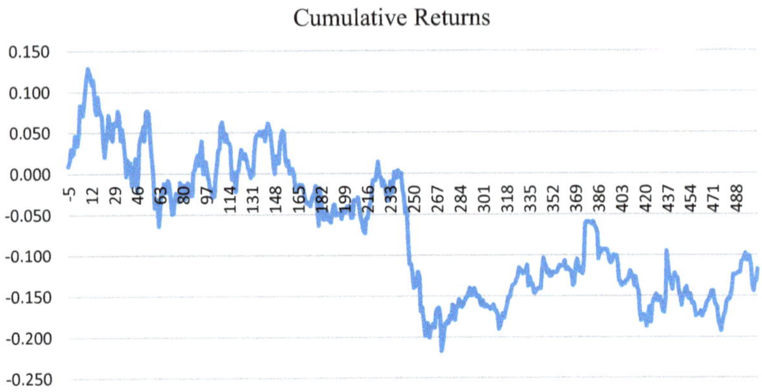

Fig. 6.1 Cumulative returns for AB InBev during SABMiller merger

Fig. 6.2 Stock price performance of target firm SABMiller

Table 6.4 Operating highlights in millions of dollars

Year	2007	2008	2009	2010	2011	2012	2013	2014	2015	2016
Revenues	19,735	23,507	36,758	36,297	39,046	39,758	43,195	47,063	43,604	45,517
Operating Income	5,872	5,340	11,569	10,897	12,346	12,747	20,443	15,111	13,904	12,882
Net Income	3,005	1,927	4,613	4,026	5,779	7,160	14,394	9,216	8,273	1,241

The year of merger completion was 2016. Hence the impact of merger could not be analyzed in terms of pre- and post-merger comparison

Table 6.5 Profitability ratios

Year	2007	2008	2009	2010	2011	2012	2013	2014	2015	2016
Gross margin %	58.9	56	53.2	55.5	57.5	58.7	59.3	60.1	60.7	60.9
Net margin %	15.23	8.2	12.55	11.09	15	18.22	33.32	19.58	18.97	2.73
Return on assets %	8.38	2.49	4.09	3.55	5.16	6.16	10.89	6.49	5.97	0.63
Return on equity %	17.78	9.11	17.49	12.28	16.1	18.42	31.46	18.37	17.96	2.19
Return on invested capital %	15.57	5.3	9.74	8.34	10.49	11.17	17.69	10.52	9.89	2.47
Interest coverage	6.19	3.01	2.56	2.8	3.75	5.37	7.08	8.01	7.48	2.03

The profitability ratios were showing a declining trend over the 10-year period (2007–2016) (Table 6.5).

References

Bray C (2016) Anheuser Busch Miller advances. https://www.nytimes.com/2016/07/30/business/dealbook/china-beer-anheuser-busch-inbev-sabmiller.html. Accessed 03 Aug 2017

Faust E (2016) http://www.mcall.com/g00/business/getsmart/mc-fast-facts-about-anheuser-busch-inbev-merger-20161005. Accessed 28 Aug 2017

Gerard B (2017) AB InBev to squeeze even more drops out of SABMiller deal. http://www.telegraph.co.uk/business/2017/03/02/ab-inbev-squeeze-even-drops-sabmiller-deal/. Accessed 04 Aug 2017

Merced MJ (2008) http://www.nytimes.com/2008/07/14/business/worldbusiness/14beer.html. Accessed 28 Aug 2017

Report (2016) Megabrew-ABInbevSabMiller Merger. http://www.chicagotribune.com/g00/business/ct-megabrew-ab-inbev-sabmiller-merger-20161010-story.html?i10c.encReferrer=aHR0cHM6Ly93d3cuZ29vZ2xlLmFlLw%3D%3D. Accessed 04 Aug 2017

Reuter (2016) AB InBev and SAB Miller expect mega brew merger to complete. https://www.reuters.com/article/us-sabmiller-m-a-abi/ab-inbev-and-sabmiller-expect-megabrew-merger-to-complete-october-10-idUSKCN10C2XC. Accessed 02 Aug 2017

Merger of Kraft and Heinz Company

7

Introduction

The Kraft Heinz Company is one of the largest food and beverage companies in the world with presence in more than 190 countries and territories. Kraft Heinz Company manufactures and markets food and beverage products which include condiments and sauces, cheese and dairy, meal meats, refreshment beverages, coffee, and other grocery products. The iconic brands of the company include Heinz, Kraft, Oscar Mayer, Planters, Philadelphia, Velveeta, Lunchables, Maxwell House, Capri Sun, and Ore-Ida. The company is co-headquartered in Pittsburgh and Chicago. In 2016, the company had sales of $26.5 billion and assets of $123 billion. The company has presence in about 40 countries. Kraft Heinz has about 200 plus brands which are sold in nearly 200 countries. This includes 8 billion dollar-generating brands in retail and food sector. The company focuses on innovation and goes to market efficiencies. The firm focuses on progressive business practices like zero-based budgeting and management by objectives. The company is listed in NASDAQ under the ticker symbol “KHC.” After the merger the new company stock began trading publicly on NASDAQ on July 6, 2016.

Following the 2015 merger, the company was reorganized into three reportable segments which were defined by geographic regions. The three regions were the United States, Canada, and Europe. The remaining businesses were combined and put under “Rest of World”. The Rest of World consists of three operating segments, namely, Asia Pacific, Latin America, Russia, India, the Middle East, and Africa. The products of Kraft Heinz were sold through sales organizations, independent brokers, agents and distributors, cooperative and independent grocery accounts, convenience stores, foodservice distributors, and institutions. In 2016, Walmart Inc. was the largest customer who accounted for approximately 20% of the sales.

During February 2017, Kraft Heinz proposed a $143 billion merger with Unilever. But the consumer goods major declined the offer.

B. R. Kumar, *Wealth Creation in the World's Largest Mergers and Acquisitions*, Management for Professionals, https://doi.org/10.1007/978-3-030-02363-8_7

Kraft Heinz Merger

Kraft and Heinz have been pioneers in the food industry for over 100 years. Through a series of transaction, the merger of Kraft Foods Group Inc. (Kraft) and the wholly owned subsidiary of H. J. Heinz Holding Corporation was consummated and completed on July 2, 2015. The new company was named the Kraft Heinz Company. Before the merger, all the common stock of Heinz was owned by Berkshire Hathaway Inc. ("Berkshire Hathaway") and 3G Global Food Holdings LP.

H. J. Heinz, offering "Good Food Every Day™," is a leading marketer and producer of foods specializing in ketchup, sauces, meals, soups, snacks, and infant nutrition. Heinz offers global branded products like Heinz® Ketchup, sauces, soups, beans, pasta, and infant foods. The other products include Ore-Ida® potato products, Weight Watchers®, Smart Ones® entrées, T.G.I. Friday's® snacks, and Plasmon infant nutrition. Heinz was bought by 3G Capital in the year 2013 and taken private. The deal was undertaken with considerable financing from Warren Buffett.

Kraft Foods Group is one of the North America's largest consumer packaged food and beverage companies. The major brands of the company include Kraft, Capri Sun, Jell-O, Kool-Aid, Lunchables, Maxwell House, Oscar Mayer, Philadelphia, Planters, and Velveeta. Kraft is listed in S&P 500 list and NASDAQ-100 indices. The combined company was co-headquartered in Pittsburgh and the Chicago area. The merged company had approximately $28 billion with 8 $1 + billion brands and 5 brands between $500 million and $1 billion. Lazard was the exclusive financial advisor for Heinz. Cravath Swaine & Moore and Kirkland & Ellis acted as legal advisors for the deal (SEC, 2015). Centerview Partners LLC served as the exclusive financial advisor for Kraft. Sullivan & Cromwell was the legal advisor for Kraft.

Terms of the Merger

Immediately prior to the consummation of the 2015 merger, each share of Heinz issued and outstanding common stock was reclassified and changed into 0.443332 of a share of Kraft Heinz common stock Annual Report Heinz Kraft Merger (n.d). All outstanding shares of Kraft common stock were converted into the right to receive on one-for-one basis shares of Kraft Heinz common stock. The deferred shares and restricted shares of Kraft were converted to deferred shares and restricted shares of Kraft Heinz, as applicable.

Under the terms of the merger, the existing Heinz shareholders held 51% stake in the newly formed company. The Kraft shareholders received 49% of shares in the combined company. To sweeten the deal for Kraft, the shareholders were offered a onetime dividend of US$ 16.50 per share. The dividend amount of $10 billion was funded by an equity investment by Berkshire Hathaway and 3G Capital. The amount of declared dividend was more than a quarter of the closing share price of Kraft as on March 24, 2015. On completion of the transaction, the Kraft Heinz Company planned to maintain Kraft's current dividend per share which was expected to increase over time. The shareholders of Kraft Group received one share of the newly combined company for each share they held. The deal was valued at approximately $45 billion. The combined firm had annual sales of over $28 billion. The chairman of Heinz became the chairman of the new company. John Cahill the Kraft chairman became the vice chairman of the combined entity. The board of directors of the combined company composed of five members who were appointed by the Kraft and Heinz board and three members each from Berkshire Hathaway and 3G Capital. The merger was not expected to increase the debt levels of the Kraft Heinz Company as the cash consideration was fully funded by the common equity from Berkshire Hathaway and 3G Capital. Berkshire Hathaway owned 27% of the stock and 3G Capital owned about 24% of the stock.

Merger Synergies

The merger resulted in the creation of the third largest food and beverage company in North America and fifth largest food and beverage company in the world. The complementary nature of the two brand portfolios provided scope for synergies which could provide a platform for market leadership for the combined company.

The combination of two companies was expected to generate synergies. Heinz had a global footprint. Heinz derived approximately 60% of its sales from regions outside North America. Approximately 25% of its sales were derived from the emerging economies. About 98% of sales for Kraft were obtained from North America. In other words, Heinz generated approximately 60% of revenues outside North America, and Kraft generated only 13% of revenues outside North America. The combination of Kraft's brands with Heinz's international brands provides a strong platform for organic growth in North America. The Heinz board considered the merger with Kraft as a strategic fit whereby they could increase Heinz's scale in North America across both retail and food service thereby creating the third largest food and beverage company in North America (Bullen, 2015). The merger could enhance Heinz's liquidity in the United States on the basis of Kraft's free cash flow generation. The merger was also aimed to diversify Heinz's category exposure across a variety of new growing and stable product categories like cheese and meats. The consolidation was also expected to create opportunities to leverage Heinz's existing international infrastructure to expand the presence of Kraft brands overseas.

The merger would provide opportunity to sell Kraft products in the global market. At the same time, Kraft had an agreement with its spun-off company Mondelez which gave the right to Mondelez to sell many of their shared brands in international market. But this deal didn't include iconic brands like A.1, Velveeta, Planters, MiO, and Lunchables. Hence the new company could focus on these brands to increase revenue growth. The merger was expected to realize cost synergies of $1.5 billion in annual cost savings by the year 2017. The transaction was expected to be EPS accretive by the year 2017.The cost synergies were attributed due to economies of scale from the North American market. On account of economies of scale, the company could drive better bargains with clients such as large retail outlets and specialty food stores and restaurants. This would lead to improved operating margins. The company could get more shelf space in retail outlets. The merger was expected to result in financial synergy. Cost savings were expected due to the new firm's capacity to refinance Heinz high-yielding debt. Kraft had a higher credit rating compared to Heinz. Hence it was expected to replace the high-risk debt of Heinz with investment grade debt which would lower the cost of capital for the new merged company. By June 2016, Heinz preferred stocks became callable and were replaced with low yield investment grade debt. The company was able to reduce the total cost of capital of the combined company (Trefis Team, 2015).

The changes in operations strategy were expected to lead to cost savings. Shutting down less efficient manufacturing facilities and implementing zero-based budgeting were part of the strategy to have cost savings. The merger led to the closure of seven plants in North America and consolidation of production in other locations which resulted in the elimination of approximately 2600 jobs. Additional savings resulted from second order effects like states started offering incentives to keep the company continue functioning in these regions. Boone County, MO, granted Kraft Heinz large tax abatements for continued operations (Calvin, 2015).

Globally the trend suggests that the intake of health foods is being outpaced by junk foods like processed meats and sweetened drinks. The merged company has adequate portfolios in both sectors.

Valuation Analysis

Centerview performed the relative value analysis for the deal taking into account the net cost synergies. Centerview estimated the ranges of the implied relative ownership of the Kraft shareholders of the combined company by allocating a low of 50% and high of 65% of the synergies to Kraft. The ranges of the implied relative ownership and implied exchange ratios are given in Tables 7.1.

The values are given in millions of dollars. The net revenue growth rates were negative in the period 2012–2014. The net earnings declined by 49.7% in the year 2011 compared to the previous year 2010. The net earnings increased by 65% in the year 2013. The year-on-year growth rates of revenues were negative in the years 2012 and 2014 (Table 7.2).

The values are given in millions of dollars. The average growth rate of net revenues for the period 2010–2014 was 1.5%. The year-on-year growth rate of revenues is decreased by 5% in the year 2014. The net income declined by 34% in the year 2014.

Thus both Kraft and Heinz were facing revenue pressures in the year before merger (Tables 7.3).

Premerger and post-merger comparison (hypothetical combination in year before acquisition).

The total assets of the company increased by two times in the year after merger (2016) compared to the year before merger (2014). The revenues declined in the post-merger period. The net income increased by 2.11 times in the post-merger period year 2016 compared to the period 2014.

Tables 7.4 and 7.5 gives the financial highlights of the company before and after merger.

Table 7.1 Valuation methodology

Valuation methodology		Range of impliedownership of thecombined company byformer Kraftshareholders	Range of impliedexchange ratio
Trading multiple analysis	Enterprise value/2015 Estimated EBITDA Stock Price/2015 Estimated EPS	45.0–51.1% 43.3–48%	0.852×–1.089× 0.796×–0.961×
Transaction multiple analysis	Enterprise value/2015 Estimated EBITDA	44.5%–55.5%	0.835×–1.300×
Discounted cash flow analysis	2015 Financial plan Upside case of the 2015 financial plan	41.6–49.3% 43.7–51.2%	0.742×–1.011× 0.807×–1.094×

https://www.sec.gov/Archives/edgar/data/1637459/000119312515126301/d898418ds4.htm

Table 7.2 Financial data for Kraft 2010–2014

Year	2010	2011	2012	2013	2014
Net revenues	17739	18576	18271	18218	18205
Net earning	3534	1775	1642	2715	1043
Capex	448	401	440	557	535
Total assets	21448	21389	23179	23148	22947
Long-term debt	31	27	9966	9976	8627
Total equity	17037	16588	3572	5187	4365

Table 7.3 Financial data for Heinz 2010–2014

Year	2010	2011	2012	2013	2014
Net revenues	10324	10559	11508	11529	10922
Net earning	882	1006	941	1027	672
Capex	278	336	419	399	399
Total assets	10076	12231	11983	12940	36763
Long-term debt	4559	3078	4780	3848	13586
Total equity	1948	3182	2811	2850	7336

Table 7.4 Financial highlights of the combined company in the year after merger 2016

	Value in millions of dollars
Revenue	26487
Net income	3632
Total assets	120480

Table 7.5 Financial highlights of the combination of acquirer and target in the year before merger 2014

	Value in millions of dollars
Revenue	29127
Net income	1715
Total assets	59170

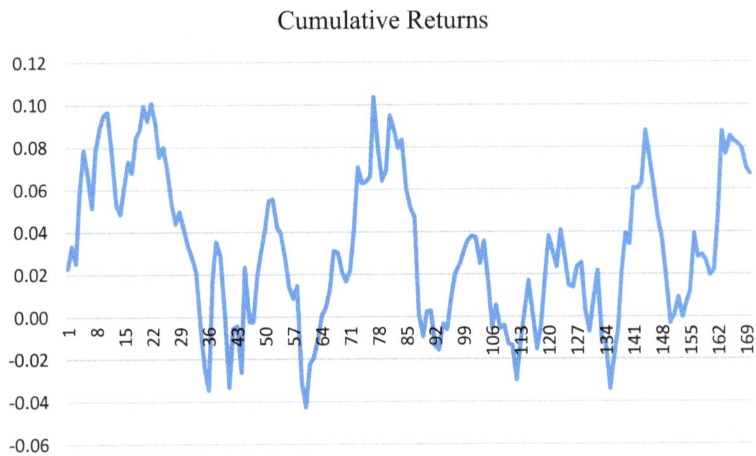

Fig. 7.1 Cumulative returns during the merger period July 6, 2015–March 2016

Effect of Merger Announcement

The merger announcement was made on March 25, 2015. The merger completion date was July 2, 2015. The analysis was based on stock price available from July 6, 2015. The cumulative returns during the period July 2015–March 2016 were approximately 7.1% (Fig. 7.1).

The cumulative returns have been fluctuating around the period of merger announcement.

References

Annual Report Heinz Kraft Merger

Bullen V (2015).Whats the brand impact of the Kraft Heinz Merger?. https://lbbonline.com/news/whats-the-brand-impact-of-the-kraft-and-heinz-merger/. Accessed 15 Sept 2017

Geoff Calvin (2015). Buy, Squeeze Repeat. http://fortune.com/kraft-heinz-merger-3g-capital/. Accessed 16 Sept 2017

http://news.heinz.com/press-release/finance/hj-heinz-company-and-kraft-foods-group-sign-definitive-merger-agreement-form-k

SEC (2015) https://www.sec.gov/Archives/edgar/data/1637459/000119312515126301/d898418ds4.htm/. Accessed 16 Sept 2017

Trefis Team (2015) Analysis of Kraft-Heinz Merger. https://www.forbes.com/sites/greatspeculations/2015/03/30/analysis-of-the-kraft-heinz-merger/#b216c26c9a8a. Accessed 15 Sept 2017

Acquisitions by Pfizer

8

Introduction

Pfizer is one of the world's largest biopharmaceutical companies engaged in the discovery, development, and manufacture of healthcare products. The portfolio of Pfizer includes medicines, vaccines, and consumer healthcare products. The company has presence in 160 countries and employed 96,500 people during the period 2016 (Pfizer Annual Report, 2017).

The two distinct businesses of Pfizer group are Pfizer Essential Health (PEH) and Pfizer Innovative Health (PIH). PEH is a global leader in non-viral anti-infectives, biosimilars, and sterile injectable medicines. PIH includes six business groups, namely, Consumer Healthcare, Inflammation & Immunology, Internal Medicine, Oncology, Rare Disease, and Vaccines. PEH offers a vast portfolio of more than 600 medicines. Pfizer has been actively engaged in the research and development of innovative medicines in the area of infectious diseases. Pfizer has commercialized more than 120 antimicrobial agents used in the treatment of bacterial, fungal, viral, and parasitic infections. The largest global antimicrobial resistance (AMR) surveillance program in the world is sponsored by Pfizer. Pfizer Injectable is a major supplier of high-quality, difficult-to-manufacture injectable pharmaceutical and surgical products. More than 220 products of this portfolio account for approximately $6 billion in annual revenues. Pfizer is one of the largest over-the-counter (OTC) healthcare companies in the world. Pfizer OTC brands are sold across more than 90 countries in the world. Pfizer is also a global leader in developing medicines for chronic immune and inflammatory diseases. Pfizer focuses on the development of potential cardiovascular disease therapies. Pfizer also focuses on the development of innovative vaccines for unmet medical needs. In a year Pfizer manufactures, packages, and distributes over 74 billion units of products in 129 countries around the world. Pfizer's top selling products include the Viagra and off-the-shelf brands like Halls cough drops and Listerine mouthwash.

B. R. Kumar, *Wealth Creation in the World's Largest Mergers and Acquisitions*, Management for Professionals, https://doi.org/10.1007/978-3-030-02363-8_8

Strategic Drivers for M&A in Pharmaceutical Industry

The major drivers for mergers and acquisitions in the pharma industry have been the need for greater scale, market share, geographical expansion, and increased technological capabilities. The need of consolidation can be basically attributed to the requirement of new pipelines and synergies in research and development. Most of the blockbuster drugs were invented during the 1960s and 1970s. Pharma companies are focusing on labs and universities throughout the world for new molecules. Megamergers like that of GlaxoWellcome and SmithKline Beecham signify the importance of how research becomes critical for the survival of pharma companies (Giordano Righi, 2016). During the period 1985–2007, 60 pharma companies consolidated to become 10 pharma companies. During the 1980s and 1990s, the pharmaceutical industry witnessed increased M&A activity. During the last decade (2000–2010), approximately 1345 mergers of pharma companies were announced.

The total deal value for M&A during the first half of year 2015 was $221 million. Some of the biggest M&A deals were Shire's $32 billion merger with Baxalta which was the global market leader in rare diseases and disorders, Teva's purchase of the generic division of Allergan for $40.5 billion, and Bayer's takeover bid of $66 billion for US seed company Monsanto.

Availability of sources of financing is an important driver for M&A in the pharmaceutical industry. Companies are also using M&A to avoid high corporate tax rates in their home country. Merging with foreign firms and transferring their headquarters have helped American pharma companies to save billions of dollars in tax revenues. On account of new US tax inversion rules, the decision of Pfizer to acquire Allergan for $160 billion which was announced in November 2015 was cancelled in April 2016. M&A have become a compelling strategy for reducing R&D costs in the pharmaceutical industry. The top 20 pharmaceutical companies spend on average 19.3% of their sales revenues on research and development. The majority of the top 50 drugs worldwide were not developed in-house. It is estimated that it takes an average of 15 years for a drug to go from concept to approval. The average amount to develop a new drug is estimated to be $2.6 billion. Very few products hit the blockbuster status of $1 billion in annual sales. Pharmaceutical companies use M&A as a strategy to fill their lacking pipelines in the context of increasing cost pressures. For many pharma companies, it would be easier and quicker to buy another business with potential breakthrough products than to invest in cost-intensive in-house R&D in order to plug in the gap for development pipeline. For example, Astra Zeneca has acquired various biotech firms during the past few years to boost the pipeline of therapeutic segments like respiratory, cardiovascular, and oncology. Strong pharma companies have acquired biotech companies for new patents as many of these companies are on verge of commercialization of their products. Pharma companies with diverse set of products use M&A as a strategy to become more specialized, for example, the Novartis divestment of its animal health division to Eli Lilly for $5.4 billion. Another example is Bayer's bid for the US seed giant Monsanto which had a value of $66 billion. Bayer's aim was to strengthen Bayer's Crop Sciences business and to enormously increase the company's market

Table 8.1 Biggest mergers and acquisitions in the pharmaceutical industry

Date	Acquirer	Target	Value in billion dollars
June 2000	Pfizer	Warner–Lambert	87
December 2000	GlaxoWellcome	SmithKline Beecham	76
January 2009	Pfizer	Wyeth	68
July 2004	Sanofi-Synthlabo	Aventis	65.5
July 2002	Pfizer	Pharmacia	60
2009	Merck	Schering Plough	41.1
2010	Novartis	Alcon	39.3
December 1998	Zeneca	Astra	37
January 1997	Ciba	Sandoz	30.1
December 1999	Monsanto	Pharmacia & Upjohn	26
December 1999	Hoechst	Rhone–Poulenc (Aventis)	21.5
2006	Bayer AG	Schering AG	21.5
November 1995	Pharmacia	Upjohn	15
January 1995	Glaxo	Wellcome	14
December 1998	Sanofi	Synthlabo	11
March 2001	Johnson & Johnson	ALZA	11
May 1997	Roche	Boehringer Manheim	11
August 1994	American Home Products	American Cyanamid	10
May 2001	Bristol Myer Squibb	DuPont Pharmaceuticals	8
March 1989	SmithKline	Beecham	7.9
February 2010	Merck	Millipore	7
May 1994	Roche	Syntex	5.3
March 2010	Teva	Ratiopharm	4.9

share within the global seed market. Bayer's focus was to create a global pharmaceutical and farm supplies specialist. The pharmaceutical industry worldwide is facing pressures on drug manufacturing, research and development on account of competitive business environment. The growth avenues are limited on account of declining prescriptions of branded drugs and advent of generic drug products. North American and European governments have squeezed their healthcare budgets for large masses with cost-effective generic products. Large pharma companies are forced to raise prices of branded drug products to cover up for declining margins. These factors have contributed to the emergence of M&A as a compelling strategy for pharmaceutical firms. Table 8.1 gives the details of the biggest mergers and acquisitions which happened in the pharma industry.

Mergers and Acquisitions by Pfizer

Pfizer has grown by megamergers and acquisitions. In the year 2000, Pfizer acquired Warner–Lambert for $111.8 billion to gain control of Lipitor. Pfizer acquired Pharmacia to acquire full rights to the product Celebrex. Pharmacia was itself formed by the series of mergers which included Upjohn, Searle, and Monsanto. In 2016, Pfizer completed the acquisition of AstraZeneca PLC's small-molecule anti-infective business primarily outside the United States which included the commercialization rights and development rights in certain markets for the newly approved

Table 8.2 M&A by Pfizer

Year	Target company	Value in billion dollars
2000	Warner–Lambert	111.8
2002	Pharmacia	60
2009	Wyeth	68
2015	Hospira	15.2
2016	AstraZeneca's small-molecule anti-infective portfolio	

EU drug Zavicefta. Pfizer acquired Hospira Inc. to create a leading provider of global sterile injectable portfolios. The combined company had a strong portfolio of drugs with revenues of over one billion. Table 8.2 lists the mergers and acquisitions undertaken by Pfizer.

Pfizer Acquisition of Warner–Lambert

In the year 2000, Pfizer acquired Warner–Lambert which was one of the fastest-growing pharma companies in the world. The acquisition added to the global strengths of Pfizer group (Melody Petersen, 2000). As a result of the acquisition, Pfizer gained product lines such as Parke–Davis branded pharmaceuticals, Listerine mouthwash, and Schick and Wilkinson sword wet shave products. Both Pfizer and Warner–Lambert traced its history back to the mid-1800s. In 1886 drug manufacturing company William R. Warner & Co was established. During the time period, Lambert Pharmacal company was established whose main product was Listerine (antiseptic). In the year 1955, Warner and Lambert combined to form Warner–Lambert. Warner–Lambert grew through acquisitions. In the year 1962, the company bought American Chicle Company which was one of the largest producers of gums and mints. In the year 1965, Warner–Lambert bought a cough tablet company and expanded the brand known as Halls "Mentholyptus." Warner–Lambert had acquired the Schick wet shave product line from Eversharp. In 1970, Warner–Lambert acquired Parke–Davis which was one of the largest drug makers. With this acquisition, Warner–Lambert refocused on three main businesses: prescription pharmaceuticals, consumer healthcare products, and gums and mints. In the year 1993, Warner–Lambert acquired Wilkinson Sword and combined it with Schick to create the world's second largest wet shave business. In 1996, Warner–Lambert entered into a co-marketing agreement with Pfizer on Lipitor which belonged to the statin class of lipid-lowering agents. Lipitor introduced by Parke–Davis was one of the largest selling pharmaceutical products in the world. In 1999, Warner–Lambert acquired Agouron which was a leader in protein-based drug design and marketer of the protease inhibitor, Viracept ® (nelfinavir mesylate). In the year before merger, Warner–Lambert had net earnings of $1.7 billion on sales of $12.9 billion, and Pfizer had net earnings of $3.4 billion on sales of $16.2 billion in sales. In January 2000, GlaxoWellcome and SmithKline announced merger plans to emerge as the largest pharma company in the world. Warner–Lambert was considered as a prize within the industry for its blockbuster products which included the cholesterol-fighting drug Lipitor marketed jointly with Pfizer.

Highlights of the Deal

The $90-billion merger deal in which Pfizer acquired Warner–Lambert resulted in the creation of the second largest pharmaceutical company in the world (Report, 2000). The deal ended the 3-month hostile battle to acquire Warner–Lambert. American Home Products which had a merger pact with Warner–Lambert agreed to terminate the deal with the receipt of a breakup fee of $1.8 billion. The combined firm called Pfizer Inc. had annual revenues of $28 billion and market capitalization in excess of $230 billion. Under the terms of the deal, Warner–Lambert stockholders received 2.75 Pfizer shares for each Warner–Lambert share which was valued at $98.31 per share (Pfizer Website, 2017a). On merger completion, Pfizer shareholders owned approximately 61% of the new company, while Warner–Lambert shareholders owned 39% of the company. On the basis of Pfizer's closing share price of $35.75, the value of the deal for Warner–Lambert was estimated at $90.27 billion.

Strategic Perspective of the Deal

Pfizer's acquisition of Warner–Lambert resulted in the combined group having eight products with greater than $1 billion in global sales and R&D budget which amounted to $4.7 billion. The deal was aimed at increasing sales, reducing costs, and sustaining growth. The combined firm was positioned for global leadership in the discovery of new medicines. The combined company was expected to have compounded 3-year annual earnings growth of 25% and achieve annual cost savings of $1.6 billion by the year 2002. The merged company was expected to spend $4.7 billion on research and development. The combination gave leadership position to Pfizer in the areas of cardiovascular, lipid control drugs, central nervous system, and infectious disease pharmaceutical segments. During the merger period, about 138 products were under development. The acquisition added a host of consumer brands like Halls cough drops, antihistamine Benadryl, the decongestant Sudafed, and Listerine mouthwash to the Pfizer portfolio. As a result of the acquisition, Pfizer increased its sales representative force by 2500 in addition to the existing force of 5000 workers. The combined company also had a research staff of 12,000 which was the largest at the same of acquisition. In the year before merger, the fastest-growing segments of Pfizer's revenue were accounted from the sales of Lipitor which was made by Warner–Lambert and from Celebrex, an arthritis drug which was made by Monsanto. One of the prime reasons why Pfizer launched a hostile bid on Warner was on account of Pfizer's co-marketing agreement with Warner–Lambert. Under the terms of agreement, Pfizer got approximately half of the profits of the drug. In the year 1999, this amount amounted to $5 billion. But when Warner–Lambert announced its plan to buy the American Products Corporation, Pfizer expected that it may lose its agreement on Lipitor. The two companies had a total workforce of 87,000 workers. The combined company had 6.3% market share. The companies had little overlap, and antitrust issues were not expected to be a factor in completing the deal. Pfizer was best known for its Viagra impotency drug and Zoloft antidepressant at the time of acquisition.

Pfizer had a more diverse therapeutic focus than Warner–Lambert. Pfizer was active in six therapy areas, while Warner–Lambert was active in three areas. The merged company held strong position within the CNS and anti-infective therapy areas mainly on account of two of Pfizer's leading products, the antidepressant Zoloft and an antibacterial Zithromax (azithromycin). Both companies also marketed treatments for diabetics. Warner–Lambert's second highest selling drug Rezulin was a diabetes drug, while Pfizer's leading diabetes drug was Glucotrol XL. The merger was expected to result in a strong cardiovascular portfolio which contains two blockbuster drugs. The combined firm was also strong in the areas of CNS and anti-infectives. Pfizer's main therapy areas – cardiovascular and CNS – were supported by the company's R&D pipeline. The acquisition also strengthened Pfizer's phase II pipeline in the therapy areas of cancer, endocrine and gastrointestinal. Scope for synergy existed between Warner–Lambert's and Pfizer's endocrine therapy areas where Warner–Lambert focused on two products for diabetes neuropathy. Pfizer was also involved in the development of a new inhaled version of insulin which complemented Pfizer's and Warner–Lambert's existing diabetes products (Melanie McCullagh, 2000). The merger was expected to result in a number of synergies with respect to therapy area focus particularly in the area of cardiovascular products. Both companies also complemented each other with respect to their R&D pipelines.

Acquisition Announcement Effect on Stock Wealth

The announcement of the deal was on February 8, 2000. The shares of Warner–Lambert rose by $2.75 to 52-week high of $97.3125. The shares of Pfizer increased by $1.25 to $37.

The announcement day (0 day) return for Pfizer was 2.2%. The price of Pfizer fell by 4.5% and −3.1% in the day after and second day after the announcement (Table 8.3). The cumulative return of the 29-day period surrounding the acquisition announcement was approximately 13%. The cumulative return for the 240-day period surrounding the acquisition announcement was 29% (Fig. 8.1).

The Pfizer stock returns have been showing increasing trend during the 1-year period of analysis surrounding the acquisition period.

Pfizer–Pharmacia Merger

The merger between Pfizer Inc. and Pharmacia Corporation was completed in the year 2003. The combined new company became the leading research-based pharmaceutical company in the world.

Table 8.3 Wealth effects on acquisition announcement

Day	Returns
−10	0.015
−9	0.000
−8	−0.011
−7	0.020
−6	0.028
−5	0.022
−4	−0.027
−3	−0.010
−2	0.004
−1	0.035
0	0.022
1	−0.045
2	−0.031
3	0.000
4	0.000
5	0.016
6	−0.051
7	0.007
8	0.000
9	−0.015
10	0.015

Fig. 8.1 Cumulative returns for Pfizer during Warner–Lambert acquisition

Pharmacia AB was established by the combination of Farmitalia Carlo Erba, Kabi Pharmacia, and Pharmacia Aktiebolaget in the year 1911. In the year 1995, Pharmacia and Upjohn merged together. The combined company became the leading pharmaceutical company focusing on human healthcare products, animal health products, diagnostics, and specialty products. In April 2000, Pharmacia merged with Monsanto and Searle to create innovative medicines. In 2002, Pharmacia spun

Table 8.4 Wealth effects of acquisition announcement

Day	Returns
−8	−0.03
−7	−0.01
−6	0.06
−5	0.00
−4	−0.04
−3	−0.06
−2	0.05
−1	−0.01
0	−0.11
1	−0.01
2	0.02
3	−0.04
4	−0.04
5	−0.03
6	0.01
7	0.07
8	0.01
9	0.05
10	0.05

Table 8.4 highlights the returns of Pfizer stock during the acquisition announcement of Pharmacia

off its agricultural subsidiary, Monsanto Company. Pharmacia Corporation had the full rights to one of the blockbuster arthritis drugs Celebrex. Pfizer the largest drug maker bought Pharmacia for $60 billion.

Strategic Advantage

The merger deal gave Pfizer the arthritis drugs Celebrex and Bextra which both Pfizer and Pharmacia co-promoted. Pfizer also added heart disease drugs like eplerenone to its cardiac market portfolio (Herper, 2002). Pfizer was already the dominant player in the cardiac market with Lipitor and Norvasc which were the leading drugs for Cholesterol and hypertension. Pfizer and Pharmacia did not face serious competition for many of their drugs. The merger was expected to enhance their earnings growth. The merger created a drug company with $46 billion in annual sales and added portfolio of leading drugs for impotence, high cholesterol, arthritis, glaucoma, and depression. The merger consolidated Pfizer's position as the number one drug maker in terms of annual sales. As a result of the union, Pfizer with a market capitalization of $256 billion became the third largest company behind General Electric and Microsoft. It had one of the largest research and development budgets of $7 billion. The merged company held 11% of the world's market for prescription drugs. Through the merger with Pharmacia, Pfizer obtained drugs like Rogaine for hair loss, Nicorette the gum for quitting smoking habits, Xalatan the drug for glaucoma treatment, Xanax for treatment of anxiety, and Detral the overactive bladder treatment drug (Reporter, 2003). Pfizer also got control of Camptosar the drug for treatment of colorectal cancer and the arthritis drug Celebrex. The merger positioned the new Pfizer to deliver a stream of innovative new products and cost-effective health solution. The combined companies manufacture products in different segments like cardiology, endocrinology, neuroscience, rheumatology, urology, ophthalmology, and oncology. The merged pharmaceutical company had 12 products with annual revenues greater than $1 billion. The combination of Pfizer and Pharmacia had an R&D pipeline of nearly 120 new chemical entities in development and more than 80 additional projects for product enhancements. This merger was relevant in the context of the patent expiry of billion-dollar blockbusters wherein large companies were increasingly finding ways to meet the impending shortfall in revenues due to the generic invasion.

Merger Highlights

The stock transaction was valued at $60 billion. Pharmacia spun off its 84% ownership of Monsanto to its current shareholders before the merger agreement. Pfizer exchanged 1.4 shares of Pfizer common stock in a tax-free transaction valued at $45.08 per Pharmacia share, based on Pfizer's July 12, 2002, closing stock price of $32.20 (Pfizer Website, 2017b). The transaction represented 44% premium based on the average closing prices of the two stocks over the preceding 30 days, adjusted for the Monsanto spin-off. Pfizer shareholders owned 77% of the combined company, and Pharmacia's shareholders owned 23% of the combined company. The merger was expected to have cost synergy of $1.4 billion, $2.2 billion, and $2.5 billion in the years 2003, 2004, and 2005, respectively. The savings was expected to come from reductions in administrative costs, purchasing, manufacturing, distribution, and research and development.

Wealth Creation in Pfizer–Pharmacia Merger

The merger announcement was made on July 15, 2002. The merger deal was completed on April 16, 2003.

The stock registered negative returns during the three-window period of −1 and announcement day. The stock price of Pfizer fell by 11% on the announcement day of merger with Pharmacia (Table 8.5). The cumulative gain registered by the stock during the 245-day period (July 1, 2002–July 5, 2003) was 7%.

The cumulative return during the different time window periods was negative except the time window period from −8 to +245 days (Fig. 8.2).

The stock price was highly fluctuating during the 1-year period of analysis.

Merger with Wyeth

Wyeth is one of the world's largest research-driven pharmaceutical and healthcare product companies in the world. It was a leader in the discovery, development, manufacturing, and marketing of pharmaceuticals, vaccines, biotechnology products,

Table 8.5 Cumulative returns during different time window period

Day	Cumulative returns
−1 to +1	−0.13
−5 to +5	−0.27
1 to +10	−0.04
1 to +100	−0.01
−8 to 245	0.07

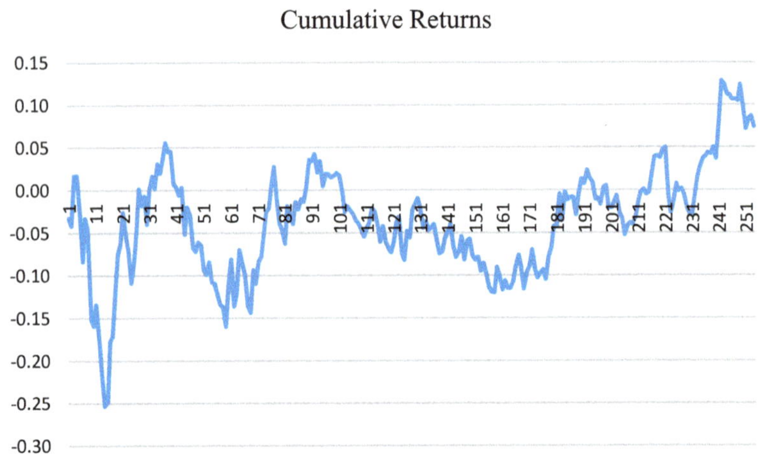

Fig. 8.2 Cumulative returns during the period of July 2002–July 2003

nutritionals, and non-prescription medicines that improve the quality of life for people worldwide. The company's major divisions include Wyeth Pharmaceuticals, Wyeth Consumer Healthcare, and Fort Dodge Animal Health.

On January 26, 2009, Pfizer and Wyeth entered into a definitive agreement under which it was proposed that Pfizer will acquire Wyeth in a cash-and-stock transaction. The deal was valued at $68 billion. The combination was aimed at creating one of the most diversified companies in the global healthcare industry. The combined company had strong product offerings in different therapeutic areas, strong product pipeline, and manufacturing capabilities. The combined company armed with broad and diversified product portfolio and reduced dependence on small molecules was expected to provide stable top line and EPS growth. It was expected that no drug of the combined firm will account for more than 10% of the total revenues by 2012.

Terms of the Merger

Under the terms of agreement, each outstanding share of Wyeth common stock was converted into the right to receive $33 in cash and 0.985 of a share of Pfizer common stock. On the basis of the closing price of Pfizer stock as of January 23, 2009, the stock component was valued at $17.19 per share. The transaction provided immediate value to Wyeth shareholders through the cash component and approximate ownership of 16% of Pfizer's common shares. The board of directors recommended for reduction of dividend to $0.16 per quarter effective from the second quarter of the year 2009. The transaction was financed through a combination of cash, debt, and stock. About $22.5 billion in debt was raised through a consortium of banks. Pfizer halved its dividend and raised $22 billion in debt to acquire Wyeth. According to the agreement, Wyeth would have had to pay Pfizer a $1.8 billion breakup free if it annulled the deal.

The lead financial advisors for Pfizer were Bank of America Merrill Lynch, Goldman Sachs, and JPMorgan. The legal advisor was Cadwalader, Wickersham & Taft LLP. The financial advisors for Wyeth were Morgan Stanley and Evercore Partners, and its legal advisor was Simpson Thacher & Bartlett LLP.

Deal Synergies

The acquisition deal was accretive for Pfizer's adjusted diluted earnings per share in the second full year after deal closing. The transaction was expected to provide cost savings of approximately $4 billion by the year 2012. The acquisition which was termed as the third largest in the drug industry since 1998 was expected to help Pfizer company to shorten the major gap in revenue in the year 2011 when its blockbuster Lipitor cholesterol drug started facing US generic competition.

Strategic Advantages

The combination of Pfizer and Wyeth created the world's premier biopharmaceutical company with diversification and scale position. The combined company became an industry leader in human, animal, and consumer health sectors (Hall & Krauskopf, 2009). It became one of the leading players in primary and specialty care and small- and large-molecule sectors. Wyeth had leadership position in attractive growth areas such as vaccines, nutritionals, and biologicals. Wyeth developed the first pneumococcal vaccine for infants. Wyeth had immense strength in biotechnology sector with products like Enbrel which is the number one biotechnology product in the world.

Pfizer and Wyeth have highly complementary businesses. The combination was aimed at enhancing the in-line and pipeline patent-protected portfolio in key invest to win disease areas such as Alzheimer's disease, inflammation, oncology, pain, and psychosis. The consolidation was also expected to make Pfizer a top-tier player in biotherapeutics and vaccines. The new company could accelerate growth in emerging markets, create new opportunities for established products, and create a lower and flexible cost base. The combined company had top-tier portfolios in key therapeutic areas like cardiovascular, oncology, women's central nervous system, and infectious diseases. The new combined company had a diverse product portfolio with 17 products with more than $1 billion each in annual revenue. With the acquisition of Wyeth, Pfizer became the world's second largest specialty care provider with products like leading biologic Enbrel, Prevnar the world's largest selling vaccine, Sutent drug for cancer, Geodon for schizophrenia, and Zyvox for infection. Pfizer had global leadership position in animal health sector with strong product lines for companion animals, biologics, and anti-infectives. The new company has one of the best resources to invest in research and development. The consolidated company had access to all leading scientific technology platforms which included vaccines, small and large molecules, nutritionals, and consumer products. The merger also brought together a robust pipeline of biopharmaceutical research and development projects which included programs in diabetes, inflammation/immunology, oncology, and pain. Significant opportunities also exist with respect to Wyeth's Alzheimer's disease pipeline which had a number of compounds in development phase which included biotech compound bapineuzumab. The merged company also achieved an enhanced ability to innovate as each business unit was given responsibility to oversee product development from clinical trials to commercialization.

In geographic terms the combination would enhance Pfizer's and Wyeth's portfolios in important growth areas. The combined company will be number one in terms of biopharmaceutical revenues in the United States with approximately 12% market share. In Europe the combined company had a market share of approximately 10%. The combined Pfizer–Wyeth had significant growth opportunities in emerging markets such as Latin America, the Middle East, and China.

The merger was completed on October 15, 2009, with the receipt of regulatory approval from all government authorities as required by the merger agreement and approval by Wyeth shareholders. Wyeth common stock ceased trading with effective from October 15, 2009. Pfizer had appointed Computershare Trust Company as exchange agent and paying agent to deal with Wyeth shareholders in connection with the merger.

Merger Announcement and Stock Wealth Impact

The merger announcement of the deal was made on January 26, 2009. The Wyeth shares dipped 0.8% on Monday immediately after the merger deal announcement. The merger was completed on October 15, 2009. The Pfizer shares fell 10.3% to $15.65 on the day of announcement. The stock price rose by 1.1% on the first day after announcement (Table 8.6).

Positive returns were registered by the Pfizer stock during period −3 day and − 1 day before merger announcement and + 1 day after merger announcement. The stock price rose by 2.1% both on +5 and + 6 days after merger announcement and by +2.3% on the 9th day after merger announcement (Table 8.6).

The cumulative return during the 251-day period −5 to +245-day period is 16%. The stock price showed increasing trend after the merger completion period. The returns surrounding the shorter window period was negative (Table 8.7).

The stock price has shown increasing trend after the merger completion period of October 2009 (Fig. 8.3).

Table 8.6 Return analysis during merger announcement period

Day	Returns (%)
−5	0.6
−4	−1.7
−3	1.6
−2	−1.5
−1	1.4
0	−10.3
1	1.1
2	−2.4
3	−2.1
4	−3.6
5	2.1
6	2.1
7	−4.1
8	−0.5
9	2.3
10	−0.9

Table 8.7 Cumulative returns during merger period

Time window	Cumulative returns (%)
−5 to 5 days	−14.75
−1 to 1 days	−7.80
0 to+20 days	−23.8
−5 to +245 days	16
+170 to +245 days	17.47

Fig. 8.3 Cumulative returns during January 2009–January 2010

Operating Performance Analysis

The year of merger (2009) is denoted as 0 in the merger period. The years after merger are denoted as 1, 2, etc. The year of merger is excluded from analysis. The average growth rate of revenues was negative (−3.27%) in the 6-year post-merger period (2011–2016). The average increase in operating income during the post-merger 6-year period (2011–2016) was 6.5%, while the net income registered a growth rate of 9.28% in the 6-year post-merger period 2011–2016 (Table 8.8).

The profitability performance of Pfizer is compared with respect to the pre- and post-merger period. The average profitability ratios in the premerger period (2007–2008) are compared with the profitability ratios in the post-merger period (2010–2016). The average gross margin declined slightly from 80% to 79.7% on comparative basis. The operating margin and net margin improved from 17.80 and 16.80% in the premerger period to 24.6 and 20.1% in the post-merger period. The average return on assets declined from 7.12% to 6.2% in the post-merger period. The return on equity and return on invested capital improved from 12.60 and 9.44% to 14.4 and 10.3%, respectively, on comparative basis (Table 8.9).

The price multiples have improved in the post-merger period. The average price-to-earnings ratio during the 2007–2008 period improved 17.1–21.5% in the post-merger period (2010–2016). The average price-to-book ratio, price-to-sales ratio, and price-to-cash flow ratio improved from 2.25, 2.9, and 9.2 to 2.4, 3.4, and 11.8, respectively (Table 8.10).

Table 8.8 Operating highlights in millions of dollars

Year	2007	2008	2009	2010	2011	2012	2013	2014	2015	2016
Merger period	−2	−1	0	1	2	3	4	5	6	7
Revenues	48,418	48,296	50,009	65,165	61,035	54,657	51,584	49,605	48,851	52,824
Operating income	7519	9694	10,827	9471	12,706	15,264	15,184	13,499	12,976	13,730
Net income	8144	8104	8635	8257	10,009	14,570	22,003	9135	6960	7215
Operating cash flow	13,353	18,238	16,587	11,454	20,240	17,054	17,765	16,883	14,512	15,901

Source of data: Morningstar

Table 8.9 Financial highlights

Merger period	−2	−1	0	1	2	3	4	5	6	7
Year	2007	2008	2009	2010	2011	2012	2013	2014	2015	2016
Gross margin in %	76.79	83.2	82.23	77.31	79.52	82.03	81.42	80.69	80.25	76.66
Operating margin in %	15.53	20.07	21.65	14.53	20.82	27.93	29.44	27.21	26.56	25.99
Net margin in %	16.81	16.78	17.27	12.18	14.84	24.7	42.65	18.42	14.25	13.66
Return on assets in %	7.08	7.16	5.33	4.05	5.23	7.8	12.3	5.35	4.13	4.26
Return on equity in %	11.96	13.24	11.71	9.29	11.78	17.84	27.94	12.38	10.24	11.62
Return on invested capital in %	9.11	9.77	8.46	7.02	8.58	12.9	19.65	8.91	7.11	7.63

Table 8.10 Price multiples

Price multiples	2007	2008	2009	2010	2011	2012	2013	2014	2015	2016
Price-to-earnings ratio	19.3	14.9	14.8	17.2	17	19.9	20.3	19.2	24.3	32.5
Price-to-book ratio	2.4	2.1	1.6	1.6	1.8	2.2	2.5	2.5	3	3.1
Price-to-sales ratio	3.3	2.5	2.6	2.1	2.5	3.2	3.9	4	4.2	3.8
Price-to-cash flow ratio	11.8	6.6	7.7	12.3	8.1	11	12.6	11.6	13.4	13.7

References

Hall J, Krauskopf L (2009) Pfizer to buy Wyeth for $68 billion. https://www.reuters.com/article/us-wyeth-pfizer/pfizer-to-buy-wyeth-for-68-billion-idUSTRE50M1AQ20090126. Accessed 23 Sept 2017

Herper M (2002) Pfizer buys Pharmacia for $60 billion. https://www.forbes.com/2002/07/15/0715pfe/. Accessed 21 Sept 2017

McCullagh M (2000) Data Monitor. Emerging from the Merger: Warner–Lambert and Pfizer. https://www.pharmaceuticalonline.com/doc/emerging-from-the-merger-warner-lambert-and-p-0001. Accessed 19 Sept 2017

Petersen M (2000) Pfizer gets its deal to buy Warner–Lambert for $90.2 billion. http://www.nytimes.com/2000/02/08/business/pfizer-gets-its-deal-to-buy-warner-lambert-for-90.2-billion.html. Accessed 18 Sept 2017

Pfizer Annual Report (2017)

Pfizer Press Release (2009) Pfizer to acquire Wyeth creating world's premier biopharmaceutical company. https://press.pfizercom/press-release/pfizer-acquire-wyeth-creating-worlds-premier-biopharmaceutical-company. Accessed 22 Sept 2017

Pfizer Website (2017a) https://www.pfizer.com/about/history/pfizer_warner_lambert. Accessed 18 Sept 2017

Pfizer Website (2017b) https://www.pfizer.com/about/history/pfizer_pharmacia. Accessed 20 Sept 2017

Report (2000) Warner–Lambert and Pfizer in a 90 billion merger deal. https://www.irishtimes.com/business/warner-lambert-and-pfizer-in-90bn-merger-1.242725. Accessed 18 Sept 2017

Reporter (2003) It's Official: Pfizer buys Pharmacia. http://money.cnn.com/2003/04/16/news/companies/pfizer_pharma/. Accessed 21 Sept 2017

Righi G (2016) Drivers of mergers and acquisitions (M&A) in life sciences. https://www.linkedin.com/pulse/drivers-mergers-acquisitions-ma-life-sciences-giordano-righi. Accessed 17 Sept 2017

ExxonMobil Merger

9

Industry Scenario

Massive changes in technology, globalization, and industry transformation have brought consolidation in the oil and gas energy sector. In the 1980s and 1990s, M&A in energy sector were concentrated in the North American region. In the 1990s oil industry witnessed consolidation when megamergers of Exxon and Mobil, BP and Amoco, and Chevron and Texaco occurred. The value of M&A deal in oil sector was approximately $88.99 billion and $66.6 billion, respectively, during the years 1997 and 1998. M&A deal activity was basically concentrated in the Exploration and Production segment. Many horizontal mergers took place during the period 1998–2001. The British Petroleum–Amoco merger in the year 1998 had projected $2 billion in savings. In December 1998 the French oil firm Total acquired Petrofina. In 1999 BP Amoco entered into an agreement to acquire Arco. The trend had been toward integrated oil industry operations where economies of scale provide significant operational efficiencies. The oil industry operations can be divided into upstream, downstream, and petrochemical operations. The oil industry is characterized by high cost of replacement assets like oil fields. The major drivers for M&A activity at the time of ExxonMobil consolidation were market share enhancement and cost minimization. Developments in the global market had resulted in low oil prices. Increases in worldwide production had led to a situation in oversupply along with a period of economic difficulties in Asia. The situation was further deteriorated as OPEC countries failed to keep their commitments to reduce production and overproduction of oil by Russia. The low price of oil was detrimental for American companies with high production costs. Upstream production of oil is a capital intensive business with substantial risks. The low oil prices were a major strategic driver for restructuring trends in the industry. The mergers were aimed at cost reductions in operations by eliminating redundant activities and provide access to more resources. The downstream business which involves the process of refining and marketing oil products was also facing huge competitive pressures.

B. R. Kumar, *Wealth Creation in the World's Largest Mergers and Acquisitions*,
Management for Professionals, https://doi.org/10.1007/978-3-030-02363-8_9

ExxonMobil Corporation

ExxonMobil Corporation is an American multinational oil and gas corporation headquartered in Texas. ExxonMobil businesses are made up of upstream, downstream, and chemical businesses.

In its over 135 years of existence, ExxonMobil has evolved from a regional marketer of Kerosene in the United States to over the largest publicly traded petroleum and petrochemical enterprise in the world. ExxonMobil was incorporated in the state of New Jersey in the year 1882. ExxonMobil and its affiliated companies operate and market different energy products throughout the world. ExxonMobil is involved in the exploration and production of crude oil and natural gas, manufacture of petroleum products, and transportation and sale of crude oil, natural gas, and petroleum products. ExxonMobil is also a major manufacturer and marketer of commodity petrochemicals which include olefins, aromatics, polyethylene, and polypropylene plastics. The divisions of ExxonMobil include ExxonMobil, Exxon, Esso, Mobil, and XTO. By 2016 end, ExxonMobil was in possession of nearly 12,000 active patents worldwide. The company had over 71,000 employees in the year ended 2016. ExxonMobil's fundamental upstream businesses include global exploration, development, production, and gas and power marketing activities. ExxonMobil's downstream operations are a large diversified business with refining, logistics, and marketing complexes around the world. The chemical businesses manufacture and sell petrochemicals of olefins, aromatics, fluids, synthetic rubber, polyethylene, polypropylene, packaging films, and other petrochemical products. ExxonMobil has a wide presence in mature markets in North America and Europe as well as in the Asia Pacific region. ExxonMobil is the largest of the world's big oil companies with daily production of 3.921 million BOE (barrels of oil equivalent). By the end of 2016, ExxonMobil's reserves were 20 billion BOE. ExxonMobil is one of the largest refiners in the world with a combined daily refining capacity of 6.3 million barrels. The company has 37 oil refineries in 21 countries. In 2009, ExxonMobil announced plans to acquire XTO Energy for $40 billion. In the United Kingdom, Exxon operates through Esso. In this region Esso and Mobil together operate about 2600 petrol stations and had a market share of approximately 25%. Table 9.1 gives the financial highlights of Exxon Mobil.

ExxonMobil Merger

This megamerger of oil industry reunited the major disintegrated divisions of the Standard Oil which had once controlled approximately 90% of oil production in the United States.

Both Exxon and Mobil were descendants of Standard Oil established by John D. Rockefeller and partners in the year 1870 as the Standard Oil Company of Ohio. In the year 1882, these companies were incorporated as the Standard Oil Trust. The Standard Oil Trust was dissolved under the Sherman Antitrust Act in 1892. In other words, Standard Oil was broken into 33 companies, of which 8 were retained under the name Standard Oil.

Table 9.1 Financial highlights of ExxonMobil

Year	2012	2013	2014	2015	2016
Revenues	451,509	420836	394105	259488	218608
Net income	44880	32580	32520	16150	7840
EPS	9.7	7.37	7.6	3.85	1.88
Cash dividend per share	2.18	2.46	2.7	2.88	2.98
Total assets	333795	346808	349493	336758	330314

Source: Annual Report 2016
The values are given in millions of dollars except per share amounts

At the time of merger, Exxon had upstream operations in 26 countries and downstream operations in 76 countries. Exxon was also the world's third largest petrochemical company and the world's largest independent non-utility power producer. In terms of size of oil and gas reserves, Exxon was second only to Royal Dutch/Shell in the year 1997. Exxon had 6.2 billion barrels of crude oil and 26.1 trillion cubic feet of natural gas by the end of the year 1997.

Mobil Corporation had its origin when Vacuum Oil Company was established in the year 1866. After a series of name changes, Standard Oil of New York became Mobil in 1966. By 1972, the former Standard Oil of New Jersey had evolved into Exxon. Mobil was present in the entire value chain of exploration, production, refining, and marketing. In year 1997, Mobil's worldwide net crude and natural gas liquid production averaged 928,000 barrels per day. Mobil was a market leader in high margin products like synthetic lubricants and premium gasolines. The proven reserves of Mobil made the company emerge as one of the five largest non-state-owned oil majors in the world.

On December 1, 1998, Exxon and Mobil announced their merger plans in a deal valued at $81 billion. The merged entity became the third largest company in the world at the time of announcement. The merged company was called ExxonMobil Corp. The new company retained both Exxon and Mobil brands. The company was headquartered in Exxon's home city of Irving, Texas. Exxon and Mobil were the largest and second largest US oil-producing companies with combined annual revenue of $193.1 billion and production of 2.5 million barrels of oil a day.

On November 30, 1999, Exxon and Mobil merger to form ExxonMobil Corporation was completed. The ExxonMobil combination represented the biggest merger at that time (Harrison, 1998). It created one of the world's preeminent oil companies with revenues of $200 billion and worldwide production of 2.5 million barrels of oil a day. The $81 billion deal was approved by the US government following the agreement that Exxon and Mobil would sell more than 2400 stations across the Northeastern United States. The deal was one of the biggest mergers in US history which eclipsed the $72.6 billion union of Travelers Group and Citicorp. The ExxonMobil deal saw the reunion of two of the seven sister companies which were forced to break up due to 1911 breakup of John D. Rockefeller's United Standard Oil Trust (Staff and Wire Report, 1998). The combined ExxonMobil with a market capitalization of $237.53 billion became the third largest company in the world behind General Electric and Microsoft.

The combined ExxonMobil had almost 21 billion barrels of oil and gas reserves. The merger placed the combined company behind only Saudi Arabia and Iran in terms of output. The merger happened in a scenario where the industry was facing historically low prices along with more global competition.

Deal Highlights

Under the terms of the agreement, Mobil shareholders received 1.32015 shares of Exxon stock (XON) for every Mobil share (MOB) held. On the basis of premerger announcement day closing price of Exxon at $75, the deal valued Mobil at $80 billion or $99.01 per share (Annual Report, 1998). This deal value represented a $13.01 premium over Mobil's premerger announcement day close price of $86 per share. Both Exxon and Mobil's share price fell on merger announcement. The fall in Exxon's share price lowered the deal value to roughly $78 billion. Shareholders of both companies cast 98% or more of its votes to approve the merger. As a result of the merger Exxon shareholders owned 70% of the new company while Mobil shareholders were left with 30% of the merged group (Staff and Wire Reports, 1999). The investment banker of Exxon was JPMorgan.

Merger Motivations

Consolidation in the energy sector was basically on account of high production costs and weak oil prices. By the merger with Mobil, Exxon focused on expansion of its presence in the regions of high potential for future oil and gas discoveries. The consolidation facilitated the combination of Exxon's rich experience in deepwater exploration with Mobil's production and exploration acreage in Nigeria and Equatorial Guinea. Exxon had strong presence in Azerbaijan. At the same time Mobil had strong presence in Kazakhstan with significant interest in the Tengiz field and Turkmenistan. Similar complementary exploration and production operations existed in regions like South America, Russia, and Eastern Canada. Synergies for the deal were expected from cost reductions or revenue enhancement. ExxonMobil deal had cost synergy due to sales of duplicate facilities and employment reductions. Cost reductions were realized by adoptions of best practices like combining advanced technologies. Revenue increases were achieved by strengthening the market positions of each firm. The joint ventures with major producing countries such as Saudi Arabia strengthened Exxon's position as a major oil producer in the world.

The merger was expected to generate savings of $2.8 billion after 2 years of deal (Deutsche Bank, 2001). The rationalization costs were expected to be $2 billion. The main components of the $2.8 billion cost-saving program were $1.1 billion of savings through rationalization of production programs, $750 million through organizational efficiencies, and $300 million through the adoption of best practices and more selective exploration program (S&P, 1998). The merger was expected to improve the return on capital of ExxonMobil by 4% within 3–5 years. The combined company aimed to reduce 7.3% of its workforce which amounted to 9000 jobs. Savings from merger was expected to be over $8 billion by the year 2003. Exxon had paid a premium of $15.5 billion. The market capitalization of the combined company increased from $234 billion to $280 billion by the end of 1999 and to $301 billion by the end of 2000. Hence, it can be stated that the capitalized value of the synergies was in the range $46 billion to $ 67 billion. In a news release in 2000, ExxonMobil had reported that synergies had reached $4.6 billion. The projected synergies of the deal were expected to be $ 7 billion by the year 2002.

Strategic Benefits from the Deal

In a scenario of low prices, profitability for firms could be achieved only through efficiency. Exxon was effective at cutting waste and streamlining its operations to achieve economies of scale. But the streamlining process became saturated, and Exxon needs to achieve substantial growth to have more scale economies. Merger with Mobil was a good strategy to achieve greater economies of scale for Exxon. With respect to research and development, Mobil had achieved significant breakthroughs in its upstream processes for extracting oil from lower-grade oil fields and downstream processes involving manufacture of improved lubricants. Mobil was also a market leader who had pioneered the carbon dioxide injection process for extending the life of existing oil fields. Mobil had also focused on development of lubricants like Mobil 1 for improving the life of automobile and industrial equipment. Thus, the merger with Mobil was expected to achieve significant R&D synergy for Exxon. Exxon also expected that Mobil acquisition would facilitate expansion into markets like Saudi Arabia where Mobil had performed substantial work with Saudi Oil Ministry (Raphael, 1999).

Regulatory Issues

Exxon and Mobil agreed to sell or reassign 1740 stations across mid-Atlantic states, 369 in California, 319 in Texas, and 12 in Guam. Among other divestitures Exxon also had to scrap an option to buy gasoline stations from Tosco Corp in Arizona. The company also had to divest its Valero Benicia Refinery in California and jet turbine oil business.

Merger Valuation

Exxon had a market capitalization of $175 billion compared with $58.7 billion before the merger. Before the merger, Exxon had a P/E ratio of 23.6 compared to 17.9 for Mobil. JPMorgan, the financial advisor for Exxon, used comparable valuation method to value Exxon. They employed relative value ratios like enterprise market value/revenues, enterprise market value/EBITDA, and enterprise market value/free cash flows. JPMorgan reviewed 38 large capitalization stock for stock transactions. JPMorgan premium analysis for Exxon was in the range of 15–25%. In its comparable valuation method, the financial advisor for Mobil used six large oil companies to value Mobil. The major two ratios used in relative valuation were price/earnings and price to cash flows. In terms of book value for Mobil in 1998, the deal value represented premium of approximately 290%.

Wealth Creation in ExxonMobil Deal

The announcement of the merger deal was made on December 01, 1998. The merger was completed on November 30, 1999.

Exxon's stock price declined by 4.5% on the day of public announcement of the deal. The stock declined in price for 3 days surrounding the public announcement of the merger. On the preannouncement day −2 and − 1, the Exxon stock increased by 2.3% and 0.8%, respectively (Table 9.2).

The cumulative return analysis for the stock during the merger period (November 1998–December 1999) shows that the stock gained during the merger completion period (Table 9.3).

Table 9.2 Announcement period returns

Day	Returns (%)
−5	0.1
−4	0.9
−3	0.0
−2	2.3
−1	0.8
0	−4.5
1	−0.5
2	−1.0
3	1.3
4	2.1
5	0.3
6	1.0
7	−0.3
8	1.2
9	−0.3
10	−0.6

Table 9.3 Cumulative returns during the merger period

Period	Cumulative returns (%)
−5 to 5 days	1.80
−1 to 1 day	−4.18
0 to 30 day	−6.18
−9 to 272 days	15.85
−5 to 272 days	15

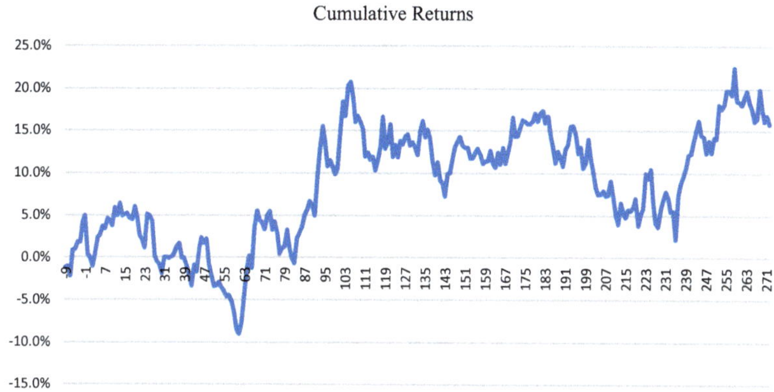

Fig. 9.1 Cumulative returns surrounding the merger period

During the shorter time window period, the cumulative returns were negative except during the 11-day period (−5 to +5 day surrounding the merger announcement period). During the entire 282-day period (−9 to 272 days) surrounding the merger period, the cumulative returns were approximately 16% (Fig. 9.1).

Operating Performance Analysis (Table 9.4)

The financial parameters analyzed are revenues, net income, total assets, and total debt of ExxonMobil during the period 1993–2006. The values are given in millions of dollars (Exxon Annual Report, 1997). The analysis is done on the basis of premerger and post-merger period. The year 1999 is the year of merger and is excluded from the analysis. The average growth rate of revenues, net income, and total assets in the premerger period (1993–1998) is compared with the average growth rate of these variables in the post-merger period (2000–2006). The five-average growth rate of revenues in the premerger period was 10.78%. During the 6-year post-merger period (2000–2006), the average growth rate of revenues declined to 8.6%. In terms of net income, synergy has been realized in the post-merger period since the average growth rate of net income in the above premerger period increased from 12.9% to 19.78% in the post-merger period. The average growth rate of assets declined to 6.8% in the premerger period compared to 12% in the post-merger period. The firm has become less risky in the post-merger period on the basis of financial leverage. The average increase in total debt during the premerger period (1993–1998) was 10.4% with the increase mainly attributed to the 76% increase in debt during the period 1997. The post-merger period witnessed a decline in total debt with an average decline of 7% during the post-merger period (2000–2006).

Table 9.4 Comparative performance in the pre- and post-merger period

Year	1993	1994	1995	1996	1997	1998	1999	2000	2001	2002	2003	2004	2005	2006
Merger period	−6	−5	−4	−3	−2	−1	0	1	2	3	4	5	6	7
Revenues	111211	113904	123920	134249	201746	169642	185527	232748	213488	200949	237054	291252	358955	365467
Net income	5280	5100	6470	7510	11732	8074	7910	17720	15320	11460	21510	25330	36130	39500
Total assets	84145	87862	91296	95527	143751	139335	144521	149000	143174	152644	174278	195256	208335	219015
Total debt	12615	12689	10025	9746	17182	17016	18972	13441	10802	10748	9545	8293	7991	8347

References

Annual Reports (1998–2005). Exxon Mobil

Deutsche Bank (2001) ExxonMobil: The Emperor's New Groove

Exxon Annual Report (1997)

Harrison M (1998) $250 billion Exxon Mobil deal is the biggest merger in history. http://www.independent.co.uk/news/business/250bn-exxon-mobil-deal-is-biggest-merger-in-history-1188674.html. Accessed 28 Sept 2017

Raphael BP (1999) Analysis of Exxon Mobil Merger. http://bobpenn.homestead.com/files/exxonmobil.pdf. Accessed 29 Sept 2017

S&P (1998) Standard & Poor's Stock Report for Exxon Corporation. December 1998

Staff and Wire Report (1998 Exxon Mobil in a 80 B deal. http://money.cnn.com/1998/12/01/deals/exxon/. Accessed 28 Sept 2017

Staff and Wire Reports (1999) Exxon-Mobil Merger Done. http://money.cnn.com/1999/11/30/deals/exxonmobil/. Accessed 28 Sept 2017

Citicorp–Travelers Group Merger 10

Consolidation in the Financial Industry

Cost savings and revenue enhancement are major driving forces for consolidation in the financial sector. Cost savings can be realized through economies of scale, economies of scope, and efficient allocation of resources. Synergies from M&A activity in this sector can be attributed to client-driven, geographic, and product-driven linkages. Economies of scope results due to cross selling by which the costs to the buyer of multiple financial services from a single supplier will be much lesser than from different supplier. The critical components driving consolidation in financial sector are advances in information technology, financial deregulation, globalization of financial markets, and real markets. The technological advancement has facilitated financial service providers to offer broader array of products and services to a wider base of clients in different geographic areas. Reforms in the legal and financial aspects have further facilitated the process of consolidation in the financial sector. Some of the major reforms include dismantling of interest rate controls, removal of barriers between banks and other financial intermediaries, and lowering of entry barriers. The adoption of euro as an integrated currency of Europe has accelerated the speed of financial integration in Europe and promoted cross-border M&A activity. In the context of price competition, reduced margins, falling spreads, and competition, financial institutions like banks are forced to adopt consolidation to enhance revenues (de Souza et al., 2009). With new structural reforms in place, the boundaries separating sectors like banking, securities, and insurance are increasingly becoming blurred. Financial institutions with mature products are using M&A to achieve growth and gain complementary skills. M&A is also used for expansion purposes. European banks have acquired smaller UK- and US-based investment banks to become global investment banks. Strategic Alliances and Ownership linkages were formed between insurance companies and investment banks during the 1980s and 1990s. This type of consolidation was for the purpose of "one-stop

B. R. Kumar, *Wealth Creation in the World's Largest Mergers and Acquisitions*, Management for Professionals, https://doi.org/10.1007/978-3-030-02363-8_10

shopping." These trends led to the concept of universal banking. Another noted trend was the modern concept of bancassurance which involved the backward integration of banks to source insurance industry products and forward integration of insurance companies to acquire distribution channels. Through this mechanism, banks were able to expand their retail banking products, while insurance companies gained an established distribution network through the bank branches. It is stated that over 10,000 financial firms were acquired in the industrialized nations during the period 1990–2001. The US banking industry itself witnessed more than 7000 mergers during the period 1980–1998. Chase Manhattan Corp and Chemical Banking Corp had merged in the year 1995 in a deal valued at $10 billion which catapulted the bank as the number one bank in the United States overtaking Citicorp.

Citigroup

Citigroup history had its origins when City Bank of New York was established in the year 1812. Citigroup is a global diversified financial services holding company which offers range of financial products and services. Citi have approximately 200 million customer accounts and does business in more than 160 countries. In 2016, Citi had approximately 219,000 full-time employees. The two primary business segments of Citigroup are Global Consumer Banking business and Institutional Clients Group and Citi Holding. Citigroup had made revenues of $69,875 million in the year 2016. Citi's Global Consumer Bank (GCB) is a global leader in credit cards, wealth management, and commercial banking. GCB serves more than 110 million customers in 19 countries. GCB operates four business lines of branded cards, retail services, retail banking, and commercial banking. In 2016, GCB held $300 billion in average deposits and managed $139 billion in average assets and $280 billion in average loans.

Acquisitions by Citi Group

Citigroup made 315 acquisitions and took stakes in 242 companies during the period 1981–2002. Citicorp over a period of time acquired stakes in international banks and brokerage firms. These included brokerage firms like Nikko Beans of Japan. Citicorp also acquired stakes in Bank Handlowy w Warszawie of Poland, Banaci Bank of Mexico, and Diner's Club of Europe. In 2001, Citi Group acquired European American Bank and added 97 branches in the New York Area. Citicorp also acquired Golden State Bancorp and added 352 branches and 1.5 million new customers. For this transaction, Citigroup paid approximately $2.3 billion in cash and issued 79.5 million Citigroup common shares. In the year 2000, Citigroup acquired the Associates First Capital Corporation, the largest American consumer finance company in a stock deal valued at $31.1 billion. Established in 1918, Associates First Capital was an important player in financial services industry which provided credit card services, home equity and mortgage loans, heavy equipment leasing, etc. With this acquisition, Citigroup became the largest provider of credit cards, home equity loans, and commercial leasing services. The combined new company had about 2000 retail branches across the United States. Citigroup exchanged 0.7334 share of its stock for each share of Associates First Capital. Associates was valued at $42.49 per share which represented a premium of 52% on stock price of the Associates First Capital. The deal resulted in cost savings of $400 million and $600 million within 2 years of the acquisition.

Travelers Companies

Travelers Group is an American insurance company with over 160 years of legacy. Travelers Group is one of the best property casualty insurers in the world. The company is a market leader in personal, business, and specialty insurance. Travelers is the second largest writer of US commercial property casualty insurance and the third largest writer of US personal insurance through independent agents. Travelers had been included in the Dow Jones Industrial Average since June 2009 replacing its parent Citi group. Travelers provides commercial and personal property, casualty insurance products, and services to businesses, government units, and individuals. Travelers offers insurance in the three major segments of personal insurance, business insurance, and bond and specialty insurance. Travelers has approximately 14000 independent agents (Travelers Annual Report, n.d.).

The Travelers was founded in 1864. In the decade of the 1990s, Travelers went through a series of mergers and acquisitions. In 1993, Primerica acquired Travelers Group but retained the Travelers name. In 1996, Travelers Group bought Aetna's property and casualty business.

In 1997 (year before the merger with Citicorp), Travelers Group acquired the investment banking powerhouse Salomon Brothers in a stock deal valued at $9 billion or $78.46 per Salomon share. Salomon was then absorbed into the Traveler's brokerage firm Smith Barney to form Salomon Smith Barney. Under the terms of the deal, Travelers issued 1.13 shares of its stock for each share of Salomon. Travelers Group expanded its foothold in investment banking thorough this acquisition. The new brokerage firm became the third largest firm in equity underwriting and fourth largest in global equity underwriting. Travelers have grown rapidly from an insurance company into a diversified financial services company with its acquisitions of the brokerage firm Smith Barney and the commodity trader and brokerage Salomon Inc.

In the year 1998, the Travelers Group merged with Citicorp to form Citigroup. When the expected synergies didn't materialize, Citigroup spun off Travelers Property and Casualty into a subsidiary company in 2002. In 2005, Citigroup sold Travelers Life and Annuity to MetLife. In 2003 Travelers bought renewal rights for Royal & Sun Alliance Personal Insurance and Commercial businesses. In 2004, St. Paul and Travelers merged to form St. Paul Travelers. The corporate name was changed to The Travelers Companies when in the year 2007, the company repurchased the rights to the famous red umbrella logo from Citigroup. In June 2013,

Travelers acquired Dominion of Canada General Insurance Company from E-L Financial Corporation. Travelers Group acquired majority interest in the property casualty business of its J. Malucelli joint venture in Brazil. In March 2017, Travelers announced plans to acquire UK-based Simply Business from Aquiline Capital Partners for approximately $490 million. Travelers had revenues of $27.625 billion in the year 2016.

Citicorp–Travelers Group Merger

On April 7, 1998, Citicorp and Travelers Group announced merger plans to create the world's largest financial services company with banking, insurance, and investment operations in 100 countries (CNN Money, 1998). The stock swap deal valued each company at $70 billion.

The combined firm with $698 billion of assets became the largest financial services company globally which was slightly larger than Bank of Tokyo-Mitsubishi. The new company was called Citigroup. The new logo featured the bank's familiar lettering followed by the red umbrella which was the symbol used by Travelers. Citigroup had a market capitalization of approximately $135 billion. The new company had yearly revenues of about $50 billion and operating income of approximately $7.5 billion. The combined company had 100 million customers in 100 countries. The thrust of the deal was to create one-stop financial shopping for consumers offering Citicorp's strengths of traditional banking, consumer finance, and credit cards along with insurance and brokerage services from Travelers and its units. The merger resulted in the first truly global financial services supermarket which offers products from traditional banking to investment broking and insurance policies. In terms of assets, Citigroup became the largest financial firm in the world (Economist, 2000). John S. Reed, chief executive of Citicorp, and Weill of Travelers served as cochairmen and co-CEOs of Citigroup. The potential for cross selling was greatest in consumer finance. Citi's strong global brand was expected to provide for selling Travelers and Salomon Smith Barney products through its branch network which spanned over 100 countries and Citi's 42 million credit card account holders. Salomon Smith Barney mutual funds have been sold to Citibank. A few months after the merger announcement, Travelers annuities were selling in the Citibank branch network. Citicorp and Travelers Group expected that the existing laws which restricted bank holding companies from participating in insurance underwriting activities would change in the foreseeable future. Travelers had to overcome hurdles to become a bank holding company. It required to dispose of some of its nonbanking holdings.

Terms of the Deal

In the stock swap deal, Citicorp shareholders received 2.5 shares in Citigroup for each of their Citicorp shares. Travelers shareholders exchanged their shares on a one-for-one basis. Citicorp and Travelers shareholders owned 50% each of the company. The merger was termed as merger of equals. The accounting for merger was done for as pooling of interests. The deal was tax-free exchange involving 2.50 Travelers shares per Citicorp share. The deal was immediately accretive to EPS with expected closing on the second half of 1998. The transaction decreased leverage and improved capitalization ratio.

On announcement of deal, Citicorp's stock price shot up $35.625 to close at $178.50. At the same time, Travelers price rose by $11.3125 to close at $73. The combined company had a valuation of approximately $170 billion which was an increase of 22% in a single day on announcement.

Strategic Motivations for the Deal

The merger deal gave Travelers the ability to market mutual funds and insurance to Citicorp's retail customers, whereas Citicorp got access to the expanded client base of investors and insurance buyers for Travelers (Mitchell Martin and International Herald Tribune, 1998). The merger facilitated Citicorp to offer investment products available to customers around the world. Citicorp had built a global retail franchise along with its worldwide corporate banking business, while Travelers was a strong investment and insurance conglomerate. The strategy was to provide one-stop shopping for financial services. The deal paved the way for the repeal of the Glass Steagall Act of 1933 which separated investment banks and commercial banks. The end of Glass Steagall ushered in an era of consolidation and integration within the financial services industry. The merger was aimed to reduce overhead and distribution costs. According to company sources, the combination was expected to increase profitability by one billion dollars. The diversity of product lines and distribution channels were expected to provide revenue synergies. Revenue synergies were expected from cross selling of products. Citicorp had 36 million US customers and Travelers had 20 million customers.

Failure of the Deal

It was one of the worst mergers of all times. The merger witnessed problems of cultural integration. Each part of Citigroup was run like a separate fief leaving the company without a single cohesive culture. Bloated costs, outmoded technology, and retention of employees were the major problems faced by Citi following the merger deal. Citigroup ran up steep losses on complex mortgage investments. John Reed the architect of the deal admitted in the year 2008 that the landmark merger failed to benefit the financial services conglomerate's investors, customers, and employees. At the time of the deal, it was hailed that the creation of Citigroup would usher in a new era in finance by creating a one-stop shop for consumer and corporate customers.

By the tenth year of the deal, Citi's shares lost more than half their value. During the period 1998–2003, Citigroup's share price had risen more than 160%, outperforming big companies like General Electric and Berkshire Hathaway. The bank was compelled to raise $30 billion to strengthen its balance sheet due to the sub-prime crisis. During the late 1980s after the real estate market collapsed, Citi was stuck with heavy leveraged transactions. There were huge technology challenges such as incompatible computer systems. Retail cross selling has been slow. The Group had a muddled internet strategy.

Merger Analysis

Citicorp had return on equity of 20.8%, 20.4%, and 20.9% in the years 1995, 1996, and 1997, respectively. The Travelers Group had a return of 15%, 19%, and 18.5% in the years 1995, 1996, and 1997, respectively. The after-tax margin for Citicorp was 17.7%, 17.6%, and 17.8%, respectively, during the years 1995, 1996, and 1997, respectively. The after-tax margin for Travelers Group for the same period was 12.4%, 12.2%, and 13.3%, respectively.

Stock Wealth Analysis Surrounding the Merger Period

The public announcement of the merger was made on April 6, 1998. The daily stock return analysis of Citicorp is done for the period March 15, 1998–April 30, 1999. The cumulative return for 279-day period for Citicorp was 35.4% (Fig. 10.1).

The announcement day return for Citicorp was 18.34%. The stock price declined in the next 2 days after the merger announcement. The stock price gained 0.09% in the third day after the merger announcement (Table 10.1).

The 2-day (−1 to 0) cumulative return was 17.98%. The 3-day (−1 to +1) cumulative return was 12.72% (Table 10.2).

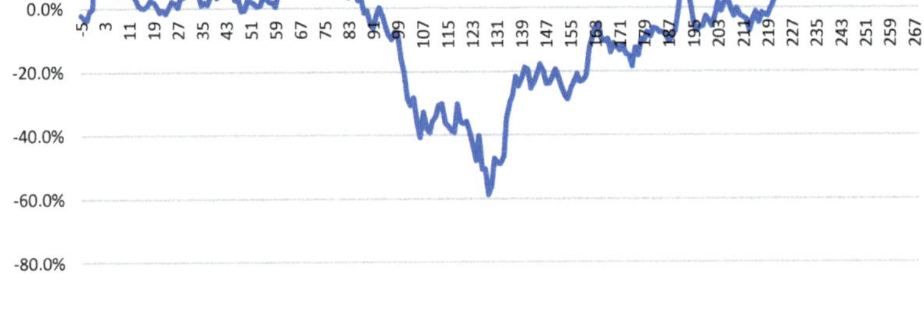

Fig. 10.1 Cumulative returns surrounding 1-year merger period

Table 10.1 Daily returns for Citicorp

Day	Returns (%)
−10	−2.32
−9	2.37
−8	0.81
−7	1.00
−6	−1.78
−5	−2.42
−4	−0.83
−3	−0.62
−2	2.73
−1	0.71
0	18.34
1	−6.34
2	−1.65
3	0.09
4	−1.21
5	0.56
6	−3.18
7	−2.22
8	2.27
9	−0.58
10	0.97

Table 10.2 Cumulative returns for Citicorp stock surrounding merger

Time window	Cumulative returns (%)
−1 to 0 days	17.98
−1 to +1 days	12.72
−5 to +5 days	9.37
−10 to +10 days	6.72
0 to +100 days	−15.79
0 to +200 days	−3.87
−10 to +268 days	35.40

Stock Returns for Travelers During Merger Period

The stock returns analysis for Travelers was done for the 279-day period surrounding the merger announcement. The period of analysis was March 16, 1998, to April 29, 1999. The cumulative return during the 279-day period surrounding the merger period −10 days to +268 days was −41.49% (Fig. 10.2).

On a public announcement of merger on April 6, 1998, the stock price increased by 1%. On the third day after the merger announcement, stock price rose by 0.4% (Table 10.3).

The merger announcement was value decreasing for Travelers Company. The cumulative stock returns were negative for Travelers in different time window intervals. The analysis suggests that the cumulative returns were negative in both shorter and longer time window periods (Table 10.4).

Fig. 10.2 Cumulative returns for Travelers in merger period

Table 10.3 Stock returns of Travelers during the merger announcement period

Day	Returns (%)
−10	−1.5
−9	−1.0
−8	−0.2
−7	0.5
−6	−0.5
−5	−1.2
−4	0.2
−3	−0.1
−2	−0.4
−1	0.3
0	1.0
1	−1.9
2	−0.9
3	0.4
4	−1.2
5	0.6
6	0.6
7	−0.6
8	−0.1
9	0.9
10	−1.1

Table 10.4 Cumulative returns for Travelers during different time window periods

Time window	Cumulative returns (%)
−1 to 0 days	−0.91
−1 to +1 days	−0.61
−5 to +5 days	−3.13
−10 to +10 days	−6.20
0 to +100 days	−28.90
0 to +200 days	−37.59
−10 to +268 days	−41.49

Table 10.5 Operating performance analysis for Citicorp

Year	1995	1996	1997	1998	1999	2000	2001	2002
Revenues	18678	20196	21616	44964	54809	63572	67367	71308
Net income	3464	3788	3591	6950	11243	13519	14216	15276
EPS	7.6	7.73	7.53	1.35	2.23	2.69	2.79	2.99
Total assets	256853	281018	310897	740336	795584	902210	1051450	1097190

The cumulative returns were in negative trend during the entire analysis period of −10 to +268 days (Fig. 10.2).

The values are given in millions of dollars except EPS (Citicorp Annual Reports, 1998–2007). The revenues of Citigroup increased from $18.678 billion in the year 1995 to $71.308 billion by year 2002 (Table 10.5). The year of merger was 1998. The average growth rate of revenues in the 2-year premerger period (1996–1997) was 7.57%. The average growth rate of revenues in the 3-year post-merger period (2000–2002) was 9.3%. The premerger growth rate in net income in the above period was approximately 2%. The post-merger growth rate in net income was 10.95% in the above period. The EPS had declined in the post-merger period compared to the premerger period.

References

Citicorp Annual Reports (1998–2007)

CNN Money (1998) Travelers Citicorp to unite. http://money.cnn.com/1998/04/06/deals/travelers/. Accessed 29 Sept 2017

de Souza I, Adolph G, Games A and Marchi R (2009) Perils of Financial Sector M&A: Seven Steps to Successful Integration, Booz & Co Report

Economist (2000) First among Equals. http://www.economist.com/node/342250. Accessed 30 Sept 2017

https://www.ft.com/content/adb7e4a6-019d-11dd-a323-000077b07658

Mitchell Martin and International Herald Tribune (1998) Citicorp and Travelers Plan to merger in record deal: A new no 1: Financial Giant. http://www.nytimes.com/1998/04/07/news/citicorp-and-travelers-plan-to-merge-in-record-70-billion-deal-a-new-no.html. Accessed 29 Sept 2017

Travelers Annual Report (2016)

11 AT&T–Time Warner Acquisition

Introduction

The telecommunications industry is one of the rapidly developing industries in the world. Telecommunications industry is a competitive market where lower prices, higher quality, and greater innovation have led to the removal of many barriers for firms to get into the markets. Strategically firms in this sector have used mergers, acquisition, or alliances to enter new markets. There were basically two waves of M&A in the telecommunication sector. The first wave was observed during the technology bubble of 1999–2000 which led to building of scale in the sector. The second wave during the period 2005–2007 led to consolidation in the US mobile market and European broadband sectors.

In the US AT&T or "Ma Bell" for decades dominated the entire telecom service value chain. Following the breakup of AT&T due to regulatory reasons in the year 1984, the sector has witnessed horizontal diversification. The numerous M&A activities during the 1990s were attributed to the revision of the American Telecommunications Act 1996, WTO agreement, and integration of the European Union. Deregulation and free competition in the European Union have also contributed to the liberalization of the global telecommunication markets.

Acquisitions Related to AT&T

The foundations of original AT&T known as the American Telephone and Telegraph Corporation were laid by Alexander Graham Bell along with Gardiner Hubbard and Thomas Sanders. AT&T was incorporated in 1885 as a wholly owned subsidiary of American Bell to build and operate the long-distance telephone network. In the year 1899, AT&T acquired the assets of American Bell and became the parent company of the Bell System. Throughout the history till the 1980s, AT&T and its Bell System functioned as a legally sanctioned regulated monopoly. In the 1970s,

B. R. Kumar, *Wealth Creation in the World's Largest Mergers and Acquisitions*, Management for Professionals, https://doi.org/10.1007/978-3-030-02363-8_11

the US government filed an antitrust suit against AT&T. As a result of the landmark settlement of the suit, AT&T had to divest itself of 22 local telephone operating companies known as Baby Bells (Kumar, 2012). The divestiture was aimed to demonopolize the telecommunications industry and create equal access to the local facilities by all long-distance carriers. In the year 1995, AT&T undertook a voluntary breakup and restructured itself into three separate public traded companies – Lucent Technologies (systems and equipment), NCR (computers), and AT&T (communication services).

SBC Communications formerly known as Southwestern Bell Corp was one of the seven regional holding companies formed after breakup of AT&T. During the period 1997–1998, SBC consolidated its position as a global communication giant by acquiring Pacific Telesis Group, Southern New England Telecommunications, and Ameritech Corporation. In the year 2006, SBC acquired AT&T to emerge as the largest telecommunications company in the world. SBC, one of the Baby Bells, reunited with the parent AT&T Ma Bell 21 years after federal regulators forced the breakup of original AT&T (Knowledge@wharton, 2005). Under the terms of agreement, the shareholders of AT&T received 0.77942 shares of SBC common stock for each common share of AT&T. The deal was valued at $16 billion. This transaction deal combined AT&T's global systems and capabilities, Internet protocol (IP)-based business with SBC's local exchange, broadband, and wireless solutions (Reardon, 2005).

In 2004, Cingular Wireless and AT&T Wireless merged in a $41 billion merger deal to create the US's biggest wireless carrier in terms of subscribers. In 2006, another Baby Bells company (BellSouth) merged with AT&T to create the largest phone company in the United States (Bajaj, 2006). The merger had reunited large parts of AT&T's former domain by consolidating BellSouth's nine state territories into AT&T's existing operations which covered the US Midwest, Southwest, and West Coast (Malik, 2006). BellSouth shareholders received 1.325 shares of AT&T for each BellSouth share or roughly $37.09 per share. In year 2011, AT&T and Deutsche Telekom entered into a stock purchase agreement under which AT&T acquired T-Mobile (the subsidiary of Deutsche Telekom) for approximately $39 billion. This deal consisted of cash offer of $25 billion and $14 billion of AT&T common stock. AT&T acquisition was timely in the scenario of formidable challenge faced by AT&T in terms of capacity constraints arising from unprecedented demand for mobile data. Mobile data traffic on AT&T network grew by 8000% during the period 2007–2010. The acquisition provided 34 million T-Mobile customers an access to robust LTE network of AT&T.

In July 2015, AT&T completed the acquisition of DIRECTV, which is a leading provider of digital television entertainment service in the United States and Latin America. The deal was valued at $47.409 billion. The acquisition was expected to provide cost and revenue synergy for AT&T in terms of bundling and integrating services. The acquisition would provide distribution scale for AT&T by means of offering consumers attractive services by combining video, high-speed broadband, and mobile services. The combined company emerged as a content distribution leader across mobile, video, and broadband platforms. Under the terms of the merger agreement, each share of DIRECTV stock was exchanged for $28.50 cash plus 1.892 shares of AT&T stock. DIRECTV shareholders held 16% stake in the new combined company.

AT&T's Acquisition of Time Warner

The modern AT&T network is the largest communication company in the world. AT&T is a fully integrated service provider which provides advanced mobile services, next-generation TV, high-speed Internet, and smart solutions. AT&T provides advanced services to 3.5 million businesses which involve nearly all of the Fortune 1000 businesses. AT&T's high-speed mobile Internet network covers over 365 million people and businesses across North America and Mexico. In the year 2016, AT&T had a consolidated revenue of $163.8 billion. The free cash flow dividend payout for the company was 70%. By the year 2016, the company had 33 years of consecutive increases in dividend payment. AT&T is the second largest provider of mobile telephone services and the largest provider of fixed telephone services in the United States. It provides broadband subscription television services to more than 25 million customers through DIRECTV.

Time Warner is a global leader in media and entertainment with an array of the world's most successful media brands. On October 22, 2016, AT&T entered into an agreement to acquire Time Warner. The deal combined Time Warner's vast resource of library of premium content for audiences around the world with the extensive distribution strength of AT&T in terms of world's largest pay-TV subscriber bases and scale in TV, mobile, and broadband distribution. AT&T acquired one of the world's best creators of premium content – Time Warner. AT&T wants to become the premier integrated communications company in the world. The combination of Time Warner's premium content with AT&T's customer relationships across mobile, TV, and broadband networks was expected to facilitate AT&T to emerge as the global leader in the converging telecom, media, and technology industry sector. The deal of acquisition of Time Warner eclipsed the $47 billion DIRECTV and had been AT&T's biggest acquisition since the $85 billion deal of BellSouth in the year 2006.

The combined business paired the AT&T's millions of wireless and pay television subscribers with Time Warner's strong brand networks such as CNN, TNT, HBO channel, and Warner Bros film and TV studio. It was a strategic initiative to use premium content on television and video to foster growth into a stalled wireless market. AT&T expects to emerge as the first wireless company to compete with cable companies by providing an online video bundle akin to a traditional pay television package. The deal will help AT&T to explore new areas of growth as its core wireless business has become saturated.

During the year 2016, AT&T lost 268,000 mainstream wireless phones customers and net 3000 video business customers. Before the acquisition announcement, Time Warner and AT&T had a market capitalization of $68 billion and $233 billion, respectively. After the completion of acquisition, the entertainment business of AT&T would account for approximately 40% of its revenues. After obtaining scale through DIRECTV acquisition, AT&T had plans to launch over the top video service which would allow users to stream programming over the web without the need for satellite dish. Thus the combination created a major colossus which would be capable of both producing content and distributing it to millions of people with wireless phones, broadband subscriptions, and satellite TV connections. The rise of online outlets like Amazon Prime, YouTube, and Netflix has compelled media companies to find out partners for consolidation. Media companies were expecting fall in fees from cable service providers and declining revenues from advertisers. The deal signified the union of Time Warner's limitless movie and television empire with AT&T's wireless network which covered 315 million people. AT&T expected to achieve $1 billion in savings within 3 years of the deal closing. AT&T aims to provide the primary TV platform by 2020 which would allow viewers to view a TV package over the Internet without a cable box or satellite dish.

In 2011, Comcast purchased NBC Universal. Technology giants like Google have encroached on traditional media by activities like live TV streaming. Netflix and Amazon doubled their yearly investments on programming between 2013 and 2015 which reached $7.5 billion. Apple also has plans to offer original services and content which can be directly accessed through its smartphones and tablets. Telecom majors like AT&T were earlier providing basic services to a steady clientele and left the creative costs and risk taking to producers, filmmakers, and studios. The core business of AT&T faces challenges as competition is tightening up for shrinking household base for TV packages and saturated audience for mobile and Internet service. The pay-TV services like DIRECTV is facing challenges from companies which are using video and entertainment options over the web. The combined company aims to become the first US mobile provider to compete with cable companies in areas of bundled mobile broadband and video in the context of a mobile network than spans more than 315 million people in the United States.

Deal Highlights

On October 22, 2016, AT&T and Time Warner entered into a merger agreement to acquire Time Warner in a 50% cash and 50% stock transaction for $107.50 per share of Time Warner common stock (Wall Street Journal, 2016). In other words, AT&T paid $107.50, a share evenly split between cash and stock. The deal was valued at approximately $85.4 billion at the date of the announcement. Taking into account the net debt of Time Warner as of September 30, 2016, the total transaction value was approximately $108,700. Each share of Time Warner was to be exchanged for $53.75 per share in cash and a number of shares of AT&T common stock equal to the exchange ratio. The merger agreement stipulated that if the average stock price at the time of closing the merger is between (or equal to) $37.411 and $41.349 per share, the exchange ratio would be the quotient of $53.75 divided by the average stock price. If the average stock price is greater than $41.349, the exchange ratio would be 1.300. If the average stock price is less than $37.411, the exchange ratio would be 1.437. The Time Warner shareholders will own between 14.4% and 15.7% of AT&T shares on a fully diluted basis based on the number of AT&T shares outstanding. The cash portion of the purchase price will be financed with new debt and cash on AT&T's balance sheet. AT&T had an 18-month commitment for an unsecured bridge term facility for $40 billion (Park & David, 2016).

If the merger failed to materialize, AT&T would have to pay $500 million, while Time Warner had agreed to pay a $1.7 billion breakup fee if another company outbids AT&T's offer (Merced, 2016). On deal announcement, Time Warner shares rose by nearly 8% to close at $89.48, while AT&T stock price declined by 3% to reach $37.49.

AT&T expected the deal to be accretive in the first year after close on both an adjusted EPS and free cash flow per share basis. By the end of the first year after closing, AT&T expects net debt to adjust EBITDA to be in the 2.5x range. On February 15, 2017, the merger agreement was approved by Time Warner shareholders.

Synergies from the Deal

AT&T expected $1 billion in annual run rate cost synergies within 3 years of the deal closing (AT&T Website, 2017). The expected cost synergies were primarily driven by corporate and procurement expenditures. Time Warner was expected to provide AT&T with significant diversification benefits (Wall Street Journal, 2016). Time Warner would provide diversified revenue mix. Time Warner revenues will constitute about 15% of total revenues of the combined company (Harwell et al., 2016). Time Warner's business requires lesser investments in capital expenditure compared to higher capital intensity business of existing AT&T's businesses. Time Warner's business is lightly regulated compared to that of AT&T's existing businesses.

Regulatory Issues

On November 21, 2017, the US Justice Department filed an antitrust suit lawsuit to prevent AT&T and Time Warner from completing the merger procedures (DW, 2017). The US government under Donald Trump was of the opinion that the merger would lead to monopoly and harm American consumers. According to the present government's view, AT&T with DIRECTV satellite operations and Time Warner's popular network would charge more for Time Warner's popular networks. AT&T challenged the lawsuit maintaining that the merger was vertical as AT&T and Time Warner were not direct competitors. According to US media reports, the Department of Justice would permit the merger if AT&T agreed to divest either Turner – the parent company of CNN and other networks – or DIRECTV Financial and operational highlights of AT&T are given in Tables 11.1 and 11.2.

Table 11.1 Financial highlights of AT&T

Year	2012	2013	2014	2015	2016
Revenues	127434	128752	132447	146801	163786
Operating income	13054	30752	12212	24785	24347
Net income	7574	18722	6736	13687	13333
EPS	1.26	3.42	1.24	2.37	2.1
Cash and cash equivalents	4868	3339	8603	5121	5788
Total assets	275834	281423	296834	402672	403821
Total debt	69638	74589	81834	126151	123513
Capital expenditures	19728	21228	21433	20015	22408
Debt ratio	42.10%	44.10%	47.50%	50.50%	49.90%

Source: Annual Report 2016
The values are in millions of dollars except EPS and debt ratio

Table 11.2 Operating highlights of AT&T

Year	2012	2013	2014	2015	2016
Total wireless customers(000)	106957	110376	120554	137324	146832
Video connections (000)	4536	5460	5943	37934	37748
Broadband connections (000)	16390	16425	16028	15778	15605
Number of employees	241810	243360	243620	281450	268540

Source: Annual Report 2016

Wealth Analysis

Acquisition Effects on AT&T

The media announcement of the acquisition was made on October 21, 2016. The cumulative returns for AT&T for 247 days (−10 to 236 days) surrounding the merger announcement period was 1.3% (Fig. 11.1).

The stock price of AT&T declined surrounding the merger announcement. AT&T stock price declined by −1.9% on the day before announcement. On announcement day, the AT&T stock price declined by 3%. The decline in stock price continued for 3 more days after merger announcement (Table 11.3).

The cumulative returns for AT&T stock during the shorter time window interval were negative, and the returns were positive during the longer time window interval. In the larger window interval (0–100 days), the cumulative returns were approximately 10% (Fig. 11.1).

Acquisition Effects on Time Warner Stock Price

The acquisition announcement gave positive returns for target firm Time Warner. On announcement day Time Warner stock rose by 7.8%. One day before announcement day, Time Warner stock rose by 4.7% (Table 11.5).

Fig. 11.1 Cumulative returns for AT&T surrounding the acquisition period

Table 11.3 Daily returns for AT&T

Day	Returns (%)
−10	−0.6
−9	0.4
−8	0.2
−7	0.6
−6	0.1
−5	−0.4
−4	0.1
−3	0.2
−2	0.1
−1	−1.9
0	−3.0
1	−1.7
2	−0.4
3	−0.7
4	0.2
5	0.0
6	0.8
7	−0.6
8	−0.5
9	0.7
10	−0.4

Table 11.4 Cumulative returns surrounding the acquisition period

Day	Cumulative returns (%)
−1 to +1	-6.5
−5 to +5	-7.5
−10 to +10	-6.8
0 to +100	10.3
0 to +236	2.5
−10 to +236	1.3

Table 11.4 highlights the cumulative returns for AT&T Stock during the acquisition announcement period

Table 11.5 Daily returns for Time Warner surrounding merger announcement

Day	Returns (%)
−10	−0.9
−9	0.5
−8	−1.0
−7	1.7
−6	−0.6
−5	0.2
−4	−0.9
−3	0.8
−2	−0.3
−1	4.7
0	7.8
1	−3.1
2	0.5
3	1.8
4	−0.5
5	−0.9
6	1.7
7	−0.8
8	−1.1
9	−0.1
10	−0.8

Table 11.6 Cumulative returns surrounding the acquisition period

Day	Cumulative returns (%)
−1 to +1	9.5
−5 to +5	10.2
−10 to +10	8.7
0 to +100	17.8
0 to +236	26.0

The Time Warner stock gave positive returns during the different time window intervals surrounding the acquisition period. During most of the time window surrounding the acquisition announcement, Time Warner stock had double digit stock returns (Fig. 11.2).

The stock price of Time Warner has shown increasing trend during the 247-day period surrounding the acquisition announcement. The cumulative returns for the time period of 247 days (−10 to 236 day) was approximately 26%.

Fig. 11.2 Cumulative returns for Time Warner surrounding the acquisition period

References

AT&T Website (2017) http://about.att.com/story/att_to_acquire_time_warner.html. Accessed 15 Oct 2017

Bajaj V (2006) BellSouth &AT&T Close deal. http://www.nytimes.com/2006/12/30/business/30tele.html. Accessed 3 Oct 2017

DW (2017) US files antitrust suit to block AT&T, Time Warner deal. http://www.dw.com/en/us-files-antitrust-suit-to-block-att-time-warner-merger/a-41460277. Accessed 20 Oct 2017

Harwell D, Fung B, Davenport C (2016) AT&T to buy Time Warner for $85.4 billion. https://www.washingtonpost.com/news/the-switch/wp/2016/10/22/report-att-to-buy-time-warner-for-more-than-80-billion/?utm_term=.9a0f7e1ad881. Accessed 15 Oct 2017

Knowledge@wharton (2005) Mother and Child Reunion: Will the AT&T/SBC Merger Build or Destroy Value?. http://knowledge.wharton.upenn.edu/article.cfm?articleid=1134. Accessed 3 Oct 2017

Kumar R (2012) Mega mergers and acquisitions, case studies from key industries, Palgrave Macmillan ISBN 978–1–137-00589-2

Malik O (2006) Ma Bell Reborn. http://money.cnn.com/2006/03/06/technology/business2_att_telecom. Accessed 3 Oct 2017

Merced MJ (2016) AT&T agrees to buy Time Warner for $85.4 billion. https://www.nytimes.com/2016/10/23/business/dealbook/att-agrees-to-buy-time-warner-for-more-than-80-billion.html. Accessed 15 Oct 2017

Park J, David J (2016) AT&T reaches deal to buy Time Warner for more than 80 billion dollar. https://www.cnbc.com/2016/10/22/att-reaches-deal-to-buy-time-warner-for-more-than-80-billion-report.html. Accessed 19 Oct 2017

Reardon M (2005) SBC closes AT&#38. Acquisition. http://news.cnet.com/SBC-closes-AT38T-acquisition/2100-1036_3-5961206.html. Accessed 2 Oct 2017

Wall Street Journal (2016) AT&T Reaches Deal to Buy Time Warner for $85.4 Billion. https://www.wsj.com/articles/at-t-reaches-deal-to-buy-time-warner-for-more-than-80-billion. Accessed 4 Oct 2017

ABN AMRO Acquisition by RFS Holding 12

ABN AMRO had its origin in the nineteenth century through the establishment of the Dutch East Indies trade (International Directory of Company Histories, 2003). The Amsterdam-based ABN AMRO is a major international bank with operations in more than 60 countries (ABN AMRO Holding, 2017). ABN AMRO is a leading foreign bank in the United States. ABN AMRO resulted from the merger of two largest banks in the Netherlands – Amsterdam–Rotterdam Bank (AMRO) and Algemene Bank Nederland (ABN) in the year 1991 (Table 12.1).

In the 1980s, the Dutch government liberalized its merger and acquisition laws. The deregulation paved the way for the national banks to pursue global operations and M&A activity. In 1991, ABN and AMRO merged to strengthen their dominance in the domestic market on account of increased competition from NMB – Postbank and Rabobank – which were the two other leading banks in the Netherlands. The merger was aimed to create economies of scale in retail bank networks and technology along with cost synergy by means of reduction in staff and overlapping businesses. With a strong combined capital base, the merged bank aimed to become a major global player in banking field. ABN AMRO became the largest bank in the Netherlands with control over half of the corporate banking market and two fifths of securities which traded on the Amsterdam Stock Exchange. As a result of consolidation, the merged ABN AMRO became the sixth largest bank in Europe and one of the top 20 banks in the world. In 1993 AMRO-owned Pierson, Heldring & Pierson and ABN-owned Mees & Hope merged to form a new bank called MeesPierson. In 1997, MeesPierson was sold to financial conglomerate Fortis Group. In 1992, ABN AMRO had acquired Hoare Govett, a UK-based international corporate investment bank (Euroweek, 1995). In 1995, the bank purchased the Nordic investment bank Alfred Berg from the Volvo Group of Sweden. In 1996, ABN AMRO acquired mortgage lender Standard Federal Bancorporation of Michigan in a deal valued $1.9 billion. The mortgage company had $15.5 billion in assets and over 180 branches in Michigan, Ohio, and Indiana. This deal made ABN AMRO the 12th largest bank in the United States. In the same year, ABN AMRO acquired a majority interest in Magyar Hitel

B. R. Kumar, *Wealth Creation in the World's Largest Mergers and Acquisitions*, Management for Professionals, https://doi.org/10.1007/978-3-030-02363-8_12

Table 12.1 Major restructuring timelines

Year	Event
1824	Netherlands Trading Society (NTS), the parent company of ABN established
1863	Rotterdamsche Bank (Robaver) is established
1948	Merger of Robaver with Incasso Bank to become Netherlands' largest bank
1964	NTS merged with 100-year-old Dutch agriculture Twentsche Bank to form Algemene Bank Nederland (ABN). Amsterdamsche Bank and Robaver merge to form Amsterdam Rotterdam Bank (AMRO)
1975	ABN acquires Dutch investment banking specialist Mees & Hope Bankiers. AMRO acquires Dutch investment bank Pierson,Heldring & Pierson
1979	ABN acquires Chicago-based LaSalle Bank and gains strong market share in the United States
1991	ABN and AMRO merger to form ABN AMRO completed. ABN AMRO acquired Talman Home Federal Savings and Loan Association
1996	ABN AMRO acquires Standard Federal Bancorporation of Michigan
1998	ABN AMRO buys Brazil's fourth largest public bank, Banco Real
2000	ABN AMRO acquires commercial bank holding company Michigan National Corporation
2002	ABN AMRO divests its investment bank and brokerage businesses in the United States. The UK-based ABN AMRO asset management and Artemis Investment Management merged with ABN AMRO as the majority shareholder of new company

Bank which was the fifth largest commercial bank in Hungary. The bank purchased Australian-based Lloyds Bank with branches in Australia and New Zealand for $868 million. In 1998, ABN AMRO acquired Brazil's fourth largest public bank Banco Real for $2.1 billion. The bank also acquired controlling interest in BANDEPE Bank. ABN AMRO also acquired 75% stake in Thailand's Bank of Asia in the same year. In 1999, the bank took 10% minority position in Italy's Banca di Roma (Forbes.com, 1999). The bank sold New York-based European–American Bank (EAB) to Citibank for $1.6 billion. ABN AMRO purchased the North American Brokerage, corporate finance, domestic equities, futures, and options businesses of subsidiary ING Barings for $275 million. The bank divested its global units in regions like Sri Lanka, Morocco, Panama, Argentina, Kenya, Bahrain, Malaysia, the Philippines, etc.

Acquisition of ABN AMRO by the Consortium Bank

During October 2007, ABN AMRO was acquired by a consortium of banks which consisted of RBS (38%), Fortis Bank (34%), and Banco Santander SA (28%). The consortium was known as RFS Holdings BV (ABN AMRO Website, 2017). The acquisition was aimed to create stronger businesses with enhanced market presence and growth prospects. The acquisition was expected to provide savings and opportunities for sustainable increases in profitable revenue. The offer terms were €30.40 in cash plus 0.844 new RBS shares for each ABN AMRO share. The total offer was €38.40 per ABN AMRO share based on RBS share price of 642.5 p at the close of business on May 25, 2007. The proposed offer was approximately 79% in cash. The deal valued ABN AMRO at €71.1billion. British bank Barclays which had earlier offered to acquire ABN AMRO withdrew its takeover offer. The deal

Table 12.2 Consideration details

	Consideration	Share of consideration (%)	Profit before tax
Fortis	€24.0 billion	33.8	€1.68 billion
RBS	€27.2 billion	38.3	€1.72 billion
Santander	€19.9 billion	27.9	€1.55 billion
Total	€71.1billion	100	€4.95billion

Table 12.3 Transaction benefits

End 2010	Cost savings per annum	Benefits per annum	Total transaction benefits per annum	Integration costs
Fortis	€1.15billion	€0.19 billion	€1.34 billion	€1.54 billion
RBS	€2.01 billion	€0.85 billion	€2.86 billion	€3.84billion
Santander	€0.86billion	€0.18billion	€1.04 billion	€1.00billion
Shared assets	€0.21billion		€0.21billion	€4.03billion
Total	€4.23billion	€1.22billion	€5.45billion	€6.80billion

involving three banks buying out ABN AMRO was one of the biggest financial services takeovers ever. Fortis of Belgium acquired ABN's Dutch operations; Banco Santander Central Hispano of Spain acquired Brazilian and Italian arms. RBS acquired the ABN investment banking arm. The consortium offer included more than €56 billion in cash (Table 12.2).

The consolidation helped Fortis to become a market leader with more than ten million customers in Benelux Retail and Commercial banking. Fortis became the third largest European private bank. Fortis was able to expand the asset management growth platform. Fortis became the top-tier asset manager with more than €300 billion AUM. The acquisition facilitated larger geographic footprint and enhanced offering third-party distributors. Through acquisition, RBS aimed to expand in corporate and institutional banking. RBS expanded presence and activities in Asia Pacific. Santander through the acquisition became one of the top three banks by network and loans. High geographical and product complementarity opportunities existed between franchises Banco Real and Santander Banespa. The pretax synergies of €1.3 billion were expected from the acquisition. For Fortis, the acquisition was expected to streamline and leverage business center network, reduce overlap in support functions, and cross sell skills such as leasing and factoring. The combination helped Fortis Bank to have a unique presence in Benelux and created the third largest network in the Netherlands. Fortis Bank would be able to capitalize on ABN AMRO's strong quality of service and brands. RBS was expected to gain from the complementary and overlapping businesses of ABN AMRO.RBS would be able to develop strong position with US mid-corporates. The acquisition will result in cost savings and revenue benefits for RBS. The cost savings would result from de-duplication of IT systems and support. In terms of revenue benefits, RBS would benefit from ABN AMRO's customer relationships using GBM management model and product strengths. The acquisition helped Santander Bank to emerge as the number two bank by total deposits and number three bank by branch network and loans. The value creation potential of this acquisition for Santander Bank was through market synergies like integration of head offices, central functions' migration to common IT platform, and optimization of distribution networks (Table 12.3).

The consortium paid three times the book value for the Amsterdam-based bank. In 2007, after acquisition of ABN, RBS was struggling under the cost of acquisition and on account of toxic assets it acquired from ABN. The government twice had to bail out RBS with rescue packages, and the treasury took 58% stake in the bank (Alston and Bird LLP, 2009). In 2010, the assets of ABN AMRO owned by RBS were demerged into two organizations – ABN AMRO Bank NV and the Royal Bank of Scotland NV (Independent, 2009). During October 2008, the Dutch government nationalized Fortis Bank Nederland which included acquisition of 34% interest in ABN AMRO Bank NV (Independent, 2009). During November 2015, the Dutch government publicly relisted the company through an IPO and sold 20% of the shares to public. The ABN AMRO operations owned by Santander in Italy and Brazil were merged with Santander, sold or eliminated.

Wealth Creation for RBS Stock

The first announcement of the deal proposal was taken on April 24, 2007, and the deal was completed on October 4, 2007.

The cumulative returns for RBS stock for the 178 days surrounding the acquisition announcement show that acquisition value was decreasing for RBS stock. The cumulative returns were – 39% during the period −4 to +173 days surrounding the acquisition period. The announcement day return was −1%. The stock price declined continuously for 5 days after the acquisition announcement (Fig. 12.1).

The cumulative returns for ABN AMRO stock for the 177 days surrounding the acquisition announcement period were approximately −15%. There were no stock gains on the day of announcement and one day after announcement of the deal. On +2 day after announcement, the stock increased by 2.9% (Fig. 12.2).

Fig. 12.1 Wealth creation for RBS stock

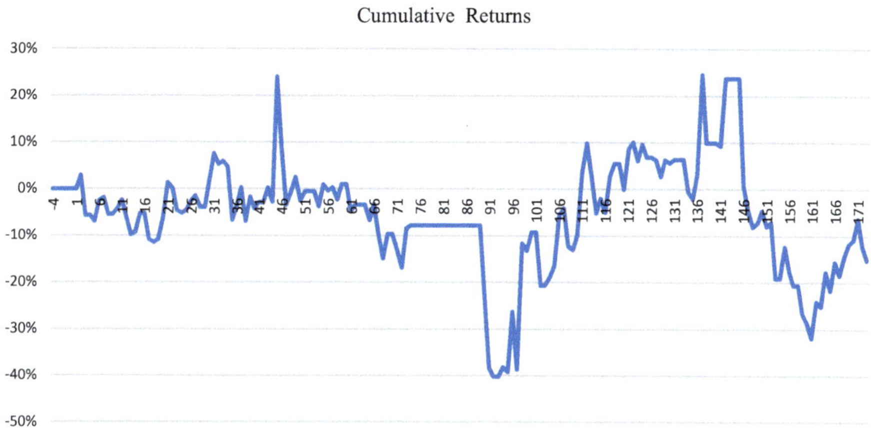

Fig. 12.2 Wealth creation for ABN AMRO

References

ABN AMRO Holding (2017) http://www.fundinguniverse.com/company-histories/abn-amro-holding-n-v-history/. Accessed 30 Oct 2017

ABN AMRO Website (2017) https://www.abnamro.com/en/footer/merger.html. Accessed 30 Oct 2017

Alston & Bird LLP (2009) ABN AMRO merger with Fortis Bank likely delayed until 2010; EU extends deadline for Dutch government to divest of certain assets before merger. https://www.lexology.com/library/detail.aspx?g=e05f77c9-aa5e-44e5-8c75-b7e7aab02370. Accessed 30 Oct 2017

Euroweek (1995) ABN AMRO in Takeover Spree, p 1

Forbes.com (1999) A Bank Ahead of Its Time. http://www.forbes.com. 14 June

Independent (2009) http://www.independent.co.uk/news/business/analysis-and-features/was-abn-the-worst-takeover-deal-ever-1451520.html. 20 Jan

International Directory of Company Histories (2003) Vol 50. St. James Press

GlaxoSmithKline Merger

13

Introduction

Over the last many decades, pharmaceutical companies were instrumental in developing and marketing a series of groundbreaking drugs with high revenues which became integral to the healthcare of millions of people around the world. In the year 1985, the ten largest firms accounted for about 20% of worldwide sales. By the year 2002, the ten largest firms accounted for approximately 48% of the sales. The top 50 pharma companies had consolidated into 10 companies during the above period. During the period 1988–2000, the pharma industry witnessed deals worth $500 billion (Danzon et al., 2003). The pharmaceutical industry witnessed increased M&A activity during the 1980s and 1990s. All the major pharma companies in the world have grown through mergers and acquisitions. The antecedents of GlaxoSmithKline include Glaxo, Wellcome, SmithKline French, and Beecham. The modern-day Pfizer is the result of consolidation of Pfizer, Warner–Lambert, Pharmacia, and Upjohn. In the pharmaceutical industry, the first wave of consolidation took place with the combination of SmithKline and Beecham. The other notable mergers include the combination of Bristol Myers and Squibb. The synergies in pharma mergers were basically meant for enhancement of revenues due to increased physician and geographical coverage. The 1990s were known as the era of horizontal mergers. One of the biggest pharmaceutical deals during this period was the Glaxo's hostile acquisition of Burroughs Wellcome in the year 1995. During the period 1985–2007, 51 large pharmaceutical companies were consolidated into 10 organizations. The strategic drivers for M&A activity in pharma sector were greater scale, market share, geographical expansion, and increased technological capabilities (Pursche, 1996). Research have become critical for survival of pharma companies. Glaxo and Wellcome had merged to create synergies in research and development. In the past decades, pharma companies had faced the major challenge of patent expiration of a large number of blockbuster drugs. By the year 2000, approximately 21 drugs became off patent which had sales of over 1 billion dollars per year in

B. R. Kumar, *Wealth Creation in the World's Largest Mergers and Acquisitions*, Management for Professionals, https://doi.org/10.1007/978-3-030-02363-8_13

1993. In the year 2013, nearly $137 billion worth of branded products lost their market exclusivity. In the last century, many of the blockbuster drugs generated huge revenues on account of its nature as it was meant for widespread afflictions like hypertension, pain management, sexual dysfunction, depression, etc. In contrast approximately 75% of the products currently developed are specialty medications which could treat fewer potential patients. The pharmaceutical industry is a highly risky business with long-term payoffs. The average time from discovery to federal drug approval (FDA) is approximately 15 years. The odds of a compound making it through this process are around 1 in 10,000 (Ravenscraft and Long, 2000). The last decade has witnessed the trend of the globalization of the pharma industry. By the year 2020, the pharmaceutical market is expected to more than double to US $1.3 trillion with the emerging countries like Brazil, China, India, Indonesia, Mexico, Russia, and Turkey to account for one fifth of the global pharmaceutical sales. The world faces the challenges for treatment of chronic diseases like diabetes. Approximately 438 million people representing 7.8% of the world's population would live by diabetics by the year 2030.

GlaxoSmithKline Beecham (GSK) is the world's leading research-based pharmaceutical and healthcare companies. GSK makes a wide range of prescription medicines, vaccines, and consumer healthcare products (GSK Website, 2017). The pharmaceutical business discovers, develops, and makes medicines to treat a broad range of the world's most common acute and chronic diseases. The vaccine business of GSK develops and distributes 1.9 million vaccines every day to people across 150 countries. The consumer healthcare business has best-selling products in pain relief, oral health, respiratory, nutrition, and skin health. The products offered by GSK can be categorized as prescription medicines, vaccines, and consumer health. The prescription medicines provide treatment for wide range of conditions such as infections, depressions, skin conditions, asthma, heart and circulatory disease, and cancer. GSK markets over 30 vaccines worldwide to fight conditions like hepatitis A, hepatitis B, diphtheria, tetanus, mumps, polio, typhoid, influenza, and bacterial meningitis. The consumer health division provides dental health products, over-the-counter medicines, and nutritional drinks. The group turnover was £30.2 billion in the year 2017.

Growth of GlaxoSmithKline Beecham (GSK) through Mergers and Acquisitions

Beecham and SmithKline Merger

The merger of Beecham and SmithKline in the year 1989 sparked a wave of mergers between pharmaceutical mergers in the next decade. SmithKline was facing revenue pressures with respect to its blockbuster drug Tagamet, while Beecham was a consumer goods company with successful initiatives in research on antibiotics. Beecham didn't have the competencies to become a serious pharmaceutical player. The combined company had created a critical mass in R&D behind major players like Glaxo.

As a part of its aim to create fully integrated healthcare provider, SmithKline Beecham purchased DPS. Drug companies focused on vertical integration as there was potential threat for the success of the managed care model and pharma companies were mere suppliers of commodity products. There were complementary advantages as SmithKline drugs in formulary lists and prescription drugs were managed by DPS. Synergies were expected from SmithKline's clinical lab divisions and DP. The acquisition of detailed patient record facilitated the improvement of the drug discovery process. Through the acquisition of DPS, SmithKline inherited the alliance with United Healthcare Corp which owned several health management organizations (HMOs) with approximately 1.6 million members. Through the alliance, SmithKline got exclusive rights among the pharmaceutical and diagnostic companies.

This merger between the Beecham Group PLC and SmithKline Beckman in the year 1989 was termed as merger of equals as both companies had equal market capitalization of £3.5 billion. The merged company facilitated international marketing presence for the merged entity. The consumer healthcare division was formed as result of merger. In the year of merger, SmithKline Beecham became the second largest drug company in the world after Merck & Company. The merged entity ranked second in worldwide prescription drug sales and nonprescription medicines. The merger was aimed to create complementary strength in research and development and global marketing. As a part of the merger deal, SmithKline sold off Allergan Inc., an eye care subsidiary. SmithKline also distributed 84% stake in Beckman Instruments to its existing shareholders. Beecham as a part of the deal sold off its cosmetics operations which included its Yardley, Margaret Astor, and Lancaster lines.

The merger deal gave shareholders of both SmithKline and Beecham equal values, dividends, and voting rights. Each SmithKline shareholder received five common shares in SmithKline Beecham and one preferred share. The shareholder was entitled to receive a special cash dividend of $5.50. In addition, each SmithKline shareholder received 0.5 share of Allergan and 0.18 share of Beckman Instruments. Beecham shareholders received 0.8784 share of SmithKline Beecham plus $1.75 or $2.96 in unsecured loan stock.

In a strategic perspective, the merger deal was aimed at realizing R&D synergy. The R&D budget of the combined pharma company was comparable to Merck's budget. SmithKline was facing revenue pressures due to slowing down of sales of its antiulcer drug Tagamet which had lost its ranking to Glaxo's Zantac with sales of $ 2 billion at the time of merger.

Glaxo Wellcome Merger

Glaxo started off as a British firm with its origins in the dried milk business and sales business in antibiotics, respiratory drugs, and nutritional supplements. Glaxo Wellcome focused on the managed care sector through its subsidiary called Wyeth–Ayerst healthcare systems. The subsidiary firm provided disease management programs, patient/member materials, outcome assessment, and support for managed care marketing. The joint venture of Glaxo with Warner–Lambert called Lambert Wellcome had given a foothold in the prescription to OTC switch market. Glaxo Wellcome group was formed due to the merger between Glaxo and Burroughs Wellcome & Company. This merger which took place in the year 1995 was termed as the biggest merger in UK corporate history. The merger was completed within 7 weeks after formal announcement. Initially the Wellcome group rejected the offer and sought a white knight. But the move became unsuccessful on account of the pledge by Wellcome Trust to sell their 40% to Glaxo. The combined companies operated in 60 countries with annual sales of £9.3 billion. This merger was in fact culturally significant as it was a transatlantic merger. For regulatory purpose, Glaxo had to divest itself of the rights to 311C90, a Wellcome compound for treating migraine that was in late-stage clinical trials. Glaxo Wellcome Inc. became one of the top three pharmaceutical companies in the world. Glaxo was the first company to manufacture and market triptans which was a new class of prescription migraine medicine. Glaxo Wellcome created over $2 billion in stock market value during the announcement period. Glaxo paid a 40.7% premium for Wellcome, increasing Wellcome shareholder value by $3.8 billion.[1] Glaxo had also acquired Affymax, a leader in combinatorial chemistry, for $592 million.

The squeeze on healthcare costs caused by recession and the expected decline in revenues due to off patents were the primary reasons for the Glaxo Wellcome merger. Glaxo and Wellcome faced the challenges of a changing industry environment and the decline of their major sources of growth since the US patents on both these drugs were expected to expire in 1997. Glaxo and Wellcome's phenomenal successes with Zantac and Zovirax turned out to be a double-edged sword. Glaxo and Wellcome were employing the classic defenses of these products including improved formulation, litigation to delay early entry, and moving to OTC status before expiration (although Zovirax was denied FDA approval for OTC). Despite these efforts, analysts estimated that both products would lose two thirds or more of sales by the year 2000. Generic drug firms were ready to move as soon as Zantac and Zovirax patents expired. One of the most obvious reasons to merge or acquire is a shortfall in the R&D pipeline. This was the position Glaxo faced in 1995 when Zantac, the world's best-ever-selling drug at the time, was coming to the end of its lifespan. Through the timely acquisition of Wellcome, Glaxo renewed its pipeline to create a substantial and innovative asset which had drugs like Seroxat.

GlaxoSmithKline Merger

The merger between Glaxo Wellcome and SmithKline created the world's largest pharmaceutical company, and the combined company became the third largest corporation in the world (New York Times, 1989). The merger was aimed to consolidate their position as a global leader in the production of pharmaceuticals and

[1] http://www.nber.org/chapters/c8653.pdf

consumer goods. The merger of Glaxo and SmithKline Beecham was termed as the merger of equals and had combined sales of approximately 24.9 billion. The merger resulted in economies of scale, complementary portfolios, operational synergies, and cost savings. The merger gave the combined company a global market share of 7.3% and a research and development budget of $ 4 billion.

The combined company had the highest R&D budget in the industry. The consolidated pharma company had one of the most extensive development pipelines in the pharmaceutical industry with a total of 30 new chemical entities (NCEs) and 19 vaccines in clinical development (phase II/III), of which 13 NCEs and 10 vaccines were in late-stage development (phase III). The combined company also became a market leader in four of the five largest therapeutic categories in the pharmaceutical industry sector. As a result of the merger, the combined firm acquired a leading position in the vaccine market and a strong position in consumer healthcare and over-the-counter medicines.

Merger Highlights

Glaxo Wellcome and SmithKline Beecham shareholders received shares in a new holding company, GlaxoSmithKline. Glaxo Wellcome shareholders received approximately 58.75% of the issued ordinary share capital of GlaxoSmithKline, and SmithKline Beecham shareholders received approximately 41.25% of the issued ordinary share capital of GlaxoSmithKline. Each Glaxo Wellcome shareholder received 1 GlaxoSmithKline share, and each SmithKline Beecham shareholder received 0.4552 GlaxoSmithKline Shares. The nominal value of the shares issued was £1556 million, and the market value of the shares at that date was £119 billion. For the American depository receipts, each Glaxo Wellcome ADS was exchanged for 1 GlaxoSmithKline ADS, and for each SmithKline Beecham ADS, 1.139 GlaxoSmithKline ADS was exchanged. The advisors for Glaxo were Goldman Sachs & Company, while SmithKline was advised by Morgan Stanley and Dean Witter & Company (International Briefs, 1995).

Merger Benefits

The merger helped the combined firm to achieve economies of scale in the pharmaceutical sector. GlaxoSmithKline Beecham (GSK) became the largest pharmaceutical company in the World, United States and Europe (Lazo, 2001). On the basis of the combined 1998 sales figure, the merged pharmaceutical firm derived approximately 45% of revenues from the United States, 33% from Europe, and 22% from other regions of the world. GSK became the world's largest producer of prescription drugs with market share of more than 7% (M&A Monitor Ltd. UK, 2002). The merger also facilitated avoidance of increased R&D costs. The R&D investment was rising with increased proportion to sales from $20 billion in the 1990s to $35 billion by 1999.The merger also enhanced the R&D capability of the combined entity. SmithKline Beecham's strong consumer healthcare and over-the-counter medicine businesses provided GlaxoSmithKline enhanced expertise in consumer-oriented marketing strategies which benefitted sales of prescription products. The merger enhanced the complementary portfolio of the two pharmaceutical companies. The merger enhanced the strength of the two companies in their common core areas of anti-infective and CNS. Synergy was expected as SmithKline Beecham's anti-infective portfolio focused on antibacterial, while Glaxo Wellcome's focus was on antivirals. On account of strengthening of cancer and gastrointestinal portfolios, significant cost savings resulted. The combination of Glaxo Wellcome's respiratory therapeutic segment with SmithKline Beecham's strength in vaccines and arthritis broadened the portfolio of offerings. Significant cost synergies were realized between Glaxo Wellcome and SmithKline Beecham's R&D pipelines, both being focused on anti-infectives, CNS, and cardiovascular products. As a result of the merger, GlaxoSmithKline became a leader in four of the five largest therapeutic areas which constituted 50% of the global pharmaceutical market. Pretax cost savings of £1.0 billion were expected from the merger. Approximately £250 million of these savings were expected from the combination of the two R&D organizations. The other cost savings were expected from reduction of overlap in administration, selling and marketing, and manufacturing facilities. The merger benefitted both companies to increase the geographic strength.

The deal was valued at $76 billion. The merged company had a stock market value of $186 billion with annual sales exceeding $25 billion. The drug portfolio of the combined firm had Glaxo's roster of top selling drugs like Zantac the ulcer drug and treatments for AIDS and asthma along with SmithKline's consumer brands like Tums antacids, Aquafresh toothpaste, and prescription drugs like Paxil for antidepressant and Augmentin, the antibiotic drugs. The combined company also became the largest seller of prescription drugs with more than $ 9 billion in prescription sales (Robert Stevens, 2000). The merger was expected to achieve annual pretax cost savings of at least $1.6 billion by the end of the year 2003 (Pharmaceutical Online, 2000).

After the merger, GlaxoSmithKline held leadership positions in major therapeutic areas of anti-infectives, central nervous system, and respiratory and gastrointestinal metabolic segments along with important vaccine market (Table 13.1). Table 13.2 lists the major acquisitions of GlaxosmithKline Beecham.

Table 13.1 Status of GSK after merger

	Market size in $ billion	GSK market share in per cent	GSK rank
Anti-infective	37	16.3	1st
Central nervous system	44	11.5	2nd
Respiratory	24	17.1	1st
Gastrointestinal GI metabolic	42	6	1st

Source IMS data

Table 13.2 Major acquisition of GlaxoSmithKline Beecham

Acquired Nanjing MeRui Pharma Co Ltd., which offers pharmaceutical medicines, medical devices, and allergy diagnostics, for 70.0 million USD
Acquired MaxiNutrition Ltd., which manufactures sports nutrition products, for 162.0 million GBP
Acquired Theravance Inc., which is involved in the development of small molecule medicines for respiratory diseases, bacterial infections, and gastrointestinal disorders, for $129.4 million
Acquired Argentina-based Laboratorios Phoenix SACyF for $253.0 million.
Acquired Dong-A Pharmaceuticals Co Ltd., which manufactures pharmaceutical products including vaccines, AIDA diagnostic kits, drinks, and OTC drugs, for 142.9 billion KRW
Acquired stakes in JCR Pharmaceuticals Co Ltd.

Table 13.3 Average returns during 10-day surrounding announcement period

Day	Returns (%)	Day	Returns (%)
−10	−0.1	1	1.0
−9	−0.8	2	−0.1
−8	−2.0	3	−2.8
−7	−1.1	4	−3.7
−6	−1.3	5	−7.9
−5	4.5	6	−7.0
−4	3.2	7	−7.1
−3	5.4	8	−8.2
−2	3.2	9	−5.6
−1	8.0	10	−8.0
0	0.2		

In the year 2000, SmithKline Beecham acquired Block Drug Company, Inc., the manufacturer of Sensodyne toothpaste and other oral healthcare and consumer products, for US $1.24 billion.

In the year 2015, GSK completed a three-part transaction with Novartis. GSK acquired Novartis's vaccine business excluding influenza business and combined the consumer healthcare business to create a new company. Novartis acquired GSK's marketed oncology portfolio and its related R&D activities.

Announcement Effects of GlaxoSmithKline Merger

The public announcement of the merger was made on 17 January 2000. SmithKline shares rose by 7% to reach 847 pence, while Glaxo stock price rose by 4.5% to reach 1818 pence. SmithKline's American depository receipts rose by $3.9375 to reach $70, while Glaxo's ADR rose by $2 to reach $60. The announcement day return was 0.2%. The returns on the day before announcement were 8% (Table 13.3).

The stock price surged ahead with increase in price ranging from 3.2% to 8% during the time window period of −5 to −1 day of announcement. The returns for the GSK stock for +1 day after announcement were 1%. The stock registered negative returns up to +10 day after the merger announcement (Table 13.3).

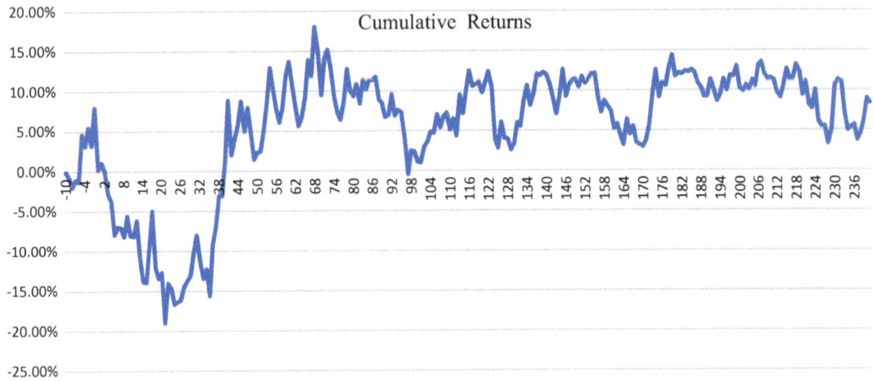

Fig. 13.1 Cumulative returns for GSK surrounding announcement period

Table 13.4 Cumulative returns during different time windows

Time interval	Cumulative returns (%)
1 to 1 days	−2.10
5 to 5 days	−6.50
10 to 10 days	−7.90
10 to 30 days	−10.25
1 to 100 days	−2.10

The cumulative returns for GSK during the 251 days' window period (−10 to 240 days) was 8.93% (Fig. 13.1). The holding period return for the above period was 0.67%.

The cumulative returns were negative for the different time window periods (Table 13.4).

The values are given in millions of pounds. The trend analysis is done with respect to 4-year pre- and post-merger. The year of merger was excluded from analysis. The sales, operating profit, profit before taxes, and net income grew by approximately 8% in the year before the merger. The average growth rate of sales and operating profit in the pre-merger period of 1996–1999 was 2.8% and 0.8%. The average profit before tax and net income during the above period was 2% and 3%, respectively. The average growth rate of sales declined to −0.15% during the post-merger period 2001–2004. At the same time, the average growth rate of operating profit, profit before tax, and net income in the post-merger period 2001–2004 was 9.4%, 11.47%, and 13.28%, respectively. It suggests that the merger had realized cost synergy and able to achieve efficiency (Table 13.5).

Table 13.5 Pre- and post-merger operating performance

Period	−4	−3	−2	−1	0	1	2	3	4
Year	1996	1997	1998	1999	2000	2001	2002	2003	2004
Sales	14,911	14,736	14,938	16,164	18,079	20,489	21,212	21,441	20,359
Operating profit	4691	4471	4412	4791	5300	4701	5569	6376	6090
Profit before taxes	4415	4242	4299	4683	5327	4484	5524	6313	6119
Net income	2938	2835	2891	3204	3697	3027	3930	4478	4302

References

Danzon PM, Epstein A, Nicholson S (2003) Mergers and acquisitions in the pharmaceutical and biotech industries. Organizational economics of health care conference, p 43

GSK Website Accessed 01 Nov 2017

International Briefs (1995) NewYork Times. http://www.nytimes.com/1995/03/17/business/international-briefs-glaxo-wellcome-merger-receives-ftc-approval.htmlJune162011. Accessed 01 Nov 2017

Lazo BB (2001) GSK a case study on the strategy of merger of equals in ethical pharmaceuticals. http://econwpa.repec.org/eps/io/papers/0211/0211017.pdf. Accessed 01 Nov 2017

M&A Monitor Ltd. UK 2002. http://www.m-a-monitor.com/xam-bin/m?mah01894. Accessed 01 Nov 2017

New York Times (1989) SmithKline Beecham to Merge. www.nytimes.com/1989/.../smithkline-beecham-to-merge.html. Accessed 01 Nov 2017

Pharmaceutical Online (2000) Glaxo Welcome and SmithKline Beecham merge at last. http://www.pharmaceuticalonline.com/article.mvc/Glaxo-Wellcome-and-SmithKline-Beecham-Merge-a-0001. Accessed Nov 2017

Pursche WR (1996) Mergers and Acquisitions–Pharmaceuticals –the consolidation isn't over. Mckinsey Quarterly. No 2

Ravenscraft DJ, Long WF (2000) The paths to creating value in pharmaceutical mergers. http://www.nber.org/chapters/c8653; http://www.nber.org/books/kapl00-1. Mergers and Productivity. University of Chicago Press. National Bureau of Economic Research

Robert Stevens (2000) Glaxo Wellcome SmithKline Beecham merger creates world's largest drug company. http://www.wsws.org/articles/2000/jan2000/glax-j22.shtml. Accessed 01 Nov 2017

Acquisitions by Royal Dutch Shell 14

Royal Dutch Shell is one of the leading energy companies in the world. The company is one of the largest independent energy companies involved in the exploration, development, production, refining and marketing of oil and natural gas as well as in the manufacturing and marketing of chemicals. Shell is one of the largest energy companies in terms of market capitalization, cash flow from operating activities and production levels. The distinctive Shell pectin a trademark is in use since the early part of the twentieth century (Annual Reports and Publications, 2017).

The operating segments of Shell Company are integrated gas, upstream, downstream, and corporate. The integrate gas manages integrated gas and the emerging opportunities of new energies. Integrated gas manages the LNG activities and the conversion of natural gas into GTL fuels and other products. The new energies is involved in the development of new fuels for transport such as advanced biofuels, hydrogen and charging for battery electric vehicles, and power from low carbon sources such as wind and solar sources. The upstream segment covers strategic themes like conventional oil and gas, deep water, and shales. The downstream segment focuses on oil products and chemicals. The downstream segment manages oil sands activities which involve the extraction of bitumen from mined oil sands and its conversion into synthetic crude oil. The projects and technology segment provides technical services and technology capability for the integrated gas, upstream, and downstream activities. Shell is a vertically integrated oil company. Shell was a heavily decentralized business worldwide especially in the downstream with companies in over 100 countries. Table 14.1 gives the segment wise details of revenues of Shell.

In 2017, Shell had research and development expenses of $922 million. The company had 10450 granted patents and pending patent applications. Shell distributed dividends of $15.6 billion in the year 2017. The company has plans for share buybacks of at least $25 billion during the period 2017–2020.

B. R. Kumar, *Wealth Creation in the World's Largest Mergers and Acquisitions*, Management for Professionals, https://doi.org/10.1007/978-3-030-02363-8_14

Table 14.1 Revenue segment wise

Year	2015	2016	2017
Integrated gas	25989	29190	36652
Upstream	33563	32936	40192
Downstream	237746	203550	268979
Corporate	96	74	51
Total	297394	265750	345874

The values are given in millions of dollars

M&A by Shell Group

In the year 1919, Shell took control of the Mexican Eagle Petroleum Company. In 1921 Shell Mex Ltd. was formed to market products under the "Shell" and "Eagle brands" in the United Kingdom. In 1929, Shell Chemicals was established.

Formation of Royal Dutch Shell Group

The Royal Dutch Shell Group was created through the amalgamation of two major rivals – the Royal Dutch Petroleum Company and the Shell Transport and Trading Company Ltd., United Kingdom, in the year 1907. The Royal Dutch Company was established in 1890. The Shell Transport and Trading Company was founded in 1897. The combined firm were operated as a dual listed company with the merged companies maintaining their legal existence but operated as a single unit partnership for business purpose. In the merged company, 60 per cent ownership was bestowed to Dutch group, while Shell Group had 40 per cent in the combined firm. Thus, from 1907 till 2005, Royal Dutch Petroleum Company and the "Shell" Transport and Trading Company PLC were existing as two public parent companies of a group of companies which were collectively called as the Royal Dutch/Shell Group. The subsidiaries of these parent companies were responsible for conducting the operating activities of these companies. In 2005, Royal Dutch Shell became the single parent company of Royal Dutch Petroleum Company and the Shell Transport and Trading Company. Royal Dutch Shell (the company) was registered as a public limited company in England and Wales and headquartered in The Hague, Netherlands. The group rapidly expanded across the world. Marketing companies were formed in Europe and many parts of Asia. Exploration and production were also extended to regions in Russia, Romania, Venezuela, Mexico, and the United States.

Following the revelation of a reporting scandal on account of overstating its oil reserves in 2004, Shell Group was restructured with the creation of new parent company named Royal Dutch Shell PLC. The primary listing was done in the London Stock Exchange and the secondary listing on the Amsterdam Stock Exchange. The unification process was completed by July 2005. The original owners delisted their companies from the respective exchanges. During July 2005, the Shell Transport and Trading Company was delisted from the London Stock Exchange, while Royal Dutch Petroleum Company was delisted from NYSE during November 2005.

On June 28, 2005, shareholders voted for the unification of Shell's Dutch and British parent companies. Approximately 96% of British and 97% of Dutch shareholders agreed to end the dual corporate structure at Shell PLC. The transaction resulted in one parent company with one board, one chairman, and one chief executive.

The former chairman of the twin headed group Jeroen van der Veer became the chief executive of the merged group. Aad Jacobs, the former chairman of the supervisory board of Royal Dutch, became the nonexecutive chairman. The unified company was worth £120 billion ($219 billion).

The unification process was completed on July 20, 2005.The shares of Shell Transport and Trading Company gained 3.2%, while Royal Dutch Petroleum Company gained 3.5% on unification news. The initial announcement of the unification process was made on October 28, 2004. The approval of Royal Dutch shareholders and Shell Transport shareholders was obtained in the annual general meeting held on June 28, 2005.

The transaction was meant for a clearer and simpler governance structure which included a single, smaller board and a simplified senior management structure with a single nonexecutive chairman and a single chief executive and clear lines of authority. The transaction was also aimed at increasing flexibility for issuing equity and debt. A single publicly traded company was expected to facilitate equity and debt issuance including on an SEC-registered basis.

Terms of the Transaction

The transaction was effected by way of an exchange offer by Royal Dutch Shell for the Royal Dutch shares and by way of a scheme of arrangement of Shell Transport under Section 425 of the Companies Act. The terms of the transaction reflected the 60:40 ownership of the Royal Dutch/Shell Group by Royal Dutch and Shell Transport. Royal Dutch Shell has two classes of ordinary shares, "A" shares and "B" shares. Under the terms of the transaction, the shareholders received two "A" shares for each Royal Dutch bearer share or Royal Dutch Hague registered share tendered. The shareholders received one 'A" ADR for each Royal Dutch New York registered share tendered. The shareholders received 0.28733 "B" shares for each Shell Transport ordinary share received. The shareholders also received 0.861 "B" ADR for each Shell Transport ADR.

The merger was completed on July 20, 2005. The stock price initially declined after merger announcement and then rose rapidly as suggested by the cumulative returns (Fig. 14.1).

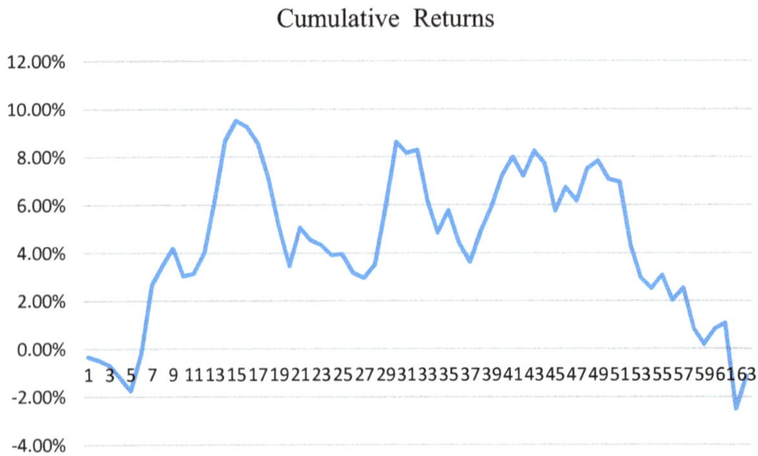

Fig. 14.1 Stock performance following merger completion

Acquisition of BG Group

BG had its origin when British Gas PLC divested Centrica and BG PLC was established in the year 1997. In 1999 the company was reorganized as BG Group PLC. BG Group PLC was a British multinational oil and gas company headquartered in Reading, United Kingdom. BG Group had operations in 25 countries across Africa, Asia, Australasia, Europe, North America, and South America. The company produced around 680,000 barrels of oil equivalent per day. The company was the largest supplier of LNG to United States. BG Group was listed on the London Stock Exchange and had been a constituent of the FTSE 100 Index. BG Group had proven commercial reserves of 2.6 billion barrels. The company was further demerged into Lattice Group and BG Group during October 2000. Lattice took ownership of the gas transporter company Transco and the gas engineering and consultancy specialist company Advantica along with property and transport companies. BG Group obtained the ownership of gas fields and related assets. In the year 2002, Lattice merged with National Grid Company to become National Grid Transco which later was renamed as National Grid in the year 2005. BG Group is basically involved in the exploration and extraction of natural gas and oil and the production of liquefied natural gas. The company sold these products to wholesale customers such as retail gas suppliers and electricity-generating firms.

On April 8, 2015, Royal Dutch Shell made public announcement of its intent to acquire BG Group for £47 billion (US$70 billion) Offshore EnergyToday.com Business Guide (2015). This acquisition catapulted Shell as the world's second largest non-state oil company after Exxon Mobil in terms of market capitalization surpassing Chevron Corporation. The acquisition was completed in February 2016. The combination of Shell and BG Group brought together two world class portfolios involving productive oil and gas projects and expertise in deep water and liquefied natural gas (LNG) (Bombey, 2016). The acquisition gave Royal Dutch Shell a dominant footprint in offshore Brazil region. BG's acquisition bolstered Shell's position in the fast-growing liquefied natural gas market and turned it into the largest foreign oil company in Brazil. Shell's main partner in Brazil is the state-run oil company Petrobras. By law Petrobras controls majority of Brazil's pre-salt oil reserves which are trapped deep under thick layers of rock and salt beneath the waters offshore Brazil. The country holds approximately 15 billion barrels of proved oil reserves which are second only to Venezuela in South America. By means of acquisition of oil field assets, Shell had profitable business plans at relatively low crude prices. BG had early mover advantage in Brazil as it was first in investment in oil-rich Santos Basin. The acquisition boosted Shell's production by 20 per cent and increased its reserves by 25 per cent (Connors and Kent, 2016). Shell had plans to cut thousands of jobs from the combined group and had plans to sell $30 billion of assets over the period 2017–2020 to finance the deal, buy back the shares, and support dividends. Shell is strategically focusing on rapid-growing LNG market in the future decade as the world was shifting toward cleaner sources of energy. The acquisition was expected to increase Shell's oil and gas production to approximately 4.7 million barrels of oil equivalent by 2020. The deal bolstered the company's position in liquefied natural gas, Brazilian oil business, and deep water assets. The company also projected annual pretax combined cost cuts and revenue improvements of $3.5 billion. The combination took place in a scenario in which oil prices were declining and job cuts were prevalent in the industry. Shell had announced reduction in jobs of about 2800 as a result of the acquisition. Approximately 99.5 per cent of BG shareholders voted in favor of the acquisition deal. About 83 per cent of the Shell's shareholders approved the deal in general shareholder meeting (Report, 2005). On the day of BG shareholders' approval for the deal (January 28, 2016), the stock price of BG went up by 3.4 per cent, while Shell B shares rose by 5.4 per cent after the vote, compared to the sector index which rose by 4.2 per cent during the above period. The acquisition was expected to result in cost savings of an amount of $3.5 billion on account of reduction in overlaps in areas of corporate, administrative, and IT operations by 2018. This acquisition was the biggest in the sector since Exxon's merger with Mobil in 1988.

The deal combined the two largest IOC LNG players to create an industry mammoth. It was estimated that by the end of the year 2018, the combined firm will control sales of 44 mmtpa making it the largest LNG seller in the world. Shell Company's focus was on deep water oil. In 2015, approximately 60% of BG's production was in gas. It was expected that this proportion of gas production will decline to 50% by 2025 as the giant Brazil pre-salt fields will come on-stream. By 2025, Brazil will be the biggest single country position in the combined portfolio accounting for 13% of BG's/Shell's total production. Thus BG added attractive deep water and integrated gas positions to the Shell portfolio. In 2016, Royal Dutch Shell announced its intention to exit oil and gas operations in about ten countries as part of a shift in strategy following its acquisition of BG Group.

Terms of Deal Agreement

The takeover became effective from Monday February 15, 2016. BG Group shareholders received 383 pence in cash plus 0.4454 Royal Dutch Shell B shares for each BG Group share they held as on Friday February 12, 2016. For products which reference BG Group shares, reference was made to Royal Dutch Shell B shares. The strike prices of Royal Dutch Shell B shares for those plans were the original BG Group strike price multiplied by 1.43599.

The theoretical closing value of BG shares on the London Stock Exchange on Friday February 12, 2016 was calculated as follows:

Theoretical BG value = 383p + (0.4454*Royal Dutch Shell B closing price on 12/02/2016)

As the closing price of Royal Dutch Shell B Shares on that date was 1526, this resulted in a value of 383 + (0.4454*1526) = 1062.68. To get the ratio to be applied to the original BG strike prices, ((1062.68–383)*(1/0.4454))/1062.68 = 1.43599.[1]

Announcement Effect on Stock Wealth

The deal was first announced on April 8, 2015. The takeover became effective from Monday February 15, 2016.

The share price of Royal Dutch Shell increased in the range of 0.2–1.9% during the period of 4 days to 1 day before the acquisition announcement. The announcement day and one day after return were – 3.4% and – 0.7%. Thereafter stock price gained in the range of 0.1–2.8% for the following days till +6 days after acquisition announcement.

Table 14.2 Returns for Royal Dutch Shell surrounding BG acquisition

Day	Return (%)
–5	–0.3
–4	0.9
–3	0.2
–2	1.9
–1	0.7
0	–3.4
1	–0.7
2	0.6
3	0.1
4	1.1
5	2.8
6	1.8
7	–0.8
8	0.2
9	–0.7
10	–0.1

[1] https://www.meteoram.com/uploads/files/Royal_Dutch_Shell_takeover_of_BG_Group.pdf

Table 14.3 Cumulative returns in different time windows

Time window	Cumulative returns (%)
−1 to 1 day	−3.40
−5 to 5 day	4
5 to 10 day	4.30
5 to 50 day	−1.50
5 day to 100 day	−11.70
5 day to 247 day	−16.30

Fig. 14.2 Cumulative returns surrounding BG acquisition announcement

The cumulative return during the 3-day window period (−1 to +1) was −3.40% (Table 14.3). In other shorter window periods, the cumulative return for the stock was positive. In longer window periods of analysis, the cumulative returns were negative (Fig. 14.2).

References

Annual Reports and Publications (2017) https://www.shell.com/investors/financial-reporting/annual-publications.html#iframe=L3JlcG9ydC1ob21lLzIwMTcv. Accessed 5 Nov 2017

Bombey N (2016) Shell completes $53B deal for BG Group. https://www.usatoday.com/story/money/2016/02/15/royal-dutch-shell-bg-group/80403694/. Accessed 7 Nov 2017

Connors W, Kent S (2016) Shell complete acquisition of BG Group, giving energy giant a large footprint in Brazil. https://www.wsj.com/articles/shell-completes-buy-of-bg-group-1455541779. Accessed 6 Nov 2017

Offshore EnergyToday.com Business Guide (2015) Shell is taking over BG.Here is what you need to know. https://www.offshoreenergytoday.com/shell-is-taking-over-bg-what-you-need-to-know. Accessed 07 Nov 2017

Report (2005) Shell shareholders vote to merge. https://www.theguardian.com/business/2005/jun/28/oilandpetrol.news. Accessed 5 Nov 2017

Bell South Merger with AT&T

15

Introduction

On March 5, 2006 AT&T and BellSouth Corporation entered into an agreement to merge two companies to emerge as an integrated provider in the wireless, broadband, video, voice and data markets. BellSouth became a wholly owned subsidiary of AT&T Inc. (Report, 2006). The acquisition was completed on December 29, 2006.

On December 30, 2006, the Federal Communication after a 7-month deadlock approved AT&T's buyout of BellSouth for $85 billion. The acquisition reunited large parts of AT&T's domain by combining Bell South's nine-state territory into AT&T's existing operations which spanned regions of Midwest, Southwest, and West Coast (Winston and Crandall, 2006). It gave AT&T compete control of Cingular Wireless which was the country's largest mobile telephone provider at the time. Earlier Cingular Wireless was a 60–40 joint venture with BellSouth. The merger streamlined the ownership and operations of Cingular Wireless by combining the Cingular, BellSouth, and AT&T networks into a single fully integrated wireless and wireline Internet Protocol network which offered a full range of advanced solutions. The combined firm had 58 million cell phone customers, 67.5 million phone lines, and 11.5 broadband users. The reported revenues were $115 billion in year 2005. The combined firm employed more than 300,000 people. The approval by regulatory authorities was based on a number of conditions including the main obligation of maintaining a "network neutrality" pledge by AT&T which allows its customers unfettered access to data and services over high-speed Internet connections. The other concessions for approval included a freeze on some fees it charges rivals for the rent of some high capacity wires which serve office buildings. The

B. R. Kumar, *Wealth Creation in the World's Largest Mergers and Acquisitions*, Management for Professionals, https://doi.org/10.1007/978-3-030-02363-8_15

other conditions include a commitment to offer high-speed Internet services to all of its local phone customers by the end of the year 2007. The conditions also stipulated allowing customers to buy high-speed Internet service without a local phone line. The merger was a big step toward putting MA Bell back together 22 years after the breakup of AT&T in 1984.

Both AT&T and BellSouth offered conventional telephone service in the United States. AT&T which was formerly known as Southwestern Bell operated in the Southwest, Far West, and the Midwest. BellSouth provided telephone service in the Southeast. Both the companies were losing subscriber lines rapidly as consumers switched to cellular phones or voice over Internet Protocol (VOIP) which were provided by the cable companies or independent providers. The new broadband (DSL) Internet services offered by these erstwhile phone companies were not sufficient to offset the revenues from traditional telephone services.

Advantages of the Merger

The combined company was able to speed up the convergence of new and improved services for consumers and businesses. The merger acted as a catalyst for the industry's shift to Internet Protocol network-based technologies. The industry was witnessing a new era of converged and bundled communications, video, and entertainment service. The merger combined the R&D work at AT&T labs coupled with BellSouth's extensive deployment of fiber networks for DSL and other broadband services. The combined company was expected to generate $130 billion in sales and serve approximately 70 million local phone customers.

The merger facilitated business customers to benefit from the expertise and innovation of AT&T Labs. The combination of AT&T's state-of-the-art national and international networks and advanced services with BellSouth's local exchange and broadband distribution platform immensely benefitted customers.

The combined AT&T became serious competitor for cable companies as it offered television service over the Internet with lower rates for its customers in its service area. AT&T offered high-speed Internet for $19.95 a month over the next 30 months without requiring customers to purchase phone service from companies. The new size gave AT&T more power to set prices for telephone and other services. AT&T had also agreed to give up some wireless licenses which were suitable for high-speed Internet so that other companies could compete. The company also froze the rates for "special access" lines which served large businesses and moved 3000 BellSouth jobs to the United States from overseas. The new AT&T with market capitalization of $225 billion became bigger than Verizon which was formed due to a $52 billion merger between GTE and Bell Atlantic.

Even though AT&T faced limited competition from other telephone operators, the real challenge was from cable and computer companies present in a complicated marketplace which encompassed television, broadband and wireless, long and local distance landline telephone service.

The merged company was able to enhance financial, technical, research and development, network, and marketing resources for serving the customers. The merger gave government customers like military and national security agencies a reliable US-based provider of integrated services.

The merger did not reduce competition in different markets since AT&T and BellSouth were not actual competitors in the local, long distance, video markets, and enterprise markets.

Terms and Conditions

Under the terms of the acquisition, each share of BellSouth common stock was converted into 1.325 share of AT&T common stock. On the basis of AT&T's closing price on March 3, 2006, the exchange ratio equaled $37.09 per BellSouth common share. This offer represented a 17.9% premium over BellSouth's closing stock price as on March 3, 2006. The deal was valued at $67 billion.

Expected Synergies of the Deal

The combination of the two leading wireline providers along with Cingular speeded up the progress in integrated wireless and wireline services. The merger allowed for closer integration of the combined firm's closer integration of the company's wireless, wireline, and IP products and services over a single global IP network. This combination facilitated the convergence of three major components of integrated services televisions, computers, and wireless devices. The expected synergies were to a tune of $18 billion with more than $2 billion in annual run rate in synergies expected in year 2008 which was expected to be $3 billion in year 2010. A major portion of the expected synergies were expected from cost reductions in operations of unregulated and interstate services and corporate staff. Synergies were also expected from productivity improvements on account of ongoing initiatives. Almost half of the cost savings were expected to result from network operations and IT as facilities and operations were consolidated and the traffic was being moved to a single IP network (Sipress and Goo, 2006). Additional savings were expected from combining staff functions and reduction of advertising and branding expenses. The deal was expected to improve AT&T's overall growth driven by wireless which represented about one third of the company's expected revenues in the year 2007. AT&T intended to use the improved free cash flow after dividends to reduce debt levels over the next 5 years.

In 1984 AT&T was broken up into seven local phone companies and one long distance company of which only three exist today: AT&T, Verizon Communications, and Qwest Communications International.

Merger Announcement and Wealth Effects

The merger announcement was made on March 5, 2006. The merger completion was on December 29, 2007. On announcement, the stock price of BellSouth rose by 4.8%. The announcement day return for AT&T was 0.7%. The cumulative returns for AT&T surrounding the merger announcement is given in the figure below (Fig. 15.1).

By the merger completion period, the share price showed consistent gains as reflected in the figure. The 247 day (−5 to +242 day) cumulative return analysis observes that the cumulative return for AT&T stock amounted to 29.8%.

Fig. 15.1 Cumulative returns for AT&T surrounding merger announcement

Post-merger Operating Performance

In the first 3 months of year 2007, AT&T earned $2.8 billion or 45 cents a share, which was up from $1.4 billion or 37 cents a share, a year earlier. The revenues also increased by 84% to reach $29 billion though sales rose a slower 1.7% to $29.4 billion adjusted for the BellSouth deal and other onetime items. In the context of adjustments for merger related costs, AT&T would have earned $4.1 billion or 65 cents a share, versus $2 billion or 52 cents a share (Bartash, 2007).

In the mobile business, AT&T added a net 1.2 million customers. The company added a record of 2.5 million in the prior quarter. The wireless revenues increased by 11% to reach $10 billion with the average user spending $49.21 a month which was a 1.4% gain from a year earlier. The income from the mobile segment increased to $1.48 billion from $773 million. Four out of every five new AT&T mobile customers fell into the valuable postpaid category. Churn rate which indicated the percentage of customers who canceled service each month dropped to 1.7% from 1.8% in the prior quarters. AT&T also provided services to 1.7 million video customers who had signed up for DirecTV or Dish Network. In the Internet market, AT&T added 691,000 broadband customers to reach the total of 12.9 million customers. On account of the acquisition of BellSouth, the operating costs rose by 79% to the amount of $24.3 billion.

The values are given in millions of dollars. The year of merger was 2006. The analysis was done with respect to the premerger period and post-merger period. The average growth rate of financial variables in the period 2003–2005 is compared with the average growth rate of variables in the post-merger period of 2008–2010. The year 2006 is excluded from the analysis. The average growth rate of operating revenue in the premerger period (2003–2005) was 0.7%, while the average increase in operating income in the post-merger period (2008–2010) was 1.5%. The average increase in operating income in the premerger period was 304% mainly on account of increase of operating income in year 2005 which amounted to 945%. The average growth rate of operating income declined in the post-merger period, due to negative growth rates of operating income in year 2008 and 2009. The growth rate of operating income in 2 years after merger was 130%. The average increase in net income in the premerger period was 0.32%, while the average increase in net income was 21%. The year-on-year comparison of growth rate in net income during the post-merger period shows that the highest growth rate of 57% was in year 2010. The average growth rate of assets in the premerger period of approximately 16% declined by 0.7% in the post-merger period. The average debt ratio in the premerger period of 2002–2005 of 36.95% increased to 39.43% in the post-merger period 2007–2010 (Table 15.1).

The operating performance measures are given in thousands. The number of network access lines has declined in the post-merger period. The number of wireless customers has shown increasing trend in the post-merger period. The number of employees has declined in the post-merger period (Table 15.2).

Table 15.1 Financial performance comparison – premerger and post-merger period

Year	2002	2003	2004	2005	2006	2007	2008	2009	2010
Operating revenue	43,138	40,498	40,787	43,862	63,055	118,928	124,028	123,018	124,280
Operating income	8623	6284	5901	61,668	10,288	20,404	23,063	21,492	19,573
Net income	5653	8505	5887	4786	7361	12,147	13,128	12,843	20,179
Total assets	95,057	102,016	110,265	145,632	270,634	275,644	265,245	268,752	269,391
Debt ratio	39.90%	32%	40%	35.90%	34.10%	35.60%	43.70%	41.30%	37.10%

Source: AT&T Annual Report

Table 15.2 Operating data comparison

Year	2002	2003	2004	2005	2006	2007	2008	2009	2010
Network access lines in service (000)	57,083	54,683	52,356	49,413	66,469	61,582	55,610	49,392	41,883
Wireless customers (000′)	21,925	24,027	49,132	54,144	60,962	70,052	77,009	85,120	95,536
Number of employees	175,980	168,950	162,700	189,950	304,180	309,050	302,660	282,720	266,590

References

Bartash J (2007) AT&T profit doubles on merger, mobile. https://wwwmarketwatchcom/story/att-profit-doubles-on-merger-mobile. Accessed 15 Nov 2017

Report (2006) AT &T Bell South Merger. https://www.nytimes.com/2006/12/30/business/30tele.html. Accessed 14 Nov 2017

Sipress A, Goo SK (2006) AT&T completes BellSouth Takeover 2006. http://www.washington-post.com/wp-dyn/content/article/2006/12/29/AR2006122901048_2.html. Accessed 14 Nov 2017

Winston C, Crandall RW (2006) The AT&T/BellSouth Merger: The breakdown of breakup. https://wwwbrookingsedu/opinions/the-attbellsouth-merger-the-breakdown-of-breakup/. Accessed 15 Nov 2017

Comcast Acquisition of AT&T Broadband 16

Comcast Corporation is a global media and technology company with two businesses – Comcast and NBC Universal. By means of transaction in the year 2011 and 2013, Comcast acquired NBC Universal. The business segments of Comcast are Cable Communications, Cable Networks, Broadcast Television, Filmed Entertainment, and Theme Parks. The latter four segments are collectively called NBCUniversal segments. Cable Communications consists of the operations of Comcast cable which is the largest providers of video, high-speed Internet, voice and security, and automation services. The cable services are provided to residential customers under the Xfinity brand name. The Filmed Entertainment division consists of operations of Universal Pictures which produces, acquires, markets, and distributes filmed entertainment worldwide. Table 16.1 gives the financial highlights of Comcast Corporation.

Acquisition of AT&T Broadband

In the year 2001, Comcast took over AT&T broadband unit for $72 billion. The deal created the biggest cable company in the United States with 22.3 million subscribers which was almost twice the size of the next biggest cable operator, AOL Time Warner (ABC News, 2001). The combined company provided lines into one fifth of US homes. AT&T Broadband was the largest cable company with 13.8 million customers. Comcast ranked third with 8.5 million customers. The transaction created the world's preeminent broadband services company. The combined company called AT&T Comcast Corporation became the leading and most powerful communications, media, and entertainment company in the world. The new combined company had subscribers in 17 of the United States' 20 largest urban markets. The combined entity became the leading provider of broadband video, voice, and data services with annual pro forma revenues of approximately $19 billion. The new

B. R. Kumar, *Wealth Creation in the World's Largest Mergers and Acquisitions*, Management for Professionals, https://doi.org/10.1007/978-3-030-02363-8_16

Table 16.1 Financial highlights in millions of dollars

Year	2013	2014	2015	2016	2017
Revenues	64657	68775	74510	80403	84526
Operating income	13563	14904	15998	16859	17987
Net income	6816	8380	8163	8695	22714
Total assets	158672	159186	166574	180500	186949
Total debt	47706	48081	52621	61046	64556

combined entity had a presence in 41 states with approximately five million digital video customers, 2.2 million high-speed data customers, and one million cable telephony customers. AT&T spun off its cable unit into a separate company and merged the newly formed entity with Comcast. The merger was the culmination of 5-month bidding war for AT&T Broadband. Initially Comcast offered $41 billion for the deal. But it was rejected. The subsequent offers from AOL Time Warner and Cox Communications were also rejected. AT&T owned 25% of Time Warner Entertainment. Microsoft owned $5 billion stake in AT&T Broadband. AT&T shareholders controlled 56% of the new company. The acquisition of AT&T Broadband enabled Comcast to deliver faster broadband speed and innovative television series to new markets.

The deal combined AT&T's cable unit which was the largest in United States with the nation's Number 3 cable operator Comcast. The number 2 cable operator at that time AOL Time Warner was one of the unsuccessful bidders.

Acquisition Highlights

Under the terms of the definitive agreement, AT&T spun off AT&T Broadband and merged with Comcast forming a new firm called AT&T Comcast Corporation. AT&T shareholders received approximately 0.34 shares of AT&T Comcast Corporation for each share of AT&T which they owned. Comcast shareholders received one share of AT&T Comcast Corporation for each Comcast share they owned. AT&T shareowners owned 56% of the new company and 66% voting interest in the new firm. The Robert family which owned Comcast Class B Shares controlled one third of the new company's outstanding voting interest. The assets of AT&T Comcast Corporation consisted of both companies' cable TV systems as well as AT&T's interest in cable television joint ventures and its 25.5% interest in Time Warner Entertainment and Comcast's interests in QVC, E! Entertainment, The Golf Channel, and other entertainment properties. The merged entity had approximately $20 billion in debt and other liabilities from AT&T and its subsidiaries. In conjunction with the transaction, Microsoft Corporation has agreed to convert the $5 billion of AT&T subsidiary trust convertible preferred securities into 115 million shares of AT&T Comcast Corporation. The aggregate value of the transaction to AT&T shareholders amounted to $72 billion. The companies put the value of the AT&T broadband unit at about $13.07 per AT&T share based on Comcast's' closing share price as of December 19, 2001. AT&T and Comcast contributed five board members to the new company (Bryer, 2001). The two companies jointly selected two additional members who had no current affiliation with either company. The AT&T Comcast closed by the end of year 2002. AT&T Comcast Corporation was headquartered in Philadelphia and maintained executive offices in the New York City area. The board of New York-based AT&T unanimously approved the deal.

The merger deal valued AT&T's cable systems at approximately $4500 per subscriber based on the closing price of Comcast stock and gave AT&T shareholders majority ownership of the combined company with an initial total aggregate value of approximately $120 billion (Beltran, 2001). The financial advisors for AT&T were Credit Suisse First Boston and Goldman Sachs. Morgan Stanley, JPMorgan, Merrill Lynch, and Quadrangle Group were financial advisors for Comcast. Wachtell, Lipton, Rosen & Katz was the legal advisor of AT&T. Davis Polk & Wardwell was the legal advisor to Comcast.

The value of $13.07 per AT&T share placed the total value of the broadband unit at about $47 billion which was a bit higher than the unsolicited $44.5 billion offer Comcast made for the company in July 2001 (The Corporate Entities and the Financial Transaction, 2001). The AT&T board rejected that bid as insufficient at that time. As a part of its efforts to block AOL Time Warner from winning the bid, Microsoft Corp provided financial assistance to both Comcast and competing cable operator Cox Communications Inc. As a part of the deal, Microsoft got $5 billion in preferred securities. AOL also was unsuccessful in its attempt to buy back AT&T's 25.5% stake in its Time Warner Entertainment unit which included Warner Bros. studios, HBO, and its cable operations. This stake became the part of AT&T Comcast along with Comcast's entertainment units such as cable shopping channel QVC and entertainment channels E! and the Golf Channel (Corporate News, 2001). AT&T shareholders owned about 56% of the combined company which also assumed about $25 billion in debt and other obligations. AT&T shareholders held approximately 66% of the voting interests. The deal represented a value per subscriber of more than $4000.

In its initial offer in July 2001, Comcast had proposed majority share ownership for AT&T, while Comcast would have had nearly 45% voting control. This offer was rejected. In the late 1990s, AT&T had paid approximately $106 billion to purchase cable business which at the time of acquisition by Comcast was sold for less than half that amount. Earlier AT&T had spun off its wireless business.

As a result of the deal, 1700 employees were laid off in the Denver area. The combined company had a total of 21 million subscribers which was nearly twice as compared to its nearest competitor, AOL Time Warner. AT&T Broadband had about 40,000 employees, and Comcast Corp's cable division had about 20,000 at the time of the merger deal. The savings from combining the two companies was expected to be at least $1.25 billion per year which could rise to as much as $2.8 billion per year (Schiesel and Sorkin, 2001).

In the year 2001, AT&T had announced plans to split itself into four companies covering the wireless, broadband (cable), business, and consumer telephone sectors. During July 2001, Comcast purchased an AT&T owned cable TV system with

115,000 subscribers for $518 million in cash. The combined company was capable of providing of cable television programs, high-speed Internet access, and telephone services. The combined firm was well positioned to roll out new generations of services like interactive television. Through this deal, AT&T ended its 3-year foray into the cable business and returned the company to its basic business of telephone and data communications services.

Merger Process

Comcast and AT&T Corporation decided to combine their broadband businesses through the following steps: AT&T contributed the assets of its AT&T broadband division including AT&T broadband phone to a new wholly owned holding company AT&T Broadband Corporation. AT&T then spun off AT&T Broadband Corporation to the shareholders of AT&T Corporation. Following this spun off, Comcast and AT&T Broadband Corporation merged into different, wholly owned subsidiaries of AT&T Comcast Corporation. At the time of the closing of deal, Comcast and AT&T shareholders exchanged their shares in the respective companies for shares in AT&T Comcast which became a publicly traded company.

Wealth Creation During Acquisition Announcement

AT&T's stock price rose by $1.41 to $18.21 on merger announcement, while Comcast price fell by $2.24 to reach $35.83. The merger announcement date was July 9 2001.When Comcast won the bid on December 19, 2001, shares of Comcast fell 94 cents or 2.41% to close at $38.09. AT&T shares rose 15 cents to $16.80.

References

ABC News (2001) Comcast, AT&T Broadband in $52 billion deal. http://abcnews.go.com/Business/story?id=87476&page=1. Accessed 22 Nov 2017

Beltran L (2001) Comcast wins AT&T Cable. http://money.cnn.com/2001/12/19/deals/att/. Accessed 23 Nov 2017

Bryer A (2003) In deal of year, Comcast buys AT&T Broadband. https://www.bizjournals.com/denver/stories/2003/03/24/focus1.html. Denver Business Journal. Accessed 24 Nov 2017

Corporate News (2001) AT&T Broadband to merge with Comcast Corporation in a $72 billion transaction. https://corporate.comcast.com/news-information/news-feed/att-broadband-to-merge-with-comcast-corporation-in-72-billion-transaction. Accessed 23 Nov 2017

Schiesel S , Sorkin AR (2001) AT&T's Cable deal: The Overview; Comcast wins bid for AT&T's Cable. https://www.nytimes.com/2001/12/20/business/at-t-s-cable-deal-the-overview-comcast-wins-bid-for-at-t-s-cable.html. Accessed 30 Nov 2017

The Corporate Entities and the Financial Transaction (2001) http://docs.cpuc.ca.gov/published/Final_decision/21056-02.htm. Accessed 30 Nov 2001

Key Mergers of JPMorgan Chase 17

JPMorgan Chase has a history dating back over 200 years. It is one of the oldest financial institutions in the world. JPMorgan Chase is a leading global financial services firm with assets of over $2.5 trillion with presence in over 100 markets. JPMorgan Chase has market leadership position in investment banking, financial services for consumers and small businesses, commercial banking, private equity, financial transaction processing, and asset management. JPMorgan Chase is a component of the Dow Jones Industrial Average. The company employs over 250, 000 employees. The foundations of JPMorgan Chase can be traced to more than 1200 predecessor institutions. The well-known predecessors of the present JPMorgan Chase include JPMorgan & Co, the Chase Manhattan Bank, Bank One, Manufacturers Hanover Trust Co, Chemical Bank, the First National Bank of Chicago, National Bank of Detroit, The Bearn Stearns Companies Inc., Robert Fleming Holdings, etc. JPMorgan Chase & Co combined two of the world's premier financial brands: JPMorgan and Chase.

The first predecessor of JPMorgan Chase, Manhattan Bank, was established in the year 1799. In 2017 JPMorgan was the first in terms of most visited bank website with the most mobile banking customers. There are 6.7 million digital customers with JPMorgan. The bank had $900 billion in debt and credit card sales volume. The bank has $5 trillion value of wholesale payments across 120 currencies. In 2017, the company earned $24.4 billion in net income on revenues of $103.6 billion. During the last 6 years, the company brought back nearly $40 billion in stock. JPMorgan is a leader in investment banking, financial services for consumers and small businesses, commercial banking, financial transaction processing, and asset management. The firm serves millions of customers throughout the world through the JPMorgan Chase brands. Table 17.1 provides the financial highlights of JP Morgan.

Table 17.2 summarizes the merger history of JP Morgan Chase. The following are the highlights of key mergers which shaped the modern emergence of JPMorgan Chase & Co.

B. R. Kumar, *Wealth Creation in the World's Largest Mergers and Acquisitions*, Management for Professionals, https://doi.org/10.1007/978-3-030-02363-8_17

Table 17.1 Financial highlights

Year	2015	2016	2017
Total net revenues in million dollars	93,543	95,668	99,624
Net income in million dollars	24,442	24,733	24,441
Net income per share	$6.05	6.24	6.35
Return on common equity	11%	10%	10%
Tier 1 capital ratio	13.3	13.9	13.8
Total capital ratio	14.7	15.2	15.7
Loans in million dollars	837.299	894.765	930.697
Total assets in million dollars	2,351,698	2,490,972	2,533,600
Deposits in million dollars	1,279,715	1,375,176	1,443,982
Market capitalization in million dollars	241,899	307,295	366,301
Total stockholder equity in million dollars	247,573	254,190	255,693

Table 17.2 Merger history

Period	Merger history
1895	J Pierpont Morgan reorganizes his family's private interests, and the New York firm is renamed JPMorgan
1901	JPMorgan buys out industrialist Andrew Carnegie and combines 33 companies to create United States steel. It was the world's first billion dollar corporation
1955	Chase National Bank mergers with the Bank of Manhattan company to form chase Manhattan Bank
1996	Chase Manhattan Corp. merges into Chemical Banking Corp.
2000	JPMorgan merges with chase Manhattan Corp. which combined four of the largest and oldest money center banking institution in New York City, JPMorgan, chase, chemical, and manufacturers Hanover, into one firm called JPMorgan Chase & Co
2004	Bank one merges with JPMorgan Chase &Co
2008	JPMorgan Chase & Co acquires bear Stearns and Washington mutual

Many of JPMorgan Chase & Co predecessors took part in the merger movement which began in the early 1990s (JPMorgan Chase, 2017). In the year 1991, Chemical Banking Corp. merged with Manufacturers Hanover Corp., keeping the name Chemical Banking Corp., which was then the second largest banking institution in the United States. In the year 1995, First Chicago Corp. merged with NBD Bancorp Inc. to form First Chicago NBD Corp., which was one of the largest banking company based in the Midwest. In 1996, Chemical Banking Corp. merged with the Chase Manhattan Corp. retaining the name the Chase Manhattan Corp. This merger created the largest bank holding company in the United States. In 1998, Bank One Corp. merged First Chicago NBD Corp. with itself. Bank One became the largest financial services firm in the Midwest by merging with Louisiana's First Commerce Corp. In the process, Bank One emerged as the fourth largest bank in the United States and the world's largest Visa credit card issuer. In 2000, the Chase Manhattan Corp. merged with JPMorgan & Co. This merger resulted in the combination of four of the largest and oldest money center banking institutions in New York City (Morgan, Chase, Chemical, and Manufacturers Hanover) into one firm called JPMorgan Chase & Co. In 2004, Bank One merged with JPMorgan Chase & Co which in fact combined the investment and commercial banking strength of

JPMorgan with the consumer banking strength of Bank One. In the year 2008, JPMorgan Chase acquired Bear Stearns Company which facilitated in strengthening its capabilities across a broad range of businesses like prime brokerage, cash clearing, and energy trading.

Chase Manhattan and JPMorgan Merger

In the year 2000, the Chase Manhattan Corp. which is the third largest banking company in United States acquired JPMorgan & Company in an all-stock deal valued at around $30.9 billion (ABC News, 2000). During the 1980s, JPMorgan had transformed itself into an investment banking firm with a blue-chip list of clients. The acquisition of JPMorgan catapulted Chase into the big leagues of investment banking. Chase and Morgan together had more than $650 billion in assets which were ranked second to Citigroup's $800 billion (ABC News, 2000).

Chase exchanged 3.7 shares of its stock for each of Morgan's share. On the basis of Chase's closing stock price of $52.50 on September 13, 2000, the proposed price was about $30.9 billion.

Chase bank's retail operations which included consumer banking and credit card business retained the Chase name. Major portion of the overlap between the two banks were in investment banking functions like underwriting stocks and bonds and trading currencies. The investment banking operations of the combined company was called JPMorgan. Chase was one of the biggest credit card issuers in the country and a major lender to individuals. Morgan had focused on serving the needs of blue chip clients. Before the merger Chase had total assets of $396 billion compared with $266 billion for Morgan (J P Morgan Chase & Co. and Bank One Corporation to Merge, 2017). Even though both companies were among the biggest five banks in the region, neither were able to reach the top tier of investment banks. At the time of the acquisition, Chase had operations in 65 countries and employed about 80,000 employees. JPMorgan had 16,000 employees. Originally Chase bank was founded in the year 1799. It has grown over a period of time through multiple mergers with Chemical Bank and Manufacturers Hanover. Chase focused on buying small investment banks to strengthen its position as an underwriter of technology companies. For example, it had acquired Hambrecht & Quist in 1999. In the year 2000, it bought the merger specialist Beacon Group and an investment banking and money management firm Robert Fleming Holdings. The latter was acquired for $7.7 billion.

The merger was expected to be successful since the two firms' array of services complemented each other. The corporate side of business consisting of the merger advisory, trading, and bond operations was known as JPMorgan while the consumer segment consisting of credit cards, Chase's large New York area branch network, mortgage banking, and insurance were known as Chase. JPMorgan had a strong presence in the investment banking area of underwriting initial public stock offerings. JPMorgan was an attractive target on account of the bank's booming money management and derivative business as well as its list of corporate clients and brand name.

On acquisition announcement on September 14, 2000, JPMorgan's stock price declined $4.19 to $181.25, and Chase Manhattan's stock price fell $2.13 to $50.69.

The speculation about JPMorgan becoming the target of acquisition pushed up the price by more than 68%.

JPMorgan Chase–Bank One Deal

Bank One was the sixth largest bank holding company in United States, with assets of $290 billion. At the time of merger announcement, Bank One had more than 51 million credit cards issued and served approximately seven million retail households and had more than 20,000 middle market customers. The bank also managed $175 billion of clients' investment assets.

At the time of merger, JPMorgan Chase had 92,900 employees and was the third largest bank holding company in the United States with $793 billion assets. JPMorgan had operations in more than 50 countries. During the merger period, Bank One had 71,200 employees and was the six largest bank holding company in the United States with $290 billion assets and 1800 branches in 14 states.

On January 14, 2004, JPMorgan Chase & Co entered into agreement to buy Bank One for $58 billion. The deal involving the merger of holding companies of JPMorgan Chase & Co and Bank One was completed on July 1, 2004. The combined company was known as JPMorgan Chase & Co. The merger created one of the largest and most globally diversified financial services companies in the world. The merger established the second largest banking company in the United States in terms of total assets after Citigroup. The combined bank had assets of $1.1 trillion, strong capital base, 2300 branches in 17 states, and leading positions in retail banking and lending, credit cards, investment banking, asset management, private banking, treasury and securities services, middle market, and private equity. JPMorgan was headquartered in New York, while Bank One was headquartered in Chicago. Bank of America Corporation had entered into a deal to acquire FleetBoston Financial Corporation for $47 billion. Table 17.3 gives the comparative financial highlights of JP Morgan and Bank One in the year of merger.

The deal helped JPMorgan to expand its reach to Midwest and Southwest. JPMorgan was able to get a strong retail and credit card presence through the merger with Bank One. Bank One had been one of the largest Visa card issuer. The combination facilitated cross selling of the products (McGeehan & Sorkin, 2000).

The merger of JPMorgan and Bank One was the third largest in US financial services after the combination of Travelers Group and Citicorp for $70.2 billion in 1998 and the purchase of BankAmerica by NationsBank for $59.2 billion to create Bank of America Corporation.

Table 17.3 Financials in the year of merger

	JPMorgan	Bank One
Assets	$793 billion	$290 billion
Net income	$1.7 billion	$3.3 billion
Employees	92,900	71,200

Source Company Reports

Terms of the Deal

The deal involved exchange of 1.32 shares of JPMorgan shares for each Bank One share. On the basis of closing price of JPMorgan Chase's common stock on the New York Stock Exchange on January 13, 2004 which was the last trading day before public announcement of the merger, the 1.32 exchange ratio represented approximately $51.35 in value for each share of Bank One common stock. On the basis of JPMorgan Chase's closing price on April 16, 2004 of $39.26, the 1.32 exchange ratio represented approximately $51.82 in value for each share of Bank One common stock. On announcement day, it equaled $51.77 a share or about $58 billion based on Bank One's roughly 1.12 billion shares outstanding. The deal created an enterprise with combined market capitalization of approximately $130 billion. The premium, based upon the average closing stock prices of JPMorgan Chase and Bank One for 1 month before announcement, was approximately 8% and about 14% based on announcement day closing prices. The financial advisors for JPMorgan Chase & Co were JPMorgan Securities Inc., and its legal advisor was Simpson Thacher & Bartlett LLP. The financial advisor for Bank One was Lazard Freres & Co, and the legal advisors for the deal was Wachtell, Lipton, Rosen & Katz.

JPMorgan Chase continued to trade on the New York Stock Exchange under the ticker symbol JPM. The Bank One stock traded till June 30, 2004.

Merger Effects

The merged company became the second largest banking institution in the United States. The deal eliminated 10,000 jobs. JPMorgan expected $3 billion of pretax merger costs and $2.2 billion of pretax savings over 3 years (Press Release, 2004). The retail financial services business which consisted of the consumer banking, small business banking, consumer lending activities, and middle market business was headquartered in Chicago. JPMorgan brand continued to be used for the wholesale business. Cost savings of $2.2 billion were expected to be achieved over a 3-year period. The merger-related pretax costs were expected to be $3 billion.

The combined banking occupied top positions across the whole spectrum of whole and retail financial services (Staff & Wire Report CNNMoney, 2004). In retail banking, the combined bank became number 4 in terms of branch network, number 2 in terms of core deposits retail lending, and number 2 in terms of credit cards. In investment banking, the combined bank occupied number 1 position in global syndicated loans and derivatives and number 2 position in investment grade corporate debt. In treasury and security services, the combined firm became number 1 US dollar clearing services. The merged entity became one of the largest private equity players in the market (Table 17.4).

Through the merger, a broad and balanced business mix was established with consumer banking and lending, mortgage, auto, small business, and middle market accounting for 33%, credit card services accounting for 16%, investment banking

Table 17.4 Financial highlights in the year of merger

	JPMorgan Chase	Bank One	Combined
Loans	$236,201	$141,710	$377,911
Assets	792,700	290,006	1082,706
Managed assets	827,015	326,769	1,153,784
Deposits	313,626	163,411	477,037
Total liabilities	747,743	267,595	1,015,338
Total equity	44,957	224,411	67,368

The values are given in millions of dollars

Fig. 17.1 Cumulative Stock returns surrounding merger announcement

accounting for 39%, and treasury and securities services accounting for 7%, while the remaining investment management and private banking accounted for 5%.

Stock Wealth Creation in Merger

The announcement date was January 14, 2004. On merger announcement, Bank One stock jumped 10%. The cumulative return for 249 days surrounding the window period −5 to +244 days was approximately 7.8% (Fig. 17.1).

The 3-day (−1 to +1) cumulative return during the announcement period was 3.47%. The announcement day and previous announcement day return was 0.7%. The 11-day (−5 to +5) cumulative return was 7.59%. The cumulative returns were positive in all time window periods except during the period −1 to +100 days (Table 17.5).

The values are given in millions of dollars. The average growth rate of total net revenues during the post-merger period 2005–2008 was 18.78%. The average growth rate of net income during the post-merger period was 55.53%. The average growth rate of deposits during the above period was 12.50%. The loans grew by 9% on average basis during the above period (Table 17.6).

Table 17.5 Cumulative returns in different time window period

Time window	Cumulative returns (%)
−1 to +1 days	3.47
−5 to +5 days	7.59
0 to +10 days	1.07
−1 to +100 days	−0.39
5 to +244 days	7.80

Table 17.6 Financial highlights in the year of merger and post-merger period

Year	2004	2005	2006	2007	2008
Total net revenue	42,736	54,248	61,999	71,372	67,252
Net income	4466	8483	14,444	15,365	5605
Trading assets	288,814	298,377	365,738	491,409	509,983
Securities	94,512	47,600	91,975	85,450	205,943
Loans	402,114	419,148	483,127	519,374	744,898
Total assets	1,157,248	1,198,942	1,351,520	1,562,147	2,175,052
Deposits	521,456	554,991	638,788	740,728	1,009,277
Total stockholder equity	105,653	107,211	115,790	123,221	166,884
Market capitalization	138,727	138,387	167,199	146,986	117,695

Table 17.7 Select performance ratios

Year	2004	2005	2006	2007	2008
EPS	1.59	2.43	4.16	4.51	1.41
Return on equity	6%	8%	12%	13%	2%
Return on assets	0.44	0.7	1.04	1.06	0.21
Tier 1 capital ratio	8.7	8.5	8.7	8.4	10.9
Total capital ratio	12.2	12	12.3	12.6	14.8

The return on equity and return on assets peaked during the year 2007. The EPS also peaked in the year 2007 (Table 17.7).

References

ABC News (2000) Chase to buy JP Morgan. http://abcnews.go.com/Business/story?id=89367&page=1. Accessed 20 Dec 2017

J P Morgan Chase &Co. and Bank One Corporation to Merge. https://www.businesswire.com/news/home/20040114005787/en/J.-P.-Morgan-Chase-Bank-Corporation-Merge. Accessed 2 Dec 2017

JPMorgan Chase. The history of JP Morgan Chase& Co. https://www.jpmorganchase.com/corporate/About-JPMC/document/shorthistory.pdf. Accessed 21 Dec 2017

McGeehan P, Sorkin AR (2000) Chase Manhattan to Acquire JP Morgan for $30.9 billion. https://archive.nytimes.com/www.nytimes.com/learning/teachers/featured_articles/20000914thursday.html. Accessed 5 Nov 2017

Press Release (2004) JP Morgan & Chase&Co. https://investor.shareholder.com/jpmorganchase/releasedetail.cfm?releaseid=144508. Accessed 2 Dec 2017

Staff & Wire Report CNNMoney (2004) $58B bank deal set. http://money.cnn.com/2004/01/14/news/deals/jpmorgan_bankone/. Accessed 2 Dec 2017

Charter Communications Acquisition of Time Warner Cable

18

Highlights of Charter Communications

Charter Communications is a leading broadband communication company and the fourth largest cable operator in the United States. Charter provides a full range of advanced broadband services which includes advanced Charter Spectrum TV® video entertainment programming, Charter Spectrum Internet® access, and Charter Spectrum Voice®. The company provides cost-effective broadband communications solutions like business-to-business Internet access, data networking, business telephone, video and music entertainment services, and wireless backhaul to firms. Charter's advertising sales and production services are sold under the Charter Media brand. As of December 31, 2017, Charter Communications provided video, Internet, and voice services to approximately 27.2 million residential and business customers. Charter Communications also sells video and online advertising inventory to local, regional, and national advertising customers. The company offers fiber delivered communications and managed IT solutions to large enterprise customers. The company also own and operate regional sports networks and local sports, news and community channels, and home management services in residential marketplace. The company had revenues of $41,581 million in the year 2017. During February 2013, Charter acquired Bresnan Communications Systems from Cablevision in a deal valued at US $ 1.63 billion. During March 2013, Liberty Media acquired 27.3% ownership in Charter making it the largest single shareholder in the company. Charter Communications is listed in NASDAQ stock exchange.

Time Warner Cable

Time Warner Cable is an American cable television company bought by Charter Communications. Prior to its acquisition by Charter, it was ranked as the second largest cable company in the United States by revenue behind only Comcast with

B. R. Kumar, *Wealth Creation in the World's Largest Mergers and Acquisitions*, Management for Professionals, https://doi.org/10.1007/978-3-030-02363-8_18

operations in 29 states in the United States. It was among the largest providers of video, high-speed data, and voice services in the United States. The major services offered by Time Warner Cable Business class include video, voice services, cell tower backhaul services to wireless carriers and enterprise class, cloud enabled hosting, etc. Time Warner Cable Media, the advertising sales arm of Time Warner Cable, offers national, regional, and local innovative advertising solutions.

Earlier the company was part of Warner Communications and then became the part of Time Warner. Time Warner spun off its cable operations in March 2009 to form an independent company called Time Warner Cable. In 2014, Comcast Corporation attempted to take over Time Warner Cable in a deal valued at $45.2 billion. In 2014, Liberty's holding in Time Warner Cable were spun off as separate holding company named Liberty Broadband Corporation.

Bright House Networks

Bright House Networks is the sixth largest operator of cable systems in the United States. It was the second largest operator in Florida. It was the tenth largest multichannel video service provider in the United States. The primary services offered by Bright House Networks included digital television, high-speed Internet, home security and automation, and voice services. Bright House Networks also owned and operated two 24-h local news operations Central Florida News 13 and Bay News 9. Florida News 13 served the Orlando area, while Bay News 9 served the Tampa Bay area. Bright House Networks Business Solutions provided a strong portfolio of video-, voice-, data-, and cloud-based solutions to the small and medium business segments. Bright House Networks Enterprise Solutions offers advanced, fiber-based telecommunication services to major industry verticals in the mid-market and carrier segments.

Acquisition of Time Warner Cable

Charter Communications acquisition of Time Warner Cable and Bright House Networks created the second largest US broadband provider and third largest pay-TV provider. The combination of Charter, Time Warner Cable, and Bright House Networks had the capacity to serve over 25 million customers in approximately 41 states in the United States. The US Federal Communications Commission approved the Charter's acquisition on May 6 2016. The combined company was marketed under the brand name Spectrum. Time Warner had more than 14 million customers. Bright House served more than two million customers. This acquisition of Time Warner Cable and Bright House Networks made Charter the second largest home Internet provider in the United States.

Earlier in 2013, Time Warner Cable had rejected unsolicited approaches by Charter. Time Warner Cable had found a white knight in Comcast to be acquired. But Comcast finally abandoned the transaction.

This acquisition was significant since the pay television industry faced stagnation on account of new competition from the over the web rivals like Netflix and Hulu. Charter and Time Warner Cable were less concerned about competition from providers like Netflix which do not offer live or current season programming. Time Warner Cable was more concerned by threats posed by companies like Sling TV and HBO NOW which offer current season content. The deal changed the face of the US pay-TV landscape. After the deal, Charter moved forward with its new cable and TV broadband services named "Spectrum." The deal also saw Charter expanding its footprint into key markets like Los Angeles and New York.

After the acquisition of Time Warner Cable, Charter became the second largest cable operator behind Comcast. The new company had 24 million subscribers which included 17.4 million video subscribers. Charter ranked as the third largest MVPD behind Comcast and DirecTV. The new company became the third largest pay-TV company which served more than 17 million video customers behind AT&T and Comcast.

Deal Highlights

The deal valued Time Warner Cable at $78.7 billion. Charter provided $100 in cash and shares of the new public parent company ("New Charter") which was equivalent to 0.5409 shares of Charter for each Time Warner share outstanding (Khatchatourian, 2016). The deal valued each Time Warner Cable share at approximately $195.71 on the basis of Charter's closing market price on May 20, 2015. The deal valued each Time Warner Cable share $200 based on Charter's 60 trading day volume weighted average price. In addition, Charter provided an election option for each Time Warner Cable stockholder other than Liberty Broadband Corporation ("Liberty Broadband") or Liberty Interactive Corporation. The election option stipulated that each Time Warner Shareholder will receive $115 of cash and New Charter shares which are equivalent to 0.4562 shares of Charter Communications.

Bright House was acquired for $10.4 billion. Liberty Broadband which had 25% stake in Charter helped the company to finance the acquisition of TWC and Bright House. Charter took over $21 billion in Time Warner Cable debt. The agreement between Charter and Advance/New house also involved the formation of a new partnership in which New Charter would own approximately 87% and Advance/New House will own 13% of the new company. After the merger, Liberty Broad band's stake went up to 19%. The Advance/New House Partnership obtained 13% stake in Charter. The deal consideration paid to Advance/Newhouse in the transaction involved common and convertible preferred partnership units in addition to $2 billion in cash. The common and convertible preferred partnership units can be exchanged into shares of New Charter. On completion of Time Warner deal, Liberty Broadband Corporation had agreed to purchase $4.3 billion of the newly issued shares of New Charter at a price equivalent of $176.95 per Charter share. On the completion of the partnership deal with Advance/New house, $700 million Charter shares at a price equivalent of $173 per Charter share were issued. Under the new agreement, Advance/Newhouse and Liberty Broadband were granted preemptive rights which allowed each of these companies to maintain their pro rata ownership in New Charter (Time Warner Cable Press Release, 2015). The Shareholder's agreement also provided for voting caps and participation in buybacks at specified caps and transfer restrictions related to governance matters.

The new board consisted of 13 directors which included 7 directors, 2 directors appointed by Advance/Newhouse, and 3 directors designated by Liberty Broadband. Goldman Sachs and Lion Tree Advisors were lead financial advisors to Charter with respect to Time Warner Cable transaction. Guggenheim Securities was also a financial advisor to Charter for the deal (Steele and Mckinnon, 2016). The main advisors for financing the transaction were Bank of America, Merrill Lynch, and Credit Suisse. The law firms Wachtell, Lipton, Rosen & Katz were the legal advisors for the deal. Morgan Stanley, Allen & Company, Citigroup and Centerview Partners were financial advisors for Time Warner.

Regulatory Approvals

The approval stipulation involved Charter's permission to allow its content providers to sell shows online and to face restrictions from the FCC for up to 7 years. The FCC approval conditions also required Charter to extend high-speed Internet access to another two million customers within 5 years with one million served by a broadband competitor. The acquisition was completed on May 17 2016. The deal also compelled the merged company not to impose data usage caps on customers for a fixed period of years. Another condition for the deal was the prohibition of the use of pay-TV contract language which made it harder for media companies to offer content online. Under the terms of the agreement with Public Service Commission, Charter was required to reduce customer complaint rates by 35% by 2020. It was reported that by January 2018, half of the gains were achieved. It was reported that in June 2017, Charter had to pay $13 million as penalty for failing to meet its requirement to build out its cable network as required in the approval of the deal.

Synergy from the Deal

The deal increased the combined firms' broadband network capacity which resulted in faster broadband speeds, better video products, and affordable phone service. The combination of Charter, Time Warner Cable, and Bright House created a leading broadband services and technology company which served about 23.9 million customers in 41 states. The combination would facilitate expansion into advanced broadband network which led to wider deployment of new competitive facilities based on Wi-Fi networks in public places and footprint expansion of optical networks aimed to serve small and medium businesses. It would lead into the creation of an environment of faster broadband speeds, better video products and high-definition channels, and better phone services in terms of affordability (Ruilson, 2018). There was also a scope of greater product innovation which could bring advanced services like Charter's spectrum guide and World Box. The teams at the three companies are credited with the invention of innovative products like video on demand, VOIP phone service, remote storage DVR, cable TV through app, and cloud-based user interface.

After the acquisition, Charter had plans to focus on Time Warner Cable' aging infrastructure and upgrade its operations to fully digital. The Time Warner Cable and Bright House Networks brand names will be phased out with the replacement by Charter's existing spectrum brand (Littleton, 2016). Charter had rolled out a cloud-based interactive channel guide across its existing subscribers. The user interface is designed to make it easier for subscribers to navigate through VOD viewing options and Internet surfing using connected TVs. Post-merger Charter had plans to hire 20,000 new employees in the United States to improve its customer service. Charter had added approximately 7000 customer service jobs since Rutledge took over the cable operator in February 2012. Time Warner Cable's offshore call centers were relocated to the United States. Charter Communications will switch its billing systems and new systems as a part of its post-merger integration strategy. (Shepardson, 2016). As a part of the regulatory approval conditions, Charter agreed to extend its cable lines and offer low-cost Internet services to poor families with children and low-income senior citizens. The company also had to agree to conditions like not to thwart the development of video streaming services and complying with open Internet rules for 3-year period (Lahman, 2017). In March 2017, Time Warner Cable was fully rebranded as Spectrum. The following table gives the financial highlights of Time Warner Cable (Table 18.1).

The values are given in millions of dollars except the ratios. The merger completion year was 2016.The revenues increased by approximately 43% in the post-merger year 2017. The average growth rate of revenues in the premerger period 2014–2016 was 9.3%. The income from operations and net income grew by 67% and 25% in the post-merger period 2017.

Wealth Creation in Charter Communication Time Warner Cable Deal

The first official announcement of the deal was made on May 26, 2015.One day after announcement, Charter Communications gained 2.43%. The +4 day announcement return was approximately 1.95% (Table 18.2).

Table 18.1 Financial highlights

Year	2013	2014	2015	2016	2017
Revenue	8155	9108	9754	29,003	41,581
Income from operations	909	971	1114	2456	4106
Net income/loss	−49	53	−331	820	1028
Investment in cable properties	16,556	16,652	16,375	144,396	142,712
Total assets	17,129	24,388	39,316	149,067	146,623
Total debt	14,031	20,887	35,723	61,747	70,231
Ratio of earnings to fixed charges	NA	1.06	NA	1.33	1.33

Table 18.2 Announcement period returns

Day	Returns (%)
−5	1.49
−4	0.12
−3	0.08
−2	−1.53
−1	0.36
0	−1.58
1	2.43
2	−1.36
3	−1.18
4	1.95
5	−0.46

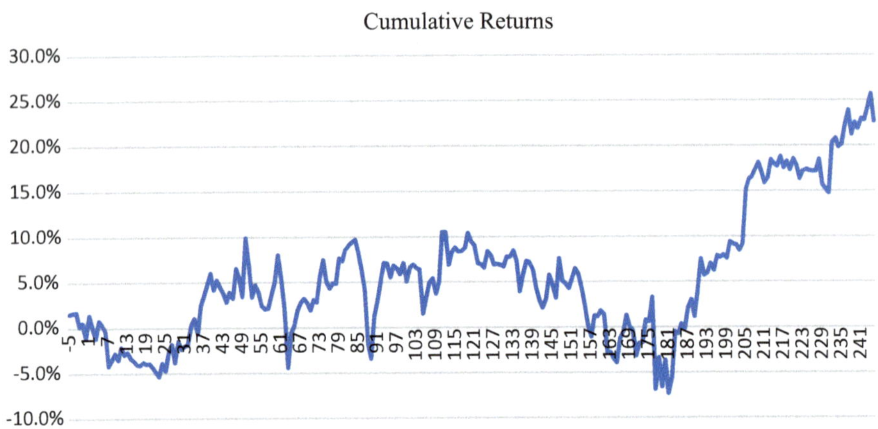

Fig. 18.1 Cumulative returns for Charter Communications during the announcement period

Table 18.3 Cumulative returns in different time window period

Day	Cumulative returns (%)
−5 to +5	0.33
−1 to +1	1.21
0 to +10	−4
0 to +100	4.50
−5 to+245	22.70

The cumulative returns for Charter Communications during the 251-day period surrounding the merger announcement (−5 day to +245 day) was 22.4% (Fig. 18.1).

The cumulative returns were negative only in the time window period of 0 to +10 day. In other periods the cumulative returns were positive (Table 18.3).

References

Khatchatourian M (2016) Charter officially acquires Time Warner Cable, Bright House. https://variety.com/2016/biz/news/charter-time-warner-cable-acquisition-official-1201777770/. Accessed 15 Dec 2017

Lahman S (2017) Time Warner is now spectrum. https://www.democratandchronicle.com/story/money/2017/03/16/time-warner-cable-now-spectrum/99257490. Accessed 20 Dec 2017

Littleton C (2016) What's next now that Time Warner Cable Merger is Complete. http://variety.com/2016/tv/news/charter-time-warner-cable-merger-completed-1201777511/. Accessed 17 Dec 2017

Ruilson L (2018) Charter says cable tv complaints are falling since merger. https://wwwtimesunioncom/business/article/Charter-says-cable-TV-complaints-are-falling-12539924php. Accessed 12 Jan 2018

Shepardson D (2016) Charter Communication completes purchase of Time Warner. https://www.reuters.com/article/us-twc-m-a/charter-communications-completes-purchase-of-time-warner-cable-idUSKCN0Y92BR. Accessed 15 Dec 2017

Steele A, Mckinnon JD (2016) Charter Communications complete acquisition of Time Warner Cable. https://www.wsj.com/articles/charter-communications-completes-55-billion-acquisition-of-time-warner-cable-1463581387. Accessed 18 Dec 2017

Time Warner Cable Press Release (2015) Charter communications to merge with Time Warner Cable and acquire Bright House networks. https://wwwtimewarnercablecom/en/about-us/press/charter-to-merge-with-time-warner-cable-and-acquire-bright-house-networkshtml. Accessed 19 Dec 2017

http://www.latimes.com/entertainment/envelope/cotown/la-et-ct-charter-time-warner-cable-20160517-snap-story.html

Actavis-Allergan Merger Deal

19

Actavis Generics

Actavis Generics is a major pharmaceutical company involved in the manufacture and commercialization of branded pharmaceutical products and generic and OTC products. Actavis has presence in over 100 countries. The company markets brand products through six franchises in key therapeutic categories. Actavis had the world's third largest generic businesses. The company had been ranked in the top 3 in 12 global markets. Actavis develops and outlicenses generic pharmaceutical products outside the United States through its Medis third-party business. Medis offers more than 200 products globally. Actavis develops biosimilar products in oncology and other therapeutic categories. Actavis have more than 40 manufacturing and distribution facilities around the world. On July 15, 2015, Actavis PLC changed its name to Allergan PLC. At the same time, the company's US and Canadian generics business continued to operate under the Actavis name. During the mid-2015 period, Allergan PLC decided to sell its generic division of the company to Teva Pharmaceuticals for $40.5 billion.

Prior to the acquisition of Allergan Inc., Actavis Generics was known as Watson Pharmaceuticals and Actavis PLC. Over the years, Actavis had grown through strategic acquisitions. The company had its IPO listing in NASDAQ exchange. In the year 1997, the company moved to New York Stock Exchange (NYSE) and began trading under the symbol WPI.

Allergan

Allergan Pharmaceuticals was established in the year 1950. Allergan developed novel formulations for specialty markets. In the year 1953, Allergan introduced the first cortisone eye drop to treat allergic inflammation and the first ophthalmic steroid decongestant. The company had its first IPO in the year 1970. In the year 1980, the

B. R. Kumar, *Wealth Creation in the World's Largest Mergers and Acquisitions*, Management for Professionals, https://doi.org/10.1007/978-3-030-02363-8_19

company was acquired by SmithKline for $259 million. In 1989, Allergan was spun off by SmithKline. In 2002, Allergan had spun off its ophthalmic surgical and contact lens care businesses into Advanced Medical Optics. During 2013, Allergan acquired MAP Pharmaceuticals for approximately $958 million. In the same year, the company sold its obesity intervention business to Apollo Endo-surgery for stock exchange of $15 million and cash payment of $75 million. Allergan had sold its generics business to Teva Pharmaceutical Industries.

Strategic Acquisitions of Actavis

In the year 2000, the pharma company acquired Schein Pharmaceutical Inc. This acquisition doubled the size of the company. In 2006, the company acquired Andrx Corporation, the Florida-based pharmaceutical company. This acquisition made Actavis the third largest specialty pharma company in the world in terms of total prescriptions. Through the Arrow Group acquisition in the year 2009, Actavis obtained international presence in more than 20 international markets. On account of the Arrow acquisition, the company also acquired the biopharmaceutical development organization Eden Bio Design of the United Kingdom. During November 2012, Watson acquired the Switzerland-based global generics Actavis Group for €4.25 billion which created the world's third largest generics company with leading positions in key established commercial markets which included the United States, United Kingdom, Nordics, Canada, Australia, and emerging markets in Central and Eastern Europe and Russia. After the acquisition, Watson adopted the Actavis' name for its global operations. During October 2013, Actavis acquired Irish pharmaceutical company Warner Chilcott PLC in a stock for stock deal valued at approximately $8.5 billion. This acquisition made Actavis the third largest US specialty pharmaceutical company with approximately $3 billion in annual revenue in year 2013. The company also achieved dominant positions in key therapeutic areas of women's health, urology, gastroenterology, and dermatology.

In 2013, Actavis completed the acquisition of Warner Chilcott which was a leading specialty pharmaceutical company involved in women's healthcare, gastroenterology, urology, and dermatology segments of branded pharmaceuticals. In the same year, Actavis had acquired Uteron Pharma for approximately $142 million in cash plus assumption of debt and other liabilities of $7.7 million and up to $ 155 million in potential future milestone payments.

During July 2014, Actavis completed the acquisition of Furiex Pharmaceuticals and Forest Transaction. There had been an increase in Actavis intangible assets as a result of the Furiex deal. Forest was a leading fully integrated specialty pharmaceutical company that marketed a portfolio of branded drug products and developed new medicines in therapeutic areas.

During 2016, Teva acquired Actavis Generics. This strategic acquisition brought together two leading generics businesses with complementary strengths, R&D, product pipelines, and portfolios. With this acquisition, Teva had 338 product registrations and FDA approvals along with leading position in the first-to-file opportunities with approximately 115 pending ANDAs in the United States. The combined company was expected to achieve at least 10% in revenue growth. Actavis projected the combined company would achieve at least 10% in revenue growth in each of the coming years.

Both Valeant and Actavis had bid for the deal for Allergan. Finally, Actavis paid $219 a share which was about 60% in cash and the rest in Actavis stock. Actavis's offer paid $85.08 a share more than the value of Allergan stock before the company was in the merger plan.

Actavis Merger with Allergan

During March 2015, Actavis completed the acquisition of Allergan Inc. in a cash and share transaction valued at $70.5 billion (Allergan News Release, 2015). The acquisition created one of the world's largest pharmaceutical companies by sales revenues. The combined company has a dominant position in global supply chain. Actavis adopted Allergan plc as its new global name and started trading under a new symbol – AGN in the New York Stock Exchange. The company name change followed the acquisition of Allergan in the year 2015.The merger created one of the top ten largest pharmaceutical companies in the world.

The company spends approximately $1.7 billion in annual R&D investment. The company have an innovative product development portfolio which exceeds 20 near term projects and world class generics pipeline. The firm has an industry dominant position in first-to-file opportunities in United States and more than 1000 marketing authorizations.

Terms of the Deal

On November 17, 2014, Actavis plc and Allergan Inc. entered into a definitive agreement under which Actavis acquired Allergan for a combination of $129.22 in cash and 0.3683 Actavis shares for each share of Allergan common stock (Press Release, 2015). On the basis of the closing price of Actavis shares on November 14, 2014, the transaction was valued approximately at $66 billion or $219 per Allergan share. The deal was unanimously approved by the Boards of Directors of Actavis and Allergan with support from both the management teams. Actavis was expected to have a new capital structure of new equity and debt of investment grade rating for long-term financial flexibility. After the merger, the Actavis shareholders owned 72% of the issued and outstanding Actavis ordinary shares. The Allergan shareholders held 28% of the issued and outstanding Actavis ordinary shares. Actavis issued approximately 128 million ordinary shares to pay the stock portion of the merger consideration to Allergan stockholders and assumed Allergan equity-based awards on closure of merger. The stock options of Allergan common stock were converted into Actavis stock. The outstanding restricted shares of Allergan were converted into a number of restricted Actavis ordinary shares. The number of restricted shares were determined by multiplying the number of shares of Allergan Restricted Shares by the Stock Award Exchange Ratio. J P Morgan was the financial advisor for Actavis, while the Bank of America, Merrill Lynch, and Goldman Sachs were the financial advisors for Allergan. The combined company were led by Brenton L Saunders, the CEO and President of Actavis. The merger agreement stipulated Actavis to pay Allergan a termination fee of $1.3 billion if Actavis terminates the merger agreement since Actavis share issuance proposal is not approved by the Actavis shareholders. The merger agreement required Allergan to pay Actavis a termination fee of $2.1 billion if Allergan terminated the merger agreement. The aggregate cash portion of the merger consideration was approximately $39 billion.

Financing of the Deal

The deal was financed through a combination of available cash on hand of Actavis and Allergan. The financing involved $8.9 billion in proceeds from the issuance and sale of common equity interests and/or mandatorily convertible preferred equity interests by Actavis and third-party debt financing in terms of senior unsecured term loan facilities, issuance, and sale of unsecured notes by Actavis Funding SCS. The senior term loan facilities consisted of a tranche of 3-year senior unsecured term loans in an original aggregate principal amount of $2.75 billion and a tranche of 5-year senior unsecured term loans in an original aggregate principal amount of $2.75 billion. The agreement stipulated issuance and sale of senior unsecured notes up to an amount of $22 billion. There was also a senior unsecured bridge facility bridge up to $30.9 billion (SEC Filings, 2015).

Benefits of Acquisition

The acquisition of Allergan created a global brand pharmaceutical business with leading positions in key therapeutic categories. The acquisition created one of the fastest and dynamic pharmaceutical companies in global healthcare. The combined company achieved dominant position in segments like eye care, neurosciences/CNS, medical aesthetics, dermatology, gastroenterology, and urology. The combination led to expansion in approximately 100 countries. The combined pharmaceutical company had six blockbuster franchises with combined revenues of approximately $15 billion which included annual revenues in excess of $3 billion in eye care, neurosciences/CNS and medical aesthetics, dermatology, and plastic surgery. The combined pharma company was in possession of a portfolio of well-known brands like Botox®, Restasis®, Juvederm®, Namenda XR®, Linzess®, and Lo Loestrin ® Fe. The combined pharmaceutical company's experienced sales and marketing organization provide support to more than a dozen medical specialists. The combined companies were able to have an expanded commercial presence in regions like Canada, Europe, Southeast Asia, Latin America, China, and India. The combined was expected to achieve growth in international markets through its enhanced portfolio of brands, generics, branded generic, and over-the-counter products. The product pipeline of both Actavis and Allergan was focused on core therapeutic areas with molecules in dermatology, aesthetics, eye care, CNS, GI, anti-infectives, and urology. The generic pipeline consisted of approximately 230 new drug application pending for FDA approval and 70 first to file applications. Allergan had a strong portfolio of well-known brands and premier pharmaceutical pipeline of medicines, generics, biosimilars, OTC products, and devices. The company was also the fourth largest distributor in the United States. The strength of Allergan lies in its fully integrated business model. The combination was expected to drive industry leading top- and bottom-line growth. The consolidated pharmaceutical company is expected to generate compound annual growth rate of at least 10%. The addition of Allergan's portfolio consisting of blockbuster therapeutic franchises doubled the revenues of Actavis' North American Specialty brand businesses. Allergan's blockbuster franchises in ophthalmology, neurosciences and medical aesthetics, dermatology and plastic surgery complemented Actavis existing blockbuster CNS, gastroenterology, and Women's Health franchises to create a major portfolio across a broad range of therapeutic areas.

Synergy

The acquisition was expected to result in $1.8 billion in operating and financial synergies. Allergan was expecting $475 million of annual savings from its Project Endurance. Actavis was expecting operating cash flow in excess of $ 8 billion in the year 2016. Rapid deleveraging was also expected from the deal. Tables 19.1 and 19.2 provides the financial highlights of Actavis and Allergan. Table 19.3 shows the pro forma combined operational data in year 2013.

Table 19.1 Financial highlights of Actavis

Year	2009	2010	2011	2012
Revenues	2793	3566.9	4584.4	5914.9
Operating income	383.9	305.4	523.4	315.7
Net income	222	184.4	260.9	97.3
EPS	2.11	1.51	2.1	0.77
Total assets	5772.4	5686.6	6698.3	14114.8
Total debt	1457.8	1016.1	1033	6433.3
Total equity	3023.10	3282.6	3562.5	3856.4

The values except EPS are given in millions of dollars

Table 19.2 Financial highlights of Allergan

Year	2009	2010	2011	2012	2013
Revenues	4503.60	4919.4	5261	5646.6	6300.4
Operating income	928	258.6	1374.6	1611	1809.3
Net income	621.3	0.6	934.5	1098.8	985.1
EPS	2.05	0	3.07	3.64	3.32
Total assets	7536.60	8308.10	8508.6	9179.3	10574.3
Total debt	1491.3	1534.2	1515.4	1512.4	2098.3
Total equity	4822.8	4757.7	5309.6	5837.1	6463.2

The values are given in millions of dollars except EPS

Table 19.3 Pro forma combined operational data in year 2013

Revenues	20,809.00
Operating income	−5310.50
EPS	−14.16
Total assets	137,447.80
Shareholder equity	68,820.00

The values are in millions of dollars

Merger Announcement Effect on Wealth Creation

The public announcement of the merger was made on November 17, 2013. The acquisition was completed on March 17, 2014.

The cumulative returns for the 228-day period (−19 to +231 days) surrounding the merger announcement is given in Fig. 19.1. The cumulative returns for the above period were 23%.

The announcement day return was 1.7%. One day after announcement, the stock price increased by 8.7%. On day 5 after announcement, the stock price increased by 2.7% (Table 19.4).

The merger announcement had a positive impact for wealth creation for Allergan stock. The stock registered positive gains in all time window periods (Table 19.5).

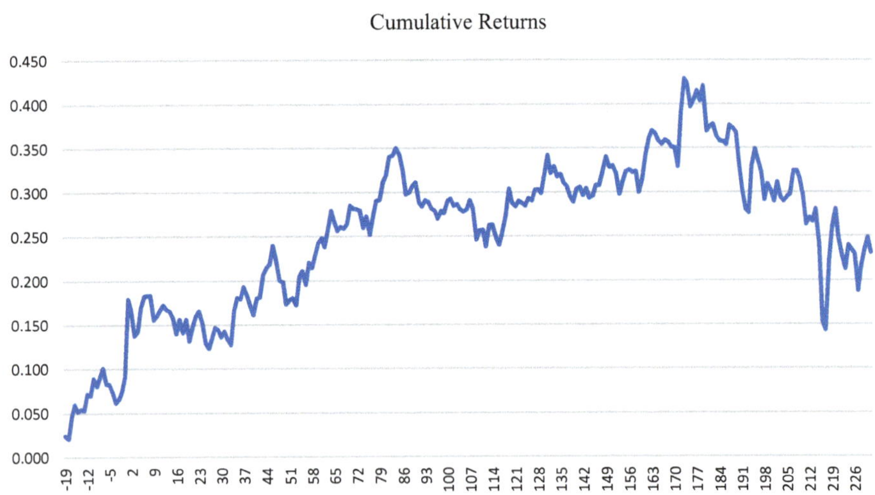

Fig. 19.1 Cumulative returns for Actavis during the merger period

Table 19.4 Returns for Allergan surrounding merger period

Time	Returns (%)
−5	−0.1
−4	−0.9
−3	−1.2
−2	0.4
−1	0.9
0	1.7
1	8.7
2	−1.3
3	−2.8
4	0.5
5	2.7

Table 19.5 Cumulative returns in different time window period

Time period	Cumulative returns (%)
1 to +1 days	11.30
3 to 3 days	6.40
5 to 5 days	8.70
10 to 10 days	9.10
15 to 15 days	9.90
19 to +231 days	23

References

Allergan News Release (2015) Actavis completes Allergan acquisition. https://www.allergan.com/news/news/thomson-reuters/actavis-completes-allergan-acquisition. Accessed 4 Jan 2017

Press Release (2015) Actavis Plc is now Allergan Plc. https://www.allergan.com/news/news/thomson-reuters/actavis-plc-is-now-allergan-plc. Accessed 4 Jan 2017

SEC Filings (2015) Form S-4/A. http://services.corporate-ir.net/SEC. Enhanced/SecCapsule.aspx? c=65778&fid=9867591

Dell's Acquisition of EMC

20

Many high-profile mergers had happened in the information technology sector. Mergers in technology industry sector like Compaq Corporation's acquisition of Digital Equipment in year 1998; Hewlett Packard Co.'s acquisition of Compaq in year 2002 and Burroughs Corp's purchase of Sperry Corp in the year 1986 were not up to expectations. The merger of Wellfleet Communications with Synoptic Communications in the year 1994 was a failed merger.

Dell

Dell was once the largest PC maker in United States. In the year 2013, Dell and private equity firm Silver Lake Partners took Dell private through one of the largest leveraged buyout valued at $24.4 billion. Dell Technologies is the world's largest privately controlled technology company in the world. Dell Technologies is a leader in the traditional technology. Dell Technologies Solutions encompasses software-defined data centers, flash arrays, hybrid cloud, converged and hyper-converged infrastructure, and cloud-native software application development tools, mobile, and security solutions. The products and services of Dell are classified into Client Solutions Group (CSG), Infrastructure Solutions Group (ISG), and VMware. The offerings of CSG include branded hardware such as personal computers, notebooks, branded peripherals, third-party software, and peripherals. Almost 50 per cent of CSG revenues are generated by sales to customers in the Americas, and the rest are accounted from customers from Europe, the Middle East, and Africa. The ISG offers comprehensive portfolio of advanced next-generation storage solutions which includes all flash arrays, scale-out file, object platforms, and software defined solutions. The server portfolio includes high-performance rack, blade, tower, and hyper scale server. ISG offerings also include software peripherals, warranty services, etc. The division also offers Virtustream product and service offerings. Virtustream's

B. R. Kumar, *Wealth Creation in the World's Largest Mergers and Acquisitions*, Management for Professionals, https://doi.org/10.1007/978-3-030-02363-8_20

cloud software and infrastructure service solutions enable customers to migrate, run, and manage critical applications in cloud-based IT environments. VMware provides compute, cloud, mobility, networking, and security infrastructure software to businesses. Approximately 50% of revenues of ISG and VMware are accounted from Americas. Other businesses of Dell Technologies include RSA, SecureWorks, Pivotal, and Boomi. RSA provides cybersecurity solutions to organizations to recue IP theft, fraud, and cybercrime. SecureWorks is a global provider of intelligence-driven information security solutions to clients to protect clients from cyberattacks. Pivotal provides cloud native platform for software development and IT operations. Boomi is involved in cloud-based integration. The R&D spends for Dell Technologies were $1.1 billion, $2.6 billion, and $4.4 billion in the year 2016, 2017, and 2018, respectively.

EMC

EMC was the largest provider of data storage systems by market share. The main competitors of EMC were NetApp, IBM, Hewlett Packard Enterprise, and Hitachi Data Systems. EMC was founded in the year 1979. The EMC was named after the founders Egan, Marion, and Curly. In the year 1981, EMC introduced its first 64 kilobyte memory boards for the Prime Computer. In the mid-1980s, EMC introduced computer data storage types and networked storage platforms. In the 1990s the company shifted its focus from memory boards to storage systems. In early 2000, the EMC business model was transformed from high-end storage platforms to a portfolio of platforms, software, and services which facilitated organizations to deliver IT as a service through cloud computing. In 2009 EMC and Cisco with financial support from VMare and Intel formed joint venture called VCE to develop products and services for the converged infrastructure and cloud computing markets. In the year 2013, EMC introduced a new company called Pivotal which combined technologies from VMare and EMC and delivered Platform – as a Service product. Unlike other corporations, EMC is structured as federation of affiliated and independent companies. The major company VMare, the virtualization giant is run entirely as a separate company to the point of being its own publicly traded stock. Another major company was Pivotal which was created to enable companies to become more digitally focused through partnership involving EMC, VMware, and GE. After the deal, EMC spun out Virtustream which was bought for $1.2 billion in year 2015.

Acquisition of EMC

On October 12, 2015, Dell made the public announcement to acquire in a cash and stock deal valued at $74 billion. The deal was the largest ever acquisition in the technology sector. The acquisition combined Dell's enterprise server, personal computer, and mobile businesses with EMC's enterprise storage business.

Financial Terms of the Deal

Dell paid $24.05 per share of EMC and $9.05 per share of tracking stock in VMware. EMC shareholders received 0.11146 shares of new tracking stock for each EMC share. There were issues related to how the deal would be taxed. Dell was expected to pay a huge debt load of $50 billion. After completing the EMC deal, Dell paid down about $9.5 billion in gross debt. Shares of the Class V Common stock were approved for listing on the New York Stock Exchange under the ticker symbol "DVMT' and began trading on September 7, 2016.

Dell Technologies financed the EMC merger transaction, the repayment of the foregoing indebtedness of EMC and Dell outstanding as of the closing of the EMC merger transaction, and the payment of related fees and expenses, with debt financing arrangements in an aggregate principal amount of approximately $45.9 billion, equity financing arrangements of approximately $4.4 billion, and cash on hand of approximately $7.8 billion.

The merger was closed on September 7, 2016. As a result of merger, EMC was renamed to Dell EMC.

Synergies from the Deal

By means of acquiring EMC, Dell Technologies focuses on offering next-generation solutions through the Client Solutions Group, Infrastructure Solutions Group, VMware Inc., RSA Information Security, SecureWorks Corp, Pivotal Software Inc., Boomi, and Virtustream Inc.

The deal brought together the leading provider of key computer storage products and top makers of servers and personal of servers and personal computers (Womack, 2017). The acquisition was to facilitate Dell to become one stop shop for business customers (Miller, 2016). The combined Dell EMC was named Dell Technologies. After the merger, Dell Technologies became world's number one seller of storage systems, number two market position with respect to servers and number three position with respect to personal computers.

The combination created $74 billion market leader with expansive technology portfolio consisting of hybrid cloud, software-defined data center, converged infrastructure, platform as a service, data analytics, mobility, and cybersecurity. The merger resulted in the creation of the world's largest privately controlled technology company. The combination created the flexibility for innovation and investment in R&D. The deal united family businesses of Dell, Dell EMC, Pivotal, RSA, SecureWorks, Virtustream, and VMare. Dell became the technology leader in 20 Gartner Magic Quadrants. The acquisition combined Dell's go to market strength with small business and mid-market customers and EMC's strength with large enterprises.

Dell Technologies serves 98 per cent of the Fortune 500 companies. The two major businesses are the Dell client solutions business and the Dell EMC infrastructure solutions. The major businesses of Dell Technologies include Boomi, Pivotal

RSA, SecureWorks, Virtustream, and VMare. The company has a portfolio of more than 20,000 patents and applications. The two company's product lines were quite complementary without many overlaps. The acquisition gave Dell a strong enterprise storage component and entry into hybrid cloud computing market. The acquisition maintained EMC's storage position while extending Dell's servers and build customer support for the converged offerings (Dell EMC PressRelease, 2016).

The focus of Dell was on hardware which was a slow growing sector of IT industry. The software sector had higher growth rates and profit margins. Among the EMC's federated holdings, VMware was the crown jewel which was driving lots of value for Dell EMC. VMware was giving Dell Technologies much relevance in the cloud computing era. After the acquisition, Dell Technologies signed on 10,000 new business customers (Barker, 2017). In one of its largest nongovernment contracts, Dell became General Electric Co.'s primary IT infrastructure supplier after the deal. After the acquisition, sales in the fiscal second quarter rose by 48 per cent from a year ago. The scope of the acquisition was to provide bigger product line and hyperconverged systems (Furrier, 2017).

Other Acquisitions

In 2018, VMware Inc. acquired VeloCloud to build on its network virtualization platform VMware NSX and expand its networking portfolio. The total purchase price was $499 million, net of cash acquired of $24 million. The purchase price included $142 million of identifiable intangible assets and $326 million of goodwill. During the second quarter of the year 2018, VMware had completed the acquisition of Wavefront and Apteligent Inc. These acquisitions were aimed to enhance the development of VMware Inc.'s Cloud services and other technologies (Ram, 2016). The aggregate purchase price for the two acquisitions was $323 million, inclusive of the fair value of the company's existing investment in Wavefront of $69 million and cash acquired of $35 million. The financial highlights of Dell Technologies is given in the following table (Table 20.1).

The share price of VMware plunged from $82.09 a day before announcement to $43.84. But later the stock recovered to trade around $73.39 a share.

Table 20.1 Financial highlights of Dell Technologies

Year	2015	2016	2017	2018
Net revenues	54,142	50,911	61,642	78,660
Gross margin	8896	8387	12,959	20,054
Cash and cash equivalents	5398	6322	9474	13,942
Total assets	48,029	45,122	118,206	122,281
Long term debt	11,071	10,650	43,061	43,998
Stockholder equity	2904	1466	13,243	9326

The values are given in millions of dollars

References

Barker C (2017) Dell and EMC one year on. How has it gone so far? https://www.zdnet.com/article/dell-emc-one-year-on-how-has-it-gone-so-far/. Accessed 07 Jan 2018

Dell EMC Press Release (2016) Historic Dell and EMC Merger Complete; forms world's largest privately controlled tech company. https://www.emc.com/about/news/press/2016/20160907-01.htm. Accessed 07 Jan 2018

Furrier J (2017) One-year birthday of $67 billion mega merger with Dell EM; Exclusive with Michael Dell. https://www.forbes.com/sites/siliconangle/2017/09/08/one-year-birthday-of-67-billion-mega-merger-with-dell-emc-exclusive-with-michael-dell/#38c653593068. Accessed 07 Jan 2018

Miller R (2016) $67 billion Dell EMC deal closes today. https://techcrunch.com/2016/09/07/67-billion-dell-emc-deal-becomes-official-today. Accessed 07 Jan 2018

Ram ML (2016) The Gamblers behind Tech's biggest deal ever. http://fortune.com/dell-emc-merger-tech-biggest-deal/. Accessed 08 Jan 2018

Womack B (2017) Dell benefits in first year after EMC merger with sales up. https://www.bloomberg.com/news/articles/2017-09-07/dell-reports-sales-of-19-billion-on-anniversary-of-emc-deal. Accessed 07 Jan 2018

Altria Group's Spin-Off of Philip Morris International Inc.

21

Philip Morris International Inc. was incorporated in 1987. Philip Morris International (PMI) is a major international tobacco company which employs 81000 people. PMI owns 6 of the top 15 international brands which include Marlboro. The company operates 46 production facilities in 32 different countries. The company employs 400 plus R&D scientists, engineers, and technicians who are working on smoke-free products (Philips Morris International Annual Report, 2017).

PMI cigarettes are sold in more than 180 markets. The international market of PMI in the year 2017 was 28%. In 2017, PMI's total cigarette and heated tobacco unit shipment amounted to 798.2 billion units. Marlboro brand of PMI is the best-selling international brand which accounted for 35% of its total cigarette shipment volume in year 2017. The other leading international cigarette brands are Bond Street, Chesterfield, L&M, Lark, and Philip Morris. Seven international cigarette brands contributed approximately 75% of cigarette shipment volume in 2017. PMI also owns a number of important local cigarette brands, such as Dji Sam Soe, Sampoerna A, and Sampoerna U in Indonesia; Fortune and Jackpot in the Philippines; Belmont and Canadian Classics in Canada; and Delicados in Mexico. The financial highlights of PMI are given in the following table (Table 21.1).

Philip Morris International Inc. Spin-Off

On August 29, 2007, Altria Group had announced its intention to spin off Philips Morris International tobacco arm (PMI) which sold Marlboro cigarettes outside the United States (Associated Press, 2007). On account of litigation, regulation, and declining sales, Altria wanted to unlock the value of (PMI) by spinning off the overseas operations into an independent entity. In the year before spin-off announcement, PMI had made profits of $8.45 billion through sales of 831 billion cigarettes

B. R. Kumar, *Wealth Creation in the World's Largest Mergers and Acquisitions*, Management for Professionals, https://doi.org/10.1007/978-3-030-02363-8_21

Table 21.1 Financial highlights of PMI

Year	2013	2014	2015	2016	2017
Net revenues	80029	80106	73908	73953	78098
Gross profit	20807	19331	17429	17294	18316
Operating income	13515	11702	10623	10815	11503
Net earnings	8850	7658	7032	7250	6341
Capital expenditures	1200	1153	960	1172	1548
Total assets	38168	35187	33956	36851	42968
Total debt	27678	29455	28480	29067	34339

The values are given in millions of dollars

with revenues of $48 billion. PMI had seven of the top ten brands which included Parliament, Bond Street, Lark, and Marlboro.

The spin-off of PMI is the second in a corporate restructuring that saw Altria spin off its Kraft Foods. During 2007, Altria Group had spun off its majority stake in Kraft Foods (Deal Book, 2011). Kraft was the world's second largest food company behind Nestle. The spin-off was expected to improve Kraft's ability to make strategic acquisitions. The spin-off created an environment for Kraft to improve their focus on businesses and enhance debt capacity of the firm. Under the spin-off plan, Altria distributed 89% stake in Kraft to shareholders. Altria shareholders received 0.7 share of Kraft for every Altria share they owned. Altria converted its class B shares of Kraft stock into Class A shares before the distribution. This spin-off was tax-free for shareholders except for those who received cash in lieu of fractional shares for amounts less than one Kraft share. The spun-off brought 1.5 billion more Kraft shares to market. In 1988, Kraft was acquired by Philip Morris. The $13 billion deal was part of a strategy adopted by Philips Morris to diversify outside tobacco. After the acquisition, the new group had a number of popular brands like Marlboro cigarettes, Miller Genuine Draft beer, and Maxwell House coffee. In 1989, Kraft acquired General Foods. In 1990, Kraft acquired Jacobs Suchard which owned Toblerone and Milka chocolates for $4.2 billion. In 2000, Philip Morris in one of the largest leveraged buyout bought Nabisco Holdings for $19.2 billion thereby enlarging the Kraft family. In the year 2001, Philip Morris sold 16% of the subsidiary thereby raising $8.68 billion. In 2002, Philip Morris sold off the Miller Brewing Company to South African Breweries. In 2003, Philip Morris changed its name to the Altria Group.

During the year 2008, Altria Group completed the spin-off of Philips Morris International Inc. (PMI) to the shareholders of Altria Group, Inc. Altria shareholders received one share of PMI for every share of Altria common stock (Altria Press Release, 2008). After the spin-off, PMI shares started trading under the symbol "PM" in different stock exchanges like New York Stock Exchange, NYSE Euronext Paris, and SWX Swiss Exchanges. Altria shares continued to trade under the symbol "MO" on the NYSE. On spin-off announcement, Altria shares rose 59 cents to $69.66. The shares had traded as high as $70.98 before the announcement.

The Philips Morris International business had better growth opportunities in emerging markets than the Philip Morris USA (Bary, 2008). The cigarette consumption has fallen steadily in the United States since 1981. PMI was perceived to be an attractive growth vehicle through mergers and acquisitions. The spin-off was part of the company strategy to improve each unit's focus on its specific market dynamics. The spin-off was aimed at insulating cigarette business from the US litigation. In other words, the spun-off cleared the international tobacco business from the legal and regulatory constraints which were faced by its domestic partner Philip Morris USA. The spin-off plan left Altria with its much smaller domestic tobacco business which still ranked as the biggest in the United States.

The spin-off saved $250 million in corporate costs between the two companies which included the closure of Altria's corporate headquarters near Grand Central Station in Manhattan. On account of the decline in the US cigarette market, Philips Morris have been experimenting in the smokeless tobacco market. Altria's competitor, Reynolds American Inc., had brought the Conwood smokeless tobacco company in the year 2006 to expand into the growing smokeless tobacco market. Altria had over 50% market share of the US cigarette market but had only 15% market share in the international market. PMI was one of the top three global players alongside China National Tobacco and British American Tobacco. PMI could target topline sales growth in emerging markets. The spun-off of PMI was intended to provide the strategic impetus for its growth (Dorfman, 2007). After the spun-off, Altria owned Philip Morris USA, Philip Morris Capital Corp., which was the finance arm of Philip Morris and 29% stake in the London-based brewer SAB Miller. Under the spin-off, Altria shareholders got shares in a stand-alone Philip Morris International. PMI oversees operations in more than 160 countries (Clark, 2007).

The spun-off of the world's largest publicly traded tobacco company was expected to deliver value for shareholders (Financial Times, 2007). Philip Morris International had a market value of more than $100 billion with operations in more than 100 countries and market share of 25% in cigarettes outside the United States excluding China. Both Altria and Philip Morris International have trailed key domestic and overseas competitors over the past few years in profit growth. During the spin-off period, Marlboro's sales volume worldwide had been down by about 4% during the past 6 years. Investors and company were worried that litigants would succeed in blocking breakups of the group. During the spin-off period, sharp drop in individual and class action claims against the industry were witnessed. In the United States, cigarette consumption was declining at a 3–4% annual rate. The focus of PMI was on China which had an estimated market of $100 billion.

After the spun-off, New Altria traded at a lower valuation than Philip Morris International. It had 13 times estimated 2008 profits of $1.66 a share, while Philip Morris International traded for 16 times estimated 2008 earnings of $3.17 a share. In 2006, PMI had operating cash flow of approximately $6.2 billion.

Philip Morris International had been slow with innovations in "light" and flavored cigarettes. Both Altria and Philip Morris International had strong balance sheets with huge annual cash flows. The New Altria also had an ambitious cost reduction program which had yielded $300 million in annual savings by 2010. Comparatively PMI sales were almost double than that of the US unit in the year before spun-off. During that period, PMI's revenues were $48.26 billion, and that of

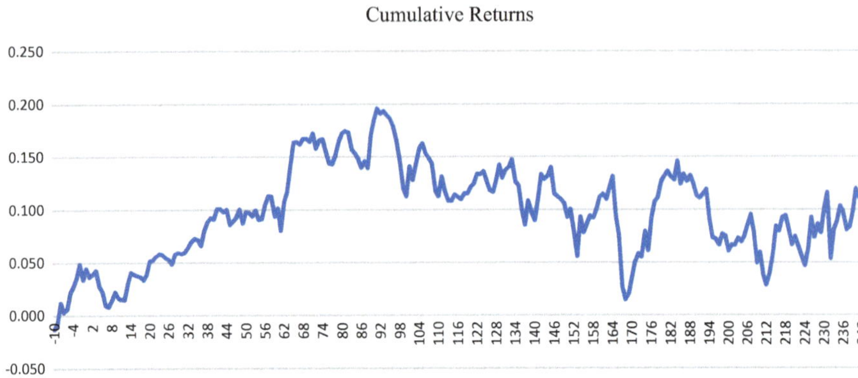

Fig. 21.1 Cumulative abnormal returns

Philip Morris USA was $18.47 billion. In 2006, PMI sold 831 billion cigarettes catapulting the company to the largest nongovernment tobacco company in terms of volume. The spin-off business was better placed for more aggressive strategy on share buybacks, cutting costs, and introduction of new products. To expand overseas, PMI acquired majority stakes in existing foreign tobacco companies in Mexico, the Dominican Republic, and Pakistan. Philip Morris USA has been focusing on marketing of moist chewing tobacco and other smokeless products. Though PMI have approximately 15% share of the international cigarette market, only 5% of its profits came from emerging markets which made up about 60% of the international cigarette market.

Stock Wealth Creation for Altria Group

The spin-off announcement date was August 29, 2007. The announcement day return for Altria was approximately 1%. The stock price declined by 1% on the day after announcement. The cumulative returns during the 252-day period (−10 to +242) days were approximately 11% (Fig. 21.1)

References

Altria Press Release (2008) Altria Group, Inc. completes spin off of Philips Morris International Inc. http://investor.altria.com/phoenix.zhtml?c=80855&p=irol-newsArticle&ID=1123169. Accessed 09 Jan 2018

Associated Press (2007) Altria to spin off Philips Morris. http://www.nbcnews.com/id/20494757/ns/business-world_business/t/altria-spin-philip-morris-international/#.Wx1tlIozbIU. Accessed 9 Jan 2018

Bary A (2008) The long awaited spin off of Philips Morris from Altria is the smart thing to do. https://www.barrons.com/articles/SB120675306208973587. Accessed 9 Jan 2018

Clark A (2007) Altria to spin off Philips International. https://www.theguardian.com/business/2007/aug/29/14. Accessed 9 Jan 2018

Deal Book (2011) Kraft, From Roll up to Spinoff. https://dealbook.nytimes.com/2011/08/04/kraft-from-roll-up-to-spin-off/. Accessed 9 Jan 2018.

Dorfman B (2007) Altria to spin off international unit.https://www.reuters.com/article/us-altria-spinoff/altria-to-spin-off-international-unit-idUSWNAS308620070829. Accessed 9 Jan 2018

Financial Times (2007) Altria to split up Philips Morris. https://www.ft.com/content/4269750e-5642-11dc-ab9c-0000779fd2ac. Accessed 9 Jan 2018

Philips Morris International Annual Report (2017) https://www.pmi.com/investor-relations/reports-filings. Accessed 9 Jan 2018

Vodafone AirTouch Merger 22

Highlights of Vodafone

Vodafone Group Plc is one of the world's major telecommunications groups with presence in Europe, Middle East, Africa, and Asia Pacific. The company has stakes in different markets through subsidiary undertakings, joint ventures, associated undertakings, and investments. In regions where the company does not hold an equity stake, Vodafone has entered into arrangements with network operators to market global products and services with varying levels of brand association. Vodafone provides mobile networks in 26 countries and fixed services in 17 countries. Tables 22.1 and 22.2 shows the financial and operational highlights of Vodafone.

Vodafone acquired Liberty Global operations in Germany, the Czech Republic, Hungary, and Romania for €18.4 billion. The acquisition was expected to yield significant potential value creation in terms of synergies amounting to €7.5 billion. This acquisition led to Vodafone becoming the next-generation infrastructure owner in Europe. It accelerated Vodafone's position as Europe's leading fixed line challenger (Vodafone Investor Presentation, 2018). This merger facilitated national cable coverage in Germany by means of merging non-overlapping regional assets. Vodafone got access to 30.8 million mobile customers, ten million broadband connections, and 14 million TV households. Through this acquisition, Vodafone aimed to deliver gigabit speeds to around 25 million German homes by 2022. Post-acquisition completion, the estimated annual cost and capex synergies from the deal was expected to be approximately €535 million. The total NPV of cost and capex synergies were estimated to be over €6 billion. The net present value of over €1.5 billion was expected in terms of revenue synergies.

B. R. Kumar, *Wealth Creation in the World's Largest Mergers and Acquisitions*, Management for Professionals, https://doi.org/10.1007/978-3-030-02363-8_22

Table 22.1 Financial metrics of Vodafone in € millions

Year	2016	2017	2018
Group revenues	49,810	47,631	46,571
Operating profit	1320	3725	4299
Profit/loss	−5122	−6079	2788

Table 22.2 Operational metrics of Vodafone in millions

Year	2016	2017	2018
European mobile customers	121.4	120.7	118.7
AMAP mobile customers	371.2	395	417.1
Group fixed broadband customers	13.4	18	19.7
Group consumer converged customers	3.1	3.8	5.5

Vodafone AirTouch Deal

On January 15, 1999, Vodafone Group Plc and AirTouch Communications Inc. announced plans to merger thereby creating one of the world's leading mobile telecommunications group (Cheyne and Hayes, 1999). The executive management of the new group was headed by Vodafone Chief Executive Chris Gent and AirTouch Chairman and CEO Sam Ginn became the Chairman of the board. The combined company was called Vodafone AirTouch Plc. The new headquarters were in Newbury, England, with San Francisco, California, as the US/Asia Pacific regional headquarters and technical center for the combined group. Vodafone Group PLC of Britain had acquired AirTouch Communications Inc. for $56 billion. At the time of the deal, AirTouch was in merger talks with Bell Atlantic Corp. Bell Atlantic declined to counter Vodafone's estimated $56 billion deal offer. The deal valued at $125 was the largest cross border merger during that period.

AirTouch was spun off in the year 1994 from Pacific Telesis Group which was acquired by SBC Communications Inc. At the time of the deal, Vodafone Group was a leading global provider of mobile telecommunications services. Vodafone had presence in mobile operations in the United Kingdom, Australia, Egypt, France, Germany, Greece, Malta, the Netherlands, New Zealand, Fiji, South Africa, Sweden, and Uganda. Vodafone Ventures served almost ten million customers on the basis of ownership share of its global ventures. The company had cellular network interests in 13 countries in Europe, Africa, and Australasia. In 1995, the company introduced cellular technology. The company employed over 11,500 employees worldwide during the period. During the merger period, the company had approximately 9.5 million customers worldwide.

During the acquisition period, AirTouch Communications was the largest wireless company in the United States based on the total number of customers served by its ventures. AirTouch owned interests in cellular, paging, and personal communications services in the United States, Belgium, Egypt, Germany, India, Italy, Japan, Poland, Portugal, Romania, South Korea, Spain, and Sweden. The company also had an interest in the Global star satellite system. AirTouch served over 17 million customers based on its ownership share of global ventures. AirTouch had cellular, PCS, and paging interest in 13 countries in North America, Europe, Asia, and Africa. AirTouch ventures were licensed to serve more than 700 million people. With 15 years' experience as mobile pioneer, AirTouch had expertise in all major technologies. In terms of international activities, AirTouch had network interests in Belgium, Egypt, Germany, India, Italy, Japan, Poland, Portugal, Romania, South Korea, Spain, and Sweden. The international interests of Vodafone were licensed to serve more than 550 million people. The company had been following the strategy of increasing interests in core cellular investments and new license opportunities.

Characteristics of Merger

Vodafone AirTouch merger was billed as the merger of equals to create mobile telecommunication leader. At the time of union, the combined market capitalization was $110 billion. The combined company became the third largest UK public company with operations in 23 countries. The combined company had 23 million mobile customers. The combination was part of the expansion strategy to achieve leadership position in next-generation mobile technology. The deal was approved by the US Federal Communications Commission. The European Commission approved the deal with the condition that Vodafone had to divest its 17. 2% stake in the German mobile operator E plus. The new merged company held double the weight of Vodafone in the FTSE 100 index. Both Vodafone and AirTouch named seven members to the merged company.

Financial Terms of the Deal

The deal envisaged equity split of approximately 50% each to Vodafone and AirTouch. AirTouch shareholders received five new ordinary Vodafone shares (0.5 ADR) plus $9 cash for each AirTouch share which represented current value for each Air Touch common share of $97. The new Vodafone shares were delivered in the form of Vodafone Air Touch ADRs which represented 10 Vodafone AirTouch ordinary shares. The financial advisors for AirTouch was Morgan Stanley Dean Witter & Co. The combined Vodafone AirTouch's shares remained listed on the London Stock Exchange and New York Stock Exchange in the form of American Depository Receipts. Goldman Sachs was the sole financial advisor to Vodafone. Goldman Sachs was the lead arranger for $10 billion senior credit facility for Vodafone to finance costs related to the merger.

Practical Issues in Merger

The merger was characterized by a number of tax and practical issues. In tax perspective, the merger was termed as reverse triangular merger which effectively allowed AirTouch's US shareholders to defer tax on gains made on AirTouch shares to the extent they received equity in Vodafone. The process involved creation of a new US subsidiary which was then merged into AirTouch. In exchange for the shares being canceled, AirTouch shareholders received American Depository Receipts in Vodafone. As Vodafone was a foreign corporation, it had to satisfy additional US tax requirements designed to ensure that US assets are not moved abroad. The merger technique used was known as reverse triangular merger. The step involved establishment of a wholly owned US subsidiary which is termed as Merger Sub. The Merger Sub merged with AirTouch under the provisions of Delaware law. The Merger Sub ceased to exist on the merger becoming effective. AirTouch became the surviving corporation. The existing shares of common stock in AirTouch were canceled and converted into the right to receive ordinary shares in Vodafone plus $9 in cash. Vodafone now known as Vodafone AirTouch issued Vodafone AirTouch shares through ADR facility to the holders of the canceled AirTouch shares. The merger agreement stipulated that AirTouch had to make a payment of US $ 1 billion to Vodafone in case the merger agreement was terminated in circumstances like failure to obtain shareholder approval of the merger. The penalty fee was also applicable when the directors of AirTouch withdrew or adversely amended their approval. Vodafone also agreed to make a payment to AirTouch of up to US$ 225 million if the transaction had been terminated for identical reasons. The new board constituted 14 board members with seven each from both Vodafone and AirTouch. The number of executive directors was six with four from Vodafone and two from AirTouch.

The cash portion of the deal was financed by Vodafone through a $10.5 billion term and revolving credit facility. Special rules were required to approve the redenomination of the change of name of Vodafone to Vodafone AirTouch according to London Stock Exchange listing rules. The merger was completed 5 months after signing of the deal. The deal also required a number of consents like antitrust, shareholder's approvals, treasury content, and listing. The deal required the approval of Federal Communications Commission of the US (FCC) under the Communications Act and the European Commission under the EC Merger Regulation Act (Laird, 1999).

Strategic Reasons for Merger

The merged company Vodafone AirTouch with a combined market capitalization of $110 billion became the largest independent wireless company in the world. The merged company had presence in 23 countries in 4 continents. The mobile communications market was undergoing rapid growth in the context of mass market service. In developed markets, mobile penetration rates were expected to be 50% by the year 2003. The mobile voice telephony was expected to replace large amounts of traffic by fixed line networks (Steven & Mehta, 1999). In the context of globalization, consolidation of telecommunication companies provided the ability to leverage scale and scope with significant operating and revenue synergies. In a scenario of mobile telephony stepping into its next phase of development of next-generation technology and mobile broadband data, consolidation was expected to position the global operators to capitalize on the new growth in the telecom industry. The alliance between Vodafone and AirTouch had been effective in different countries, for example, in Sweden and Egypt. The combination was expected to have an unparalleled global footprint of mobile telephony assets with significant management, operational, and technical expertise.

The combination created a global mobile group with significant presence in the United States, Europe, Asia, Africa, and Australia. It provided a complete pan European footprint with holdings in 11 European countries which included all major markets (Vodafone Media Release, 1999). The combined group emerged as an attractive partner for other international fixed and mobile telecommunication providers. The combined group could focus on two of the fastest-growing segments – mobile voice and data communications (CNET News Staff, 2002). The new group became well positioned for the 3G next-generation services. The merger was in line with Vodafone's strategy to account half of the company's revenues from outside the United Kingdom by early 2000.

Bell Atlantic was also bidding for AirTouch. But the transaction deal would be more dilutive for Bell Atlantic's earnings. Compared to Bell Atlantic, Vodafone had a smaller stock market capitalization but had a higher price to earnings ratio. Thus the deal was more beneficial to Vodafone as its financial position would be strong without diluting its own earnings.

AirTouch and Vodafone competed each other overseas. Vodafone and AirTouch were partners in Global star, a satellite-based mobile phone system which provided a global wireless service to high-end customers (CNNMoney deals, 1999). They were competitors in the German wireless market. AirTouch and Mannesmann together held Mannesmann Mobilfunk with approximately 5.2 million customers for its D2 mobile phone network. Vodafone held 17.25% in D2 rival E-Plus.

The combination created a pan European network. Vodafone operated in United Kingdom and held shares in operators in France, Greece, Sweden, and the Netherlands. With AirTouch acquisition, Vodafone extended its reach to Belgium, Italy, Poland, Portugal, Romania, and Spain. Vodafone held stakes in Australian and Hong Kong Carriers. Through the deal, Vodafone also acquired AirTouch's stakes in markets like Japan, South Korea, and India (Douglass, 1999).

Synergistic Effects

The new group realized significant cost and revenue synergies over several years. In March 1988 Vodafone's EBITDA was $1516 million, while AirTouch's proportionate EBITDA was $1869 million. On a pro forma basis for the year ended March 1998, the combined group had proportionate revenues of $9892 million and EBITDA of $3386 million. With a combined market capitalization of approximately $110 billion, the combined entity became the third largest publicly traded company in the United Kingdom and one of the top ten global telecommunications company by market capitalization. By 2002, the merger was expected to have post-tax cash flow savings of approximately $330 million with net present value of $3.5 billion.

Table 22.3 Sales in million pounds

Year	1997	1998
Vodafone	1749	2471
AirTouch	1599	2252
Total	3348	4723

The values are given in million pounds

Table 22.4 Operating profit in million pounds

Year	1997	1998
Vodafone	539	686
AirTouch	361	599
Total	900	1285

The values are given in million pounds

Table 22.5 Asset and debt highlights in year 1998

	Vodafone	AirTouch
Intangible assets	170	5188
Tangible assets	1725	2327
Investments and other long-term assets	331	2308
Total	2226	9823

The values are given in million dollars

Additional cash flow benefits were expected from revenue enhancements and new products. The merger resulted in global purchasing and operating efficiencies which included volume discount on worldwide purchases of cellular handsets and infrastructure. The combined company also achieved cost savings in the development and acquisition of 3G next-generation mobile handsets, infrastructure, and software (Sanchez, 1999). The merger resulted in the creation of a European transit network and lower leased line costs. Revenue enhancement resulted through optimization of European, transatlantic, and global roaming. There had been improved coverage of global corporate accounts.

Pro forma financial highlights in year before merger (Tables 22.3, 22.4, and 22.5).

Stock Market Wealth Effects on Deal Announcement

On acquisition announcement, the stock price of Vodafone rose sharply. In New York Stock Exchange, Vodafone's ADR rose to $174.625. The merger announcement was made on January 15, 1999. The Vodafone stock rose by approximately 16% on the day after announcement in London stock exchange. The stock again rose by 0.8% on the +2 day after the announcement of the deal. The 250-day period daily cumulative return analysis surrounding the merger announcement shows that the stock gained only 1.08% for the period −10 to +261 day (Fig. 22.1).

The cumulative returns for the 3-day period (−1 to +1 day) was 13.59%. The cumulative returns were positive in different time window period of analysis except for the 11-day period (−10 through +10) (Table 22.6).

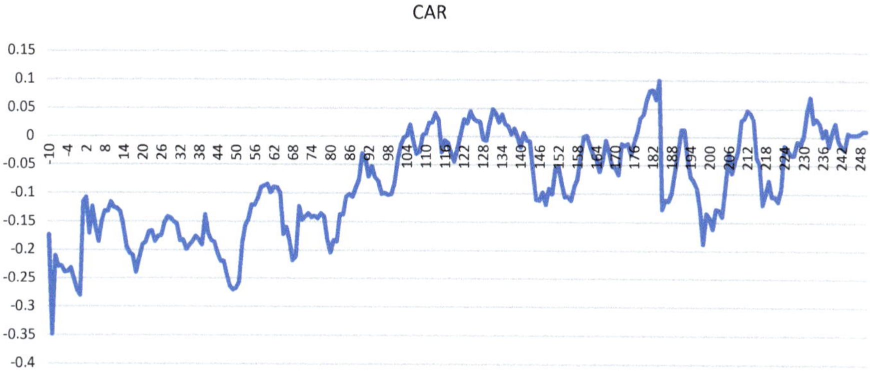

Fig. 22.1 CAR analysis for Vodafone surrounding the merger announcement for 1-year period

Table 22.6 Cumulative abnormal returns in different time window period

Days	CAR (%)
−5 to +5	6.80
−1 to +1	13.59
−10 to +10	−11.50
−1 to +100	17.60
−10 to +261	1.08

References

Cheyne D, Hayes C (1999) Linklater's and Alliance. Vodafone AirTouch: a global merger. https://uk.practicallaw.thomsonreuters.com/7-101-0373?transitionType=Default&contextData=(sc.Default)&firstPage=true&bhcp=1. Accessed 10 Jan 2018

CNET News Staff (2002) Vodafone wins war for Air Touch. https://www.cnet.com/news/vodafone-wins-war-for-airtouch/. Accessed 11 Jan 2018

CNNMoney deals (1999) Vodafone wins Air Touch. http://money.cnn.com/1999/01/15/deals/bellatlantic/. Accessed 11 Jan 2018

Douglass E (1999) Vodafone Air Touch Merger. http://articles.latimes.com/1999/may/28/business/fi-41841. Accessed 11 Jan 2018

Laird L (1999) US authorities clear Vodafone merger with Air Touch. https://www.theguardian.com/business/1999/jun/24/20. Accessed 11 Jan 2018

Sanchez J (1999) Analysts favor Air Touch Combo. https://wwwcomputerworldcomau/article/46417/analysts_favour_vodafone_airtouch_combo/. Accessed 11 Jan 2018

Steven L, Mehta S (1999) Vodafone Group makes an offer to Buy Air Touch for $45 billion. https://www.wsj.com/articles/SB915496102703942000. Accessed 11 Jan 2018

Vodafone Investor Presentation (2018) Acquisition of Liberty's global operations in Germany, the Czech, Hungary and Russia. file:///C:/Users/Admin/Documents/Casebook%20on%20Mega%20Mergers/Vodafone%20AirTouch%20Merger/Investor%20Presentation%20-%20FINAL.PDF. Accessed 15 June 2018

Vodafone Media Release (1999) Vodafone and Air Touch merger to create global mobile. http://www.vodafone.com/content/index/media/vodafone-group-releases/1999/press_release17_01.html. Accessed 10 Jan 2018

Bell Atlantic- GTE Merger

23

Introduction

Verizon Corporation was created on June 30, 2000, by the merger of Bell Atlantic and GTE Corp in one of the largest mergers in US history. Verizon Communications Inc. is one of the leading providers of communications, information, and entertainment products (CNN Money News, 1998). The company provides services to consumers, businesses, and governmental agencies. Verizon offers voice, data, and video services and solutions on wireless and wireline networks. By the end of 2017, the company had approximately 155,400 employees. The strategic focus of the company is on leveraging network leadership, increasing high-quality customer base along with profitability, and enhancing ecosystems in media and telematics. The company is also consistently deploying new network architecture and technologies to extend the leadership position in fourth-generation (4G) and fifth-generation (5G) wireless networks. The two reportable segments of Verizon are the Wireless and Wireline which are operated and managed as strategic business units and organized by products, services, and customer groups. The Wireless segment known as Verizon Wireless provides wireless communications, products, and services across major wireless networks in the United States. The Wireline segment provides voice, data, and video communications products and enhanced services which include broadband video and data services, corporate networking solutions, security, managed network services, and local and long-distance voice services. The following tables give the financial highlights, operating revenues and operating statistics of Verizon Communication (Tables 23.1, 23.2, and 23.3).

GTE Corp formerly known as General Telephone & Electronics Corporation was one of the largest independent telephone companies in the United States during the Bell System era. In the year 2000, Bell Atlantic completed the acquisition of GTE Corp. The combined company was renamed as Verizon. GTE provided local telephone service to different regions in the United States through operating companies.

B. R. Kumar, *Wealth Creation in the World's Largest Mergers and Acquisitions*, Management for Professionals, https://doi.org/10.1007/978-3-030-02363-8_23

Table 23.1 Financial highlights of Verizon Corporation

Year	2013	2014	2015	2016	2017
Operating revenue	120,550	127,079	131,620	125,980	126,034
Operating income	31,968	19,599	33,060	27,059	27,414
Total assets	273,184	232,109	244,175	244,180	257,143
Long-term debt	89,188	110,029	103,240	105,433	113,642

The values are given in millions of dollars

Table 23.2 Operating revenues

Year	2015	2016	2017
Service	70,396	66,580	63,121
Equipment	16,924	17,515	18,889
Other	4360	5091	5501
Total	91,680	89,186	87,511

The values are in millions of dollars

Table 23.3 Operating statistics

Year	2015	2016	2017
Retail connections	112,108	114,243	116,257
Retail postpaid connections	106,528	108,796	110,854

The values are given in millions of dollars

In 1991 GTE acquired the third largest independent company Continental Telephone. In 1997, GTE acquired BBN Planet which was one of the earliest Internet service providers. The acquired division named as GTE Internetworking was later spun off into an independent company called Genuity in order to satisfy Federal Communications Commission requirement with respect to GTE Bell merger to form Verizon. In regions like Canada, GTE operated via stakes in subsidiary companies like BC Tel and Quebec Telephone. When BC Tel got merged with Telus to form BCT. Telus, GTE's Canadian subsidiaries were merged into a new parent company, thereby making it the second largest telecommunications carrier in Canada. The new Verizon company became the only foreign telecommunications company with more than 20% stake in a Canadian telecommunication company. In 2004, Verizon completely divested its stakes in the Canadian carrier. Prior to its merger with Bell Atlantic, GTE maintained an interactive television service joint venture called GTE mainStreet and an interactive entertainment and video game publishing operation called GTE Interactive Media. In the 1990s, GTE restructured itself into three business groups – telecommunications products and services, telephone operations, and electrical products. In 1984, Bell Atlantic was formed from the breakup of the original AT&T as the local phone monopoly for the mid-Atlantic states. After the deregulation of the telecommunications in the year 1996, Bell Atlantic acquired the Nynex Corporation which served most of the region between New York and Maine.

Merger Between Bell Atlantic and GTE

Bell Atlantic completed the acquisition of GTE on June 30, 2000, and the new entity was named as Verizon Communications. Bell Atlantic Corp acquired GTE in an all-stock deal valued at $52.8 billion combining Bell Atlantic's local and wireless phone service with GTE's local, long-distance, wireless, and Internet businesses (Freer, 2000). The merged companies build upon GTE's and Bell Atlantic's complementary strengths. Bell Atlantic through this merger acquired long-distance business and data assets. The merger was in line with the focused strategy to offer one bundled telecommunication service to customers in which local, distance, cellular, and Internet services were to be combined. Bell Atlantic and GTE served over 10.6 million wireless customers in the United States. By means of acquiring GTE, Bell Atlantic became US largest local phone company serving more than 63 million customers. GTE was the third largest local company service provider in the United States behind Bell Atlantic and SBC Communications. Together Atlantic and GTE employed more than 250,000 people. The GTE operating companies retained by Verizon were collectively known as Verizon West. The remaining smaller operating companies were sold off or transferred into the remaining companies. In the year 2010, Verizon sold many of its GTE properties to Frontier Communications. In this transaction, each Verizon stockholder received one share of Frontier common stock for every 4.165977 shares of Verizon common stock. The fractional shares which resulted from the spin off were sold at a price of $7.1846 per share. Bell Atlantic was also part of PrimeCo Personal Communications LP Wireless Alliance. Bell South was another bidder in the fray for GTE's acquisition.

The merger with GTE was the second major deal done by Bell Atlantic since the passage of the Telecommunications Act of 1996. Bell Atlantic had acquired NYNEX for $25 billion. The deal was announced the next day after AT&T Corp agreed to merge its overseas operations with British Telecom in a $10 billion joint venture.

Deal Highlights

GTE shareholders received 1.22 Bell Atlantic shares for each GTE share. Based on Bell Atlantic's closing price of $45 on July 28, 1998, the deal was valued at $52.8 billion. The deal didn't offer any premium for GTE based on the closing price on the day of announcement. The pricing came to $54.90 per GTE share based on Bell Atlantic's closing price. It was lower than the market value for GTE shares which closed on the day before the announcement at $55.75. Analysts had priced GTE at approximately $55 per share. The exchange ratio was 1.22 shares of Verizon Communications common stock for each share of GTE common stock owned. Fractional shares resulting from the exchange of GTE stock certificate were converted into Verizon Communication shares at a price of $55 per share. After the announcement, the GTE shares fell by more than 5% to $52.88 as investors gave a thumbs-down to the deal.

The deal had a breakup fee of up to $2 billion if either company decided to pursue another merger opportunity. The deal faced regulatory scrutiny as the Telecommunications Act of 1996 prohibited the Baby Bells from selling long-distance service unless they opened their local networks to potential competitors. This merger was also in line with the series of consolidation witnessed in the sector where the merged entity was offering a variety of integrated services from cable television to cell phone and local and long-distance calling. As a part of regulatory approval, GTE had to spin off 90.5% of the Genuity while retaining 9.5% (Labaton, 2000). The merger was completed on the basis of approval from 27 state regulatory commissions, the Federal Communications Commission, and the Justice Department (Goodman, 2000).

Merger Benefits

The new Verizon company controlled a third of the US local telephone market with approximately 63 million local lines and 25 million cell phone customers in 40 states of the United States. The merger yielded economies of scale and cost synergy in which Verizon was able to offer packages of services like wireless and wired telephone service as well as high-speed Internet on one bill. The merger combined the complementary assets of both the companies (Kane, 1998). Through the deal, six of the eight equal-sized local telephone companies were consolidated into two superregional monopolies of Bell Atlantic and SBC. The merger consolidated Bell Atlantic's local telephone dominance in the northeastern and mid-Atlantic states with GTE's local systems spread out throughout the United States. The merger facilitated Verizon Communications to intensify its drive toward selling complete package of communications offerings which ranged from long-distance and local telephone service to wireless and high-speed Internet service. The new Verizon was positioned to expand into areas such as video entertainment and interactive gaming thereby leveraging its direct route into large number of homes and businesses. The deal also added GTE's roughly four million wireless phone customers to Verizon Wireless. Verizon Wireless was formed by the joint venture of Bell Atlantic with Vodafone Air Touch to become the largest wireless operator in the United States. The merger added 25 million wireless customers to Verizon which were more than twice than that of the next biggest wireless operator AT&T Corp. The merged firm had a market value of approximately $150 billion and revenue of $60 billion a year. The GTE acquisition was a major step for Bell Atlantic for its transformation from a regional provider of basic telephone service into a major industry player. On account of synergy from the deal, it was expected that the revenues would increase by $2 billion, and costs drop by $2 billion. The merged entity became the largest wireless and cellular company in the United States with the ability to offer local, long-distance, wireless, and data services. The combined company had the financial, operational, and technological resources to compete effectively against major telecom companies like AT&T/TCI, SBC/Ameritech, and WorldCom/MCI.

Merger Announcement and Wealth Effects

The merger of Bell Atlantic and GTE was announced on July 28, 1998. The stock price of Bell Atlantic fell by approximately 3% on merger announcement. The cumulative returns during the 252-day period surrounding the merger announcement (−18- to +233-day period) were 32.5% (Fig. 23.1).

The Bell Atlantic stock registered positive returns during the shorter time window period and the longest time window period of analysis. The stock registered negative returns during the time window period −5- to +10- and −10- to +10-day period (Table 23.4).

Fig. 23.1 Cumulative returns for Bell Atlantic surrounding merger announcement period

Table 23.4 Cumulative returns during different time window periods

Window period	Cumulative returns
−1 to +1	1.17%
−3 to +3	3.04%
−5 to +5	3.74%
−5 to +10	−9.56%
−10 to +10	−12.07%
−18 to +233	32.50%

References

CNN Money News (1998) Bell Atlantic buying GTE. http://money.cnn.com/1998/07/28/deals/gte/. Accessed 17 January 2018

Freer J (2000) It's Official: Bell Atlantic, GTE merger. https://washingtontechnology.com/articles/2000/06/30/its-official-bell-atlantic-gte-merge.aspx. Accessed 18 January 2018

Goodman PS (2000) GTE, Bell Atlantic cleared to merger. https://www.washingtonpost.com/archive/politics/2000/06/15/gte-bell-atlantic-cleared-to-merge/014abb92-a232-4075-91b0-78ce209d4263/?noredirect=on&utm_term=.6a7c1c4077e4. Accessed 18 January 2018

Kane M (1998) Merger mania: Bell Atlantic, GTE to combine in $53 B deal. https://www.zdnet.com/article/merger-mania-bell-atlantic-gte-to-combine-in-53b-deal/. Accessed 18 January 2018

Labaton S (2000) FCC approves Bell Atlantic – GTE merger, creating No.1 phone company. https://www.nytimes.com/2000/06/17/business/fcc-approves-bell-atlantic-gte-merger-creating-no-1-phone-company.html. Accessed 18 January 2018

Verizon Annual Report (2017) https://www.verizon.com/about/investors/annual-report

British Petroleum Merger with Amoco 24

Introduction

British Petroleum (BP) is a global energy business company with operations in Europe, North and South America, Australasia, Asia, and Africa. The company had $240 billion sales in the year 2017. The profit for the company was $3.4 billion. By the end of 2017, BP had operations in 70 countries worldwide, produced around 3.6 million barrels per day of oil equivalent, and had total proved reserves of 18.441 billion barrels of oil equivalent. The company had 18,300 service stations worldwide. BP merged with Amoco to become BP Amoco in the year 1998 and acquired ARCO and Burmah Castrol in the year 2000. The company was renamed as BP plc in the year 2001. During the period 2003–2013, BP was a partner in the TNK-BP joint venture in Russia. During the early 2000, BP became the leading partner of the Baku Tbilisi-Ceyhan pipeline which marked the beginning of a new oil transportation route in the Caspian region. In 2017, BP made an announcement to acquire 43% stake in the solar energy developer Lightsource Renewable Energy and renamed it as LightSource. In the same year, the company acquired Clean Energy's bio methane business and assets. Butamax, the subsidiary of BP, purchased Nesika Energy, an isobutanol production company in the year 2017. The following table gives the financial highlights of BP (Table 24.1).

The Merger of BP Amoco

On August 12 1998, BP announced plans to merge with Amoco in a deal valued at $48.2 billion. At that time, it was billed as the largest oil industry merger ever. The deal was also the largest takeover of an American company by a foreign company. The merged company became the third largest multinational oil company in terms of net income after Exxon Mobil Corporation and the Royal Dutch/Shell Group of

B. R. Kumar, *Wealth Creation in the World's Largest Mergers and Acquisitions*,
Management for Professionals, https://doi.org/10.1007/978-3-030-02363-8_24

Table 24.1 Financial highlights of British Petroleum

Year	2013	2014	2015	2016	2017
Total revenues	396,217	358,678	225,982	186,606	244,582
Profit before interest and taxes	31,769	6412	(7918)	(430)	9474
Profit	23,758	4003	(6400)	172	3468
Total assets	305,690	284,305	261,832	263,316	276,515

The values are in millions of dollars

Companies. During the period, it was ranked as the world's largest combination of industrial companies surpassing the $36 billion transatlantic deal of Daimler–Chrysler merger. After the merger, BP Amoco became the largest company in Britain with more than $140 billion in market capitalization and one of the world's top three oil majors. Before the merger, Amoco was the fifth largest oil company in the United States with roughly 9300 gasoline stations. During the period, BP was the third largest oil company with a network of 17,900 stations. The merger resulted in job cuts of 6000 worldwide. The merger took place against a backdrop of depressed world oil prices which had fallen to the lowest levels in over a decade Ibrahim (1998). At the time of announcement of deal, the price of a barrel of Brent crude fell to $11.8 which was the lowest price in 25 years during that period.

Merger Highlights

The merger deal was a share swap deal whereby Amoco shareholders were offered 3.97 BP Shares for each share of Amoco common stock. The deal involved exchange of American depository receipts equivalent to 3.97 of its shares for each Amoco share. On the basis of BP's closing price of $7.73 on the day of announcement, the value of deal was estimated to be $48.2 billion with $50.15 for each Amoco share. The shares were delivered in the form of BP Amoco American Depository Receipts (ADRs). Each ADR represented six BP ordinary shares. Each Amoco share was about 0.66 ADR when expressed in terms of ADR. The merger was accounted for on a pooling of interest's basis. Amoco shareholders received a 25% premium above the BP's market value at the time of merger announcement.

JPMorgan Chase & Co and Sullivan & Cromwell were the advisors for British Petroleum. Amoco was advised by Morgan Stanley Dean Witter and Wachtell, Lipton, Rosen & Katz law firm.

The merged company was governed by a team composed of members from both companies. The new board based in London had 13 British Petroleum directors and 9 Amoco directors. Amoco Chairman and CEO Laurence and BP Chairman Peter Sutherland became the cochairmen of the board of BP.

The merger agreement stipulated that if Amoco breaks the agreement, then it had to pay $950 million. If BP backs out, then the company had to pay $ 1 billion as fine charges.

The deal was completed on December 31, 1998. The US Federal Trade Commission approved the deal with the condition to sell 134 gasoline stations and 9 terminals and ensure that 1600 independent gasoline stations switch suppliers.

Chicago became the headquarters for the new company's North American operations in refining, marketing, and transportation and worldwide chemicals business. Amoco was the fourth largest company in the Chicago area. Exploration and production operations for the Western Hemisphere were managed from Houston. After the completion of the deal, the American depositary shares of BP Amoco were subsequently listed on the New York Stock Exchange and the Pacific, Chicago, and Toronto stock exchanges. All BP retail outlets in the United States adopted the Amoco brand name. BP retail sites outside the United States continued to retain the BP name.

Expected Synergy from the Deal

The combined exploration prowess of the company resulted in larger supply of crude oil. There were a lot of operational synergies from the deal as a result of complementary strengths. BP's strength lays in its exploration skills, while the company was weak in the business of refining oil into products and chemicals as well as in areas of marketing and distribution. Amoco had strong marketing and distribution network. The merger consolidated the combined company's spending on exploration which exceeded that of Exxon and Royal Dutch Shell. The deal facilitated both the companies to become more competitive in regions like the former USSR, China, and Latin America.

The combined company employed a total of 99,450 workers worldwide. BP employed 56,450 employees.

The merged company benefitted from both companies' complementary strategic and geographic strengths. The merger was expected to realize operational synergies and cost savings of at least $2 billion pretax by year 2000. The merged company had combined production resources of about three million BOE and reserves of 14.8 billion BOE. The combined entity obtained oil leadership position in Alaska, the Gulf of Mexico, the North Sea, and the Caspian Sea. BP Amoco also had a leading position in the US gasoline market and chemical businesses. Substantial cost savings were expected from the merger. The estimates suggested that additional synergies from increased organizational efficiency at line and staff levels were expected to be $ 1 billion (Oil and Gas Journal, 1998). Cost savings were obtained from more focused exploration, streamlining business processes, and extra buying power. Synergies of focused exploration were expected to be $300 million. Streamlining of business process was expected to realize $200 million. Improved procurement and rationalization of duplicate operations resulted in cost synergies of $500 million. The combined bottom line was expected to increase by more than 20%. The group had combined reserves of around 14.8 billion barrels of oil and gas, daily production of three million barrels with active presence in all main exploration areas. The BP Amoco group became the leading company in the areas of chemicals, petrochemicals, and solar energy.

Both BP and Amoco's assets and market positions were a strategic fit to each other. In upstream sector, BP was the largest oil producer in the United States, United Kingdom, and North Sea. Amoco was the largest private natural gas producer in North America and the second largest gas reserve holder. In the downstream sector, BP had refineries in the United Kingdom, France, Spain, the United States, Australia, South Africa, and Singapore. Amoco had five refineries in the United States with a total capacity of about one million barrel per day. The European refineries of BP which were involved in joint venture with Mobil Corp were excluded from the merger with Amoco. Worldwide BP had almost 18,000 service stations, and Amoco had 9300 service stations. In the chemical sector, BP produced 9.4 million metric tons of chemical products every year. During the merger period, BP was the leading producer of polyethylene in Europe and supplied more than 90% of the acrylonitrile technology in use worldwide. BP was also one of the largest manufacturers of Styrenics in Europe and a leading producer of polybutene. During the same period, Amoco had chemical capacity of 13 million metric tons per year. Amoco was the largest producer of purified terephthalic acid, paraxylene, polybutene, and polyalphaolefins. It was also a major producer of linear – olefins and polypropylene.

The merger was a strategic fit as both BP and Amoco operations were purely complementary in nature. It made Amoco less sensitive to natural gas and chemicals and BP less sensitive to crude oil. Earlier BP had no base in gas operations in the United States. The merger gave BP access to the US natural gas market. The merger gave Amoco access to huge oil supplies overseas and in Alaska. In downstream sector, the merger gave BP access to the US market (Oil and Gas Journal, 1999). The merger happened in a scenario of low oil prices and lower refining margins. Hence one of the strategic reasons of the deal was to reduce costs.

Though the deal was stated as merger, in fact it had been an acquisition whereby BP controlled 60% of the new merged company. BP also assumed $4.86 billion in long-term debt of Amoco. The merger was completely friendly in nature.

The combined company had 9.2 billion barrels of crude oil in reserves. In an effort to move away from its saturated American market, Amoco was refocusing its growth strategy. In 1997, the company sold about one third of its domestic oil and gas properties.

Through the acquisition, BP acquired 9300 retail gasoline outlets. The new company became the largest natural gas producer in North America. After the merger, BP became the largest company in Britain surpassing GlaxoSmithKline (BBC News, 1998).

During the year before merger, Amoco's net income declined to $673 million from $1 billion, and revenues had dropped from $17.6 billion to $15.4 billion. The stock price had also declined by 12% during the year before merger announcement.

It was stated that BP achieved its projected $2 billion in cost savings within the first year, ahead of schedule. The stock of BP emerged as a top performer which rose by 11% during the first hundred days after the merger announcement and outperformed the oil and gas stock index by 17% 1 year after the deal was announced.

The merger between British Petroleum and Amoco in the year 1998 was followed by the acquisition of ARCO and Burmah Castrol. The union of BP, Amoco, ARCO, and Burmah Castrol created a global enterprise in the oil industry known as "Super Major."

Stock Reaction to Merger Announcement

The merger was announced on August 12, 1998. The BP Amoco merger announcement coincided with a significant drop in oil prices globally as the markets were flooded with supplies. The reasons attributed were economic slowdown in Asian economies, a mild winter, and overproduction by the OPEC. As the deal was announced, the average oil price around the world hit a 10-year low at about $10 per barrel which adjusted for inflation was lower than the price of oil about 25 years ago. The shares in BP surged 1.5% after the news announcement of the merger. By the close of trading on the announcement day, BP shares increased 22 pence to $7.95, thereby increasing the value of the deal to $49.7 billion. During the announcement day of the deal, the shares of the target company Amoco which had closed at $41 climbed as high as $52.125 in early trading before closing at $46.875 on the New York Stock Exchange.

The trading of the new shares started on January 4, 1999. Immediately after listing, the share price of the new company began to rise against the general downward trend in petroleum stocks. On January 4, 1999, BP Amoco shares rose by 21.5 pence to close at $15.25 per share. On that day BP Amoco shares were the most traded shares in the market.

The announcement day return based on the closing price was 0.32%. The stock price increased by approximately 1% in the NYSE on 1 day after merger announcement. Two days after merger announcement, the stock price increased by approximately 3.5%. The cumulative returns for BP during the 253-day period (−10 to +242) interval were approximately 39% (Fig. 24.1).

The cumulative returns were positive in all time window periods except 11-day period of −10 to +10 day. The cumulative returns were 39% for the longest time window period of −10 to +242 days. Hence it can be concluded that the merger was net positive present value activity for British Petroleum (Table 24.2).

Fig. 24.1 Cumulative returns surrounding the merger announcement for BP stock

Table 24.2 Cumulative return analysis for BP stock

Time window	Cum returns
−10 to +10 day	−2.20%
−5 to +5 day	5.20%
−1 to +1 day	4.20%
−1 to +20 day	5.03%
−1 to +100 day	20%
−10 to+242	39%

References

BBC News (1998) Business: the company file BP and Amoco in oil mega merger. http://news.bbc.co.uk/2/hi/business/149139.stm. Accessed 22 January 2018

Ibrahim Y (1998) British Petroleum is buying Amoco in a $48.2 billion deal. https://www.nytimes.com/1998/08/12/business/british-petroleum-is-buying-amoco-in-48.2-billion-deal.html. Accessed 22 January 2018

Oil and Gas Journal (1998) BP Amoco merger creates third supermajor. https://www.ogj.com/articles/print/volume-96/issue-33/in-this-issue/general-interest/bp-amoco-merger-creates-third-39supermajor39.html. Accessed 22 January 2018

Oil and Gas Journal (1999) BP Amoco finish merger after FTC approval. https://www.ogj.com/articles/print/volume-97/issue-2/in-this-issue/general-interest/bp-amoco-finish-merger-after-ftc-approval.html. Accessed 22 January 2018

Qwest Merger with US West

25

Growth Strategy of Qwest Telecommunications

In the year 1988, SP Telecom was established as a fiber-optic network building subsidiary of the Southern Pacific Transportation Co. Qwest Communications International was established as a subsidiary of this giant railroad company. In 1988, Anschutz Corp acquired Southern Pacific from Santa Fe Industries. Qwest International offered local and long-distance telephone services as well as a broad range of Internet, multimedia, data, and voice services which were sold to business, consumers, and government customers. Qwest Communications International, Inc. operated as a broadband Internet communications company and provided communications services and construction services (Funding Universe, 2018).

The company went for an IPO during June 1997 and renamed itself as Qwest Communications International. The IPO offer raised $297 million on the sale of 13.5 million shares. The company had an initial market capitalization of $2.1 billion. Only 14% of the company shares were offered to the public, and the rest were held by railroad billionaire Philip Anschutz. The IPO had raised $297 million. The company had completed the construction of its 18500-mile national fiber-optic network in the year 1999 and added 4300 route miles in Canada and Mexico. Qwest focused on its strategy of building its nationwide fiber-optic network on the premise that ground-based networks were more reliable for the transmission of data than satellite-based networks. It was expected that the demand for high-speed networks for data transmission was set to explode over the next decade. The deregulation in telecommunication sector especially in the long-distance market was expected to bring down the costs for fiber and equipment dramatically. Qwest had grown through a series of mergers and acquisitions. In 1997, Qwest acquired Colorado's largest Internet service provider (ISP), SuperNet Inc., for $ 20 million. SuperNet was the state's oldest ISP which was originally founded by the Colorado Advanced Institute of Technology. Eyeing on the dramatic increase in Internet usage in the late 1990s, Qwest focused on plans to take advantage of the expansion of voice over

B. R. Kumar, *Wealth Creation in the World's Largest Mergers and Acquisitions*, Management for Professionals, https://doi.org/10.1007/978-3-030-02363-8_25

Internet protocol (IP) services. In December 1997, Qwest offered IP-based services to users in nine Western cities.

In the year 1998, Qwest acquired the Virginia-based long-distance carrier LCI International for $4.4 billion. The deal created the fourth largest long-distance carrier in the United States behind AT&T, MCI, WorldCom, and Sprint Corp. This acquisition gave Qwest approximately 2 million long-distance customers and a strong sales force. Qwest also purchased EUNet a European ISP based in Amsterdam with approximately 60,000 customers for $154 million. The acquisition of ISP EUNet gave Qwest data services. The company also offered voice services by making deals with established carriers in Europe. In September 1998, Qwest acquired Icon CMT of Weehawken, New Jersey, for $185 million. The deal was share based. Icon CMT provided Internet-based services such as web hosting, intranets, online stock trading, and online publications. Qwest also established a 3-year alliance with Netscape Communications to provide Netscape's Web Portal Net Center which provided a range of telecommunications services. During December 1998, Qwest and Microsoft Corp entered into an agreement whereby Microsoft invested $200 million in Qwest, thereby taking 1.3% minority interest in the company. Qwest got access to Microsoft Windows NT Server OS for usage of its electronic commerce, web hosting, streaming media, managed software, and virtual private networking services.

In 1999, Qwest received $3.5 billion investment from BellSouth and aimed for takeover of US West and Frontier Communications. In the year 2000, the company completed the acquisition of US West.

US West

US West was one of the seven "Baby Bells" – the regional Bell operating companies – which was created in the year 1983 as a result of the antitrust breakup of AT&T. US West provided local telephone, intraLATA long-distance services, data transmission services, cable television services, wireless communication services, and related telecommunication products in regions like Arizona, Colorado, Idaho, Iowa, Minnesota, Nebraska, New Mexico, North Dakota, Washington, and Wyoming. US West was a holding company for three Bell operating companies, namely, Mountain Bell, Northwestern Bell, and Pacific Northwest Bell until the 1990s. In the year 1991, Northwestern Bell and Pacific Northwest Bell merged into Mountain Bell and was renamed to US West Communications. US West had the distinction of being the first regional Bell operating to consolidate its Bell operating companies. In the year 1998, US West was split into two separate companies. The major business of telephone properties was retained by US West, while the remaining operations like cable, wireless, and international businesses were transferred to MediaOne. The split process was structured in such a way that MediaOne Inc. became the legal successor to US West and US West was spun off.

On June 30, 2000, US West merged with Qwest. The US West brand was replaced by the Qwest brand. On April 1, 2011, Qwest merged with CenturyLink. After the merger completion, Qwest brand was replaced by the CenturyLink brand.

Qwest Acquisition of US West

The hostile acquisition bid announcement for US West was made by Qwest when rumors were ripe that Qwest might be a long-term acquisition target for BellSouth which had a 10% interest in Qwest (Bloomberg News, 1999). Qwest made announcement bid for US West and Frontier Communications. US West, one of the regional Bell operating companies, had local phone customers in 14 Western states. Frontier Communications was the fifth largest US long-distance carrier at that time. In fact, US West was already the target of a $52 billion takeover bid from Global Crossing Ltd, a Bermuda-based company involved in establishing an undersea fiber-optic network. On announcement bid, Qwest stock price fell by more than 20%. The initial offer was valued at $35 billion. The initial offer of Qwest was rejected by US West as the latter reaffirmed its willingness to Global Crossing. Qwest increased its offer price to $69 a share for US West and $68 a share for Frontier (Bloomberg News, 2000). The renewed deal offer to US West was valued at $48 billion. Global Crossing's offer had been $11 billion for Frontier and $30 billion for Qwest. Soon Qwest and US West reached an agreement to acquire US West. As a part of the deal, Qwest agreed to forego providing long-distance service in US West's territory. As a result of the acquisition, Bell South's stake in the merged company declined from 10% to 3.5%. Quest withdrew its offer for Frontier, and Frontier was acquired by Global Crossing for $10.9 billion (Bloomberg News, 2000).

Before the merger in 1999, Qwest had about 8700 employees, while US West had 55000 employees. Through the acquisition, Qwest gained a huge workforce. Qwest also gained 25 million local phone customers of US West in 14 Western states.

The acquisition of US West by Qwest was cleared by different regulatory agencies like the US Department of Justice, the Federal Trade Commission, the Federal Communications Commission, and public service commissions in 7 of the 14 states served by US West. As a part of regulatory approval, the Federal Communications Commission approved the sale of Qwest's long-distance assets in US West territory to Touch America, a subsidiary of the Montana Power Company for $193 million. The sold operations represented approximately 6% of Qwest's customers and accounted for $300 million in annual revenue. The new merged company retained the Qwest name (CBSMARKETWATCH.COM, 1999).

As a result of breakup of the deal, Global Crossing received $420 million in cash and capacity on long-distance networks. In reality the amount was half of the breakup fee written in the original agreement between Global Crossing and US West.

The deal was based on share exchange. Each share of US West was exchanged for 1.72932 shares of Qwest common stock which was priced at $49.6875. Qwest issued 882 million shares in exchange for US West shares which represented about 53% of the combined company's shares.

Strategic Advantages of the Merger

Qwest added about 25 million customers and regional phone networks to it kitty as a result of its merger with US West. The combined company had a market capitalization of approximately $85 billion. The merger brought together one of the six largest and oldest local phone carriers and the next-generation long-distance carrier thereby creating a giant company for the delivery of high-speed data, video, and voice transmissions. This combination is of great significance in the context of exponential demand for high-speed broadband and world wide web services. The combined company was expected to erase $12.5 billion in expenditure over 5.5 years by eliminating redundancies and achieving economies of scale.

Stock Market Reaction

On the announcement day, the shares of US West closed at $54.875 which was up by 56.25 cents compared to the previous day before the announcement. In Nasdaq where Qwest was listed, the stock price rose by $1 to close at $44.875.

CenturyLink Acquires Qwest

CenturyLink is the third largest telecommunications company and leader in network services market in the United States. CenturyLink provides broadband, voice, and wireless services to consumers and businesses across the United States. The company also offers advanced entertainment services under the Century CenturyLink™ Prism™ TV and DIRECTV brands. The company also offers data, voice, and managed services to businesses, government, and wholesale customers in different markets through its advanced fiber-optic network and multiple data centers. CenturyLink is an S&P 500 company and is among the Fortune 500 list of America's largest companies (CenturyLink Website, 2018).

On April 22, 2010, CenturyLink and Qwest announced that the board of directors have approved a definitive agreement under which CenturyLink will acquire Qwest in a tax-free, stock-for-stock transaction. Under the terms of the agreement, Qwest shareholders received 0.1664 CenturyLink shares for each share of Qwest common stock they owned at closing. CenturyLink shareholders owned 50.5% and Qwest shareholders owned 49.5% of the combined company (CenturyLink News Release, 2010). On the basis of the closing price of CenturyLink on April 21, 2010, the per-share consideration received by Qwest shareholders was equivalent to $6.02 of CenturyLink stock which represented a premium to Qwest shareholders of approximately 15% over Qwest's closing price as of April 21, 2010. On the basis of the closing stock price of CenturyLink on April 21, 2010, the deal reflected an enterprise value of Qwest of approximately $22.4 billion which included the assumption of $11.8 billion of Qwest net debt outstanding as of December 31, 2009. The deal was expected to generate annual operating and capital synergies of approximately

$625 million over 3- to 5-year period after merger completion. The transaction was also aimed at realizing operating cost synergies of $575 million within a 5-year period. The key drivers of synergies were to be sourced from reduction of corporate overhead, elimination of duplicate functions and systems, and increased operational efficiencies.

The new company's board of directors included current CenturyLink board members plus four members of Qwest board. The all-stock deal was valued at $12.2 billion. The consolidation in the sector was a response to the trend of steady cancellation of landlines in favor of reliance on cell phones or cable phone services. Qwest was the larger company. Qwest was facing problems with its US West acquisition due to accounting troubles. The high debt load of Qwest left it unable to be the acquirer company. CenturyLink had acquired Embarq in the year 2009 (Vuong, 2011).

CenturyLink and Qwest served local markets in 37 states with approximately 5 million broadband customers, 17 million access lines, 1415000 video subscribers, and 850000 wireless consumers. The combined company employed 47500 people.

Qwest is one of the three universal service providers for Networx which was the largest communications service contract company in the world. Qwest also served 95% of Fortune 500 companies. The combined company was able to deliver a broader range of communication services via its 190,000 route mile fiber network.

References

Bloomberg News (1999) Qwest Expected to Buy US West; Global to Acquire Frontier. http://articles.latimes.com/1999/jul/17/business/fi-56766. Accessed 25 January 2018

Bloomberg News (2000a) Qwest completes merger of US West. https://www.nytimes.com/2000/07/03/business/qwest-completes-purchase-of-u-s-west.html. Accessed 25 January 2018

Bloomberg News (2000b) Qwest US West merger a done deal. https://www.cnet.com/g00/news/qwest-us-west-merger-a-done-deal/?i10c.encReferrer=aHR0cHM6Ly93d3cuZ29vZ2xlLmFlLw%3D%3D&i10c.ua=1&i10c.dv=14. Accessed 25 January 2018

CBSMARKETWATCH.COM (1999) Telecom saga ends; Qwest wins US West. https://www.marketwatch.com/story/telecom-saga-ends-qwest-wins-u-s-west. Accessed 25 January 2018

CenturyLink News Release (2010) CenturyLink and Qwest agree to merge. http://news.centurylink.com/2010-04-22-CenturyLink-and-Qwest-Agree-to-Merge. Accessed 25 January 2018

CenturyLink Website (2018) www.centuryLink.com. Accessed 25 January 2018

Funding Universe (2018) Qwest Communications International Inc History. http://www.fundinguniverse.com/company-histories/qwest-communications-international-inc-history/. Accessed 25 January 2018

Vuong A (2011) The DenverPost. CenturyLink completes purchase of Qwest. https://www.denverpost.com/2011/04/01/centurylink-completes-purchase-of-qwest/

WorldCom's Acquisition of MCI

26

Introduction

WorldCom, a telecommunication giant, had faced one of the biggest accounting scandals in the history of the United States. The company also had one of the biggest bankruptcies. In the year 2002, the company filed for bankruptcy. In the accounting scandal, about $3.3 billion in profits were improperly recorded on its books from 1999 to the first quarter of 2002. These scandals led to the Sarbanes–Oxley Act in July 2002 which dealt with disclosure requirements and penalties for fraudulent accounting. On July 21, 2002, WorldCom filed for Chap. 11 bankruptcy protection in the largest such filing in the United States during that time period.

MCI Communications Corp was an American telecommunications company founded in the year 1963. Over a period of time, the company grew to become the second largest long-distance provider in the United States. The company was purchased by WorldCom in 1998. The new company was renamed as MCI WorldCom. Following the WorldCom's financial scandals and bankruptcy, the company's name was changed to MCI Inc. in the year 2003. On the account of the bankruptcy reorganization agreement, the company paid $750 million to the SEC in cash and stock in the new MCI. The company emerged from Chap. 11 bankruptcy during the year 2004 with approximately $5.7 billion in debt and $6 billion in cash. In the year 2006, MCI was acquired by Verizon.

WorldCom MCI Deal

On November 10, 1997, WorldCom and MCI agreed to merge in a deal valued at $37 billion. WorldCom finally won the takeover battle with British Telecommunications Plc and GTE Corp for the control of MCI Communications Corp (Associated Press, 1998). The merger created a telecommunication

B. R. Kumar, *Wealth Creation in the World's Largest Mergers and Acquisitions*, Management for Professionals, https://doi.org/10.1007/978-3-030-02363-8_26

conglomerate with estimated revenues of $30 billion in the year 1998. The deal combined the second and fourth largest US long-distance service providers to create a major powerhouse in global telecommunications and Internet services. The new company was renamed as MCI WorldCom (Hiltzik and Shiver Jr, 1997). The WorldCom MCI deal eclipsed the largest US merger deal of Bell Atlantic Corp and Nynex Corp at that time period. The Bell Atlantic Corp and Nynex Corp deal was valued at $25.6 billion. MCI Communications, the number 2 long-distance telephone company at that time, agreed to the deal with WorldCom, the fourth largest distance carrier company rejecting the bid offers of $28 billion from the big local telephone company GTE and $19 billion bid from the overseas major British Telecommunications. The new MCI WorldCom became the second largest long-distance carrier behind AT&T Corporation. The new merged MCI WorldCom controlled about 25% of the long-distance market compared with approximately 50% share of AT&T. MCI WorldCom became the world's largest carrier of Internet traffic (CNNMoney News, 1997). The new company became the backbone network operator from which other online carriers leased capacity. MCI WorldCom became one of the largest companies offering a range of services from local and long-distance to Internet services to over 22 million clients in over 200 countries. In November 1997, WorldCom shares were trading at 90 times its earning. WorldCom strategically focused on growth through acquisitions. At the time of the deal acquisition, WorldCom had earlier acquired 40 companies during the period 1992–1997. After the deregulation in the telecom industry, the industry had witnessed a series of megadeals which included the $22 billion merger of Bell Atlantic Corp and Nynex Corp and the $15.7 billion combination of SBC Communications Inc. and Pacific Telesis Group. In 1997, WorldCom acquired CompuServe Inc., an online service company. WorldCom also acquired Brooks Fiber Properties which was a provider of local telephone services in about 40 markets for $2.4 billion. WorldCom had added local service with the acquisition of MFS Communications, the bypass company which ran fiber-optic lines directly into office buildings (Schiesel, 1997; Shiver Jr, 1997; The Economist, 1997).

Terms of the Deal

MCI Communications accepted the sweetened takeover bid from WorldCom Inc. in a $37 billion deal rejecting a $28 billion all cash offer from GTE Corp. The initial bid offer of WorldCom was $41.50 a share. MCI shareholders received $51 in WorldCom common stock for each MCI share they owned. British Telecommunications received $465 million as termination fee as MCI broke its previous contract to merger with British Petroleum in a $24 billion deal. British Petroleum also received $7 billion or $51 per share in cash from WorldCom for its 20% stake in MCI (Kupfer, 1998). The transaction including the breakup fee represented a pretax gain on British Petroleum's investment in the region of $2.25 billion.

British Petroleum held control of Concert Communications Services, a joint venture with MCI. British Petroleum had 75.1 per stake in Concert and had an option on the 24.9% owned by MCI. GTE Corp had offered MCI an amount of $28 billion or $40 per share. But WorldCom's offer was well above the GTE offer. The deal was accounted for as a purchase. It was structured as tax-free to MCI shareholders. MCI shareholders owned about 45% of the combined company WorldCom MCI. WorldCom also assumed $5 billion of debt of MCI. WorldCom's aggressive offer for MCI outpaced the cash bid by GTE Corp by $9 billion and represented $20 billion premium over the revised offer of British Petroleum.

MCI Chairman Bert Roberts became the chairman of the new company. MCI WorldCom had a 15-member board consisting of 8 from WorldCom, 5 from MCI, and 2 additional members. MCI WorldCom had joint headquarters in Washington and Jackson. The advisors for WorldCom were Salomon Brothers Inc. and Cravath, Swaine & Moore. MCI's advisors included Lazard Freres & Company, Lehman Brothers Inc., and Thacher & Bartlett.

Stock Market Reaction

On the announcement of the deal, MCI's shares gained $4.625 to close at $41.50 on the Nasdaq stock market. WorldCom's shares fell by $2.125 to $31.GTE's stock rose by $1.25 to $44.875 on the New York Stock Exchange.

Reasons for the Merger

The deal was a result of the Telecommunication Act of 1996 which largely deregulated the telecom industry. Deregulation had unleashed a wave of mergers and consolidation in the telecommunications sector. Young companies like WorldCom was looking for growth through acquisitions in the context of surging demand for the Internet access, advanced communication services, and vicious price competition. MCI was one of the telecom industry's most valued companies. MCI pioneered competition by battling to break up the AT&T monopoly and was effective in resisting the incumbent phone companies. But lately MCI was not performing well in the consumer long-distance market, and its investment in wireless and local phone markets had lagged behind many competitors. In 1996, half of the MCI's revenues of $18.6 billion came from residential long-distance service. WorldCom's revenues during the same period were only $4.5 billion. The attractive crown jewel assets of MCI were its international network traffic, fiber optic networks, and wholesale Internet services.

During the consolidation period, world telecom networks were less evenly divided between data and voice signals. In future it was expected that data's shares were to grow at a rate of 95%, and voice traffic was expected to grow at 15% a year.

Advantages of Merger

The deal acted as a catalyst to speed the advent of all-in-one packages of telecommunication services which ranged from long-distance and local telephone to the Internet access on a single monthly bill. WorldCom had increased its offer by 23% compared to its initial offer. During the due diligence, the cost savings as a result of the combination were revised to $5.5 billion a year. The cost savings were expected from savings in the international business and cost of installing domestic lines. The consolidation was like a vertical merger. The new MCI WorldCom was vertically integrated with all assets of modern telecom networks like local, satellite, long-distance, and Internet services. Since WorldCom owned local networks, the combined new company was not required to pay the margin sapping 45% tariff to the regional Baby Bells on long-distance revenues which MCI had paid. The merged company was able to offer a complete service for businesses to meet the capacity which was needed to carry ever-increasing volumes of data. WorldCom had a competitive edge since its subsidiary UUNet was in a dominant position in providing Internet services. WorldCom was better placed to lead the next telecom wave. MCI had the marketing power, name recognition, and vast customer base. The marketing prowess of MCI along with WorldCom's strong presence in local telephone services to businesses was a source of synergy. The deal established MCI WorldCom as the second largest telecommunications firm in the United States behind AT&T.

Verizon Communication's Acquisition of MCI

On February 14, 2005, Verizon Communications reached an agreement to acquire MCI for $7.6 billion (Reardon, 2018). After the announcement by Verizon, MCI became the target of an intense bidding war between Verizon and Qwest Communications. The acquisition of MCI gave Verizon an international long-distance network and several large corporate customers (Bartash, 2006).

The telecommunication market consolidation facilitated the advent of new company that provided a full suite of communication services such as local, long-distance, wireless, and high-speed Internet access and television programming. The advent of Internet protocol technologies had changed the landscape of the telecommunications industry sector in which telecom giants like AT&T and Verizon Communications faced stiff competition from cable operators which offered voice calling, high-speed Internet access, and TV service (Richtel and Sorkin, 2005). Qwest had submitted several increasing bids for MCI ever since the bidding war started. West final bid amounted to $7.3 billion. But MCI board chose Verizon over Qwest since it had concerns regarding Qwest's ability to finance the transaction. Through MCI acquisition, Verizon got access to more than 14 million residential customers and one million corporate clients, a robust national voice and data network along with a strong sales force. Verizon also got access to $5.6 billion cash reserves of MCI. MCI which emerged from bankruptcy protection after the massive accounting scandal of WorldCom secured a new financial partner and new lease of life through Verizon acquisition. Under the terms of the agreement, MCI stockholders received 0.5743 shares of Verizon for each MCI share they owned. In addition, Verizon made a cash payment of $2.738 per MCI share. The value of the deal thus estimated was $20.40 per share.

References

Associated Press (1998) Worldcom deal for MCI Backed. https://www.nytimes.com/1998/09/15/business/worldcom-deal-for-mci-backed.html. Accessed 03 February 2018

Bartash J (2006) Verizon completes MCI acquisition. https://www.marketwatch.com/story/verizon-completes-mci-acquisition. Accessed 03 February 2018

CNNMoney News (1997) WorldCom wins MCI. http://money.cnn.com/1997/11/10/deals/worldcomwins/. Accessed 02 February 2018

Hiltzik M, Shiver J Jr (1997) WorldCom makes $30 billion offer to take over MCI. http://articles.latimes.com/1997/oct/02/news/mn-38328. Accessed 03 February 2018

Kupfer A (1998) MCI Worldcom: it's the biggest merger ever. Can it rule Telecom? http://archive.fortune.com/magazines/fortune/fortune_archive/1998/04/27/241525/index.htm. Accessed 03 February 2018

Reardon M (2018) Verizon closes book on MCI merger. https://www.cnet.com/g00/news/verizon-closes-book-on-mci-merger/?i10c.encReferrer=aHR0cHM6Ly93d3cuZ29vZ2xlLmNvbS8%3D&i10c.ua=1&i10c.dv=14. Accessed 03 February 2018

Richtel M, Sorkin AR (2005) Verizon agrees to acquire MCI for $6.6 billion, beating Qwest. https://www.nytimes.com/2005/02/14/technology/verizon-agrees-to-acquire-mci-for-66-billion-beating-qwest.html. Accessed 03 February 2018

Schiesel S (1997) The battle for MCI: The offer; MCI accepts offer of $36.5 billion; deal sets record. https://www.nytimes.com/1997/11/11/business/the-battle-for-mci-the-offer-mci-accepts-offer-of-36.5-billion-deal-sets-record.html. Accessed 03 February 2018

Shiver J Jr (1997) MCI, WorldCom agree to record $37 billion merger. http://articles.latimes.com/1997/nov/11/news/mn-52599. Accessed 03 February 2018

The Economist (1997) WorldCom and MCI engaged. https://www.economist.com/business/1997/11/13/engaged. Accessed 03 February 2018

Microsoft's Acquisition of LinkedIn

27

Microsoft the technology company was founded in the year 1975. Microsoft develops, licenses, and supports a wide range of software products, services, and devices that provide value to millions of people around the world. The strategy of Microsoft is to build best in class platforms and productivity series for an intelligent cloud infused with artificial intelligence. The products offered by Microsoft include operating systems, cross-device productivity applications, server applications, business solution applications, desktop and server management tools, software development tools, video games, and training and certification of computer system integrators and developers. Microsoft also designs, manufactures, and sells devices which include PCs, tablets, gaming, and entertainment consoles. Microsoft also offers an array of services which include cloud-based solutions which provide customers with software, services, platforms, and content. Microsoft operates worldwide in over 190 countries.

In 2017, the company made $90 billion in revenues and $22.3 billion in operating income. According to 2017 statistics, more than 100 million people use Office 365 commercial. Approximately 27 million consumers use Office 365 Home & Personal across devices. More than 53 million members are active on Xbox. More than 500 million LinkedIn members use the LinkedIn network. Windows 10 is active on more than 500 million devices around the world. In 2017, Dynamics 365 customers grew more than 40 percent year over year. During fiscal years 2017, 2016, and 2015, research and development expense for the company was $13.0 billion, $12.0 billion, and $12.0 billion, respectively.

Microsoft operate its business using three segments: Productivity and Business Processes, Intelligent Cloud, and More Personal Computing. The Productivity and Business Processes segment primarily comprises Office Commercial, Office Consumer, LinkedIn, and Dynamics Business Solutions. The Office Commercial included Office 365 subscriptions and Office licensed on premises which comprised Office, Exchange, SharePoint, Skype for Business, Microsoft Teams, and related

B. R. Kumar, *Wealth Creation in the World's Largest Mergers and Acquisitions*, Management for Professionals, https://doi.org/10.1007/978-3-030-02363-8_27

Client Access Licenses. Office Consumer segment included Office 365 subscriptions, Office licensed on premises, and Office Consumer Services which included Skype, Outlook.com, and OneDrive. LinkedIn includes Talent Solutions, Marketing Solutions, and Premium Subscriptions. Dynamics Business Solutions includes Dynamics ERP, Dynamics CRM, and Dynamics 365. The Intelligent Cloud segment offered server products and cloud services which included Microsoft SQL, Windows Server, Visual Studio, System Center, related CALs, and Azure. Enterprise Services included Premier Support Services and Microsoft Consulting Services. The More Personal Computing segment consists of Windows including Windows OEM licensing; Windows Commercial; Devices which include Microsoft Surface; Gaming which includes Xbox hardware, Xbox software, and services; and search advertising. The following table provides the financial highlights of Microsoft (Table 27.1).

The values are in millions of dollars except per share data. On December 8, 2016, Microsoft acquired LinkedIn. The acquired company results have been incorporated in the consolidated results of operations in year 2017 starting on the acquisition date. The following table lists the ten biggest deals of Microsoft (Table 27.2).

Table 27.1 Financial highlights

Year ended June 30	2017	2016	2015	2014	2013
Revenue	$89,950	$85,320	93,580	86,833	77,849
Gross margin	55,689	52,540	60,542	59,755	57,464
Operating income	22,326	20,182	18,161	27,759	26,764
Net income	21,204	16,798	12,193	22,074	21,863
Diluted earnings per share	2.71	2.10	1.48	2.63	2.58
Cash dividends declared per share	1.56	1.44	1.24	1.12	0.92
Cash and cash equivalents	132,981	113,240	96,526	85,709	77,022
Total assets	241,086	193,468	174,303	170,569	140,890
Long-term obligations	104,165	62,114	44,574	35,285	24,531
Stockholders' equity	72,394	71,997	80,083	89,784	78,944

Source: Microsoft Annual Report (2017)

Table 27.2 Microsoft's ten biggest deals

SL	Year	Company	Deal value in billion dollars
1	2016	LinkedIn	$28
2	2011	Skype	$8.5
3	2018	Github	$7.5
4	2013	Nokia	$7.2
5	2007	Aquantive	$5.9
6	2014	Mojang	$2.5
7	2002	Navision	$1.3
8	1999	Visio	$1.3
9	2000	Great Plains Software	$1.3
10	2012	Yammer	$1.2

Source: Dealogic

LinkedIn

It is the world's largest professional network on the Internet with more than 562 million users in more than 200 countries and territories worldwide. This business- and employment-oriented service operates via websites and mobile apps (Microsoft Annual Report, 2018). The company was launched in the year 2005. LinkedIn offers services which are used by customers to transform the way they hire, market, sell, and learn. LinkedIn allows members to create profiles and connections to each other in an online social network which represent real-world professional relationships. LinkedIn has a diversified business with revenues from membership subscriptions, advertising sales, and recruitment solutions.

Along with LinkedIn's free services, LinkedIn offers three categories of monetized solutions: Talent Solutions, Marketing Solutions, and Premium Subscriptions which include Sales Solutions. Talent Solutions consists of two segments – Hiring and Learning and Development. Hiring segment enables recruiters to attract, recruit, and hire talent content. Learning and Development provides subscription to enterprises and individuals to access online learning content. Marketing Solutions facilitate firms to advertise to LinkedIn's member base. Premium Subscriptions enables professionals to manage their professional identity and connect their talent through additional services like premium search. Premium Subscriptions also include Sales Solutions which facilitate sales professionals that find, qualify, create sales opportunities, and accelerate social selling capabilities. LinkedIn revenue is mainly determined by demand from enterprises and professional organizations for subscriptions to Talent Solutions and Premium Subscriptions offering as well as member engagement.

Microsoft's Acquisition of LinkedIn

On June 13, 2016, Microsoft Corp and LinkedIn entered into a definitive agreement under which Microsoft acquired LinkedIn for $196 per share in an all-cash transaction valued at $26.2 billion which was inclusive of LinkedIn's net cash (Aitken, 2016). LinkedIn retained its distinct brand, culture, and independence. Jeff Weiner remained as the CEO of LinkedIn reporting to Satya Nadella, CEO of Microsoft. LinkedIn was continuously building a strong and growing business. In 2015, the company launched a new version of its mobile app which led to increased member engagement and enhanced LinkedIn newsfeed to deliver better business insights. LinkedIn had acquired a leading online learning platform called Lynda.com to enter a new market and rolled out a new version of its recruiter product to its enterprise customers. These strategic initiatives had resulted in increased membership. The year witnessed 19% growth year over year to more than 433 million members worldwide. The company also witnessed 9% year-on-year growth to more than 105 million unique visiting members per month. It had also registered 49% growth year-on-year to 60% mobile usage. There had been 34% growth year-on-year to more than 45 billion quarterly member page views and 101% year-on-year growth to more than seven million active job listing.

The acquisition was officially closed on December 8, 2016, after getting the final pending approval from the European Commission. Microsoft had to make concessions to the European Commission about how it would work to allow other social networking sites to integrate on its platforms. Governments of the United States, Canada, and Brazil had earlier approved the deal.

Morgan Stanley acted as exclusive financial advisor to Microsoft, and Simpson Thatcher & Bartlett LLP acted as legal advisor to Microsoft. Qatalyst Partners and Allen & Company LLC acted as financial advisors to LinkedIn, while Wilson Sonsini Goodrich and Rosati, a professional corporation, acted as legal advisor to the deal.

Deal Highlights

Microsoft paid $196 per share in cash which represented a 50% premium over LinkedIn's closing price before announcement. This amounted to $9 billion premium which was paid to LinkedIn's market value. Fitch Ratings, one of the Big Three credit rating agencies, placed Microsoft's long-term IDR and senior unsecured debt both at AA+ on deal announcement. Microsoft issued $19.75 billion of debt securities across seven maturities to finance its LinkedIn takeover (Microsoft News Centre, 2016). This bond issuance represented the fifth biggest corporate bond sale on record in the United States. With a $26.2 billion valuation, the LinkedIn's monthly active users were valued at $248 which was 23% more than Facebook's users and over 7.5x of Twitter's active users.

Strategic Drivers for the Deal

The LinkedIn's acquisition took place after high-profile failures such as Microsoft's doomed $6 billion acquisition of the Nokia. In 2003, when LinkedIn was founded, 4500 members joined after its first month. The new deal meant that Microsoft could embed LinkedIn with Skype, its email system, and other enterprise products. Microsoft acquired one of the world's most influential, specialized, highly read, and constantly updated digital media company (Feller, 2016). LinkedIn had 433 million users with more than a quarter of them in the United States alone. Now two members joined every second. In the first quarter of 2016, there were 45 billion page views which were 37 billion the previous quarter. Microsoft's largest ever acquisition was aimed to fit into a strategy of building up the Microsoft Office suite of workplace productivity products and its cloud computing business.

LinkedIn has over 500 million users on its professional network, most of whom use it for free. This service contributed to Microsoft's revenues through its three business divisions. The biggest of them "the Talent Solutions" helps recruiters find job for subscribers. It also derives revenue from advertisements on its platform. The company also offers paid subscription for online courses and premium access on its network. The platform users include sales representatives who use it as a tool for "social selling" or targeting prospective customers through their trusted social networks and connections (Lunden, 2016). Microsoft exploration into LinkedIn's professional network's database of work histories and detailed information would provide the strategic thrust for growth opportunities. Cross-selling opportunities existed for Office 365 or LinkedIn upgrades (Zolciak, 2016). New opportunities exist for monetization through individual and organization subscriptions and targeted advertising. Social media will also become source of new leads. LinkedIn would become a central professional profile that will be available within Outlook, Skype, Office, and Windows. The deal positioned Microsoft as a leader in data in the professional world both at organizational and individual level (Rosoff, 2016). The companies were expecting annual savings of $150 million by the year 2018. Synergy from the deal was expected through the integration of LinkedIn Sales Navigator tool for sales representatives into Microsoft's customer relationship management tool, Dynamics.

Post-acquisition Integration

The process of integration involved manifold initiatives like application of LinkedIn identity in Microsoft Outlook and the Office suite, LinkedIn notification within the Windows action center, etc. (Associated Press, 2018). The other integrative initiatives involved enabling members drafting resumes in word to update their profiles and apply jobs on LinkedIn. The other areas of integration involved extending the reach of sponsored content across Microsoft properties, Enterprise LinkedIn lookup powered by Active Directory and Office 365. There were opportunities for LinkedIn learning to be made available across the Office 365 and Windows ecosystem. Another area of importance was the strategizing social selling through the combination of Sales Navigator and Dynamics 365.

Microsoft have been focusing on growing LinkedIn after the acquisition. In its first year after acquisition, LinkedIn focused on its feed, adding video, overhauling its message platform, and the major focus on active job seekers than passive candidates (Foley, 2018).

Stock Market Reaction to Acquisition Announcement

The announcement date of the deal was June 13, 2016. Microsoft stock returns on the announcement day were −5% approximately. The stock price of Microsoft declined by 6% in the +1 and + 2 day after announcement. But the deal was value creating for Microsoft on the basis of cumulative returns for the 252-day period (−8 to +243 day) surrounding the acquisition announcement. The cumulative returns for Microsoft stock were 28.8% (Fig. 27.1).

The cumulative returns during the 7-day period (−3 to +3) were 3.28%. Microsoft stock registered negative gains in the short-term window periods. However, in the long window periods, the stock gained significantly (Table 27.3).

Fig. 27.1 Cumulative returns for Microsoft stock

Table 27.3 Cumulative returns for Microsoft in different time window period

Day	Cumulative returns (%)
−3 to +3	−3.28
−1 to +1	−3.49
−5 to +5	−3.30
−5 to +10	−6.50
−1 to+100	14.80
−8 to +243	28.80

LinkedIn was delisted from NYSE on December 19, 2016. The shares of LinkedIn traded for the final time on December 18, 2016 officially closed at $195.96. The stock, which in 2015 traded at around $260 and was priced at $131 prior to Microsoft offer, ended the year 2016 down 12.94% compared to 9.90% year-to-date rise in the S&P500 Index.

References

Aitken R (2016) Microsoft's $26 billion LinkedIn deal begs immaterial social media valuation. https://www.forbes.com/sites/rogeraitken/2016/08/14/microsofts-26bn-linkedin-deal-begs-immaterial-social-media-valuation-questions/#65b84e115412. Accessed 22 Feb 2018

Associated Press (2018) How Microsoft's marriage with LinkedIn working out. https://www.cbsnews.com/news/microsoft-linkedin-how-marriage-is-working-out/. Accessed 15 Feb 2018

Feller G (2016) This is the real reason Microsoft bought LinkedIn. https://www.forbes.com/sites/grantfeller/2016/06/14/this-is-the-real-reason-microsoft-bought-linkedin/#269edd03f04a. Accessed 5 Feb 2018

Foley M (2018) Microsoft and LinkedIn: When next to No News is Good. https://redmondmag.com/articles/2018/02/26/microsoft-and-linkedin-no-news.aspx. Accessed 15 Feb 2018

Lunden I (2016) Microsoft officially closes its $26.2 billion of LinkedIn. https://techcrunch.com/2016/12/08/microsoft-officially-closes-its-26-2b-acquisition-of-linkedin/. Accessed 5 Feb 2018

Microsoft Annual Report (2018)

Microsoft Annual Report (2017) https://www.microsoft.com/investor/reports/ar17/index.html

Microsoft News Centre (2016) Microsoft to acquire LinkedIn. https://news.microsoft.com/2016/06/13/microsoft-to-acquire-linkedin/. Accessed 5 Feb 2018

Rosoff M (2016) Microsoft just finalized its deal for LinkedIn –here's what happens next. http://www.businessinsider.com/microsoft-linkedin-acquisition-closes-next-steps-2016-12. Accessed 22 Feb 2018

Zolciak A (2016) Why Microsoft bought LinkedIn and what it means? https://brand24.com/blog/microsoft-bought-linkedin/. Accessed 20 Feb 2018

http://www.chicagotribune.com/g00/business/sns-bc-us--microsoft-linkedin-20180131-story.html?i10c.encReferrer=aHR0cHM6Ly93d3cuZ29vZ2xlLmFlLw%3D%3D&i10c.ua=1&i10c.dv=14

Procter & Gamble's Acquisition of Gillette

28

Introduction

Procter & Gamble Co. (P&G) is an American multinational consumer goods company headquartered in downtown Cincinnati, Ohio. The company was founded in the year 1837 by William Procter and James Gamble. The Company has five reportable segments: Beauty; Grooming; Health Care; Fabric and Home Care; and Baby, Feminine, and Family Care (P&G Website, 2018). P&G's ten-category portfolio includes Fabric Care, Home Care, Grooming, Oral Care, Baby Care, Feminine Care, Family Care, Personal Health Care, Hair Care, and Skin and Personal Care. P&G products are sold in more than 180 countries and territories mainly through mass merchandisers, grocery, stores, membership club stores, drug stores, department stores, distributors, wholesalers, baby stores, specialty beauty stores, e-commerce, high-frequency stores, and pharmacies. Approximately 16% of total sales of the company in 2017 were accounted by sales to Walmart Stores and its affiliates. Segment-wise Baby, Feminine, and Family Care accounted for 28% of the net sales in year 2017. Beauty segment accounted for 18%, while Fabric and Home Care accounted for 32% of the net sales. Health Care segment accounted for 12%, while Grooming segment accounted for 10% of the net sales in the year 2017.The research and development expenses of the company amounted to $1.9 billion in year 2017 and 2016. The total number of employees of the company was 95,000 as of 2017. The business model of P&G depends on the continuous growth and success of existing brands and products as well as the creation of new products. In 2014, P&G announced that it was streamlining and strengthening its product portfolio by selling off 105 brands to focus on the remaining 65 brands which produced 95% of the company's profits. During the last 2-year period, P&G divested, discontinued, or consolidated these 105 brands. In 2017, developed markets accounted for 65% of its sales, while the developing markets contributed the remaining 35% of the sales. In total, P&G returned nearly $22 billion of value through dividends, share exchanges, and share repurchases. The company paid $7.2 billion in dividends in 2017 which

B. R. Kumar, *Wealth Creation in the World's Largest Mergers and Acquisitions*,
Management for Professionals, https://doi.org/10.1007/978-3-030-02363-8_28

reflected a 3% increase thereby marking the 61st consecutive annual increase in dividends made by the company. P&G has consistently paid dividends for 127 years since the year of establishment. P&G had acquired Gillette Company in the year 2005. P&G had also acquired other brands as a part of its strategy for growth. P&G had undertaken major acquisitions with the focus on transformation of the company from heavy reliance on household products to overwhelming focus on beauty and personal care. In this context P&G acquired Germany's Wella AG hair care line in year 2003 for $5.7 billion. P&G had also acquired Clairol from Bristol Myers Squibb for its hair care lines in 2001. The company had acquired Iams Co. for its pet foods in the year 1999. The following table gives the financial highlights of P&G (Table 28.1).

Gillette

Gillette is a brand of men's and women's safety razors and other personal care products including shaving supplies owned by P&G. The Gillette Company was founded by King C Gillette in the year 1901 as a safety razor manufacturer. The Gillette Company continued as a supplier of products under various brands until its merger with P&G in the year 2005. The Gillett's assets were incorporated into a P&G unit known as "Global Gillette." In the year 2007, Global Gillette was dissolved and incorporated into two major divisions of P&G – P&G Beauty and P&G Household Care. The Gillette Company had $10.5 billion sales with net income of $1.7 billion in the year 2004. Gillette is a market leader in the shaving business. The following table gives the timeline of introduction of gillette products (Table 28.2).

Gillette's Acquisition by P&G

On January 28, 2005, P&G announced the largest acquisition in its history to buy Gillette in a $57 billion deal (Isdore, 2005). The deal combined some of the world's top brands. P&G was the largest consumer products company in the world. P&G products ranged from Crest toothpaste to Head & Shoulders shampoo. The major products of Gillette included its signature razors, Duracell batteries, Braun, and

Table 28.1 Financial highlights

Year	2017	2016	2015	2014	2013
Sales	$65	$65.30	$70.70	$74.40	$73.90
Operating income	$14	$13.40	$11	$13.90	$13.10
Net earnings	$15.30	$10.50	$7.00	$11.60	$11.30
Diluted EPS	$5.59	$3.69	$2.44	$4.01	$3.86
Operating cash flow	$12.80	$15.40	$14.60	$14.00	$14.90
Total assets	120.41	127.14	129.50	144.27	139.26

Source: P&G Annual Report (2017)
The values are given in billions of dollars except per share amounts

Table 28.2 Timeline of Gillette products

Year	Events
1901	Breakthrough innovation of disposable blades based on King C Gillett idea
1920	Gillette® set out to create the first mechanical innovation
1957	The first adjustable razor with three settings was introduced for light, medium, and heavy beards
1965	Techmatic, the first system razor with a "continuous band," spooled and retractable features introduced
1971	Gillette® produces the Trac II®, the first twin-blade shaving system
1977	Gillette introduces the Atra/Contour system, the first twin-blade shaving cartridge with a pivoting head
1985	Gillette Atra Plus/Contour Plus – the first razor with a lubricating strip – is launched
1990	Gillette launches Sensor® – the first razor with twin blades individually mounted on highly responsive springs
1998	Gillette breaks the performance barrier with the MACH3®, the first three-blade technology
2006	Gillette Fusion® razors debut in manual and power versions
2015	The Gillette Fusion ProGlide® with FlexBall™ Technology Razor is introduced
2017	Gillette Fusion ProShield® with lubrication is introduced

Oral-B brands dental care products. The merger created the largest consumer products company in the world. Berkshire Hathaway was Gillette's largest shareholder with 96 million shares which represented 9% of the company. The deal gave P&G more control over shelf space at the nation's retailers and grocers and real estate which was at premium. P&G added Duracell batteries, Right Guard deodorant, and Gillette razors to more than 300 consumer brands which included Ivory soap, Head & Shoulders shampoo, Pringles, Crest toothpaste, and Bounty paper towels. The acquisition was expected to vault P&G's sales to more than $60 billion annually.

The acquisition enabled Gillette and P&G to get better shelf space and distribute their products more cheaply.

Deal Highlights

P&G paid 0.975 share of its common stock for each share of Gillette common stock. On the basis of the closing price of $55.32 per share on January 28, 2005, the deal valued Gillette at about $54 per share which represented an 18% premium over its closing price. P&G had also announced plans to buy back $18 to $22 billion of its stock in within a time window of 2 years. On the basis of this plan, the deal was to be finally financed through 60% stock and 40% cash.

Strategic Advantages of the Deal

With the acquisition of Gillette, P&G became a more balanced company (Neff, 2005). Approximately half of P&G sales came from the Baby, Family, and Household categories, while the other half came from Beauty and Health businesses. With Gillette acquisition, P&G had 10 billion dollar brands in Beauty and Health and 12 billion dollar brands in Baby, Family, and Household segments. The deal involved reduction by about 4% of the combined work force of 140,000 employees. The job reductions were to come from eliminating management overlaps and consolidation of business support functions.

The value of the planned cost savings was expected to be in the range of $14–$16 billion. The combined company was expecting cost savings of more than $ 1 billion by the third year after merger. On consolidation, P&G with 16 brands having sales of more than $ 1 billion each and Gillette with five major brands was positioned to have greater leverage in negotiation with retailers for the all-important display space. The consolidation helped the companies to get further savings from broadcasters and other media companies on advertising purchases. At the time of acquisition, P&G was the largest television advertiser in the United States, while Gillette spend almost $ 1 billion a year on advertisements which primarily targeted men rather than P&G's traditional female customers. The combined company was able to see savings from manufacturing as well as the logistics of moving productions from plants to stores. P&G became one of the top US advertising spenders with addition of Gillette's more than $200 million in US advertisement spending. The deal added billion dollar global brands such as Gillette, Duracell, and Right Guard to P&G's existing 16 to create a stable of 21 billion dollar brands.

At the time of the deal, P&G had the largest lineup of leading brands in the industry of which 17 were billion dollar brands and 13 brands with sale of $500 million or more. These 13 brands had the capability of crossing the billion dollar mark in the next few years. P&G focused on the same strategy and leveraged the same core strengths. The acquisition of Gillette accelerated the shift of P&G's business mix toward faster-growing, higher-margin, and more asset-efficient businesses of beauty and health. The combined company brought together many of the industry's most successful brands. With the purchase of Gillette, P&G had 22 billion dollar brands. The combined company was able to offer retailers a larger, more profitable mix of brands, broader, and deeper consumer and shopper knowledge. The consolidation also led to more product and marketing innovation and more supply chain solutions. The combination also provided Gillette access to P&G's larger distribution networks in major developing markets where P&G had the presence in approximately 2000 cities and more than 11,000 towns and villages. Gillette became one of the biggest growth opportunities for P&G. P&G revised its annual sales growth forecast through 2010 on account of Gillette's leadership position in fast-growing categories and expected synergies.

Gillette's razors and blades had a global market share of more than 70% which was nearly five times higher than the nearest competitor. Braun was the number one global brand in the premium electric shaver market. Oral-B had a strong portfolio in manual, battery, rechargeable toothbrushes. Oral-B was the market leader with 36% share of market.

Both Gillette and P&G were delivering strong top and bottom line growth. The acquisition combined Gillette's and P&G's healthy brand franchises and core strengths. The unique flexibility of P&G's organization structure facilitated the integration of Gillette's business into P&G. P&G's organization structure consisted of Global Business Unit (GBU), Market Development Organization (MDO), and Global Business Services (GBS). Gillette's businesses took advantage of P&G's GBU, MDO, and GBS organization structure.

The acquisition identified more than a billion dollars in cost synergy opportunities. P&G eliminated administrative overlap by integrating Gillette's and P&G's corporate staff.

Significant synergy opportunities existed in purchasing, manufacturing, logistics, marketing, and retail selling (Vries, 2005). After acquisition, the focus of P&G was on expansion of Gillette brands into channels and markets with little presence like China. P&G also leveraged Gillette's strong in store presence in channels and with customers where P&G brands are not fully developed such as home improvement channels.

Gillette and P&G had similar cultures and complementary core strengths in branding, innovation, scale, and go to market capabilities which turned out to be a strategic fit.

P&G and Gillette shareholders approved the deal on July 12, 2005, with more than 96% of voting shareholders in favor of the acquisition.

Stock Market Reaction

The announcement date for the deal was January 28, 2005. On announcement day, P&G stock went down by approximately 2%, while Gillette stock jumped about 12% in afternoon trading of the announcement day. Gillette shares closed at $45.85 which was a new 52 weeks high for the company.

P&G stock declined by 2% on the day of announcement and 1 day after announcement. The cumulative returns for the 251-day period surrounding the merger announcement date (−8 to +242 day) were approximately 6% (Table 28.3).

The cumulative returns were negative in the shorter time window period and positive in the longer time window period (Fig. 28.1).

Table 28.3 Cumulative returns for P&G in different time window period

Time window days	Cumulative returns (%)
−1 to +1	−4
−5 to+5	−7
−5 to +10	−8
−1 to +100	2
−8 to +242	6

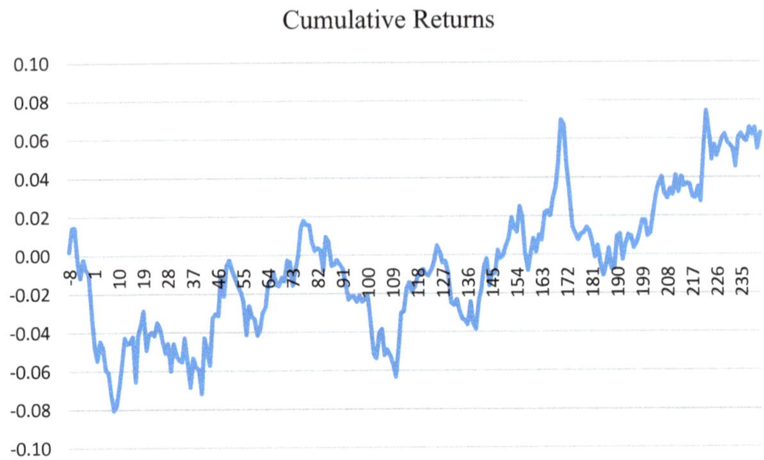

Fig. 28.1 Cumulative returns for P&G stock

Operating Performance

During the announcement period, both companies had reported strong earnings. P&G registered strong quarterly earnings with a 12% increase in net income from $1.8 billion to $2.04 billion. In the same quarter, the sales increased by 7% to reach $14.45 billion. Gillette also reported increase of income from $416 million to $475 million in the same quarter.

The operating performance is analyzed by comparing the average growth rate of financial variables like sales, operating income, and net earnings in the premerger period compared to the post-merger period. The year of merger (2005) is excluded from analysis. It has to be noted that 3 years of the post-merger period were recessionary period (Table 28.4).

The values are given in millions of dollars except net earnings margin which are stated in percentage (Annual Reports of P&G, 2005–2010). The average growth rate values of financial parameters like net sales, operating income, net earnings, and total assets were compared in the post-merger period (2006–2010) in relation with the premerger period (2001–2004). The average growth rate of net sales of 9.6% in premerger period declined to 5.4% average growth rate in the post-merger period. The average growth rate of operating income and net earnings of 27.91% and 31.02% in the premerger period declined to 6.5% and 10.4% in the post-merger period. The average growth rate of assets in the premerger period which was approximately 18% declined to −1.3%. The average net earnings margin in the post-merger period improved to 13.6% from 10.7% in the premerger period. The average capital expenditure in the premerger period was $1917.75 million and $2992.6 million in the post-merger period.

Table 28.4 Comparative operating performance in pre- and post-acquisition period

Merger period	−4	−3	−2	−1	0	1	2	3	4	5
Year	2001	2002	2003	2004	2005	2006	2007	2008	2009	2010
Net sales	39,244	40,238	43,377	51,407	56,741	64,416	72,441	79,257	76,694	78,938
Operating income	4736	6678	7853	9827	10,927	12,551	14,485	15,979	15,374	16,021
Net earnings	2922	4352	5186	6481	7257	8684	10,340	12,075	13,436	12,736
Net earnings margin	7.40%	10.80%	12%	12.60%	12.80%	12.70%	13.30%	14.20%	13.90%	13.90%
Total assets	34,387	40,776	43,706	57,048	61,527	135,695	138,014	143,992	134,833	128,172
Capital expenditure	2486	1679	1482	2024	2181	2667	2945	3046	3238	3067

References

Annual Reports of P&G 2005–2010

Isdore C (2005) P&G to buy Gillette for $57 B. http://money.cnn.com/2005/01/28/news/fortune500/pg_gillette. Accessed 26 Feb 2018

Neff J (2005) P&G acquires Gillette for $57 billion. http://adage.com/article/news/p-g-acquires-gillette-57-billion/41996/. Accessed 26 Feb 2018

P&G Annual Report (2017). http://www.pginvestor.com/CustomPage/Index?KeyGenPage=1073748359

Vries L (2005) Procter & Gamble acquires Gillette. https://www.cbsnews.com/news/procter-gamble-acquires-gillette/. Accessed 26 Feb 2018

Oracle's Hostile Takeover of PeopleSoft 29

Introduction

Oracle was founded in 1976 by Larry Ellison. Oracle Corporation provides products and services for corporate information technology (IT) environments consisting of applications, platform, and infrastructure (Annual Reports Oracle Corporation, 2005). The applications, platform, and infrastructure offerings are delivered to customers worldwide through a number of flexible and interoperable IT deployment models like cloud-based, on-premise or hybrid models. The company has a customer network of around 430,000 based in 175 countries. Oracle Cloud offerings provide a comprehensive and fully integrated tack of applications, platform, compute, storage, and networking services. The Oracle Cloud services like Oracle Cloud SaaS, PaaS, and IaaS integrate the software, hardware, and services on customer's behalf in IT environments. Oracle is a world leader in the core technologies of cloud IT environments which include database and middleware software as well as enterprise applications, virtualization, clustering, large-scale system management, and related infrastructure. The company invested $6.1 billion in R&D expenses in the year 2018. Oracle has three business segments. The cloud and license business include Oracle cloud service offerings, cloud license, and on-premise license offerings and license support offerings. The cloud and license business accounted for 82% of the total revenues in the year 2018. The hardware business included hardware products and related hardware support service offerings. The service business segment accounted for 8% of the total revenues in the year 2018. The following table provides the financial highlights of Oracle Corporation (Table 29.1).

Oracle has made over 125 acquisitions over a period of time. The largest acquisitions by Oracle is given in the following table (Table 29.2) (Butler, 2016).

B. R. Kumar, *Wealth Creation in the World's Largest Mergers and Acquisitions*, Management for Professionals, https://doi.org/10.1007/978-3-030-02363-8_29

Table 29.1 Select financial highlights

Year	2018	2017	2016	2015	2014
Total revenues	39,831	37,728	37,047	38,226	38,275
Operating income	13,679	12,710	12,604	13,871	12,759
Net income	3825	9335	8901	9938	10,955
Earnings per share	$0.90	$2.21	$2.07	$2.21	$2.38
Total assets	137,264	134,991	112,180	110,903	90,266

The values are given in millions of dollars except per share amount

Table 29.2 Largest acquisitions by Oracle

SL	Year	Target	Deal value	Strategic assets acquired
1	2005	PeopleSoft	$10.3 billion	SaaS platform for human resource,finance, supply chain, and CRM
2	2016	NetSuite	$9.3 billion	SaaS platform for enterprise resource planning (ERP)
3	2008	BEA systems	$8.5 billion	Application development and middleware software platform
4	2010	Sun	$7.4 billion	Java, MySQL database, servers, storage, and networking
5	2006	Siebel systems	$5.85 billion	Customer relationship management
6	2014	Micros systems	$5.3 billion	Retail and hospitality hardware/software systems
7	2007	Hyperion Corp.	$3.3 billion	Enterprise performance management software
8	2013	Acme packet	$2.1 billion	Networking hardware for telecommunication providers
9	2012	Taleo	$1.9 billion	Talent management software
10	2011	RightNow technologies	$1.5 billion	CRM SaaS

Source: Collated from various sources/Networkworld.com

PeopleSoft

Many companies use PeopleSoft's applications to manage their human resources, customer relationship, and accounting functions. PeopleSoft Inc. was a global leader in enterprise application software (Sikora, 1999). The company provided human resource management systems, financial management solutions, supply chain management, customer relationship, and enterprise performance management. PeopleSoft also provides PeopleSoft Campus Solution which is a separate package developed as a student information system for colleges and universities around the world. It existed as an independent corporation until its acquisition by Oracle Corporation in 2005. The company had exponential growth rate in the 1990s which slowed down in the 2000s.

Industry Scenario

Enterprise resource planning (ERP) is a subset within the computer software industry. ERP companies develop applications that automate the process of managing functions across a firm such as accounting, human resources, order processing, scheduling, distribution, and inventory management. SAP, Oracle, PeopleSoft, and Seibel Systems were the major ERP players. In the 1990s, ERP software business grew at 30%. In the 2000s, the business started shrinking. In the year 2003, the growth rates declined from double digit to single digit. The value of business was estimated as $36 billion. The sector was rapidly moving from the growth phase to mature phase. In the changing scenario, many ERP vendors moved beyond their core strengths in finance, human resources, and operations to offer broader set of applications. They focused on niche applications like customer relationship management (CRM) and supply chain management (SCM). The ERP industry was moving toward the universal concept of "one-stop shopping." Selection and implementation of ERP system is a time-consuming process (Miller and Hamerman, 2003). The licensing of ERP system usually takes a time span of 1.5–2 years.

The Takeover Battle

On June 6, 2003, Oracle had announced a hostile takeover of PeopleSoft. Oracle had offered to buy PeopleSoft's shares at a price of $16 per share which represented a premium of 6% over the company's price the week before the announcement (Dicarlo, 2003). The deal was valued at $5.3 billion. It was a major deal announcement after IBM bought Lotus Development in the year 1995.

The all-cash deal signified that the shareholders of PeopleSoft would not get a stake in the new company (PR Newswire, 2003). It was also announced that once the merger was complete, Oracle would discontinue PeopleSoft products. The plan was to merge PeopleSoft's application developers with those of Oracle and advance Oracle's eBusiness Suite of software. This strategic move came 4 days after PeopleSoft announced that it would buy JD Edwards for $0.17 billion (Reporter, 2004).

The software sold by PeopleSoft were complex in nature in terms of installation. The subsequent customization and ongoing vendor consulting and technical support system were also complicated.

As the revenues of its FlagShip database had flattened, Oracle had pegged its growth to business application. SAP was having the dominant market share of 17% in the market.

PeopleSoft turned down Oracle offer on June 12, 2003, stating the antitrust authorities would block the deal and Oracle's decision to discontinue PeopleSoft's products would damage the company. On June 16, 2003, PeopleSoft amended its bid for JD Edwards in such a way that it is not required to put the merger plan to a vote for PeopleSoft shareholders. On June 18, 2003, Oracle raised its bid to $19.50 and also filed a suit against PeopleSoft alleging that the board's actions which included its refusal to dissolve the firm's strong "poison pill" antitakeover defense breached its fiduciary duties to shareholders. Two PeopleSoft executives had developed a plan to give customers an incentive to make substantial investment which was required in purchasing People Software. The plan which was known as PeopleSoft's Customer Assurance Program (CAP) aimed to provide customers with a contractual assurance that they would be reimbursed for certain software-related costs if the acquirer did not support and upgrade PeopleSoft's products.

The board of PeopleSoft formed a transaction committee out of a group of independent directors. The purpose of this committee was to evaluate Oracle's offer. The transaction committee came to the conclusion that Oracle's $16 offer undervalued PeopleSoft's stock and offered premium of only 6% to stockholders based on PeopleSoft's June 5 closing stock price of $15.11. In hostile takeovers 40% of the bids were stated to result in at least a 50% premium. PeopleSoft had offered 60% premium in its proposed acquisition of software firm Vantive. The committee felt that the Oracle offer would lead to a long regulatory approval process and the merger may not be approved by the regulatory authorities. The Committee further opined that offer would erode shareholder value and have negative consequences in relation to financial performance.

The board decided to pursue two action plans to thwart Oracle's hostile takeover attempt. One of the plans was the usage of flip-in poison pills. If a single shareholder acquired over 20% of PeopleSoft's stock, then the firm would issue new shares to other existing shareholders at a heavily discounted price. PeopleSoft would continue to issue shares until the acquirer's shares were diluted by 50%. The pill could be triggered multiple times. Flip-in plans can effectively block any acquisition of PeopleSoft unless the board approved the deal and rescinded the pill. The board also adopted the Customer Assurance Plan to derail the takeover attempt of Oracle Corp. The plan stipulated that customers would receive a money back guarantee of two to five times what they paid for the software in the case of acquisition of PeopleSoft and the acquirer did not maintain or continue the PeopleSoft products. This plan was attractive to improve sales and would become expensive for a company to acquire PeopleSoft (Landgrave, 2004). It was estimated that the assurance plan would create potential liabilities of an amount of more than $2 billion.

Many analysts observed that Oracle's intention was to thwart the PeopleSoft-JD Edwards merger. Oracle was serious about its intention to acquire PeopleSoft (Knowledge@Wharton, 2013). The company wanted to incorporate advanced features from the PeopleSoft's products into future versions of the Oracle eBusiness Suite. Oracle expected substantial cost savings and minimal business integration risk. Oracle was attracted toward PeopleSoft's larger installed base of applications (Smith, 2013). In 2002, PeopleSoft's revenue amounted to $700 million. The PeopleSoft was projecting that they were acting in the best interests of PeopleSoft's shareholders. Analysts believed that SAP could be the real winner in a long drawn-out battle between PeopleSoft and Oracle (Daines et al., 2006).

PeopleSoft filed a lawsuit in Alameda on June 14 seeking an injunction to block Oracle's offer. The suit alleged that Oracle's bid had interfered with PeopleSoft's agreement to acquire JD Edwards. On June 16, PeopleSoft and JD Edwards revised the terms of their merger agreement to prevent Oracle's bid for PeopleSoft. The revamped offer included $863 million in cash. The enhanced value of the deal to JD Edwards stockholders became $1.75 billion. The original offer had been an all-stock deal. From PeopleSoft perspective, the JD Edwards deal would increase the size of the prospective deal for Oracle by almost 30%. In August 2003, the PeopleSoft adopted another antitakeover defense mechanism by adopting golden parachutes involving large cash payments related to severance policies to senior executives in the event of change of control due to acquisition (The Economist, 2003). On account of all these antitakeover defenses, Oracle couldn't acquire PeopleSoft directly through a tender offer. PeopleSoft continued to be firm in its unwillingness to negotiate. During November 2003, Oracle nominated five candidates to stand for election on its behalf for election to the PeopleSoft board of directors and proposed a bylaw change which would expand the board to nine from the present eight. The contest offered the opportunity to take control of PeopleSoft by electing a majority of its directors at its annual meeting scheduled on March 25, 2004. Oracle raised its offer to $26 per share in cash on February 4, 2004. This rise was a 63% increase over the initial bid. The total value of the deal became $9.4 billion. PeopleSoft again dismissed Oracle's revised bid citing regulatory concerns and inadequacy of the revised offer for shareholders. The Department of Justice joined by seven states filed suit to block the deal on antitrust grounds on February 26, 2004. Oracle withdrew its nominees for board posts and dropped its proxy contest the same day. PeopleSoft's stock was continuously declining ever since the Department of Justice announcement of file suit against the takeover. On May 14, 2003, Oracle lowered its bid to $21 based on the market conditions at that time (PeopleSoft Corporation, 2003). On September 9, 2004, the District Court of Northern District of California ruled that the Department of Justice has failed to prove that the consolidation of Oracle and PeopleSoft would lessen competition in the business application software market segment. On September 30, 2004, the other board members voted unanimously to remove Conway as CEO. Conway resigned from board and received $13.7 million severance package. Oracle had brought a suit before the Delaware Court of Chancery seeking the removal of PeopleSoft's poison pill and an injunction to stop the CAP program (PeopleSoft Court Brief, n.d.). On November 1, 2004, Oracle through its Operation "Bump and Rush" increased its cash offer from $21 to $26.5 per share which was described by Oracle as the best and final offer. But Oracle made a condition that it will withdraw the offer unless a majority of PeopleSoft shareholders accept the offer by November 19, 2004. PeopleSoft again rejected the offer and advised shareholders not to tender their shares. By November 19, 2004, approximately 61% of PeopleSoft's shares were tendered. Finally, 97% of PeopleSoft's stockholders were ready to sell their outstanding stock which amounted to about 388.7 million shares. Oracle's final offers of $26.5 per share in cash were accepted by PeopleSoft's board of directors on December 12, 2004. The deal value was finally estimated as $10.3 billion. The 3% remaining PeopleSoft shareholders who did not tender their shares were paid the $26.50 offer price. This final offer represented approximately 10% premium over PeopleSoft's closing price. Finally, the 18-month struggle between the two companies ended. PeopleSoft, the number two supplier of enterprise application software, became the wholly owned subsidiary of Oracle Corporation. The Delaware trial and another lawsuit filed by PeopleSoft were dropped as part of the sale (Millsstone and Subramanian, 2017). The merger was completed on January 7, 2005. The merger made Oracle the world's second largest seller of business application software behind SAP AG (Kane, 2004).

Reasons for Acquisition

The enterprise industry was getting matured, and PeopleSoft had the competitive edge to survive. Oracle was one of the largest providers of database software but was lacking the customer relationship management (CRM) domain. Oracle wanted to avoid competition as PeopleSoft would have become bigger than Oracle if the deal with JD Edwards materialized. Oracle would gain market share and get new products once PeopleSoft comes into its kitty. In other words, Oracle could expand its own business while preventing a rival company from expanding at the same time. Through PeopleSoft acquisition, Oracle could focus toward the goal of one-stop shopping where all services are provided. Oracle was able to provide customers with a stronger support system through the deal with PeopleSoft (Knowledge@ Wharton, 2003). The merger was a step toward consolidation in the telecom industry sector. The acquisition of PeopleSoft gave Oracle the size it required to compete effectively in the application market. The merger led to increase in the number of customers (Landgrave, 2004). The newly merged company became the number one application vendor in North America. The combined company had number one market position in banking application and strong presence in healthcare sector (Mcmillan and Niccolai, 2005).

Stock Market Reaction to Deal

On announcement, PeopleSoft's shares rose sharply and were trading at $3 higher than what Oracle was offering. This section analyzes the stock returns for Oracle during the entire takeover period. The date of hostile takeover announcement was June 6, 2003.The merger was completed on January 07, 2005.

The Oracle share declined in value during the immediate period surrounding the hostile takeover announcement. The stock price declined by 2% each on the −1,0, + 1 day during the announcement period. The stock price increased by 1% and 2% on day +2 and + 3 of the announcement period (Table 29.3).

The stock price gained approximately 17.2% during the 410 days (−8 day to +401 day) surrounding the takeover announcement period (Table 29.4).

The cumulative returns for Oracle stock were positive for most of the time window period (Fig. 29.1).

Table 29.3 Announcement period return for Oracle stock

Day	Returns (%)
−5	1
−4	−2
−3	2
−2	4
−1	−2
0	−2
1	−2
2	1
3	2
4	0
5	1

Table 29.4 Cumulative returns for Oracle stock in different time window periods

Time window in days	Cumulative returns (%)
−1 to+1	−5.40
−3 to +3	3.80
−5 to +5	5.20
−5 to +10	1.10
−1 to+100	−9.40
−8 to +401	17.20

Fig. 29.1 Cumulative returns for Oracle in different time window periods

References

Annual Reports Oracle Corporation (2005–2010)

Butler B (2016) A look at Oracle's 10 biggest. https://www.networkworld.com/article/3101876/software/a-look-at-oracle-s-10-biggest-acquisitions.html. Accessed 5 Mar 2018

Daines R, Drabkin D, Nair V (2006). Case: CG-4A, Oracle's hostile takeover of PeopleSoft (A), Stanford Graduate School of Business

Dicarlo L (2003) Oracle goes hostile after Peoplesoft. https://www.forbes.com/2003/06/06/cx_ld_0606orcl.html#1fd61b1a4451. Accessed 3 Mar 2018
Kane M (2004) Oracle buys PeopleSoft for $10 billion. https://www.cnet.com/news/oracle-buys-peoplesoft-for-10-billion/?i10c.encReferrer=aHR0cHM6Ly93d3cuZ29vZ2xlLmFlLw==&i10c.ua=1&i10c.dv=14. Accessed 17 Mar 2018
Knowledge@Wharton (2003) What's behind Oracle's unwelcome bid for Peoplesoft. http://knowledge.wharton.upenn.edu/article/whats-behind-oracles-unwelcome-bid-for-peoplesoft/. Accessed 9 Mar 2018
Knowledge@Wharton (2013) What's behind Oracle's unwelcome bid for PeopleSoft. 14 June
Landgrave T (2004) Who benefits if Oracle buys peoplesoft. https://www.techrepublic.com/article/who-benefits-if-oracle-buys-peoplesoft/. Accessed 17 Mar 2018
Mcmillan R and Niccolai J (2005) Its official –Oracle closes on PeopleSoft acquisition. https://www.computerworld.com/article/2568706/enterprise-applications/it-s-official%2D%2Doracle-closes-on-peoplesoft-acquisition.html. Accessed 17 Mar 2018
Miller B, Hamerman P (2003) Market overview 2003: comprehensive enterprise applications. Giga Information Group Inc (Forrester Research, Inc)
Millsstone D, Subramanian G (2017).Oracle Versus PeopleSoft: a case study, Harvard Negotiation Law Review, Vol 12–1
PeopleSoft Corporation (2003) Annual Report. p 56
PeopleSoft Court Brief p 15
PR Newswire (2003) Oracle to Launch Cash Tender Offer to PeopleSoft for$16 per share, PR Newswire. 6 June
Reporter (2004) Oracle to acquire PeopleSoft for 103 billion. https://www.nytimes.com/2004/12/14/technology/oracle-to-acquire-peoplesoft-for-103-billion-ending-bitter-fight.html?mtrref=www.google.ae&gwh=FCC179B4B16CC7C8B8F9243816317564&gwt=pay. Accessed 15 Mar 2018
Sikora M (1999) Tender offers. Plugged in: PeopleSoft marries late. Barrons Chicopee 79(42):53
Smith R (2013) Why did Oracle acquire PeopleSoft. http://www.peoplesoft-planet.com/oracle-acquire-peoplesoft/. Accessed 10 Mar 2018
The Economist (2003) Oracle Versus Peoplesoft. Barbarians in the valley. https://www.economist.com/business/2003/06/26/barbarians-in-the-valley.Accessed 5 Mar 2018

Mergers and Acquisitions by Bank of America 30

Introduction

Bank of America's acquisition of Countrywide Financial Corporation had been ranked as one of the worst financial decisions in US business history as by 2016; Bank of America's mortgage business had lost more than $50 billion since the purchase of Countrywide Financial. The acquisition of Merrill Lynch catapulted Bank of America into number one underwriter of global high-yield debt and the third largest underwriter of global equity. Among the six acquisition announcements analyzed, only the acquisition of US Trust resulted in a positive gain of 0.09% on the announcement day. Positive returns were registered for the Bank of America for the acquisition of FleetBoston, MBNA, and Countrywide for the day before announcement.

The Bank of America is a global leader in wealth management, corporate, and investment banking and trades across a broad range of asset classes. The Bank of America serves governments, corporations, institutions, and individuals throughout the globe. The Bank of America is a Delaware incorporated bank holding company (BHC) and financial holding company. In the United States alone, the bank serves approximately 47 million consumer and small business relationships. The bank serves clients in more than 35 countries. The Bank of America provides a diversified range of banking and nonbanking financial services and products through four business segments: Consumer Banking, Global Wealth and Investment Management, Global Banking, and Global Market. The remaining operations are recorded in All Other. As of December 2017, the corporation had approximately $2.3 trillion in assets and headcount of approximately 209,000 employees. The Bank of America has approximately 4500 retail financial centers and around 16,000 ATMs. The Bank of America has leading banking platforms with approximately 35 million active users and 24 million mobile active users. The bank offers support to approximately three million small business owners. The wealth management businesses with client

B. R. Kumar, *Wealth Creation in the World's Largest Mergers and Acquisitions*, Management for Professionals, https://doi.org/10.1007/978-3-030-02363-8_30

Table 30.1 Financial highlights of the Bank of America

Year	2017	2016	2015	2014	2013
Net interest income	44,667	41,096	38,958	40,779	40,719
Non-interest income	42,685	42,605	44,007	45,115	46,783
Total revenue	87,352	83,701	82,965	85,894	87,502
Net income	18,232	17,822	15,910	5520	10,539
Return on average assets	0.80%	0.81%	0.74%	0.26%	0.49%
Market capitalization	303,681	222,163	174,700	188,141	164,914
Total loans and leases	918,731	900,433	876,787	898,703	918,641
Total assets	2,268,633	2,190,218	2,160,536	2,145,393	2,163,296
Total deposits	1,269,796	1,222,561	1,155,860	1,124,207	1,089,735
Shareholder equity	271,289	265,843	251,384	238,317	233,819

The values are in millions of dollars except return on average assets which is stated in percentage

balances of nearly $2.8 trillion provide customized solutions to clients through a broad range of investment management, brokerage, banking, trust, and retirement products. The following table gives the financial highlights of Bank of America (Table 30.1).

Acquisitions by Bank of America

In the year 1998, the Bank of America was formed by the merger between the NationsBank and Bank of America. This union created a bank with assets of $ 570 billion and extensive network of 4800 branches. During the period 2004–2007, the Bank of America bought FleetBoston Financial for $47 billion, credit card giant MBNA for $35 billion, US Trust for $3.3 billion, and LaSalle Bank for $21 billion. In 2008, Bank of America acquired Countrywide Financial for $4.1 billion and Merrill Lynch for $50 billion which was an all-stock deal (Frankel, 2015).

Merger of NationsBank and Bank of America

In 1997, the Bank of America suffered huge losses as its client D. E. Shaw & Co., a large hedge fund, suffered significant losses after the 1998 Russian bond default. In October 1998, NationsBank of Charlotte acquired the Bank of America which was termed as the largest bank acquisition in history at that time. The holding company was renamed as Bank of America Corporation. In technical terms, the deal was a purchase of the Bank of America Corporation by NationsBank. But the deal was structured as merger. The deal was valued at $60 billion.

The NationsBank merged with Bank of America to form Bank of America N.A. as the remaining legal bank entity. NationsBank had undertaken a series of acquisitions to become the largest and fastest-growing financial institution in North Carolina. In the 1980s, NationsBank had acquired First National Bank of Lake City and First Republic Bank of Dallas. In the 1990s, NationsBank acquired Sovran Corp, Boatmen's Bank, and Barnett Bank, thereby expanding its presence in regions of Georgia, Missouri, and Florida.

The Bank of America has also used acquisition strategy. The Bank Holding Company Act 1956 forced the Bank of America to split off its insurance program. The Bank of America introduced the first bank credit card – the BankAmericard which later became Visa. In 1983, the Bank of America acquired Seafirst Corp. of Seattle. In the 1990s, the Bank of America acquired Security Pacific Corp, Continental Illinois National Bank, and Trust Company of Chicago. Through these acquisitions, the Bank of America emerged as the second largest deposit-based financial corporation after NationsBank. The consolidation led to the establishment of the first coast to coast interstate retail and commercial retail giant in US history.

Acquisitions by Fleet Group

FleetBoston Financial was created by the merger of Fleet Financial Group and BankBoston in the year 1999. In the year 2004, FleetBoston Financial merged with Bank of America. Fleet was founded as Providence Bank in the year 1791. Providence Bank joined the national banking system in the year 1865 as Providence National Bank. In the year 1951, Providence bank merged with Union Trust Company to form Providence Union Bank and Trust Company. In 1954, the bank acquired Industrial Trust Company to form Industrial National Bank. By the year 1968, the bank became the leading subsidiary of Industrial National Corporation. In the mid-1970s, the Industrial National bank began to diversify into nonbank financial services. The bank changed its name to Fleet Financial Group in the year 1982. The banking subsidiary became Fleet National Bank. In the year 1988, Fleet merged with New York-based Norstar Bancorp to form Fleet/Norstar Financial Group. In 1991, Fleet/Norstar acquired the Bank of New England. In 1992, the company readopted the Fleet Financial Group name. In 1995, Fleet merged with the Shawmut National Corp. The newly formed bank became a major regional bank and the ninth largest bank in the United States. Fleet acquired the US branch network of the British National Westminster Bank, the discount brokerage bank Quick & Reilly, and its discount online subsidiary Suretrade in the year 1996 and 1998, respectively. In 1999 Fleet merged with BankBoston. This was the biggest deal done by Fleet Group. BankBoston was formed by the merger between Bank of Boston and BayBank. The combined new bank FleetBoston became the seventh largest bank in the United States with asset size of $197 billion in the year 2003. The combined bank had approximately 20 million customers worldwide and revenues of $12 billion per year. For regulatory approval, Fleet had to divest 306 New England branches. In the year 2000, Fleet acquired New Jersey-based Summit Bancorp. In the same year, Fleet sold 278 of its New York England branches to Sovereign Bank as a part of the divestiture plan required by regulators to allow the 1999 acquisition of BankBoston.

Bank of America's Acquisition of Fleet Boston

On October 27, 2003, Bank of America made announcement to acquire FleetBoston for $47 billion in a stock deal. The deal consolidated Bank of America's position as US's second largest bank ranked by assets behind Citigroup. Bank of America became the bank with most retail outlets in the United States. The deal gave Bank of America a foothold in the Northeast. The combined financial company had the largest retail banking network with 5700 branches across 29 states. The deal gave the new bank an entry into the number one market New York as well as market leadership position in Massachusetts, Rhode Island, Connecticut, and New Jersey. At the time of acquisition, FleetBoston the number seven bank was focusing on repositioning itself as a consumer bank after suffering losses in Latin America and due to loans to troubled companies like Enron (Department of Justice, Press Release 1999). At the time of acquisition, Bank of America was number three bank with approximately 33 million customers and 2.5 million business clients in 35 countries. The strategic acquisition was aimed to blend Bank of America's operations in Southern and Western States with FleetBoston's dominant position in New England (Bank of America, Financial Releases, 2004).

The merger created the fourth most profitable company in the world on the basis of 2003, pro forma results. It also created the world's second largest banking company. The merged bank had approximately $96.5 billion in equity and $166 billion market capitalization. The merged bank had wide retail distribution in 29 states in the United States. It also became the largest small business and middle market lender in the United States (PR Newswire Press Release, 1999). The merger diversified Bank of America's revenue mix in terms of both geography and different business lines. The merger combined banks with assets of $930 billion. The Bank of America with $737 billion in assets was the third largest bank behind Citigroup with approximately $1 trillion and JPMorgan with $740 billion. The combined bank had about 5200 branches. The following table gives the comparative financial highlights of Bank of America and FleetBoston in the year before merger (Table 30.2).

The deal valued FleetBoston at about $45.46 a share. Fleet shareholders received 0.5553 share of Bank of America for each of their shares. The deal price represented a premium of 43% for Fleet based on Fleet's closing price on the day of announcement.

The Bank of America expected an $800 million after tax restructuring charge and $1.1 billion of after tax savings by 2005 on account of deal (Reuters, 2003). The combined company's shares continued to be listed on the New York, Pacific, and

Table 30.2 Financial highlights in the year before merger (2002)

	Bank of America	FleetBoston
Assets	$737 billion	$196 billion
Net income	$9.25 billion	$1.2 billion
Number of ATMs	13,100	3400
Employees	132,583	50,000
Headquarters	Charlotte, NC	Boston

London Stock Exchanges as Bank of America Corporation under the ticker symbol BAC.C (Vries, 2003). On announcement of the deal, the shares of FleetBoston increased by 25% to $39.20. Bank of America's stock fell by 12.5% to $73.57.

Bank of America's Acquisition of MBNA Corporation

MBNA Corporation was the bank holding and parent company of wholly owned subsidiary MBNA America Bank NA. MBNA was founded in the year 1982 as Maryland Bank NA, a subsidiary of Maryland National Bank. In 1989, Maryland Bank was renamed MBNA America Bank. In the year 1991, MBNA Corporation was spun off from Maryland National. Maryland National was acquired by NationsBank in the year 1993. MBNA was the world's largest independent credit card issuer with leadership position in affinity marketing. It is an international financial services company which provides lending, deposit, and credit insurance products and services. MBNA credit cards and related products are endorsed by more than 5000 organizations worldwide. In the year 2006, MBNA was acquired by Bank of America. In December 2016, UK-based Lloyds Banking Group purchased MBNA from the Bank of America for £1.9 billion.

On June 30, 2005, the Bank of America announced the definite agreement to acquire MBNA Corporation. The acquisition combined US largest domestic bank with a leading provider of credit card and payment products. The acquisition enhanced Bank of America's product mix and customer reach. Bank of America became one of the largest credit card issuers in the United States with $143 billion in managed outstanding balances and 40 million active accounts. Bank of America added more than 20 million new customer accounts as well as affinity relationships with more than 5000 partner organizations and financial corporations. The acquisition facilitated the Bank of America to deliver innovative deposit, lending, and investment products and services to MBNA's customers. The deal resulted in the creation of US's largest retailer of financial services with improved distribution efficiencies.

Under the terms of the deal, MBNA shareholders received 0.5009 shares of Bank of America common stock for each of their shares plus a cash component of $4.125 per share. The deal was valued at $35 billion in total or $27.50 per MBNA share on the basis of share price of the Bank of America at the close of business as on June 28, 2005.

The deal was expected to result in overall expense efficiencies of $850 million after tax by the year 2007. Cost reductions were realized from job reductions, elimination of overlapping technology, vendor leverage, and marketing expense.

As a result of the deal, Bank of America became the leading worldwide payment service company. It also became the largest issuer of credit, debit, and prepaid cards based on total purchase volume. Bank of America had 40 million active credit card accounts.

The acquisition made Bank of America the fourth most profitable company in the world. Bank of America got access to the attractive portfolio, products, and services as well as the marketing capabilities of MBNA. The deal allowed the Bank of America to get a foothold in markets of Canada, the United Kingdom, Spain, and Ireland.

Both the firms got the opportunity to cross sell their products. The merger created one of the largest credit card portfolios and gave the consolidated firm access to new marketing channels. Significant synergy opportunities existed due to the combination of Bank of America's distribution platform and customer base with MBNA's products, affinity relationships, and marketing expertise. The merger gave MBNA more powerful distribution channel. Approximately 55% of the combined company's earnings came from global consumer and small business banking, 17% were accounted from global business and financial services, and 11% were from global capital markets and investment banking. The remaining 10% were accounted from global wealth and investment management. The consolidation had created a diverse business mix which was less dependent on market-sensitive businesses. The deal came nearly a year after the JPMorgan Chase & Co union with Bank One Corp. On January 01, 2005, the merger was completed.

Lloyds Bank Acquires MBNA

Lloyds Banking Group bought the MBNA credit card business from Bank of America for 1.9 billion pounds ($2.4 billion). The acquisition was aimed at reducing Lloyds' reliance on mortgage lending. It was the first major acquisition for biggest mortgage lender of the United Kingdom which was partly owned by government (Bank of America Investor Relations, Financial Releases, 2003). Lloyds Bank was bailed out during the 2007–2009 crisis (Jessop and White, 2016). The acquisition increased Lloyds' presence in the UK credit card market with multi-brand strategy. The acquired MBNA business comprised gross assets of £7 billion. Lloyds believed that the MBNA brand and portfolio were a good fit for its existing credit card business.

Acquisition of US Trust by Bank of America

On November 20, 2006, the Bank of America announced the intention to acquire Charles Schwab's private banking division, US Trust for $ 3.3 billion in cash. Schwab had bought US Trust for about $2.8 billion in the year 2000. US Trust serves as manager, executor, and trustee of personal and corporate funds (Associated Press, 2006).

The deal heralded Bank of America's entry into the private banking industry sector which had been a competitive strength for other major banks like JPMorgan Chase and Citibank (Lipton, 2006). The merger made Bank of America's private banking unit the second largest in the United States on the basis of assets under management which was approximately $261 billion. US Trust was founded in 1853 (Bank of America Investor Relations, Financial Releases, 2006). The company had

33 offices with approximately 2100 employees. It had approximately $94 billion of assets under management.US Trust was one of the top wealth managers for ultra-high net worth individuals with more than $50 million in investable assets in United States. The target clients of US Trust were high net worth households and ultra-high net worth households with more than $two million in investable assets. US Trust had approximately 13,600 relationships with individuals and families (Merced, 2006). The Private Bank of America had almost 2300 associates in 150 offices across US with clients with more than $three million in investable assets. As of September 30, 2006, the Bank had $167 billion in assets under management. Both Bank of America and US Trust had highly complementary strengths and business models. As a result of the merger, US Trust clients gained access to Bank of America's broad-based services and distribution platform (Wyant, 2007).

The stock market reaction to the deal announcement was positive for both the acquirer and target company. Schwab shares rose 38 cents to $18.94 in which Bank of America shares also witnessed increase of 5 cents to $54.90. The deal was completed on July 2, 2007.

Bank of America's Acquisition of LaSalle Bank

LaSalle Bank Corporation was the holding company for LaSalle Bank NA and LaSalle Bank Midwest. LaSalle Bank was an indirect subsidiary of Netherlands-based ABN AMRO Bank NV. LaSalle Bank had its origin when National Builders Bank of Chicago was founded in the year 1927. In 1940, the name was changed to LaSalle National Bank. In the 1960s, LaSalle acquired the Mutual National Bank of Chicago. In 1979 ABN AMRO acquired LaSalle Bank. At the time of deal with Bank of America, LaSalle was a top 20 US bank holding company with $113 billion total assets. The subsidiaries of LaSalle Bank had retail and commercial operations in 20 states and 26 cities across the United States.

On April 23, 2007, Bank of America entered into a definitive agreement with ABN AMRO, the parent company of LaSalle Bank, and its subsidiaries to acquire LaSalle Bank (Bank of America Investor Relations, 2007). The union of LaSalle and Bank of America created a leading banking franchise in metropolitan Chicago which was the number three banking market in Michigan. Bank of America paid $21 billion in cash to ABN AMRO. The net cost of the deal was $16 billion after return of $5 billion in excess capital. Through the acquisition, Bank of America got approximately 17,000 commercial banking clients of LaSalle Bank. Bank of America consolidated its position in the Chicago area. The Bank of America also got access to 1.4 million retail customers, 411 banking centers, and 1500 ATMs in regions like Chicago, Michigan, and Indiana. The acquisition also marked Bank of America's entry into Michigan with a 23% deposit market share. Bank of America also got possession of six banking offices of LaSalle Bank in Indiana region. With the deal, Bank of America gained more than 14% of the deposit market share in metropolitan Chicago region (Yerak, 2010). Commercial and corporate clients of LaSalle bank benefitted from the greater access to global capital markets and investment banking and global treasury services of Bank of America. Innovative products from the Bank of America like Keep the Change, Business 24/7, and $0 Online Equity supported LaSalle's strong areas. The financial advisor for Bank of America was Banc of America Securities. As a result of the deal, Bank of America and LaSalle customers could access US's largest network of more than 18,500 ATMs to make cash withdrawals with no ATM fees. By October 2007, Bank of America Corp.'s deposit market share in the Chicago area increased to 14.6% from 1.7% after acquiring LaSalle Bank.

The legal advisor for Bank of America was Wachtell, Lipton, Rosen & Katz. ABN AMRO was advised by UBS. The legal advisor for LaSalle Bank was Davis Polk & Wardwell. The deal was completed on October 1, 2007.

Acquisition of Countrywide by Bank of America

On January 11 2008, Bank of America announced that it would buy Countrywide Financial for $4.1 billion in an all-stock deal. The company was purchased by the Bank of America in a scenario of spiraling housing market toward collapse due to bad lending and speculation (Ellis, 2008). The deal officially closed on July 1, 2008. The acquisition created the US's leading mortgage originator and servicer (Bank of America Investor Relations, Financial Releases, 2007). Bank of America would focus on responsible home lending, serving as a reliable source of mortgages for American consumers. It was expected that cost reductions would come from elimination of overlap of technology, vendor, and marketing expenses. The deal made Bank of America the biggest mortgage lender and loan servicer. The Bank of America expected $670 million in after tax cost savings in the transaction or 11% of the expense base of the two companies' mortgage operations (National Public Radio, 2008).

On announcement of the deal, Countrywide shares tumbled 15% trading on New York Stock Exchange after soaring 51% on speculation that the deal was forthcoming. Bank of America's stock closed 2% lower on acquisition announcement. In the year before acquisition, Countrywide shares fell approximately 79% making it the second worst performer in the S&P 500.

Under the terms of agreement, shareholders of Countrywide received 0.1822 of a share of Bank of America stock in exchange for each share of Countrywide. On the basis of preannouncement day closing price, the deal valued Countrywide at $4 billion or $7.16, a share which was approximately 7.5% discount on the countryside share price. As a part of deal, the Bank of America absorbed Countrywide's massive albeit troubled loan portfolio. In the year before acquisition, Countrywide had $408 billion in mortgage originations and serviced nine million loans worth $1.5 trillion. Countrywide had shut down its subprime lending operations to focus on originating loans that conform to Fannie Mae and Freddie Mac guidelines regarding safe investments.

In 2013, Countrywide was found guilty of defrauding federal mortgage giants like Fannie Mae and Freddie Mac. These mortgage companies made a gross loss of $848 million on suspect loans which they bought from Countrywide.

By 2016, Bank of America's mortgage business had lost more than $50 billion since the purchase of Countrywide Financial (Eiiff.com, 2016). The bank had to pay $3.6 billion to Fannie Mae and bought back $6.75 billion in loans which the Countrywide banking unit had sold to the Fannie Mae during the period 2000–2008. Bank of America's acquisition of Countrywide Financial corporation had been ranked as one of the worst financial decisions in US business history.

Acquisition of Merrill Lynch by Bank of America

On September 14, 2008, the Bank of America made the announcement regarding the decision to acquire Merrill Lynch & Co. Inc. in an all-stock deal valued at $50 billion (Gasparino, 2008). Bank of America was reportedly in talks to purchase Lehman Brothers. But the talks were called off as government guarantees were lacking for Lehman Brothers. Merrill Lynch was the world's largest and most widely recognized stockbroker. Merrill Lynch dominated the retail stockbroking sector with a strength of 16,000 brokers around the globe. In April 2008, Merrill Lynch had announced 4000 job cuts after incurring losses of $24 billion due to subprime lending crisis (Inman, 2008).

The Bank of America bought approximately $44 billion of Merrill's common shares as well as $6 billion of options, convertibles, and restricted stock units. The price offered of $29 per share represented a 70% premium to Merrill's share price of $41.705 on the trading day before announcement. Merrill Lynch shares had been witnessing sharp decline ever since its liquidity started declining. Merrill Lynch shares were trading over $90 at the beginning of January 2007 and at $50 in May 2008.Bank of America issued 1.71 billion common shares. Merrill shareholders received 0.8595 of a Bank of America common share for each of their common share.

Three Merrill Lynch directors joined the Bank of America Board. Shareholders of both companies approved the acquisition on December 5, 2008, and the deal closed on January 1, 2009. The acquisition created a global financial service giant which dealt from fixed income trading to stock underwriting to credit lending. The combined firm became one of the largest banks in the United States in terms of assets. The Bank of America was able to offer Merrill's retail stock brokering services to its customer base.

The acquisition catapulted Bank of America into number one underwriter of global high-yield debt and the third largest underwriter of global equity. Bank of America became the ninth largest adviser on global merger and acquisitions. The combined company also became the largest in terms of brokerage, credit cards, investment banking, mortgage, and wealth management operations. Bank of America also acquired 50% stake of Merrill Lynch in BlackRock Inc.

The losses at Merrill Lynch subsidized once the credit crisis eased out and the subsidiary generated $3.7 billion profits for Bank of America by end of first quarter in the year 2009. In 2021, Bank of America settled the class action lawsuit over the Merrill Lynch acquisition. Bank of America received $20 billion as a part of the federal bailout from the US government through the Troubled Asset Relief Program (TARP) and a guarantee of $118 billion in potential losses at the company in the year 2012.Bank of America also received $25 billion in Fall 2008 through the TARP. In 2009, Bank of America received an additional $5.2 billion in government bailout which was channeled through American International Group.

In a 2013 study by *The Wall Street Journal*, Merrill Lynch acquisition have been profitable for the Bank of America since Merrill Lynch earned six times the profits of the total bank since 2009. But the bank had to settle for $2.43 billion a shareholder lawsuit as the bank had failed to provide sufficient disclosures to investors.

Effect of Acquisition Announcement on Wealth Creation

In this section the impact of acquisition announcement on wealth creation in stock market is examined. The stock returns for the Bank of America during different acquisitions are analyzed (Tables 30.3 and 30.4).

The return analysis is done for Bank of America for different acquisitions made in different period of time. The time window period of analysis is an 11-day period (−5 to +5) surrounding the acquisition announcement. The acquisition of Countrywide and Merrill Lynch were done during the economic crisis wherein all stocks were affected. Among the six acquisition announcements analyzed, only the

Table 30.3 Event dates

SL	Target	Announcement day
1	FleetBoston	27-Oct-03
2	MBNA	30-Jun-05
3	US Trust	20-Nov-06
4	LaSalle Bank	23-Apr-07
5	Countrywide	11-Jan-08
6	Merrill Lynch	14-Sep-08

Table 30.4 Return analysis

Day	FleetBoston (%)	MBNA (%)	US Trust (%)	LaSalle Bank (%)	Countrywide (%)	Merrill Lynch (%)
−5	−0.35	−1.2	−0.57	1.20	−1.1	−3.3
−4	−0.48	−0.2	0.68	0.67	0.1	−2.2
−3	0.01	0.0	−0.64	0.31	−3.7	12.2
−2	0.93	0.2	0.77	−1.01	0.9	−3.4
−1	0.10	0.6	−0.09	−0.79	1.4	−3.4
0	−10.13	−2.5	0.09	−0.02	−2.0	−2.7
1	−0.98	−2.2	−0.33	−0.14	1.9	5.7
2	2.07	0.1	−0.16	0.50	−3.4	−17.3
3	1.09	0.2	−0.13	0.30	2.1	−5.8
4	0.74	−0.9	−1.17	−0.49	−4.6	6.1
5	0.34	0.6	0.65	0.73	−2.5	1.3

Table 30.5 Cumulative returns in different time window periods

Time window	FleetBoston (%)	MBNA (%)	US Trust (%)	LaSalle Bank (%)	Countrywide (%)	Merrill Lynch (%)
−1 to +1 day	−11	−4.2	−0.3	−0.95	1.3	−0.37
−3 to +3 day	−7	−3.6	−0.5	−0.85	−2.9	−14.70
−5 to +5 day	−7	−5.3	−0.9	1.25	−11.0	−12.90
−5 to +10 day	−7	−2.6	−3.7	2.25	3.1	12.78
−5 to +243 day	9	−1.8	−21.4	−23.59	−63.8	55.50

acquisition of US Trust resulted in a positive gain of 0.09% on the announcement day. Positive returns were registered for the Bank of America for the acquisition of FleetBoston, MBNA, and Countrywide for the day before announcement. The −1-day announcement return for Countrywide was 1.4%.

The cumulative returns for the Bank of America in different time window period for six acquisition announcements are examined in this section. The time window period included shorter duration of 3 days like −1 to +1 through the announcement day. The other shorter time window periods included −3 to +3 day, −5 to +5 day, and −5 to +10-day period. The longer time window period included 249 days (−5 to +243-day period). The cumulative returns were negative in all most all acquisition time window period for most of the acquisition announcements. For FleetBoston, the cumulative returns were 9% in the longest time window period. For Merrill Lynch acquisitions, the stock gained approximately 55% on cumulatively basis during the long window period. Positive gains of 1.25% and 2.25% were observed for LaSalle Bank acquisition announcement during the time window period of −5 to +5 day and −5 to +10 day (Table 30.5).

References

Associated Press (2006) Schwab agrees to sell U.S. Trust to Bank of America. http://articles.latimes.com/2006/nov/21/business/fi-schwab21. Accessed 05 April 2018

Bank of America, Financial Releases (2004) Bank of America completes FleetBoston merger. http://investor.bankofamerica.com/phoenix.zhtml?c=71595&p=irol-newsArticle&ID=510909#fbid=iVtaLK7Y2Hw. Accessed 04 April 2018

Bank of America Investor Relations (2007) Bank of America agrees to acquire LaSalle Bank. http://investor.bankofamerica.com/phoenix.zhtml?c=71595&p=irol-newsArticle&ID=988431#fbid=iVtaLK7Y2Hw. Accessed 10 April 2018

Bank of America Investor Relations, Financial Releases 2003. Bank of America to acquire MBNA. http://investor.bankofamerica.com/phoenix.zhtml?c=71595&p=irol-newsArticle&ID=725228#fbid=iVtaLK7Y2Hw. Accessed 04 April 2018

Bank of America Investor Relations, Financial Releases 2006. Bank of America to acquire US Trust. http://investor.bankofamerica.com/phoenix.zhtml?c=71595&p=irol-newsArticle&ID=1171009#fbid=hO26elG1Pot. Accessed 04 April 2018

Bank of America Investor Relations, Financial Releases. 2007. Bank of America completes countywide financial http://investor.bankofamerica.com/phoenix.zhtml?c=71595&p=irol-newsArticle&ID=1171009#fbid=hO26elG1Pot. Accessed 10 April 2018

Department of Justice, Press Release (1999) Justice Department requires Fleet Financial and Bank Boston to divest 306 branches in four new England States. Accessed 04 April 2018

Eiiff.com (2016) Bank of America merger. http://www.eiiff.com/merger-acquisition/bank/bank-americas.html. Accessed 04 April 2018

Ellis D (2008) Countrywide rescue: $4 billion. https://money.cnn.com/2008/01/11/news/companies/boa_countrywide/. Accessed 10 April 2018

Frankel M (2015) The biggest mergers and acquisitions in banking. https://www.fool.com/investing/general/2015/04/22/the-biggest-mergers-and-acquisitions-in-banking.aspx. Accessed 04 April 2018

Gasparino C (2008) Bank of America to buy Merrill Lynch for $50 billion. https://www.cnbc.com/id/26708319. Accessed 10 April 2018

Inman P (2008.) WallStreet Crisis: Bank of America buys Merrill Lynch. https://www.theguardian.com/business/2008/sep/15/merrilllynch.wallstreet. Accessed 10 April 2018

Jessop S, White L (2016) Lloyd Bank's on credit card growth with $2.4 billion MBNA buy. White https://www.reuters.com/article/us-lloyds-banking-mbna/lloyds-banks-on-credit-card-growth-with-2-4-billion-mbna-buy-idUSKBN1490N3. Accessed 04 April 2018

Lipton J (2006) Bank of America to buy US Trust. https://www.forbes.com/2006/11/20/bank-of-america-markets-equity-cx_jl_1120markets12.html#78367384621d. Accessed 04 April 2018

Merced M (2006) Bank of America to acquire US Trust. https://dealbook.nytimes.com/2006/11/20/bank-of-america-to-acquire-us-trust-for-33-billion/. Accessed 04 April 2018

National Public Radio (2008) Bank of America to buy Countrywide. https://www.npr.org/templates/story/story.php?storyId=18022987. Accessed 10 April 2018

PR Newswire Press Release (1999) Sovereign Bank New England announces acquisition of Fleet/BankBoston branches, Philadelphia and Boston. Newswire. Accessed 04 April 2018

Reuters (2003) BofA nabs Fleet for $47 billion. https://money.cnn.com/2003/10/27/news/companies/ba_fleet/. Accessed 04 April 2018

Vries L (2003) Bank of America buys FleetBoston. https://www.cbsnews.com/news/bank-of-america-buys-fleetboston/. Accessed 04 April 2018

Wyant C (2007) Bank of America completes acquisition of US Trust. https://www.bizjournals.com/twincities/stories/2007/07/02/daily4.html. Accessed 05 April 2018

Yerak B (2010) Bank of America Chief says LaSalle Bank acquisition was worth the money. http://articles.chicagotribune.com/2010-01-13/news/1001120353_1_lasalle-bank-wealth-and-investment-management-new-york-mellon. Accessed 10 April 2018

Gaz de France Merger with Suez

31

On July 16, 2007, Gaz de France (GDF) was acquired by ENGIE SA in a reverse merger deal. ENGIE has operating presence in approximately 70 countries worldwide and offers innovative solutions to personal customers, urban authorities, and companies. In the year 2017, the revenues of the ENGIE amounted to 65 billion euros. ENGIE is listed in Paris and Brussels. The company GDF Suez through its subsidiaries operates as an independent power producer throughout the world. GDF Suez is involved in the generation of electricity from renewable energies and distributes gas and electricity to consumers, companies, and local authorities. The company is also involved in the exploration, distribution, and supply of oil and liquefied natural gas (S&P Global Market Intelligence, 2008). The company also has operations in regasification of terminals, gas terminals, and gas storages. GDF Suez also manages and operates natural gas transportation networks. The company also operates as energy trader. The firm also provides engineering consultancy services for nuclear, gas plants, and industries. The company is involved in the operation and management of electrical engineering, mechanical engineering, and climate-controlled facilities. The company is also involved in the design and implementation of solutions to optimize energy consumption through integration of production and distribution of energy.

Gaz de France Merger with Suez

The merger between two companies was originally announced in February 2006 as a defensive move when Suez was facing the prospect of hostile bid by Italy's Enel along with France-based Veolia. The deal then got bogged down partly since the two firms were of unequal size. Suez's sales were approximately 50% higher than that of GDF which was contrary to the envisaged merger of equals. Another hindrance could be attributed to the refusal by Suez's head Mestrallet to change his dual

B. R. Kumar, *Wealth Creation in the World's Largest Mergers and Acquisitions*, Management for Professionals, https://doi.org/10.1007/978-3-030-02363-8_31

strategy on focus on two divisions – energy distribution and environmental activities like water and waste treatment. Negotiations turned acrimonious at times. Finally, the deal happened with the strong support of then French President Nicholas Sarkozy (Gumbel, 2007).

On September 3, 2007, European giant Gaz de France and Suez made the announcement to merge in a €70billion (£47billion) deal which created the world's fourth largest energy company. GDF Suez with market capitalization of 70 billion euros after the spin of Suez's water and waste division was placed behind Russia's Gazprom, France's Electricite de France, and Germany's E.ON (Hotten, 2007).

This merger created Europe's second largest electricity and gas group. The merger was engineered as a part of a deal to thwart a possible foreign takeover attempt from Enel, the Italian utility firm. The final deal came after approximately 2.5 years of the merger saga marked by takeover attempts, political disputes over privatization policy in France, and union opposition over the financial terms of the deal. As a part of the deal, Suez had to divest 65% of its environment activities (Gaz de France, Merger Prospectus 2008). Suez spun off its water and waste businesses which were valued at €20 billion. The remaining assets of the company were valued at €90 billion. Initially Suez Chairman resisted selling the water assets. The spun off created equal-sized companies and avoided overly diluting the stake of the government which held 80% stake in Gaz de France. Gaz de France was Europe's largest natural gas operator. The merger implied the privatization of Gaz de France which was strongly opposed by unions and opposition socialists. French Government held approximately 35% in GDF Suez compared to its 80% stake prior to merger.

At the time of the deal Gaz de France Group was a major energy player in Europe. The company employed nearly 50,000 people. In 2007, the sales revenues for the company amounted to €27 billion. Gaz Group held a portfolio of approximately 14 million clients of which 11 million were French clients. Gaz de France was listed on the Paris Stock Exchange and formed part of the CAC 40 and Dow Jones Stoxx 600 indices (Reuters, 2008).

Suez had its roots originated with the establishment of the Societe Generale des Pays-Bas in the year 1822 and Universal Company for the Maritime Channel of Suez in the year 1858. Suez was the company that was involved in building Suez Canal. Suez was a major global industrial and services group which designed sustainable and innovative solutions for the management of public utilities as a partner of public institutions, businesses, and individuals. The Group was involved in offering services in electricity, natural gas, water and waste management. The Group employed 149,000 people globally and had sales revenues of €47.5 billion in the year 2007. Approximately 89% of its revenues were generated in Europe and North America. Suez was listed on the Brussels, Luxembourg, Paris, and Zurich stock exchanges and is represented in the major international indices: CAC 40, BEL 20, DJ STOXX 50, DJ EURO STOXX 50, Euronext 100, FTSE Eurotop 100, MSCI Europe, and ASPI Euroz.

On announcement of the deal, the shares of both companies fell to the bottom of the CAC 40 Index in Paris with Gaz de France falling by 2.7% to close at 35.81

euros and Suez fell by 3.3% to close at 40.36 euros. During the period between the original announcement and the final announcement of the deal, GDF and Suez had gained 26% and 54%, respectively, in stock prices.

Terms of the Deal

Gaz de France swapped 21 of its shares for 22 of Suez. In other words, the share exchange ratio was 0.9545. The merger was via the absorption of Suez by Gaz de France. Gaz de France retained approximately 40% of the merged company. Approximately 65% of the capital of Suez Environment was distributed to Suez shareholders who received one Suez Environment share for four Suez shares. Suez Environment Company was the legal name of the firm holding Suez Environment (Reuters Business News, 2007).

The distributed shares of Suez Environment were listed on Euronext Paris and Euronext Brussels. The issued shares of GDF Suez were listed on Euronext Paris, Euronext Brussels, and Luxembourg Bourse. The merger had received the approval of the French privatization authority, the Commission des Participations et des Transferts. The deal offered Suez shareholders a jump of four euros a share compared with the original plan. Both companies had to sell its stakes in Belgium's Distrigas and power producer SPE as a part of European Commission's regulatory obligations. The commission felt that the merged GDF Suez could hamper competition in Belgium. GDF Suez and the main Suez shareholders held approximately 35% and 12% of the environment activities of Suez after the deal.

The new board consisted of 24 directors. GDF was advised by Societe Generale and Merrill Lynch, while Suez was advised by BNP Paribas, JP Morgan, and Rothschild. Suez head Gerard Mestrallet became the chairman and chief executive of the new group and GDF chief Jean Francois Circelli as the new Group's Vice Chairman.

Strategic Drivers for the Merger

The merger between Gaz de France and Suez created a global energy leader with leadership position in natural gas and electricity (Laurent, 2007). The combined firm created a diversified, flexible energy supply stream with high-performance electricity production base. The combined company became the Europe's largest purchaser of natural gas with 25% market share and the world leader in LNG. GDF Suez also became Europe's number one natural gas transmission and distribution network operator. The merged entity achieved strong positions in the United States, Brazil, and Middle East. The Group also became the number two storage and LNG terminal operator in Europe.

The merger equipped the combined company to develop capacity to meet the future energy challenges of Europe in terms of renewable energy and greenhouse gas reduction. On account of strong complementarity between Gaz de France and Suez, the new combined group became active on the entire value chain – from upstream to downstream in natural gas and electricity, nuclear energy, and services. The strategy of GDF Suez was to become a major player in the gas and electric sector with an energy supply portfolio which is secure, diversified, and flexible.

The industrial strategy of the combined group was strengthened by the increased production capacity. The combined group acquired six cogeneration plants in Italy with an installed capacity of 370 MW. The other acquisitions included acquisition of Teesside Power Limited in England, the largest CCGT in Europe with a capacity of 1875 MW and acquisition of 79% stake in Elettrogreen, a wholesale electricity market operator in Italy with wind energy development projects in Canada, France, and Portugal. The combined group also strengthened its position in natural gas, LNG, and infrastructure with the acquisition of new natural gas reserves and discovery of natural gas in Egypt and natural gas production startup in Norway and the United Kingdom. The combined group also obtained new supply contracts with Norsk Hydro for 3.2 billion m3 of natural gas over 4 years in the United Kingdom. The group also had obtained new contract with Shell for a volume of 10 billion m3 of natural gas. GDF Suez also acquired new energy services and environment contracts in France and in other regions of world.

Financial Performance After Merger

The liquidity and financial leverage position of the group improved after the merger. The pro forma group revenues in the year 2007 was EUR 74.3 billion while the EBITDA was EUR 13.1 billion and the operating income was EUR 8.3 billion. The proforma net income of the group was EUR 5.6 billion. The merger was expected to yield operational synergies of EUR one billion by the year 2013. The group expected synergies of approximately one billion euros on account of financial synergy.

References

Gaz de France. Merger Prospectus (2008) AMF Approval of Merger Prospectus Shareholder Meeting. http://www.engie.com/wp-content/uploads/2012/05/amf-approval-of-the-merger-prospectus.pdf. Accessed 28 April 2018

Gumbel P (2007) How France's Sarkozy muscled a merger through. http://archive.fortune.com/2007/09/04/magazines/fortune/gumbel_sarkozy.fortune/index.htm. Accessed 28 April 2018

Hotten R (2007) Suez and Gaz de France in £47bn merger. https://www.telegraph.co.uk/finance/markets/2815018/Suez-and-Gaz-de-France-in-47bn-merger.html. Accessed 28 April 2018

Laurent L (2007) Gaz de France, Suez Ink marriage of almost equals. https://www.forbes.com/2007/09/03/suez-gdf-energy-markets-equity-cx_ll_0903markets06.html#7a19b9a370ee. Accessed 28 April 2018

Reuters (2008) Timeline key dates in Gaz de France Suez Merger. https://www.reuters.com/article/us-suez-gdf/timeline-key-dates-in-gaz-de-france-suez-merger-idUSL1572930220080715. Accessed 28 April 2018

Reuters Business News (2007) FACTBOX: Details of Suez GDF French Energy Merger. https://www.reuters.com/article/us-suez-gdf-terms/factbox-details-of-suez-gdf-french-energy-merger-idUSL0329339120070903. Accessed 28 April 2018

S&P Global Market Intelligence (2008) Company Overview of Gaz de France. https://www.bloomberg.com/research/stocks/private/snapshot.asp?privcapId=874603. Accessed 28 April 2018

Sanofi–Aventis Merger

32

Sanofi is a leading global healthcare company involved in research, development, manufacture, and marketing of therapeutic solutions. The pharma company focuses on its strategy to emerge as one the world's top three innovative and diversified human healthcare companies by the year 2025.The company employs more than 100,000 people in 145 countries. Sanofi has presence in over 100 countries with 81 manufacturing sites. Sanofi has access to 82 healthcare programs in 65 countries with over 35 million patients receiving diagnosis and vaccination. The company had trained approximately 346,000 healthcare professionals. The five global business units of Sanofi are diabetes and cardiovascular, consumer healthcare, Sanofi Pasteur (vaccine segment), Sanofi Genzyme (rare diseases, multiple sclerosis, oncology, and immunology), and General Medicine & Emerging Markets. The company invested 5.5 billion in R&D in the year 2017 which represented 15.6% of the company sales. There were 74 R&D projects under development as of April 2018. In 2008 Sanofi–Aventis acquired the Czech generic drug maker Zentiva NV for $2.6 billion.

In year 2010, Sanofi–Aventis acquired 100% stake in Chattem Inc. and strengthened its presence in the US consumer healthcare market. This acquisition provided Sanofi–Aventis new channels for maximizing the potential for conversion of Sanofi–Aventis' prescription medicines to over the counter (OTC) products (PRNewsWire, 2010). In 2011, Sanofi–Aventis completed its acquisition of Genzyme Corporation which became its wholly owned subsidiary. During March 2018, Sanofi–Aventis completed the acquisition of Bioverativ Inc. for $105 per share in cash. The acquisition of Bioverativ provided Sanofi–Aventis a strong position in the growing hemophilia market and presence in specialty care market (Sanofi Press Release, 2018). The following table gives the financial highights of Sanofi-Aventis (Table 32.1).

B. R. Kumar, *Wealth Creation in the World's Largest Mergers and Acquisitions*, Management for Professionals, https://doi.org/10.1007/978-3-030-02363-8_32

Table 32.1 Financial highlights

Year	2013	2014	2015	2016	2017
Net sales	30,693	31,380	34,060	33,821	35,055
Gross profit	20,989	21,769	23,942	24,006	24,593
Operating income	4982	6064	5624	6534	5803
Net income	3716	4390	4287	4709	8434
Total assets	96,055	97,392	102,321	104,672	99,826

The values are given in millions of dollars

Sanofi–Aventis Merger

In the year 2004 after a bitter takeover battle, France's largest drug maker, Aventis agreed to be absorbed by a smaller rival company Sanofi-Synthelabo SA in a cash and stock deal valued for Euro 55.2 billion ($65 billion) (CNN Money News International, 2004). At the time of the deal, the consolidation created the world's third largest pharmaceutical company with a market capitalization of approximately 90 billion euros behind US-based Pfizer and Britain's GlaxoSmithKline. The combined company had a strong diversified portfolio consisting of Aventis' leading drugs like allergy pill Allegra, cancer treatment drug Taxotere, and anti-blood clotting drug Lovenox along with Sanofi's top drugs like anti-stroke medicine Plavix, sleeping pill Ambien, and cancer therapy Eloxatin. The French government had pushed for the consolidation of Sanofi and Aventis similar to the all French mergers which created Total SA, the world's fourth largest oil company.

In early 2004, Sanofi-Synthelabo made a hostile takeover bid worth €47.8 billion for Aventis. Aventis had initially fought off Sanofi's hostile bid and sought a white knight offer from Novartis. Aventis enacted a poison pill provision and invited Novartis to enter the merger negotiations. The 3-month-old hostile battle was converted into a friendly deal when Sanofi offered a friendly bid of €54.5 billion in place of the earlier offer. The French government put pressure on Sanofi-Synthelabo to raise its bid for Aventis and for Aventis to accept the offer. Sanofi under pressure from French government sweetened its offer under the scenario, whereby Aventis invited Novartis to become a "white knight" to acquire Aventis (Timmons and Bennhold, 2004; Hoffmann, 2004). Initially Aventis had rejected Sanofi's offer in January 2004 citing low deal price.

Novartis failed to put a bid for Aventis after announcing that it was prepared to enter merger negotiations with French drug maker. Thus France's largest drug maker Aventis stayed under French control after the smaller company raised its bid to $64.2 billion thus turning a hostile bid into a friendly acquisition.

Terms of the Deal

Under the terms of the revised bid, Sanofi offered five of its shares for each Aventis shares held plus €120 in cash which was equivalent to €66.6 per Aventis share based on Sanofi's closing stock price on the trading day before the announcement of the deal. There was a subsidiary all cash offer of €68.93, but the cash offer was limited to 29% of the total offer. In the initial offer, the cash part was capped at 19%. Based on Sanofi's closing price of €55.95 on Friday before the deal announcement, Aventis was valued at €66.6 a share in cash and stock. The total deal value was estimated at €53.2 billion. Sanofi increased its offer value by 14% compared to its original offer. On announcement of the deal, Sanofi shares fell by 8.9%, while Aventis share fell by 5.6% in early afternoon trading (Raghavan et al. 2004). Aventis shares were trading at substantial premium to Sanofi's original offer as Novartis entered the fray for bidding Aventis. Kuwait Petroleum, one of the largest stakeholder in Aventis, had abstained from voting on the new Sanofi bid.

Sanofi was advised by Merrill Lynch and BNP Paribas; Goldman Sachs, Morgan Stanley, and Rothschild advised Aventis.

The combined company had a 17-member board with 9 members from Sanofi and 8 members from Aventis side. Jean Francois de Beca the Sanofi-Synthelabo's CEO became the chairman and chief executive. The new merged company was named as Sanofi–Aventis.

Stock Market Returns During the Announcement of Deal

The initial offer was made in January 2004. The announcement of the final deal was made on April 26, 2004. During the −78 to +173 (254-day merger period) covering January 1, 2004–January 2005, the stock gained 9.20% on cumulative basis (Fig. 32.1).

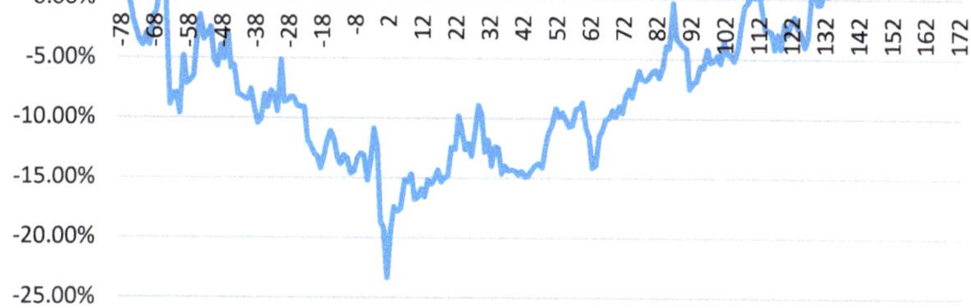

Fig. 32.1 Cumulative returns for Aventis during merger period

Table 32.2 Announcement returns

Day	Returns (%)
−5	−0.12
−4	−2.14
−3	1.60
−2	2.77
−1	−1.59
0	−6.21
1	−0.52
2	−4.15
3	3.88
4	1.97
5	−0.32
6	0.26
7	2.32
8	−0.16
9	0.72
10	−2.16

The announcement period returns were negative. On the day before announcement, the stock fell by approximately 1.59%. On announcement day, the stock price of Sanofi fell by approximately 6%. The down spree continued for the next 2 days. The stock gained by approximately 4% on +3 day of announcement (Table 32.2).

References

CNN Money News International (2004) Sanofi lands Aventis for $64B. https://money.cnn.com/2004/04/26/news/international/aventis_sanofi/. Accessed 29 April 2018

Hoffmann C (2004) Merger of Sanofi Synthelabo and Aventis to create Sanofi Aventis. http://www.firstwordpharma.com/node/217045?tsid=17#axzz5MfubeAdr. Accessed 29 April 2018

PRNewsWire (2010) Sanofi Aventis successfully completes the acquisition of Chattem Inc. http://www.news.sanofi.us/press-releases?item=118517. Accessed 29 April 2018

Raghavan A, Carreyrou J, Naik G (2004) Sanofi to swallow Aventis in a deal set at $65 billion. https://www.wsj.com/articles/SB108291923112092711. Accessed 29 April 2018

Sanofi Press Release (2018) Sanofi completes acquisition of Bioverativ Inc. https://mediaroom.sanofi.com/en/press-releases/2018/sanofi-completes-acquisition-of-bioverativ-inc/. Accessed 8 March 2018

Timmons H, Bennhold K (2004) France helped broker the Aventis Sanofi deal. https://www.nytimes.com/2004/04/27/business/france-helped-broker-the-aventis-sanofi-deal.html. Accessed 29 April 2018

Bayer's Acquisition of Monsanto

33

Bayer Group

Bayer is a life science company with more than a 150-year history. The company had core competencies in the areas of healthcare and agriculture. The Bayer Group is managed as a life science company with three divisions – pharmaceuticals, consumer health and crop science, and animal health business unit (Bayer Media News, 2016). The corporate functions, the business services, and the service company Curenta support the operational business. In the year 2017, the Bayer Group consisted of 237 consolidated companies in 79 countries globally. The company also provides a reliable supply of high-quality food-, feed-, and plant-based raw materials. The pharmaceuticals segment focuses on prescription products for cardiology, women's healthcare, and on specialty therapeutics in the areas of oncology, hematology, and ophthalmology. The division also deals with radiology business which markets diagnostic imaging equipment. The consumer health segment markets non-prescription medicines, medical products, and cosmetics in the dermatology, nutritional supplement, analgesic, digestive health, allergy, cold, foot care, and sun protection categories. Crop science division of Bayer is the world's leading agriculture enterprise with businesses in crop protection, seeds, and nonagricultural pest control. The crop protection/seeds unit markets a broad portfolio of high-value seeds and innovative pest management solutions. The environmental science unit provides products and services for professional nonagricultural applications such as vector and pest control and forestry. Animal health division develops and markets products and solutions for the prevention and treatment of diseases in companion and farm animals. In connection with the planned acquisition of Monsanto, a new structure became effective in the year 2018 where all strategic business entities like herbicides, fungicides, insecticides, and seed growth businesses were organizationally located below the crop science segment. The following table provides the financial highlights of Bayer Group (Table 33.1).

B. R. Kumar, *Wealth Creation in the World's Largest Mergers and Acquisitions*, Management for Professionals, https://doi.org/10.1007/978-3-030-02363-8_33

Table 33.1 Financial highlights of Bayer Group

Year	2013	2014	2015	2016	2017
Sales	40,157	41,339	46,085	34,943	35,015
EBITDA	7830	8315	9573	8801	8563
EBIT	4934	5395	6241	5738	5903
Net income	3189	3426	4110	4531	7336
R&D expenses	3406	3537	4274	4405	4504
Ratio of R&D expenses to sales in %	15.80%	15.60%	16%	16.70%	16.20%
Net financial debt	6731	19,612	17,449	11,778	3595
Capital expenditures	2155	2484	2554	2627	2418
Total dividend payment	1737	1861	2067	2233	2315

Source: Annual Report (2017)
The values are given in millions of euros

Table 33.2 Financial highlights of Monsanto Co

Year	2013	2014	2015	2016	2017
Net sales	$14,861	$15,855	$15,001	$13,502	$14,640
Income from operations	3570	4075	3523	2375	3212
Net income	2482	2740	2314	1336	2260
Total assets	20,651	21,918	21,920	19,736	21,333
Long-term debt	2048	7465	8429	7453	7254

The values are given in millions of dollars

Monsanto

Monsanto is a global agricultural Fortune 500 company. It is headquartered in St Louis, MO. It employs over 20,000 people globally. The company has facilities in 69 countries. Monsanto was established in year 2002 when it was divested from Pharmacia Corporation. Monsanto is the first agricultural company to introduce a second-generation biotechnology trait product.

Monsanto's seeds biotechnology trait products, herbicides, and digital agriculture products provide farmers with solutions that help improve the productivity and reduce the cost of farming. There are two reportable segments – seeds and genomics and agricultural productivity. Seeds and genomics segment produces leading seed brands which include DEKALB, Asgrow, Deltapine, Seminis, and De Ruiter. Monsanto develops biotechnology traits which help farmers in controlling insects and weeds and digital agricultural products to assist farmers in decision-making. Agricultural productivity segment manufactures Roundup brand herbicides and other herbicides and provides lawn and garden herbicide products for the residential market. In 2004, Monsanto Co.'s holding company American Seeds Inc. had acquired seed company Channel Bio Corp. for $120 million cash. Monsanto had formed American Seeds to support regional seed businesses with capital, genetics, and technology investments. Channel owned and managed Crow's Hybrid Corn Co., Midwest Seed Genetics Inc., and Wilson Seeds. The following table gives the financial highlights of Monsanto Co. (Table 33.2).

Bayer's Acquisition of Monsanto

Industry Scenario

Agriculture supply industry has witnessed consolidation with the three major mergers of which Monsanto–Bayer merger was the biggest. The other two mergers were DowDuPont and Syngenta–ChemChina mergers. Through the three major mergers, approximately 61% of the global seeds and pesticide production were consolidated in the three major corporations. There were seven big agrichemical companies earlier which got consolidated into four. Skeptics argued that the consolidation would lead to monopoly in agrochemicals and GMO crop species which would leave the farmers globally with no real choices about how to grow their crops in a profitable manner. The agricultural industry faces the challenge of feeding an additional 3 billion people in the world by the year 2050 in an environmentally sustainable way. According to US Department of Agriculture, farm production has shifted focus from smaller farms to larger farms. In 1987 approximately 15% of cropland was held by farms with at least 2000 acres, but by the year 2012, that percentage increased to 36%.

In May 2016, Bayer the German pharmaceutical and drug company made an unsolicited offer to buy Monsanto, the US agrichemical giant at $122, a share which was approximately valued at $66 billion at that time of the deal. Bayer and Monsanto had formally announced the deal finalization in September 2016. The acquisition was aimed to boost agriculture research and innovation for doubling the world's food supply by 2050. The Bayer–Monsanto deal was the second biggest deal in year 2016 after the AT&T–Time Warner deal. The deal required approval from regulators in 30 countries. The deal was the largest overseas deal ever by a German company. It was also the largest all cash buy out on record. With the merger, Bayer became the single biggest supplier of seeds and crop protection chemicals in the world. The acquisition reinforced Bayer's leadership position as a global innovation-driven life science company.

On September 14, 2016, Bayer and Monsanto signed the definitive merger agreement under which Bayer will acquire Monsanto for USD 128 per share in an all-cash transaction. Monsanto's Board of Directors, Bayer's Board of Management, and Bayer's Supervisory Board had unanimously approved the agreement. Bayer will remain as the company name. Monsanto will no longer be the company name. The acquired products will retain their brand names and become part of the Bayer portfolio.

Farmers were skeptical about the consolidation with respect to prices and future businesses. Farmer unions were worried since they believed that the merger was motivated by profit alone and would lead to price rises. National Farmers Union (NFU) opined that the deal involving Bayer's acquisition of Monsanto was disappointing since "the consolidation will among the handful of companies which would control both US and global agricultural markets". Environmentalists were critical of Monsanto's policy with respect to development of genetically modified seeds which would promote monocultures whereby farmers are trapped into a cycle of dependence as well as increased reliance on chemicals. They were highly critical of controversial chemical such as Agent Orange and the weed killer glyphosate. About 70 environmental organizations had petitioned European commission stating that Bayer–Monsanto will become the largest player in the field of agricultural data platforms and pose risks and problems to farmers similar to those observed in existing data platforms like Google, Amazon, and Facebook.

In the year 2018, Bayer completed its takeover of Monsanto (Bayer News Media, 2018). On May 29, 2018 Bayer won approval from the US Justice Department to buy the agricultural giant Monsanto. Under the proposed settlement required for deal approval, Bayer had agreed to sell its seed and herbicide business to German chemical company BASF. These business included soybean, canola, vegetable seed, and cotton seed businesses as well as its glufosinate weed killer which was a direct competitor to Roundup, the flagship brand of Monsanto's business. Bayer was also required to divest its Liberty herbicide business which rivaled Monsanto's Roundup herbicide. According to settlement, Bayer has to divest certain intellectual property and research capabilities which included R&D projects, as well as its nascent "digital agriculture" business which focuses on effective sensor technology, smart analytics, and selective spray systems. The divesting assets were estimated of value $9 billion (£6.7 billion). The European Union had earlier approved the deal. Through the settlement, approximately more than 15% of the acquired firm's assets were divested. Hence analysts were of the opinion that this process involved the elimination of a substantial amount of competition.

The last major regulatory hurdle was cleared after almost 2.5 years of initial announcement. Bayer had committed to a USD 2 billion reverse antitrust break fee (Detrick, 2018). On June 7, 2018, Bayer successfully completed the acquisition of Monsanto. Shares of Monsanto were to be delisted on New York Stock Exchange with Bayer becoming the sole owner of the company. The Global Seeds and Traits and North American commercial headquarters were based in St. Louis, Missouri. The global crop protection and divisional crop science were headquartered in Manheim, Germany. The digital farming business of the combined firm would be based in San Francisco, California.

Motivation for the Acquisition

The two companies were very strong companies offering similar products and had strong R&D capabilities (Bohme, 2018). Under the current system, it was stated that it takes approximately 10 years for a company to develop and get approval for a new herbicide. Similarly it takes the same time period to make a seed trait which responds to the new chemical. The merger would facilitate Bayer and Monsanto's combined resources to develop the paired products in a shorter period of time. Monsanto had partnership and joint ventures with other companies to develop innovative products which in turn resulted in profit sharing. The consolidated new company would be in a better position to develop in house innovative products which don't require a revenue sharing partnership. Both firms intended to invest $16 billion on research and development globally over a 6-year period. For Monsanto, data acquisition was the key motive for the deal. In the year 2013, Monsanto purchased The Climate Corp., a data company which provide farmers with weather data and predictions for approximately $1 billion. By 2014, more than one third of all US farmland was using this technology. Monsanto's "farm-to-fork" data platform called Climate FieldView is a strategic growth driver for the company. This platform uses tractors fitted with sensors and GPS, algorithms, and data drones to monitor field conditions and advise farmers in real time. The merger gave a "first-mover" advantage for Bayer–Monsanto to create the biggest platform which would facilitate Bayer–Monsanto to control the food value chain in terms of which pesticides to be used and which seeds to be planted (Varinsky, 2018). The deal brought together leading seeds and traits, crop protection, biologics, and digital farming platforms (Nelson et al., 2016). The consolidation provided synergistic benefits through the combination of Monsanto's leadership in seeds and traits and Bayer's broad crop protection. In a geographic sense, the combination was complementary in nature which expanded Bayer's presence in America, Europe, and Asia Pacific. The consolidation was beneficial for customers in terms of broad product portfolio and the deep R&D pipeline. The consolidation provided consumers with enhanced solutions in seeds and traits, digital agriculture, and crop protection. The consolidation brought together both companies leading innovation capabilities and R&D technology platforms with annual pro forma R&D budget of approximately EUR 2.5 billion.

Deal Value

The deal was valued at $128 per share all cash offer and valued at $ 62 billion. The acquisition created a leading integrated agriculture business with broad product portfolio to provide innovative solutions. The deal value represented a substantial premium of 37% over Monsanto's closing share price of $89.03 as of May 09, 2016. The value also represented 36% premium over the 3-month volume-weighted average share price and 33% premium over the 6-month volume-weighted average share price. It was also equal to 12 months EBITDA multiple of 15.8x as of February 29, 2016 (Trager, 2018). The transaction was financed through a combination of debt and equity. The expected equity portion of approximately $19 billion was expected to be raised through an issuance of mandatory convertible bonds and through a rights issue with subscription rights. Bridge financing for US $57 billion was offered by BofA Merrill Lynch, Credit Suisse, Goldman Sachs, HSBC, and JPMorgan. Bayer had targeted an investment grade credit rating post-closing and is committed to the single "A" credit rating category over the long term.

Bank of America Merrill Lynch and Credit Suisse were the lead financial advisors for Bayer along with Rothschild as an additional financial advisor. Bayer's legal advisors were Sullivan & Cromwell LLP and Allen & Overy LLP. Morgan Stanley & Co. and Ducera Partners were the financial advisors for Monsanto. Wachtell, Lipton, Rosen & Katz was the legal advisor for Monsanto.

Synergies

Total synergies of approximately $1.5 billion after 3 years of merger were expected along with additional integrated benefits. The combination was expected to provide Bayer's shareholders with accretion to core EPS by a mid-single-digit percentage in the first full year after closing and a double-digit percentage thereafter. The pro forma sales of the combined agricultural business amounted to EUR 23 billion in the year 2015.

Impact of Acquisition on Stock Market

The announcement of the deal was made on May 10, 2016. The deal was finally closed and became effective on June 7, 2018. The analysis of stock returns for Bayer was done for the entire period since the day of initial announcement of the deal till the completion of the acquisition. The cumulative returns for the entire period of 539 days surrounding the acquisition period (−5 to +531 day) were approximately 6.72% (Fig. 33.1). The day before the announcement, the stock return for Bayer was 0.6%. On the announcement day, the stock price increased by 2.3% approximately.

During the announcement day, the return for the target stock Monsanto was approximately −0.31%. However, the stock gained 2.21% on +1 day after announcement and further increased by approximately 10% on the +2 day after announcement. The Monsanto stock's cumulative return during the entire acquisition period was approximately 33.66%. The analysis was done for the 533-day period (−5 to +524 day) surrounding the merger announcement. The cumulative return for Monsanto stock during the time window period 0 to +25 day period was approximately 19.50% (Fig. 33.2). It can be concluded that Monsanto stock gained significantly compared to the acquirer firm Bayer during the acquisition period.

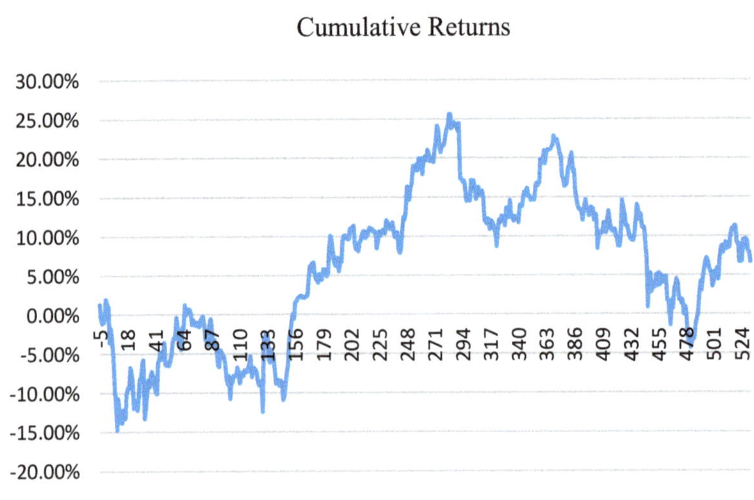

Fig. 33.1 Cumulative returns for acquirer Bayer stock during the acquisition period

Fig. 33.2 Cumulative returns for target Monsanto stock during the acquisition period

References

Bayer Annual Report (2017) http://www.annualreport2017.bayer.com/management-report-annexes/about-the-group/corporate-structure.html. Accessed 30 May 2018

Bayer Media News (2016) Bayer offers to acquire Monsanto to create a global leader in agriculture. https://media.bayer.com/baynews/baynews.nsf/id/Bayer-Offers-to-Acquire-Monsanto-to-Create-a-Global-Leader-in-Agriculture. Accessed 30 May 2018

Bayer News Media (2018) Bayer closes Monsanto acquisition. https://monsanto.com/news-releases/bayer-closes-monsanto-acquisition/. Accessed 30 May 2018

Bohme H (2018) Opinion: The Bayer-Monsanto merger. https://www.dw.com/en/opinion-the-bayer-monsanto-merger/a-44110352. Accessed 18 May 2018

Detrick H (2018) The Justice department is going to let Bayer buy Monsanto. Here's why it matters. http://fortune.com/2018/04/10/bayer-monsanto-deal-doj-approval/. Accessed 18 May 2018

Nelson A, Monsanto, Bayer are set to merge (2016) Here's why you should care. https://www.huffingtonpost.com/entry/monsanto-bayer-merge_us_5afeef96e4b07309e0578b5e. Accessed 30 May 2018

Trager R (2018) https://www.chemistryworld.com/news/bayermonsanto-merger-momentum/3009088.article. Accessed 30 May 2018

Varinsky D (2018) The $66 billion Bayer Monsanto merger just got a major green light-but farmers are terrified. https://www.businessinsider.com/bayer-monsanto-merger-has-farmers-worried-2018-4. Accessed 1 June 2018

Roche Holding's Acquisition of Genentech

34

Roche Holding

Roche Holding was established in the year 1896 by Fritz Hoffman-La Roche as the successor company to Hoffmann Traub & Co. in Basel, Switzerland. Roche is the world leader in in vitro diagnostics and drugs for cancer and transplantation and is a market leader in virology. It is also active in other major therapeutic areas such as autoimmune diseases, inflammatory and metabolic disorders, and diseases of the central nervous system. Through in-house combination of pharmaceuticals and diagnostics, Roche delivers personalized healthcare. In the year 2017, the pharmaceutical division sales amounted to CHF 53.3 billion, while the diagnostics division sales was CHF 12.1 billion. Approximately 137 million patients were treated with Roche medicines. Around 19 billion tests were conducted with Roche Diagnostics products. Among the 400 drugs included in the WHO Model List of Essential Medicines, 30 of them are from Roche. In 2017, Roche conducted clinical trials with more than 295,000 patients. Roche currently has 41 new partnerships in diagnostics and 118 new partnerships in pharmaceutical sector (Roche Annual Report, 2017).

Genentech

Genentech Inc. is a biotechnology corporation which became the subsidiary of Roche in the year 2009. The company was founded by venture capitalist Robert A. Swanson and biochemist Herbert Boyer. Boyer was considered as a pioneer in the field of recombinant DNA technology. In 1990 Hoffmann-La Roche AG acquired a majority stake in Genentech. In the year 2006, Genentech acquired Tanox. Tanox had initiated the development of the drug Xolair and later completed in collaboration with Novartis and Genentech (Fierce Biotech, 2006). In 2009, Roche acquired Genentech. In the year 2014, Genetech/Roche had acquired Seragon for its pipeline

B. R. Kumar, *Wealth Creation in the World's Largest Mergers and Acquisitions*, Management for Professionals, https://doi.org/10.1007/978-3-030-02363-8_34

of small molecule cancer drug for $725 million cash up front with an additional $ 1 billion of payments based on the successful development of products in Seragon's pipeline (Gen News Highlights, 2014).

Roche's Acquisition of Genentech Inc.

Roche had alliance with Genentech since the 1980s and had acquired controlling stake in the company in the year 1990. Roche had owned 55.9% of all outstanding shares. Roche bought the stake in Genentech for $2.1 billion. In the 1980s Genentech had research collaboration with Roche. On March 12, 2009, Roche announced a $46.8 billion deal to buy South San Francisco-based Genentech (Cage, 2009). Genentech over the years were transformed from a startup to an entrepreneurial company which had developed Roche's best-selling drugs like Avastin, Herceptin, and Rituxan. Roche wanted to absorb the biotech firm's DNA into its corporate culture.

During this merger period, Pfizer bought Wyeth for $68 billion in year 2009, and Merck acquired Schering-Plough for $41 billion. These companies had adopted the M&A strategy in an effort to diversify before facing the expiration of patents on a number of their blockbuster drugs. The agreement that allowed Roche first rights to market Genentech drugs outside the United States was set to end in the year 2015. Many of the late-stage clinical trials conducted by Roche involved Genentech products. It was expected that Roche's main growth could come from expanded uses of Avastin. Unlike Pfizer and Merck, Roche had no interest in generic drugs or consumer products. Roche have become a leader in diagnostics.

During the period of acquisition, Roche employed approximately 78,000 people while Genentech employed 11,000 people. In the year before acquisition, Roche had net income of $9.33 billion compared to Genentech's net income of $3.6 billion. In the 1990s, Genentech was fully focused on R&D with 50% of employees accounted by R&D division (Fisher, 2000). By 2008, 75% of Genentech employees were in manufacturing or commercial and administrative divisions.

A complete acquisition of Genentech was one of the options considered by Roche. Another option before Roche was to increase its percentage ownership stake. But this option was declined by Genentech. On July 21, 2008, Roche went public with an offer of $43.7 billion or $89 a share of the 44% share of Genentech that it did not own (Roche Investor Update, 2008). On announcement, the share price of Genentech went up from $80 to $94. A committee consisting of three independent Genentech board members rejected the offer citing undervaluation of Genentech. It was the time when economic recession had hit hard the economy. Lehman Brothers had filed the largest Chap. 11 bankruptcy petition in US history. Genentech then did a counterbid offer of $112 per share. Roche sold $16 billion in bonds to fund its takeover of Genentech. The negotiations between Roche and Genentech were not fruitful. On January 30, 2009, Roche announced a hostile bid on Genentech by directly going to the Genentech shareholders with an offer of $86.50 a share which was approximately 3% lower than its initial offer in July 2008. Genentech urged shareholders to reject Roche's new offer. Analysts were skeptical since fears were expressed that the process might alienate Genentech scientists and witness exodus of these scientists from the company which would be wholly owned by Roche. Roche raised the offer to $93 a share. Finally, on March 12, 2009, Roche made announcement to acquire the remaining portion of Genentech for $95 per share with deal value of $46.8 billion (Knowledge@Wharton, 2010). Genentech's offer was equivalent to 22 times forecast 2010 earnings, against 14 times what Pfizer had paid for Wyeth and 12 times what Merck & Co. had paid for Schering-Plough Corp. Roche had successfully raised $39 billion in the bond market. The savings are expected to be $750 million to $850 million a year. The acquisition was aimed to improve coordination on product development. With the deal, Roche obtained access to Genentech's product pipeline beyond the year 2015 and gained access to Genentech's cash pool of approximately $10 billion (Genentech Media Release, 2009).

One of the biggest integration challenges was in terms of combining the cultures. The manufacturing and commercial operations of the two firms were combined. The research culture of Genentech was adopted across the merged firm. The acquisition of Genentech made Roche the largest biotechnology company in the world.

The combined US commercial business of both companies was based at Genentech's headquarters in South San Francisco.

Key Benefits of Acquisition

The combination was expected to enhance innovation by adoption of diversity of research approaches and sharing of intellectual property and technologies, partnerships, and other key assets. The consolidation is expected to improve operational efficiency which results from reduced complexity, elimination of duplications, and increased scale in the United States. Genentech continued to operate as an independent research and early development center within Roche from its existing campus in South Francisco by retaining its talent and approach to discovering and progressing new molecules. The structure of the combined company allowed for diversity of approaches in research and early development which led to overall innovation within the Group. Roche's Disease Biology Area approach allowed five diverse groups to manage their innovative portfolios. Sharing of technologies like RNAi and novel protein architectures, assets like chemical libraries, intellectual property like antibody production, and know-how of the combined research organization strengthened the group's ability for innovation (Pollock, 2009). Elimination of duplicative functions in areas of development, manufacturing, corporate administration, and support functions resulted in well-aligned structures and lean processes. The combined company became the seventh largest US pharmaceutical company in terms of market share. The combined company generated more than US $ 15 billion in annual revenues. The new combined company with broad portfolio and commercial operations enhanced its ability to successfully commercialize emerging new medicines in US healthcare market.

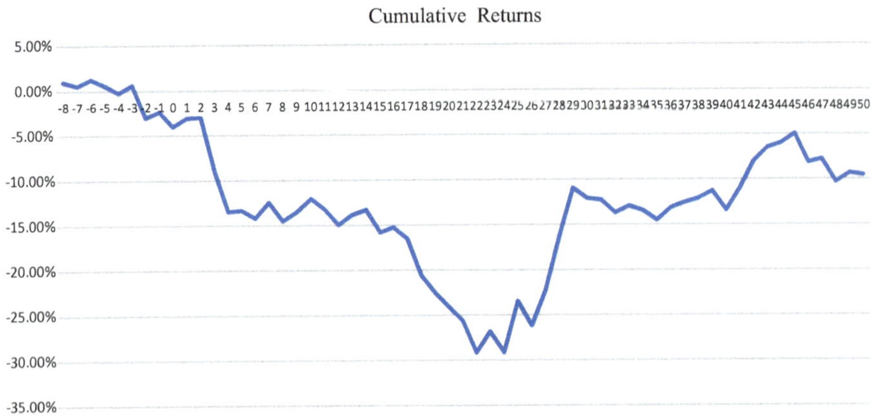

Fig. 34.1 Cumulative returns during the acquisition period

Greenhill & Co. acted as the financial advisor to Roche. Davis Polk & Wardwell was the legal counsel for Roche. Genentech was delisted from New York Stock Exchange after March 26, 2009.

Stock Market Reaction to Final Acquisition Offer

On final deal announcement, Roche's shares went up 1.3% to trade at CHF 147.70. The DJ Stoxx European healthcare sector index, SXDP, went up by 1%. Genentech shares rose by 2% to reach $94.01.

The final deal announcement date was March 12, 2009. The initial hostile bid was on January 30, 2009. The merger was completed on March 26, 2009.On initial hostile bid announcement, the shares of Roche fell by 4% on the announcement of the offer followed by 3% on the following day. On the final deal announcement, the stock of Roche rose by 5.34%. On the −1 and −2 days before the final deal announcement, Roche stock rose by 5.96% and 3.94%. The cumulative return during the entire acquisition period (initial hostile bid announcement to deal completion) was approximately −9.59%. The analysis covered the acquisition period of 58 days (−8 to +50 day) (Fig. 34.1).

References

Cage S (2009) Roche's $46.8 billion Genentech deal outshines others. https://www.reuters.com/article/us-roche-genentech-sb/roches-46-8-billion-genentech-deal-outshines-others-idUS-TRE52B1DN20090312. Accessed 10 June 2018

Fierce Biotech (2006) Genentech strikes $919M deal to buy Tanox, Nov 9

Fisher LM (2000) Genentech: survivor strutting its stuff. The New York Times, Oct 1

Gen News Highlights (2014) Genentech acquires Seragon for up to $1.725B. Genetic Engineering & Biotechnology News https://www.genengnews.com/gen-news-highlights/genentech-acquires-seragon-for-up-to-1-725b/81250056/. Accessed 10 June 2018

Genentech Media Release (2009) Roche completes acquisition of Genentech. https://www.gene.com/media/press-releases/12007/2009-03-26/roche-completes-acquisition-of-genentech. Accessed 10 June 2018

Knowledge@Wharton (2010) Anatomy of a merger: hostile deals become friendly in the end, Right. http://knowledge.wharton.upenn.edu/article/anatomy-of-a-merger-hostile-deals-become-friendly-in-the-endright/. Accessed 2 June 2018

Pollock A (2009) Roche agrees to buy Genentech for $46.8 billion. https://www.nytimes.com/2009/03/13/business/worldbusiness/13drugs.html. Accessed 10 June 2018

Roche Annual Report (2017) https://www.roche.com/dam/jcr:78519d71-10af-4e02-b490-7b4648a5edb8/en/ar17e.pdf

Roche Investor Update (2008) Roche makes offer to acquire all outstanding shares of Genentech for US$89 per share in cash. https://www.roche.com/investors/updates/inv-update-2008-07-21b.htm. Accessed 10 June 2018

France Telecom SA–Orange PLC Merger 35

During October 1999, the German conglomerate Mannesmann AG acquired Orange for US $ 33 billion. Vodafone made a hostile takeover bid for Mannesmann. Orange was originally owned by Hutchison Whampoa of Hong Kong. In February 2000, Vodafone acquired Mannesmann for approximately US $ 183 billion. Vodafone gained control of Orange following its acquisition of Germany's Mannesmann. As a part of regulatory approval from European Union, Vodafone had to divest Orange.

Orange was founded in 1991 and is headquartered in Paris, France, with presence in 30 countries. Orange being a digital operator offers mobile and Internet services in Europe and Africa and corporate telecommunication services worldwide. The group operates under the brand name Orange Business Services (OBS), both in France and internationally, in the business communication and IT services markets (Crunchbase, 2018).

On May 30, 2000, France Telecom SA and London-based mobile phone operator Orange PLC announced their US$ 40.2 billion merger to become Europe's second largest wireless telecommunications company (BBC News, 2000). Finally, in August 2000, France Telecom bought Orange PLC from Vodafone for a total estimated cost of €39.7 billion. France Telecom had also brought stakes in several other international firms like Global One, Equant, Internet Telecom, Freeserve, EresMas, NTL, and Mobilcom. After the merger France Telecom became the fourth largest global operator. The mobile telephone operations of Orange PLC were merged with the majority of mobile operations of France Telecom to form the new group called Orange SA.

Orange was merged with France Telecom's existing mobile operations which included Itineris. The company continued its operation under the brand name "Orange." The merger between Orange and France Telecom was similar to Mannesmann AG's buyout of Orange in the year 1999 for 19.8 billion pounds. Dutch Telecommunications operator Koninklijke KPN NV and US-based MCI Communications Corp. were the unsuccessful bidders for Orange. The combined

B. R. Kumar, *Wealth Creation in the World's Largest Mergers and Acquisitions*, Management for Professionals, https://doi.org/10.1007/978-3-030-02363-8_35

group had over 21 million mobile phone customers. In year 2000, KPN had acquired Germany's third biggest mobile phone company, E-Plus from France Telecom.

Mannesmann had paid $33 billion for Orange in 1999 when it had approximately four million customers. French Telecom paid 6741 euros per Orange subscriber vis-a-vis 9500 euros payment for Mannesmann.

France Telecom evinced interest in Orange acquisition after the British operator won one of the five 3G mobile phone licenses in Britain which allowed mobile phone companies to offer services such as high speed, always on Internet, quality video, and television. Vodafone had projected that its 3G mobile services would boost its average revenue per user by 25% in the year 2004.

In the year 2016, Orange had bought majority stake in Groupama Banque for gaining entry into French banking sector through its mobile services. The deal enabled Orange to launch Orange Bank a full-fledged mobile banking service in France. Orange already had 28 million mobile clients in France at the time of the deal (Financial Times, 2008).

In the year of announcement of deal, Vodafone had a profit before tax of £2.4 billion compared to £1.8 billion in the year before acquisition announcement. As of March 31, 2000, Vodafone had more than 39.1 million mobile customers worldwide, up from 25.4 million in the previous year.

France Telecom acquired Bharti Airtel's in Burkina Faso and Sierra Leone. The company had also entered into an agreement to acquire Cellcom Telecommunications' subsidiary in Liberia (The East African, 2016).

Deal Terms

Under the terms of deal, France Telecom paid Vodafone AirTouch PLC 25.1 billion pounds in a mixture of cash and shares. France Telecom also took on 1.8 billion pounds in Orange debt. As part of Orange's debt acquisition, France Telecom paid the UK government 1.8 billion pounds for the third-generation (3G) mobile license bid which it won. Vodafone received a total of 25.1 billion pounds from France Telecom. Cash payment of 13.8 billion pounds was paid to Vodafone on the completion of the sale (Rohde, 2000). Under the terms of the deal, Vodafone took a stake of approximately 10% in France Telecom which it intended to sell within a 2-year period after the 6-month lockup period ended. The French government's stake in France Telecom was cut from 61% to 54%.

France Telecom made public a minority portion of Orange stock on the London, Paris, and New York stock exchanges in 2001. On February 2001, Orange SA was listed on the Euronext Paris stock exchange with initial public offering of 95 Euros per share with secondary listing in London. In May 2001, Orange SA was listed on the CAC 40. In June 2001, the France Telecom Mobile brands Itineris and Mobicarte were replaced by the Orange brand.

Merger Advantages

The acquisition of Orange and the formation of New Orange were major steps of France Telecom toward the strategy of internationalization to become European leader and global player.

The deal made France Telecom the second largest mobile phone company in Europe after Vodafone with operations in Britain, France, Belgium, Portugal, Germany, Italy, and Eastern Europe. The deal place France Telecom on equal standing with its rival Dutch competitor Deutsche Telekom which already owned another UK mobile phone company, One2One.

Through the deal, Vodafone got good price, and France Telecom became one of the leading mobile phone consolidators in Europe. The merger was in line with France Telecom's strategy to have presence in 50 countries with access to 1 billion customers across 6 continents. France Telecom wanted Orange to play an active role in M&A activity and seek US presence so as to emerge as Vodafone's biggest global competitor. France Telecom expected to have 30 million customers for Orange by the end of the year 2000. Orange acquisition was expected to yield cost savings of more than 800 million euros for France Telecom by the end of year 2003.

The Orange merger with France Telecom was also advantageous for its partner firm NTL Group the UK-based cable company. There existed scope for synergy between cable company and mobile operator. Vodafone planned to use the proceeds of the sale of Orange to fund its acquisitions of 3G licenses across Europe (Vaughan, 2000). France Telecom sold its stake in the US-based Sprint Corp. as well as its shares of Deutsche Telekom AG and the Mexican telecommunications company Teléfonos de México SA de CV (Telmex). The proceeds from those sales were used to pay off the bank loans for the acquisition of Orange.

Orange through its subsidiary, Network Related Services, had acquired 59.10% stake of the capital of Business & Decision owned by the Bensabat family group at a price of 7.70 euros per share. This acquisition was a part of Orange Business Services' strategy to become a worldwide player in digital transformation and a leader across the entire value chain in data services.

Stock Market Reaction

France Telecom was trading at 148 euros per share on announcement day which represented a gain of 2.42%. On announcement day France Telecom was trading at 147.8 euros per share on Paris stock exchange which represented a gain of 2.35%. Shares of Vodafone rose by 7.6% in London Stock Exchange.

The announcement date of the deal was May 30, 2000.

The Orange stock gained during the merger announcement window period. The announcement day return was approximately 7%. The highest single gain of 10.19%

Table 35.1 Daily returns for Orange stock during merger announcement period

Day	Returns (%)
−1	3.41
0	6.98
1	3.99
2	3.83
3	10.19
4	−5.14
5	1.44

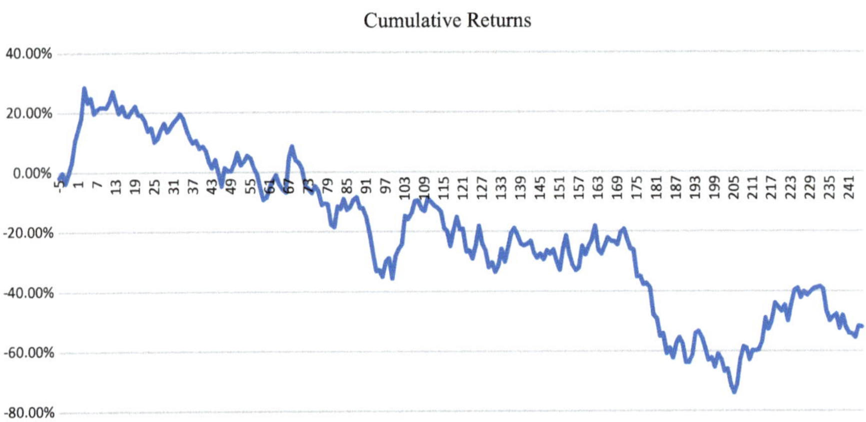

Fig. 35.1 Cumulative returns for Orange stock during merger period

for the stock was observed on the third day after merger announcement (Table 35.1). The cumulative returns for the stock for the 6-day period surrounding the merger announcement (−2 day to +3 day through zero being the announcement) was approximately 32%.

The cumulative returns were analyzed for 250-day period surrounding the merger window (−5 to +245 day). The stock deteriorated in stock market performance after the merger announcement in the longer period. The cumulative returns were approximately −52% during the above period (Fig. 35.1).

References

BBC News (2000) Business. France Telecom clinches Orange deal. http://news.bbc.co.uk/2/hi/business/769293.stm. Accessed June 15 2018

Crunchbase (2018) Company Orange https://www.crunchbase.com/organization/orange#section-overview. Accessed June 15 2018

Financial Times (2008) 1 Orange buys 65 per stake in Groupama Banque https://www.ft.com/content/6b4160d6-0872-11e6-b6d3-746f8e9cdd33. Accessed 17 Aug 2017

Rohde L (2000) France telecom, Orange detail US $40B Merger. https://www.computerworld.com.au/article/98008/france_t_l_com_orange_detail_us_40b_merger/. Accessed 10 June 2018

The East African (2016) France Telecom goes on Africa buying spree after exit from Kenya. http://www.theeastafrican.co.ke/business/France-Telecom-goes-on-Africa-buying-spree-/2560-3034502-5pa9e0z/index.html. Accessed June 15 2018

Vaughan G (2000) France Telecom acquires Orange. https://www.marketwatch.com/story/france-telecom-acquires-orange-for-377-billion. Accessed 17 Aug 2017

Merck–Schering-Plough Corp Merger 36

Merck

Merck & Co. Inc. is a global healthcare company which delivers innovative health solutions through medicines, vaccines, and biological and animal health products. The company conducts operations through four operating segments which are the pharmaceutical, animal health, healthcare services, and alliance segments. The pharmaceutical segment is the only reportable segment. It includes human health pharmaceutical and vaccine products. Human health pharmaceutical products consist of therapeutic and preventive agents, generally sold by prescription, for the treatment of human disorders. Focus on research and development is a major strategic thrust for the company. The company employs approximately 12,650 people in research activities. The research and development expenses were $10.2 billion in year 2017, $10.1 billion in 2016, and $6.7 billion in year 2015 (Merck Investor Relations, 2015). Merck's clinical pipeline includes candidates in multiple disease areas including cancer, cardiovascular diseases, diabetes, infectious diseases, neurosciences, obesity, pain, respiratory diseases, and vaccine. The following table provides the financial highlights of the Consolidated Merck group (Table 36.1).

Alliances, Mergers, Spin-Off, and Divestitures by Merck & Co.

In 1994, Merck and Sanofi Pasteur had established an equally owned joint venture to develop, market, and distribute combination vaccines for Europe. The joint venture was operated through Sanofi Pasteur MSD ("SPMSD") JV. SPMSD supplies a complete range of 45 vaccines to protect patients from 20 infectious diseases. On August 19, 2003, Merck & Co. spun off all of the outstanding stock of Medco Health Solutions Inc. ("Medco Health") to Merck shareholders of record as of the close of business on August 12, 2003. As a result of the spun off, the shareholders received 0.1206 shares of Medco Health common stock for each share of Merck

B. R. Kumar, *Wealth Creation in the World's Largest Mergers and Acquisitions*, Management for Professionals, https://doi.org/10.1007/978-3-030-02363-8_36

Table 36.1 Financial highlights of Merck & Co. Inc. and subsidiaries

Year	2013	2014	2015	2016	2017
Sales	44,033	42,237	39,498	39,807	40,122
Profit before tax	5545	17,283	5401	4659	6521
Income after tax	4517	11,934	4459	3941	2418
R&D expenses	7503	7180	6704	10,124	10,208
Total assets	105,370	98,096	101,677	95,377	87,872
Long-term debt	20,472	18,629	23,829	24,274	21,353
Total equity	52,326	48,791	44,767	40,308	34,569
Number of employees	77,000	70,000	68,000	68,000	69,000

Source: Merck Annual Report (2017)
The values are given in millions of dollars except for the last row variable

common stock which shareholders owned. In year 2009, Schering-Plough merged into Merck. Merck had also undertaken a number of product divestitures. On November 15, 2013, Merck sold the US rights to three branded ophthalmic products to Akorn, Inc. for $52.8 million. During April 2014, Merck sold the US rights of ZIOPTAN® to Akorn, Inc. for $11 million. On January 17, 2014, Merck sold the US rights to SAPHRIS® (asenapine), a treatment for adult patients with schizophrenia or acute bipolar mania, for $240 million. During October 2013, Merck sold its active pharmaceutical ingredient (API) manufacturing business, including the related manufacturing facility, in the Netherlands to Aspen Holdings (Aspen). The 2013 annual sales accounted from API business were approximately $150 million.

On May 6, 2014, Merck had entered into an agreement to divest its consumer care business to Bayer AG for $4.2 billion. During July 2014, Merck sold its ophthalmology business segment consisting of nine branded ophthalmic products in Japan, Europe, and Asia Pacific to Santen. Santen made an upfront payment of approximately $600 million for the deal and would make additional payments based on defined sales milestones.

Schering-Plough

Originally Schering-Plough was the US subsidiary of the German company Schering AG which was founded in the year 1851. It became an independent company as a result of nationalization in the year 1951. In the year 1971, Schering Corporation merged with Plough to form Schering-Plough. Schering-Plough had manufactured several pharmaceutical drugs like the allergy drugs Claritin and Clarinex, anticholesterol drug Vytorin, and brain tumor drug Temodar. Schering-Plough owned and operated major foot care brand Dr. Scholl's and the skin care line Coppertone. Centocor Inc. and Schering-Plough Corporation had a distribution agreement with respect to development, commercialization, and distribution of both Remicade (infliximab), an antitumor necrosis factor (anti-TNF) alpha therapy for chronic inflammatory disorders, and golimumab, Centocor Inc.'s next-generation, human, anti-TNF alpha therapy which is in phase III trials. Schering-Plough Corporation's marketing rights to both products extended for 15 years after the first golimumab commercial sale.

Merck-Schering-Plough Merger

On March 9, 2009 Merck and Schering-Plough made the announcement of a definitive agreement under which Merck and Schering-Plough merged to form Merck in a stock and cash deal (BusinessWire, 2009). On November 3, 2009, Merck and Schering-Plough Corp announced the completion of their $41.1 billion merger. The new company was based at Merck's headquarters in Whitehouse Station.

Terms of the Deal

Under the terms of the agreement, Schering-Plough shareholders received 0.5767 shares of the newly combined company and $10.50 in cash for each share of Schering-Plough. Each Merck common share became the common share of the newly combined company. On the basis of the closing price of Merck stock on March 6, 2009, Schering-Plough shareholders were valued at $23.61 per share. The deal was valued $41.1 billion on average. This offered price represented a premium to Schering-Plough shareholders of approximately 34% on the basis of the closing price of Schering-Plough stock as on March 6, 2009. The consideration also represented a premium of approximately 44% based on the average closing price of the two stocks over the last 30 days of trading during the merger announcement.

On merger completion, Merck shareholders owned approximately 68% of the combined company, and Schering-Plough shareholders owned 32% of the company.

Merck appointed Wells Fargo shareowner services as agent to exchange the Schering-Plough common stock. The financial advisor for Merck was JPMorgan. Fried, Frank, Harris, Shriver and Jacobson LLP were the legal advisors for Merck. Goldman Sachs & Co. and Morgan Stanley acted as financial advisors to Schering-Plough. Wachtell, Lipton, Rosen & Katz acted as legal advisor to Schering-Plough.

Financing of the Deal

The aggregate consideration comprised of approximately 44% cash and 56% stock. The cash portion of the deal was financed through a combination of $9.8 billion from existing cash reserve balances, and the remaining $8.5 billion was provided by JPMorgan. The transaction was structured as a "reverse merger' wherein Schering-Plough became the surviving corporation Schering-Plough renamed as Merck continued as the surviving public corporation. Schering sold the arthritis drug Remicade outside the United States and also had some rights to another in late-stage development, golimumab, under a partnership with Johnson & Johnson, which made

Remicade. Schering had been generating approximately $2 billion a year from the above deal. The merger was structured as a reverse merger to avoid triggering provisions in the J&J deal which might lead to loss of revenue from the deal.

The exchange ratio was calculated based on an agreed price of $26.25, with $10.50 in cash and $15.75 in Merck stock, based on a trailing 30-day volume-weighted average price of $27.3109. The receipt of shares by Schering-Plough shareholders and the conversion of Merck shares into combined company shares under the transaction were tax-free as per US federal income tax purposes. Schering-Plough shareholders were subjected to tax on the cash received up to the amount of gain realized on the shares exchanged.

Merck sold half of its stake in the Merial pet care business for $4 billion to Sanofi Aventis for regulatory approval. Schering-Plough had acquired the rights to Remicade and Simponi from Johnson & Johnson which sold Remicade in the United States.

During the announcement period, Moody's Investors Service backed its Aa3 credit rating for Merck but revised its outlook on the rating to negative from stable. Standard & Poor's reaffirmed Merck's "AA," long-term rating.

Strategic Merger Benefits

Consolidation among big drug makers became the trend as the blockbuster drugs of the 1990s lost patent protection which were complicated by the dearth of new drugs. Schering-Plough, however, has patent protection for key products until the middle of the next decade.

The deal between Merck and Schering-Plough created the world's second largest prescription drug maker. The deal united the maker of asthma drug Singulair with the maker of allergy medicine Nasonex. Merck and Schering had partnership for well-known cholesterol drugs like Vytorin and Zetia.

The merger created a strong broad-based global healthcare pharmaceutical company which immensely benefitted from research and development pipeline, portfolio of medicines, and presence in major international markets specifically in high-growth emerging markets. Merck had cost savings from the Schering-Plough merger by cutting 15% of the combined workforce of both companies. Through the merger, Merck acquired a large number of Schering-Plough drugs. Schering-Plough scientists have built an outstanding clinical development pipeline. Schering-Plough's significant biologics expertise complemented Merck's novel proprietary biologics platform. The combination had a major biologics presence in global markets. Merck was a top maker of pills and vaccines. The acquisition of Schering-Plough gave Merck the prized portfolio of biologic drugs, which are made from living cells. Through the acquisition, Merck became one of the world's biggest animal health businesses and obtained a sizable consumer health division that includes products such as allergy pill Claritin, Dr. Scholl's foot products, and the Coppertone sun-care line.

The merger resulted in complementary product portfolios and pipeline with focus on key therapeutic areas. Merck was able to derive additional revenue opportunities through the combined company's expanded product offerings. The consolidated pharma company expanded opportunities for life cycle management through the introduction of potential new combinations and formulations of existing products. The consolidated company had high-potential early mid- and late-stage pipeline molecules. Together the combined company had 18 medicines in the phase III development. The combined company had a more diverse portfolio across important therapeutic segments like cardiovascular, respiratory, oncology, neuroscience, infectious disease, immunology, and women's health (Singer, 2009). The addition of Schering-Plough's cholesterol drugs Zetia and Vytorin into Merck's cardio vascular portfolio provided ample opportunities for the combined company to leverage the cholesterol market through new drug combination. Schering-Plough's potential first-in-class antiplatelet therapy drug thrombin receptor antagonist complemented Merck's phase III cardiovascular development portfolio. The merger also enhanced Merck's strong respiratory franchise with multiple complementary products for treatment of asthma and allergic rhinitis. Schering-Plough's strong R&D capabilities in neuroscience complemented Merck's development portfolio in the area with drug molecules for migraine and sleep product. Schering-Plough had several promising potential last-stage molecules like Saphris which was an antipsychotic drug for treatment of schizophrenia and bipolar disorder. The other potential drug candidate of Schering-Plough in the area included Bridion which was a novel anesthesia reversal agent. The merged pharma company was expected to leverage the scientific and commercial strength of both the acquirer and target firm for the treatment of human immunodeficiency virus (HIV) and hepatitis C virus (HCV). Schering-Plough had a strong portfolio of HCV candidates like Boceprevir which strategically fitted with Merck's infectious disease programs. Through the merger, Schering-Plough brought distribution rights outside the United States to its well-known biological product Remicade which is used for inflammatory/immunological diseases. Both firms had a strong portfolio of women's health products. Schering-Plough brought to the combined company a strong portfolio of vaccines and small molecules in animal health business. Both the firms had proven track record of research and scientific discovery to deliver innovative promising drug candidates. The merger expanded the global presence of the combined firm with diverse revenue base. Schering-Plough generated approximately 70% of its revenues outside of the United States (The Associated Press, 2009). The revenue generation of Schering-Plough in emerging markets accounted for approximately $2 billion annually. Schering provided Merck access to international markets. Merck was able to penetrate emerging markets through this consolidation. With diverse geographic mix of business, the combined company aimed to generate more than 50% of its revenues outside the United States.

The merged company had a strong cash and investment balance of approximately $8 billion. The merger expected to realize substantial cost savings of approximately $3.5 billion annually beyond the year 2011. The cost savings were attributed from all segments of the combined pharma company particularly from the full integration of the Merck/Schering-Plough Pharmaceuticals cholesterol joint venture (Reuters Deals, 2009).

Schering had invested heavily in developing biotechnology drugs (biologics) derived from living cells. It would be difficult for potential generic makers to copy biological drugs than small molecule chemical compounds. Hence investment in biologics provides scope for competitive advantage in terms of entry barriers. In the year 2007, Schering paid $14.4 billion for Organon, a biotechnology firm which had several novel drugs under last-stage clinical trials. These drugs included fertility treatment drugs. At the time of merger, Merck has about 55,200 employees, and Schering-Plough had approximately 50,800.

Wealth Reaction in Merger Event

The public announcement date of the merger was March 09, 2009. The merger completion date was November 3, 2009. On merger announcement, Schering-Plough's shares gained, while acquirer Merck's shares fell in value. Schering shares jumped $2.63, or 15%, to $20.26, and Merck shares fell $2.19, or 9.6%, to $20.55. On merger completion announcement, Merck shares were down to 41 cents at $30.85 in afternoon trading on the New York Stock Exchange. Schering-Plough Shares declined by 13 cents to $28.27 on its final day of trading on NYSE.

The announcement day return for the Merck stock was −9.84%. One day after the announcement, the stock gained by 7.34%. The +4 and +5 days after announcement were 10.98% and 11.21% (Table 36.2). The 22 day gain in stock returns was 17.35% during the announcement window period of −1 to +20 day.

The cumulative returns for the 251-day period surrounding the merger window event (−5 to +245 day) period was 48.57%. Hence, the merger announcement was a value-creating activity from the perspective of the acquirer firm Merck (Fig. 36.1).

Table 36.2 Announcement period returns for Merck

Day	Returns (%)
−1	−1.11
0	−9.84
1	7.34
2	2.36
3	−1.26
4	10.98
5	11.21

Fig. 36.1 Cumulative returns for the Merck surrounding the merger event

References

BusinessWire (2009) Merck and Schering Plough to merge. https://www.businesswire.com/news/home/20090309005463/en/Merck-Schering-Plough-Merge. Accessed 10 July 2018

Merck Annual Report (2017). https://investors.merck.com/financials/annual-reports-andproxy/default.aspx

Merck Investor Relations (2015) Frequently asked questions and answers. http://s21.q4cdn.com/488056881/files/doc_downloads/other/Merck_Asset_Divestitures_FINAL_March.pdf. Accessed 10 July 2018

Reuters Deals (2009) Merck, Schering-Plough set to complete merger. https://www.reuters.com/article/us-merck-scheringplough/merck-schering-plough-set-to-complete-merger-idUSTRE5A23YZ20091103. Accessed 01 July 2018

Singer N (2009) Merck to buy Schering Plough for $41.1 billion. https://www.nytimes.com/2009/03/10/business/10drug.html. Accessed 10 July 2018

The Associated Press (2009) Merck agrees to merge with Schering Plough in a $41 B deal. https://www.nj.com/news/index.ssf/2009/03/merck_plans_to_buy_scheringplo.html. Accessed 10 July 2018

Astra–Zeneca Merger

37

AstraZeneca is a global innovation-driven biopharmaceutical business which focuses on the discovery, development, and commercialization of prescription medicines for the treatment of cardiovascular, metabolic, respiratory, inflammation, autoimmune, oncology, infection, and neuroscience diseases (AstraZeneca, 2016). AstraZeneca operates in over 100 countries. Zeneca Group was formed by the demerger of the pharmaceutical operations of Imperial Chemical Industries in the year 1993. AstraZeneca was formed in the year 1999 through the merger of the Swedish Astra AB and the English Zeneca Group. AstraZeneca has a primary listing on the London Stock Exchange and is a constituent of the FTSE 100 Index. It has secondary listings on the New York Stock Exchange and the OMX exchange. The following table gives the financial highlights of AstraZeneca (Table 37.1).

Astra AB

Astra AB was founded in the year 1913 and was headquartered in Sweden. Astra was an international pharma group which focused on research, development, manufacture, and marketing of pharmaceutical products in four main product categories of gastrointestinal, cardiovascular, respiratory, and pain management. Astra also marketed a range of other pharmaceutical products which included anti-infective products.

Zeneca Group Plc

Zeneca was formed as the result of demerger of three business divisions by Imperial Chemical Industries in the year 1993 (Blake, 2012). The three divisions were Pharmaceuticals, Agrochemicals, and Specialties. Imperial Chemical Industries

B. R. Kumar, *Wealth Creation in the World's Largest Mergers and Acquisitions*, Management for Professionals, https://doi.org/10.1007/978-3-030-02363-8_37

Table 37.1 Financial highlights of AstraZeneca

Year	2015	2016	2017
Revenues	24,708	23,002	22,465
Operating profit	4114	4902	3677
Net profit	2826	3406	2868
Total assets	60,056	62,526	63,354
Loans and borrowing	14,137	14,501	15,560
Total equity	18,509	16,669	16,642

The values are given in millions of dollars

was founded in the year 1926. Zeneca became a major international bioscience group involved in the manufacture and marketing of pharmaceuticals, agricultural chemicals, and specialty chemicals. In 1994, Zeneca acquired 50% of Salick Health Care, an operator of cancer care centers in the United States. Following this acquisition, Zeneca became strong in the therapeutic area of oncology, where its key products included Casodex, Nolvadex, and Zoladex. In 1998, Zeneca sold off Specialties division, which included products in biocides, industrial colors, life science modules, and performance and intermediate chemicals. Zeneca was the second-leading maker of cancer drugs behind Bristol-Myers Squibb of the United States. It also had a large agrichemical business.

Corporate Restructuring by AstraZeneca

In 2006, AstraZeneca purchased Cambridge Antibody Technology for a deal valued at $1.3 billion. The acquisition expanded AstraZeneca's activities in biological medicines (PharmaTimes, 2006). Before the complete acquisition, AstraZeneca had 19% stake in Cambridge Antibody Technology which was the United Kingdom's biggest biotechnology company.

In 2007 AstraZeneca acquired MedImmune for $15.6 billion in an all cash deal. This acquisition bolstered AstraZeneca's product pipeline and supplemented its portfolio of biologic drugs (Pollock, 2007). In 2013, MedImmune, the subsidiary of AstraZeneca, acquired the privately held biotech company Spirogen for $440 million. Spirogen focused on antibody drug conjugate technology for oncology.

MedImmune paid $200 million up front for all of Spirogen's shares, plus an additional of up to $240 million tied to undisclosed development milestones. The acquisition was aimed at strengthening AstraZeneca's pipeline of cancer treatment. In 2013 AstraZeneca acquired Pearl Therapeutics which focused on the development of inhaled small-molecule therapeutics for respiratory diseases (AstraZeneca Media Release, 2013). The acquisition gave AstraZeneca access to potential new treatment for chronic obstructive pulmonary disease (COPD) which was in late-stage development and inhaler and formulation technology which provided a platform for future combination products. In the year 2015, AstraZeneca completed the acquisition of ZS Pharma. This acquisition strengthened AstraZeneca's cardiovascular and metabolic disease (CVMD) portfolio with the addition of potassium-binding compound ZS-9, a potential best-in-class treatment for hyperkalemia. In 2015,

AstraZeneca acquired the rights to Actavis' branded respiratory business in the United States and Canada. During 2014, AstraZeneca's subsidiary and biologic research and development arm MedImmune completed its acquisition of Definiens, a privately held company which had pioneered a world-leading imaging and data analysis technology known as Tissue Phenomics. This technology improved the identification of biomarkers in tumor tissue. In 2016 AstraZeneca acquired the core respiratory business of Takeda Pharmaceutical Company. In the year 2018, AstraZeneca spun out a new autoimmune company called Viela Bio.

Zeneca–Astra Merger

In 1999, Zeneca and Astra merged to form a new company called AstraZeneca. The merger deal was valued at $67 billion. It was billed as one of the largest ever European mergers at the time of the deal. The deal made UK-based Zeneca and Sweden-based Astra the fourth largest drug company in the world with $14 billion in sales. Under the British accounting rules, the AstraZeneca deal was classified as a merger of equals (Cowell, 1998).

Percy Barnevik, the Swedish industrialist who was the chairman of Astra's biggest shareholder, Investor AB, became the chairman of the new company. Zeneca chief executive Tom McKillop became chief executive of the new group. The new company had its headquarters in London, while Research and Development was based in Sweden. Astra shareholders received 0.5045 AstraZeneca shares for each Astra A or B share they held. Under the terms of the deal, Zeneca shareholders received 53.5% of the new company, while Astra shareholders received 46.5% of the new company (BBC News, 1998). The merger was intended to build the scale to match the global leaders like GlaxoWellcome and Merck. Zeneca made the leading hypertension drug Zestril (Seely, 1998). Astra possessed the world's bestselling prescription drug for Ulcer – Prilosec. The two companies were market leaders in anticancer drugs and anesthetics. Zeneca was well known for its cancer medicines. Astra and Zeneca had highly complementary product portfolios as well as sales and marketing organizations. Both companies also are active in anesthetics and treatments for respiratory and cardiovascular diseases (CNNMONEY News International, 1998).

Portfolio-wise Zeneca had strong oncology medicines, anesthetics, and cardiovascular and respiratory ailment drugs. Approximately 30% of its total sales came from oncology products, 44% from cardiovascular, and 16% from sales of central nervous system products. About 7% of sales were derived from anti-infectives. The leading drugs of Zeneca included antipsychotic Seroquel, cancer drugs Nolvadex and Zoladex, the ACE inhibitor Zestril, and the antiasthma medication drug Accolate. Before the deal Astra had consolidated its portfolio by combining Astra Merck and Astra USA. Astra brought a profitable cardiovascular portfolio to the deal along with antiasthma, antiulcer, and anesthetic products (Emmett, 2000).

The merger achieved cost savings of $1.1 billion. Approximately 6000 jobs were cut worldwide over the 3 years after merger. Before the merger Astra came out of the joint venture it had with Merck, and AstraZeneca paid Merck $740 million as part of the settlement. The deal also envisaged payment of $950 million for a future option to buy out Merck's remaining interest in drug products.

Astra had overcome resistance from its biggest shareholder, the Wallenberg family, who owned 12% of the company.

AstraZeneca had market capitalization of $67 billion based on the closing price on the day of announcement. The proforma sales totaled $15.9 billion. Of the total sales, drug sales accounted for 67%. The new company's R&D spending of $1.9 billion was the third highest among the drug firms.

The consolidation made sense since both companies' drug patents were set to expire in 2001. The US patent protection was set to lapse on the best-selling drugs of both companies during the year 2001. The advent of generic competition for Astra's Losec and Zeneca's flagship heart drug Zestril was expected to hit hard the sales of both companies by the year 2002.

These midsized companies needed more scale. Moreover, the pharma industry witnessed massive consolidation. A chain of consolidation events was announced in pharma industry during the period of Astra–Zeneca Merger. The announcement of Astra–Zeneca merger came a week after the public announcement of Hoechst–Rhone-Poulenc merger to form Aventis. Two days after Astra–Zeneca merger announcement, the merger between Sanofi and Synthelabo was announced to the public. This wave of merger consolidation was basically driven by the huge R&D costs involved in the pharma industry.

At the time of the deal, AstraZeneca deal was the largest drug merger in Europe which surpassed the $28 billion combination of Ciba–Geigy and Sandoz to form Novartis in the year 1996. The merger improved operating efficiencies by eliminating duplicate infrastructure through better asset utilization and effective exploitation of economies of scale. Annual pretax cost savings of $1.1 billion were expected by the third year of merger completion. The combination of Astra and Zeneca provided a strong base for expansion in research and development and geographical presence. The new AstraZeneca focused on five therapeutic areas of gastrointestinal, cardiovascular, respiratory, oncology, and anesthesia. The merger was attractive for both scientists and physicians since the therapeutic focus areas of the combined company increased. The merger gave about 50,000 employees and concentration of scientific and laboratory talent (Lipin and Stephen, 1998; Pharmaceutical Online News, 1998).

AstraZeneca was able to introduce several partnerships like the one with Incyte Pharmaceuticals of Palo Alto, California, on gnome libraries and chemical targets. The combined company was able to achieve "critical mass" strength in gastrointestinal disease, oncology, respiratory, cardiovascular, central nervous system (CNS), and pain and infection. The company established a new infection and oncology research center in Boston while focusing on CNS research in Wilmington, Del. The merger facilitated the combined company to create a market presence in the United States (PharmaExec.com, 1999).

Fig. 37.1 Announcement returns for AstraZeneca for merger period

Stock Market Reaction on Merger Event

The stock market reacted favorably to the merger announcement. Shares of Zeneca rose sharply on the London Stock Exchange. The shares of Astra increased more sharply by 22% on the day of announcement. The merger was announced on December 09, 1998. The merger was completed on April 06, 1999.

The analysis was done for 1 year which included the period of merger announcement to post-merger period (January 12, 1998–January 12, 1999) (Fig. 37.1). The cumulative return for the entire period of analysis was 10.20%. On the preannouncement day, Zeneca's price increased by 4.33%, and on announcement day, the stock price increased by 6.82%.

References

AstraZeneca (2016) Annual Report. https://www.astrazeneca.com/content/dam/az/Investor_Relations/Annual-report-2016/AZ_AR2016_Full_Report.pdf. Accessed 12 July 2018

AstraZeneca Media Release (2013) AstraZeneca to acquire Pearl Therapeutics to strengthen respiratory portfolio. https://www.astrazeneca.com/media-centre/press-releases/2013/astrazeneca-pearl-therapeutics-respiratory-disease-10062013.html#. Accessed 12 July 2018

BBC News (1998) Business. The company file: Zeneca and Astra merge to form drug giant. File. http://news.bbc.co.uk/2/hi/business/231213.stm#sa-link_location=story-body&intlink_from_url=https%3A%2F%2Fwww.bbc.com%2Fnews%2Fbusiness-27391124&intlink_ts=1533325358737-sa. Accessed 12 July 2018

Blake H (2012) A history of AstraZeneca. https://pharmaphorum.com/views-and-analysis/a_history_of-_astrazeneca/. Accessed 12 July 2018

CNNMONEY News International (1998) Another drug giant created. https://money.cnn.com/1998/12/09/europe/zeneca/. Accessed 12 July 2018

Cowell A (1998) Zeneca buying Astra as Europe consolidates. https://www.nytimes.com/1998/12/10/business/zeneca-buying-astra-as-europe-consolidates.html. Accessed 12 July 2018

Emmett A (2000) The Urge to merge. https://www.the-scientist.com/news/the-urge-to-merge-56057. Accessed 12 July 2018

Lipin S, Stephen D (1998) Zeneca Group, Astra unveil merger valued at $35 billion. https://www.wsj.com/articles/SB913210382327981500. Accessed 12 July 2018

Pharmaceutical Online News (1998) Astra, Zeneca to merge. https://www.pharmaceuticalonline.com/doc/astra-zeneca-to-merge-0001. Accessed 12 July 2018

PharmaExec.com (1999) Zeneca, Astra announce plans to merge. http://www.pharmexec.com/zeneca-astra-announce-plans-merge. Accessed 12 July 2018

PharmaTimes (2006) AstraZeneca to buy Cambridge Antibody Tech. http://www.pharmatimes.com/news/astrazeneca_to_buy_cambridge_antibody_tech_996847. Accessed 12 July 2018

Pollock A (2007) AstraZeneca buys MedImmune for $15.6 billion. https://www.nytimes.com/2007/04/24/business/24drug-web.html. Accessed 12 July 2018

Seely R (1998) Drug Makers Zeneca Astra to merge. https://www.apnews.com/40aad2d37254f6580c1505f0733e8ca6. Accessed 12 July 2018

HP Compaq Merger

38

HP is a leading global provider of personal computing and other access devices, imaging and printing products and related technologies, solutions, and services. HP sell to individual consumers, small- and medium-sized businesses, and large enterprises. HP was incorporated in the year 1947. On November 1, 2015, HP completed the separation of Hewlett Packard Enterprise Company ("Hewlett Packard Enterprise") which consisted of enterprise technology infrastructure, software services, and financing businesses. As a result of separation, the Hewlett-Packard Company changed its name to HP Inc. ("HP"). For financial reporting purposes, HP is organized into three segments: Personal Systems, Printing, and Corporate Investments (HP Annual Report, n.d.). The Personal Systems segment offers commercial and consumer personal computers ("PCs"), workstations, thin clients, commercial tablets and mobility devices, retail point-of-sale ("POS") systems, displays and other related accessories, software, support, and services for the commercial and consumer markets. The Printing segment provides consumer and commercial printer hardware, supplies, solutions, and services, as well as scanning devices. Corporate investments include HP Labs and certain business incubation projects. Table 38.1 gives the financial highlights of HP and subsidiaries. Table 38.2 lists the mergers and acquisition undertaken by HP.

Compaq Computer Corporation

Compaq Computer Corporation was a leading global provider of information technology products, services, and solutions for enterprise customers. It was founded in the year 1982. Compaq Computer Corporation, together with its consolidated subsidiaries (collectively "Compaq"), was involved in the design, development, manufacture, and marketing of information technology equipment, software, services, and solutions, including industry-leading enterprise storage and computing solutions, fault-tolerant business-critical solutions, communication products, personal

B. R. Kumar, *Wealth Creation in the World's Largest Mergers and Acquisitions*, Management for Professionals, https://doi.org/10.1007/978-3-030-02363-8_38

Table 38.1 Financial highlights of HP Inc. and subsidiaries

Year	2013	2014	2015	2016	2017
Net revenues	55,273	56,651	51,463	48,238	52,056
Net earnings	5113	5013	4554	2496	2526
Total debt	20,884	18,109	8842	6813	7819
Total assets	105,629	103,158	106,853	28,987	32,913

The values given are in millions of dollars

Table 38.2 M&A by HP

Year	Company
2000	Spin circuit (joint venture)
2001	Bluestone
2001	Compaq computer corporation
2001	Storage apps
2002	Indigo
2003	Intria
2003	Pipebeach
2003	Extreme logic; select access, Talking Blocks
2004	Persist, DGS, Triaton, Novadigm, Tru-Logica, Consera, Riverstone Networks XGS (sponsored by ProCurve) Synstar
2005	Snapfish, AppIQ, RLX technologies, CGNZ Ltd. Peregrine, Scitex Vision
2006	Trustgenix, PIXACO, OuterBay, TTP, Mercury Interactive, Silverwire, VoodooPC
2007	Knightsbridge, Bitfone, Polyserve, Bristol, Tabblo, Logoworks, SPI Dynamics, Opsware, Neoware, AOME, EYP Mission critical facilities, MacDermid Colorspan
2008	Opelin, Exstream, NUR Macroprinters, tower software, Colubris, EDS, Lefthand Networks
2009	IBRIX
2010	3Com, Palm, Melodeo Phoenix technologies, Inc., Assets of Motionbox, ArcSight, Stratavia, Fortify Software, 3PAR
2011	Vertica, Printelligent, Autonomy Corporation Plc
2012	Hiflex Software GmbH
2014	Eucalyptus systems, Inc.
2015	Voltage security, Inc., ConteXtream, Inc.

Source: www.hp.com

desktop and notebook computers, and personal entertainment and Internet access devices (Compaq Annual Report, 2002). Compaq products and services are sold in more than 200 countries directly and through a network of authorized Compaq marketing partners. Compaq's three reportable business segments were Enterprise Computing, Access, and Compaq Global Services.

In the year 1997, Compaq had acquired Digital Equipment Corporation along with its powerful 64-bit Alpha RISC chip and Windows NT/Digital UNIX servers which were successful in high-performance computing environments. In February 1999, Compaq acquired Shopping.com ("SDC") for an aggregate purchase price of $257 million. In April 1999, Compaq acquired Zip2 Corp. ("Zip2") for an aggregate purchase price of $341 million. These acquisitions were part of Compaq's strategy to become a global leader in Internet access and infrastructure through superior technology, services, and partnerships. In August 1999, Compaq sold an 81.5% equity interest in AltaVista Company, SDC, and Zip2 (collectively "AltaVista") to CMGI, Inc. ("CMGI") for CMGI stock and other considerations totaling $1.8 billion in an effort to accelerate AltaVista's move to a world-leading portal network. In February 2000, Compaq acquired certain configuration and distribution assets of InaCom Corp. ("Inacom"), a provider of information technology services and products, for approximately $370 million in cash. This acquisition was aimed to provide best-in-class complex configuration capabilities along with end-to-end order management and direct fulfillment capacity to the worldwide marketplace. Compaq subsequently established Custom Edge Incorporated ("CEI") (doing business as Compaq Direct) as a wholly owned subsidiary to operate the assets acquired from Inacom. In 2001, CEI was merged with Compaq Computer Corporation. The folowing table provides the financial highlights of Compaq before the merger period (Table 38.3).

HP Compaq Merger

On September 2, 2001, Compaq and Hewlett-Packard Company ("HP") announced that a definitive merger agreement was unanimously approved by both board of directors subject to approval by regulators and shareholders. The new HP offered most complete set of IT products and services for both businesses and consumers to serve customers with open systems and architectures. The combined firm valued at $87 billion had number 1 position globally in servers, access devices (PCs and handheld), imaging, and printing. The combined entity also had leading revenue positions in IT services, storage, and management software. The merger was expected to generate cost synergies of approximately $2.5 billion annually. The combined new HP had a proforma asset of $56.4 billion, annual revenues of $87.4 billion, and annual operating earnings of $3.9 billion. The combined company had operations in more than 160 countries and employed over 145,000 employees. Carly Fiorina, the chairman and chief executive of HP, became the chairman and CEO of the new HP. On completion of the deal, four members of Compaq's board joined the new HP board.

Under the terms of agreement, Compaq shareholders received 0.6325 of the newly issued HP share for each outstanding share of Compaq common stock. The transaction was accounted as purchase transaction. The deal was valued at $25

Table 38.3 Financial highlights of Compaq before merger

Year	1997	1998	1999	2000	2001
Revenues	24,584	31,169	38,447	42,222	33,554
R&D expenses	817	1353	1660	1469	1305
Net income (loss)	1855	–2743	569	569	–785
Total assets	14,631	23,051	27,277	24,856	23,689
Long-term obligations		422		575	600
Stock holder equity	9429	11,351	14,834	12,080	11,117

The values are given in millions of dollars

billion. HP shareowners owned approximately 64%, and Compaq shareholders owned 36% of the merged company (HP Press Release, 2001). The transaction was accounted as purchase and tax-free to shareholders of both companies for US federal income tax purposes. The anticipated synergies resulted from product rationalization, efficiencies in administration, procurement, manufacturing and marketing, and savings from improved direct distribution of PCs and servers. The merged entity was headquartered in Palo Alto. The new HP was structured around four operating units consisting of imaging and printing franchise, access devices business, infrastructure business, and service business.

Many large shareholders opposed the merger including Walter Hewlett, one of the company directors and son of the company's cofounder who had engaged in a proxy battle to prevent the takeover. The major objection of the opponents to the merger was that Compaq had many overlapping product lines and would get the company involved in the low margin PC business.

The merger was considered a failure. Under the leadership of CEO Carly Fiorina, the merged HP lost half of its market value, and the company incurred heavy job losses. Fiorina stepped down in the year 2005 (ZDNET editors for between the lines, 2016). HP's shareholders paid $24 billion in stock to buy Compaq and in exchange got relatively lower value from the deal. HP had to write off a chunk of the $14.5 billion in goodwill assets that it had set up on its books after the deal (Loomis, 2011).

On August 1, 2015, HP was split into two companies – HP Enterprise consisting of servers, storage, services, and software businesses and HP Inc. which sold PCs, printers, and other consumer products. The below table gives the proforma financial highlights of HP and Compaq in the year of merger (Table 38.4).

Operating Performance Analysis: Pre- and Post-merger Period (Table 38.5)

The year of merger consolidation is given as zero. Merger periods +1, +2, +3, etc. denote post-merger years. −1, −2, −3, etc. denote the premerger years. The performance is analyzed using the average growth rates of the financial parameters during the 4-year period in the pre- and post-merger period. The average 4-year growth rate of revenues of HP during the period 1998–2001 was 6.71%. The average growth rate of revenues of HP during the 4-year post-merger period of 2003–2007 was 9.3%. The average growth rate of earnings during the above period increased from −12.23% in the premerger period to 37.5% in the post-merger period. The average growth rate of total assets increased from 2.42% in the premerger period to 4.4% in the post-merger period.

Table 38.4 Proforma financial highlights in the year of merger

Key facts	HP	Compaq	Proforma combined
Total revenues	$47	$40.40	$87
Assets	$32.40	$23.90	$56
Operating earnings	$2.10	$1.90	$4

The values are given in billions of dollars

Table 38.5 Financial highlights of HP in the pre- and post-merger period

Merger period	−5	−4	−3	−2	−1	0	1	2	3	4	5
Year	1997	1998	1999	2000	2001	2002	2003	2004	2005	2006	2007
Net revenues	35,358	39,330	42,371	48,870	45,226	56,588	73,061	79,905	86,696	91,658	104,286
Net earnings	3476	3456	3818	4025	1439	−1012	2896	4227	3473	6560	8719
Total assets	29,852	31,708	35,297	34,009	32,584	70,710	74,716	76,138	77,317	81,981	88,699

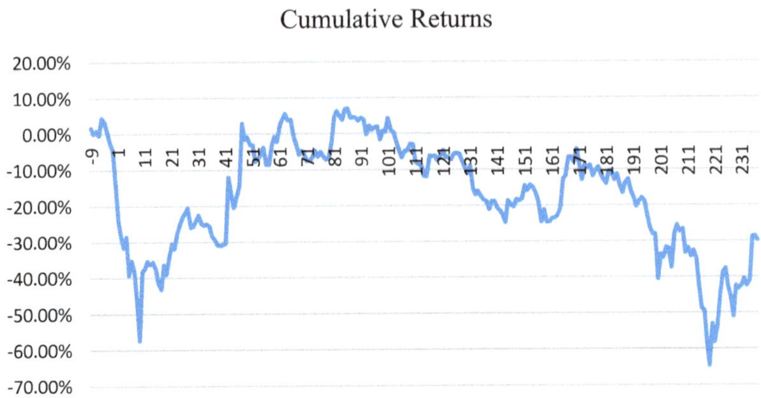

Fig. 38.1 Stock returns for HP during the announcement period

Stock Market Reaction to Merger Announcement

The deal was announced on September 2, 2001. Compaq stock fell by 10% on the day of announcement and then by 16% on the day after announcement. HP's announcement day return was –8.64%. On +1 day after announcement, the stock price fell by approximately 11%. The daily stock price return analysis for HP stock was made for the 1-year period surrounding the merger announcement period (August 20, 2001, to August 20, 2002, with September 2, 2001, the announcement date for merger). Cumulatively the stock lost 29.81% in value during the above period of analysis (Fig. 38.1).

The return analysis was done for the time window of 246 days surrounding the merger announcement (–9 to +236 days).

References

Compaq Annual Report (2002). http://h30261.www3.hp.com/financial/annual-reports-compaq.aspx

HP Annual Report (2017). http://h30261.www3.hp.com/financial/annual-reports-and-proxies/2017.aspx

HP Press Release (2001) Hewlett-Packard and Compaq agree to merge, creating $87 billion global technology leader. http://www8.hp.com/us/en/hp-news/press-release.html?id=230610#.W2X2aSgzbIU. Accessed 10 June 2018

Loomis C (2011) Why Carly's big bet is failing. http://fortune.com/2011/08/21/why-carlys-big-bet-is-failing-fortune-classics-2005/. Accessed 10 June 2018

ZDNET editors for between the lines (2016) Worst tech mergers and acquisitions: HP and Compaq. https://www.zdnet.com/article/worst-tech-mergers-and-acquisitions-hp-and-compaq/. Accessed 10 June 2018

Major Acquisitions by Facebook 39

Facebook is an American online social media and social networking service company based in Menlo Park, California. On February 4, 2004, Mark Zuckerberg and co-founders Dustin Moskovitz, Chris Hughes, and Eduardo Saverin launched the website for Facebook. The founders initially limited the website membership to Harvard students. Later they expanded it to the higher education institutions in the Boston area, the Ivy League schools and Stanford University. The mission of Facebook is to "give people the power to build community and bring the world closer together." Facebook focusses on the strategy to build useful and engaging products which enable people to connect and share with friends and family through mobile devices, personal computers, and other surfaces. Facebook enables people to share their opinions, ideas, photos, and videos and stay connected by accessing Facebook's products. The products offered by Facebook include Facebook, Instagram, Messenger, WhatsApp, and Oculus (Facebook Annual Report, 2017). Facebook enables people to connect, share, discover, and communicate with each other on mobile devices and personal computers. The most important way to engage with people on Facebook is through News Feed which displays an algorithmically ranked series of stories and advertisements individualized for each person. Instagram is a community for sharing visual stories through photos, videos, and direct messages. Messenger is a messaging application which makes it easy for people to connect with other people, groups, and businesses across a variety of platforms and devices. WhatsApp is a simple and reliable messaging application used by people around the world to stay connected. Oculus virtual reality technology and content platform power products facilitate people to enter a completely immersive and interactive environment to train, learn, play games, consume content, and connect with others. The business environment of Facebook is characterized by innovation, rapid change, and disruptive technologies. The initial public offering (IPO) of Facebook was offered in February 2012. The company was valued at $104 billion.

B. R. Kumar, *Wealth Creation in the World's Largest Mergers and Acquisitions*, Management for Professionals, https://doi.org/10.1007/978-3-030-02363-8_39

Table 39.1 Financial highlights of Facebook

Year	2013	2014	2015	2016	2017
Revenue	7872	12,466	17,928	27,638	40,653
Income from operations	2804	4994	6225	12,427	20,203
Net income	1500	2940	3688	10,217	15,934
Cash and cash equivalents	11,449	11,199	18,434	29,449	41,711
Total assets	17,858	39,966	49,407	64,961	84,524
Total stockholder equity	15,470	36,096	44,218	59,194	74,347

The values are given in millions of dollars

Facebook generates revenues from selling advertisement placements to marketers. As of June 30, 2018, Facebook had 30,272 employees. As of June 30, 2018, Facebook had on average 1.47 billion daily active users and 2.23 billion monthly active users. The following table gives the financial highlights of Facebook (Table 39.1).

Acquisitions by Facebook

Facebook have acquired 66 companies. The largest acquisition was WhatsApp messenger acquisition. Other notable acquisition of Facebook includes that of Instagram and Oculus virtual reality (Table 39.2).

In 2011, Facebook bought Snaptu, an Israeli startup which enabled people to use smartphone-like applications on simpler "feature" phones which formed the majority of mobiles in use globally (Arthur, 2011). Feature phones offered huge untapped market to companies such as Facebook and Twitter. Since such phones typically lack Internet capabilities, they needed apps written that are tailored to their operating software. Feature phones make up 80 per cent of the mobile phones. One of the reasons cited for Snaptu acquisition is that its technology worked on more than 2500 different mobile devices (Parr, 2011).

During April 2012, Facebook acquired mobile photo-sharing app Instagram for approximately $1 billion in cash and stock. After acquisition, Instagram remained as an independently branded standalone app which was separate from Facebook. At the time of acquisition, Instagram was increasingly positioning itself as a social network with 27 million users on IOS alone rather than a social network. Through the deal Instagram gained massive design and engineering resources. Instagram's investors included Benchmark Capital, Greylock Capital, Thrive Capital, and Andreessen Horowitz, along with angel investors including Quora's Adam D'Angelo, Lowercase Capital's Chris Sacca and Square, and Twitter's Jack Dorsey. At the time of acquisition, Instagram had just 30 million users and zero revenue. By 2017, Instagram had more than 600 million users with future focus on multibillion dollar advertisement business (Wagner, 2017). In 2012, Instagram was growing at a rapid pace that Facebook believed could have undermined its appeal in photo-sharing position (Techcrunch.com Contributor, 2012). Moreover, Instagram was basically focusing toward mobile rather than desktop which emerged as the future trend. Facebook allowed Instagram to grow organically. By 2014 Instagram had

Table 39.2 Acquisitions by Facebook

No	Year	Target company	Deal value	No	Year	Target company	Deal value
1	Aug-05	AboutFace	$200,000	34	Feb-13	Atlas	<$100 million
2	Jul-07	Parakey	Undisclosed	35	Mar-13	Osmeta	Undisclosed
3	Jun-08	ConnectU	$31 million	36	Mar-13	Hot Studio	Undisclosed
4	Aug-09	FriendFeed	$47.5 million	37	Apr-13	Spaceport	Undisclosed
5	Feb-10	Octazen	Undisclosed	38	Apr-13	Parse	$85 million
6	Mar-10	Divvyshot	Undisclosed	39	Jul-13	Monoidics	Undisclosed
7	May-10	Friendster	$40 million	40	Aug-13	Jibbigo	Undisclosed
8	May-10	ShareGrove	Undisclosed	41	Oct-13	Onavo	Undisclosed
9	Jul-10	Nextstop	$2.5 million	42	Dec-13	SportStream	Undisclosed
10	Aug-10	Chai Labs	$10 million	43	Jan-14	LittleEyeLabs	$15 million
11	Aug-10	Hot Potato	$10 million	44	Jan-14	Branch	$15 million
12	Oct-10	Drop.io	$10 million	45	Feb-14	WhatsApp	$19 billion
13	Nov-10	FB.com domain name	$8.5 million	46	Mar-14	Oculus	$2 billion
14	Jan-11	Rel8tion	Undisclosed	47	Mar-14	Ascenta	$20 million
15	Mar-11	BELGUA	Undisclosed	48	Apr-14	Liverail	$500 million
16	Mar-11	snaptu	$70 million	49	Apr-14	ProtoGeo Oy	Undisclosed
17	Mar-11	RECrEC	Undisclosed	50	Jun-14	Pryte	Undisclosed
18	Apr-11	DayTum	Undisclosed	51	Aug-14	PrivateCore	Undisclosed
19	Jun-11	Sofa	Undisclosed	52	Aug-14	WaveGroup Sound	Undisclosed
20	Jun-11	MailRank	Undisclosed	53	Jan-15	Wit.ai	Undisclosed
21	Aug-11	Push Pop Press	Undisclosed	54	Jan-15	Quickfire	Undisclosed
22	Oct-11	Friend.ly	Undisclosed	55	Mar-15	TheFind	Undisclosed
23	Nov-11	Strobe	Undisclosed	56	May-15	Surreal Vision	Undisclosed
24	Dec-11	Gowalla	Undisclosed	57	Jul-15	Pebbles	$60 million
25	Apr-12	Instagram	$ 1 billion	58	Mar-16	Masquerade	Undisclosed
26	Apr-12	Tagtile	Undisclosed	59	Mar-16	Two Big Ears	Undisclosed

(continued)

Table 39.2 (continued)

No	Year	Target company	Deal value	No	Year	Target company	Deal value
27	May-12	Glancee	Undisclosed	60	Sep-16	Nascent Objects	Undisclosed
28	May-12	Lightbox.com	Undisclosed	61	Oct-16	Infiniled	Undisclosed
29	May-12	Karma	Undisclosed	62	Nov-16	Crowd Tangle	Undisclosed
30	Jun-12	Face.com	$100 million	63	Nov-16	Faciometrics	Undisclosed
31	Jul-12	Spool	Undisclosed	64	Jul-17	Ozlo	Undisclosed
32	Jul-12	Acrylic Software	Undisclosed	65	Oct-17	tbh	Undisclosed
33	Aug-12	Threadsy	Undisclosed	66	Aug-17	Fayteq	Undisclosed

Source: Collated from various sources /https://www.techwyse.com/blog/infographics/facebook-acquisitions-the-complete-list-infographic/

approximately 300 million users who were sharing 70 million photos and videos every day (Heisler, 2016).

In June 2012, Facebook acquired the Israeli start-up facial recognition company Face.com in a deal valued at approximately $100 million. Facebook's facial recognition technology was already used to offer auto tag suggestions when users upload photos to Facebook. Face.com also had a mobile photo app called Kli (D'Orazio, 2012; Murph, 2012). In 2013, Facebook acquired Parse to mark its entry into the new business segment of paid tools and services for developing mobile apps. The Parse deal facilitated Facebook to offer back-end services for data storage, notifications, and user management. This offered a brand new kind of revenue stream for Facebook. At the time of acquisition, Parse had 60,000 apps and almost the same number of developers (Cutler and Constine, 2013).

In 2014, Facebook acquired Oculus VR, the leader in immersive virtual reality technology for $2 billion. At the time of deal, Oculus had received more than 75,000 orders for development kits for the company's virtual reality headset, the Oculus Rift. Facebook acquired Oculus with the strategic aim to extend Oculus' existing advantage in gaming to new verticals which included communications, media and entertainment, education, and other areas (Constine, 2014). There exists immense scope for virtual reality technology to emerge as the next social and communications platform. Facebook paid Oculus $400 million in cash and roughly $1.6 billion in stock. An additional $300 million in cash and stock incentives were to be awarded to Oculus for achievement of certain milestones (PRNEWSWIRE, 2014). The $ 1.6 billion in stock payment was on the basis of average share price of $69.35 from the 20 trading days preceding March 2, 2014. Facebook owned Oculus acquired Pebbles Interface in the year 2015 which develops advanced motion sensors meant to recreate physical objects within digital realm irrespective of the angle or range. In 2014, Facebook acquired the San Francisco-based video ad-tech company, LiveRail, for a reported $400–$500 million to facilitate video advertising. LiveRail helped the publishers sell their advertisement space to the highest bidder and provided analytics to help optimize the advertisement performance (O'Reilly, 2016).

Facebook's Acquisition of WhatsApp

WhatsApp was founded by Jan Koum and Brian Acton in the year 2009. WhatsApp is a cross-platform mobile messaging app which enables users to exchange messages for free. WhatsApp has over 1 billion mobile active users who send approximately 60 billion messages per day. WhatsApp started as an alternative to SMS. WhatsApp supports, sends, and receives a variety of media – text, photos, videos, documents, and location as well as voice calls. WhatsApp is similar to traditional text messaging. The unique feature of WhatsApp is that instead of racking up texting fees, WhatsApp sends the actual messages over mobile broadband. This mechanism made WhatsApp cost effective in terms of communication with people overseas.

WhatsApp was acquired by Facebook in the year 2014. The deal was valued at $19 billion (Covert, 2014). WhatsApp continued to run its operation completely independent since its acquisition. In other words, Facebook kept WhatsApp as a separate service just as it did with Instagram. WhatsApp services were not based on any monetization model. With approximately 450 million monthly active users, WhatsApp allowed users to send text messages to other users for free without advertisements. The company offers the app for free, but to aid in the cost of the service users pay $0.99 every year. According to Forbes estimates, WhatsApp makes money by charging $1 a year subscription in a couple of countries which have clear carrier billing systems and where credit card penetration is high thus accounting $20 million in annual revenue at the time of acquisition. After acquisition Facebook scrapped the annual fee charged by WhatsApp.

Facebook supposedly paid more than double its annual revenue for WhatsApp that had very less revenue. Analysts pointed out that the purchase price was slightly more than the market value of Sony Corp at the time of deal.

The acquisition of WhatsApp bolstered Facebook's strong position in the messaging arena. Facebook's a standalone messaging app for mobile devices was second only to WhatsApp with respect to its share of the smartphone market (Olson, 2014).

As a part of the deal, Facebook paid WhatsApp $4 billion in cash and $12 billion in stock. WhatsApp founders Han Koum, Brian Acton, and staff were eligible to receive another $3 billion in stock grants if they remained employed by Facebook for 4 years. Koum also got a membership on the Facebook board. Facebook awarded 177.8 million shares of its Class A common stock and $4.59 billion in cash to WhatsApp's shareholders. The deal also involved 45.9 million shares (restricted stock units) to WhatsApp's employees (Reuters, 2014; Rowan, 2018).

Five years after launch, WhatsApp became the world's most popular and profitable phone apps. More than 18 billion messages were send via WhatsApp in year 2014 when it was acquired.

By May 2018, approximately 1.5 billion users were sending 65 billion messages via the WhatsApp mobile app and web client per day up from 1 billion users when the company was launched (Bhardwaj, 2018). The acquisition gave Facebook the most popular messaging service in the world. It was particularly significant since users were avoiding one product competitors like Snap and Skype and choosing one of the many services offered by Facebook. The acquisition of WhatsApp provided major benefits to Facebook in terms of large user base in the direct messaging area, smartphone engagement, and penetration across various geographical regions. The acquisition boosted Facebook's access to emerging markets like India and Mexico. India was WhatsApp's biggest customer base with more than 40 million active users. Mexico had over 30 million users. Facebook had fallen behind in mobile phone messaging apps in emerging markets where users were accessing the Internet on fast-growing 3G mobile networks on smartphones.

Facebook is the leading global social sharing utility. The aim of acquisition was to facilitate Facebook to emerge as the global communication utility. WhatsApp was much stronger than Facebook Messenger in Europe, Latin America, Africa, and Australia. Facebook paid WhatsApp $42 per user when the market value per user was $170 for Facebook and $212 for Twitter. At the time of deal, WhatsApp's user base was less than half of Facebook's users, but the WhatsApp's users were more active. According to usage statistics in 2014, on any given day, approximately 70 percent of WhatsApp users were active compared with 62 per cent for Facebook.

Stock Performance on Acquisition Announcement of WhatsApp

The WhatsApp acquisition by Facebook was made on February 19, 2014.On announcement day the stock price of Facebook increased by 0.16%. The stock price increased by 1% and 3% approximately on the +1 day and +2 day after the announcement. The cumulative return analysis for Facebook stock was done for 1-year period surrounding the acquisition window period (10/2/2014–10/2/2015). The analysis was done for the time window of 251 days (−5 to +245 interval). The cumulative return during the period was 19.87% (Fig. 39.1).

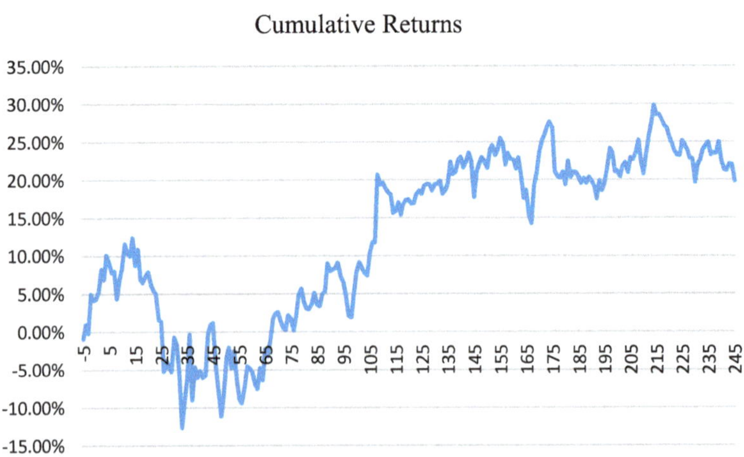

Fig. 39.1 Cumulative returns for Facebook during the WhatsApp acquisition period

References

Arthur C (2011) Facebook buys Snaptu. https://www.theguardian.com/technology/2011/mar/21/facebook-buys-snaptu. Accessed 15 July 2018

Bhardwaj P (2018) The number of messages sent via WhatsApp each day has tripled since Facebook bought it four years ago. https://www.businessinsider.com/whatsapp-messages-tripled-facebook-acquisition-charts-2018-5. Accessed 18 July 2018

Constine J (2014) Facebook's $2 billion acquisition of Oculus closes, Now Official. https://techcrunch.com/2014/07/21/facebooks-acquisition-of-oculus-closes-now-official/. Accessed 15 July 2018

Covert A (2014) Facebook buys WhatsApp for $19 billion. https://money.cnn.com/2014/02/19/technology/social/facebook-whatsapp/index.html. Accessed 18 July 2018

Cutler KM, Constine J (2013) Facebook buys Parse to offer mobile development tools as its first paid B2B service. https://techcrunch.com/2013/04/25/facebook-parse/. Accessed 18 July 2018

D'Orazio D (2012) Facebook acquires Face.com, brings facial recognition technology in house. https://www.theverge.com/2012/6/18/3094832/facebook-acquires-face-com. Accessed 15 July 2018

Facebook Annual Report (2017). http://www.annualreports.com/company/facebook

Heisler Y (2016) Once mocked, Facebook's $1 billion acquisition of Instagram was a stroke of genius. https://bgr.com/2016/12/29/facebook-instagram-acquisition-1-billion-genius/. Accessed 15 July 2018

Murph D (2012) Face.com acquired by Facebook for an estimated $80 million+, facial tagging clearly at the forefront. https://www.engadget.com/2012/06/18/face-com-acquired-by-facebook-for-80-million-recognition/. Accessed 18 July 2018

O'Reilly L (2016) Pullbacks, delays, ad fraud: the story of Facebook's '$500 million' LiveRail acquisition. https://www.businessinsider.com/why-facebooks-liverail-changed-course-2016-3. Accessed 18 July 2018

Olson P (2014) Facebook closes $19 billion WhatsApp deal https://www.forbes.com/sites/parmyolson/2014/10/06/facebook-closes-19-billion-whatsapp-deal/#3e276ff25c66. Accessed 18 July 2018

Parr B (2011) Facebook acquires Snaptu to bring social networking to feature phones. https://mashable.com/2011/03/20/facebook-snaptu/#eSk68olpTqqc. Accessed 15 July 2018

PRNEWSWIRE (2014) Facebook to acquire Oculus. https://www.prnewswire.com/news-releases/facebook-to-acquire-oculus-252328061.html. Accessed 15 July 2018

Reuters (2014) Facebook's $19B WhatsApp buy makes sense to Wall Street. https://nypost.com/2014/02/20/facebooks-19b-whatsapp-buy-makes-sense-to-wall-street/. Accessed 18 July 2018

Rowan D (2018) The inside story of Jan Koum and how Facebook bought WhatsApp. https://www.wired.co.uk/article/whats-app-owner-founder-jan-koum-facebook. Accessed 18 July 2018

Techcrunch.com Contributor (2012) Facebook buys Instagram for $1 billion, turns budding rival into its standalone photo app. https://techcrunch.com/2012/04/09/facebook-to-acquire-instagram-for-1-billion/. Accessed 15 July 2018

Wagner K (2017) Here's why Facebook's $1 billion Instagram acquisition was such a great deal. https://www.recode.net/2017/4/9/15235940/facebook-instagram-acquisition-anniversary. Accessed 15 July 2018

JDS Uniphase Corp and SDL Inc. Merger 40

JDS Uniphase (JDSU) is a high-technology company which designs, develops, manufactures, and distributes a large number of products for the fiber-optic communications market. The fiber-optic components of the company are used by system manufacturers to develop advanced optical networks for the telecommunications and cable television industries. JDS Uniphase specializes in wavelength division multiplexing (WDM) technology. On August 2015, JDSU split into two companies to form Viavi Solutions and Lumentum Holdings. The restructuring was done by undertaking a tax free spinoff of its optical components and commercial laser division and the remaining company to focus more on software and services.

JDS Uniphase Merger

In 1981 JDS Fitel Inc. was established. In March 1996, JDS Fitel raised 93.6 million Canadian dollars through its initial public offering. Furukawa Electric Co., Ltd. of Japan had retained a majority stake of 55% in the company following the IPO. In 1997 JDS Fitel entered into a strategic alliance with Optical Coating Laboratory Inc. (OCLI) to exploit the increasing opportunities in the dense wavelength division multiplexing (DWDM) business. In May 1998, the company acquired a 68% interest in FITEL-Photomatrix (Canada) Inc. from the Furukawa Electric Co., Ltd. Later in the year, it acquired the remaining stake of 32% in the company. In 1998, JDS Fitel acquired the Akzo Nobel Photonics business unit from the Netherlands-based Akzo Nobel N.V. which was a world leader in waveguide technology for optical switching.

Uniphase Corporation was formed in 1979 and became publicly traded in 1992. The company was involved in the manufacture of red helium and blue argon gas lasers for printing, biomedical, and other applications. The helium–neon lasers were used in bar code readers. In 1995, Uniphase acquired the United Technologies

B. R. Kumar, *Wealth Creation in the World's Largest Mergers and Acquisitions*, Management for Professionals, https://doi.org/10.1007/978-3-030-02363-8_40

Photonics Division which became the core of Uniphase Telecommunications Products (UTP). In 1997, Uniphase acquired Australian-based Index which was a leader in fiber-optic reflection filters for wavelength division multiplexing (WDM). In March 1997, Uniphase acquired the laser diode manufacturing unit of IBM, located in Zurich, Switzerland, and renamed it Uniphase Laser Enterprise AG. In November 1998 Uniphase acquired Broadband Communications Products and formed Uniphase Broadband Products, Inc.

In 1999, Uniphase Corporation and JDS Fitel Inc. merged in a stock swap deal valued at approximately $3.2 billion (Lipin et al., 2000). The deal created one of the biggest manufacturer of parts used in phone equipment (Bloomberg News, 1999). Uniphase made lasers and computer chips which helped fiber-optic phone networks to carry more information. JDS Fitel made components used in systems such as filters. JDS Fitel had market capitalization of US $3.08 billion, and Uniphase had market capitalization of $3.13 billion at the time of merger. The combined company had sales of $420 million and more than 3600 employees worldwide. Both companies had little overlap in products while the two companies shared an immense overlap in customers. The merger facilitated the creation of an independent supplier with a broader portfolio of components and modules for modern communications systems.

In 1999 and 2000, the stock had soared 451% and 44%, respectively. The shares of JDS Uniphase were traded on the NASDAQ under the symbol JDSU, while the shares of JDS Uniphase Canada Ltd were traded on the Toronto Stock Exchange under the symbol JDU. JDS Uniphase had grown over the years through a series of mergers and acquisitions. In September 1999, JDS Uniphase had acquired AFC Technologies, a Quebec-based developer of optical amplifiers and broadband instruments. During October 1999, JDS Uniphase acquired Ramar Corporation which was a developer of lithium niobate-based integrated optical components. In November 1999, JDS Uniphase acquired Optical Coating Laboratory for approximately $2.8 billion in stock. During the same period, JDS Uniphase acquired EPITAXX Inc., a New Jersey-based supplier of optical detectors and receivers for fiber-optic telecommunications and cable television networks for a stock deal valued at $400 million. In December 1999, the company acquired SIFAM, a United Kingdom-based maker of fused component products. During June 2000, JDS Uniphase completed the buyout of E-Tek Dynamics which made fiber-optic network equipment for $15 billion. In the same year, JDS entered into an agreement to acquire Cronos Integrated Microsystems, Inc., a North Carolina-based provider of optical MEMS devices to the telecommunications industry for $750 million in stock.

SDL made optical equipment for fiber-optic networks for volumes of Internet traffic. SDL produces semiconductors, lasers, and amplifiers to boost signal strengths on optical network.

JDS Uniphase: SDL Merger

The optical networking industry had been witnessing consolidation through a series of acquisitions by Cisco Systems, Corning Inc., and JDS Uniphase.

The definitive merger agreement between JDS Uniphase and SDL was announced on July 10, 2000. The deal was valued at $41 billion based on July 7 closing price of JDS Uniphase. The acquisition of SDL was the continuation of the aggressive merger strategy pursued by JDS Uniphase (ABC News, 2000).

On February 16, 2001, JDS Uniphase Corp and SDL Inc. announced the completion of their merger. Each outstanding share of SDL common stock was exchanged for 3.8 shares of JDS Uniphase common stock. SDL became a wholly owned subsidiary of JDS Uniphase. The deal represented a 49% premium for SDL shareholders (CNN Money Deals, 2000). The transaction valued SDL's shares at $441.5125 a share which represented approximately 50% premium for SDL shareholders (CNN Money Deals, 2000). The acquisition created a technology giant on the basis of the strength of the fast-growing market for high-speed networks which send data on light impulses over thin glass fibers.

The union was aimed to increase the technological expertise and economies of scale and offer customers new innovative module offerings (Matsumuto, 2000). The increased demand for bandwidth required faster telecommunication network capacity and flexibility. The merger was expected to expedite the development and deployment of high-capacity, flexible optical networks by speeding up the delivery of optical amplifiers, lossless optical switches, integrated optical modules, and other innovative solutions. The combination was expected to bring together world class technical and manufacturing teams which delivered best in class products. Both JDS Uniphase and SDL manufactured products which were needed for high-capacity fiber-optic networks which facilitated increased telecommunications traffic. The demand for such products was growing as high-speed audio and video transmission became prevalent on the Internet. The deal was in line with the trend whereby major manufacturers were consolidating to add capacity and develop higher-performing products to keep up the demand for fiber-optic equipment. SDL made lasers and amplifiers for fiber-optic communications systems. JDS also made lasers but bought some from SDL. The acquisition of SDL added pump lasers and arrayed wave guides to its product mix. The merger combined the company's manufacturing capabilities which were particularly relevant in the context of persistent component shortages. The acquisition enabled the combined company to offer a complete line of components to run optical networks. Adding SDL to its portfolio gave JDS 80% market share for some types of optical networking component. Both JDS Uniphase and SDL benefitted from the booming construction of fiber-optic networks which were necessitated by the high demand for more internet bandwidth. It was estimated by the telecom market research firm RHK Inc. that the worldwide market for optical components which were used in long distance and cable television applications would increase to $23 billion in 2003 compared to $6.6 billion in the year 1999.The fastest growing segment of the market was Dense Wave Division Multiplexing (DWDM) which enabled 128 light signals to be carried on a single optical fiber. JDS

Uniphase had a competitive advantage for DWDM. The combined company dominated certain segments of the laser pump business like 980 nanometer laser pump business (Photonics.com, 2000, 2001; Pillar, 2000).

JDS Uniphase was headquartered in San Jose California and employed more than 17,000 people at the time of merger announcement. SDL was headquartered at San Jose California and employed 1700 people with multiple locations in Massachusetts, Philadelphia, and Canada. JDS Uniphase's co-chairman and chief executive officer, Donald Scifres, and SDL's chief executive became the co-chairman of the board.

Stock Market Reaction to the Deal

On merger announcement, JDS Uniphase shares fell by $15.063 to $101.125 on the NASDAQ stock market, while shares of SDL rose by $25.375 to $320.688. JDS shares fell nearly by 13%, and SDL shares increased by approximately 9%. The stock return analysis for JDS Uniphase was done for the entire merger period. The merger announcement was done on July 10, 2000. The merger was completed on February 16, 2001. The cumulative return analysis for JDS Uniphase stock was done for 1-year period (1/7/2000 to 1/7/2001) covering 251 days of analysis. The merger event window was −4 to +246-day period. On the day before announcement, the stock price of JDS Uniphase fell by approximately 4%. One day after announcement, the stock price increased by 3.15% but again fell by 4.7% on +2 days of announcement. On +3 and +4 days of announcement, the stock price increased by approximately 5%. Hence the JDS Uniphase stock price was highly fluctuating in the immediate period surrounding the merger announcement. On a cumulative basis during the time window event of analysis for merger, the JDS Uniphase stock declined by approximately 150% (Fig. 40.1).

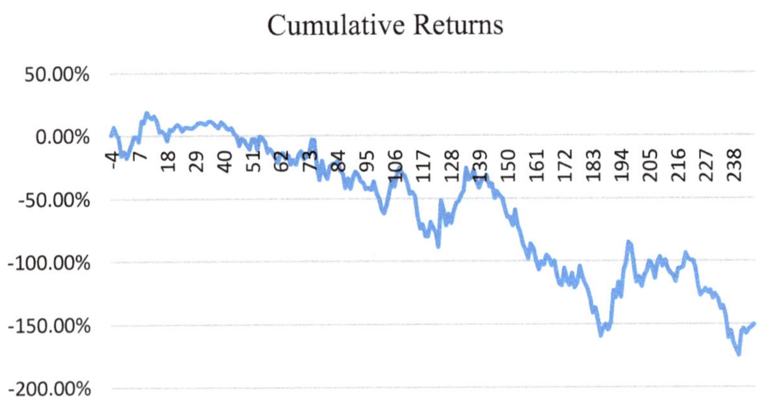

Fig. 40.1 Cumulative returns for JDS Uniphase stock for the merger event period

References

ABC News (2000) JDS Uniphase to acquire SDL for $37 billion. https://abcnews.go.com/Business/story?id=89676&page=1. Accessed 20 July 2018

Bloomberg News (1999) Uniphase and JDS Fitel agree to merge. https://www.nytimes.com/1999/01/29/business/uniphase-and-jds-fitel-agree-to-merge.html. Accessed 20 July 2018

CNN Money Deals (2000) JDS offers $41B for SDL. https://money.cnn.com/2000/07/10/deals/jds/. Accessed 20 July 2018

Lipin S, Deogun N, ThurmStaff S (2000) JDS Uniphase agrees to purchase rival SDL for $41 billion in stock. https://www.wsj.com/articles/SB963200491536854074. Accessed 20 July 2018

Matsumuto C (2000) JDS Uniphase plans SDL purchase. https://www.eetimes.com/document.asp?doc_id=1141939. Accessed 20 July 2018

Photonics.com (2000) JDS Uniphase and SDL Inc. Announce $41 billion merger. https://www.photonics.com/a6668/JDS_Uniphase_and_SDL_Inc_Announce_3641. Accessed 20 July 2018

Photonics.com (2001) JDS Uniphase and SDL merger completed. https://www.photonics.com/a8363/JDS_Uniphase_And_SDL_Merger_Completed. Accessed 20 July 2018

Pillar C (2000) JDS Uniphase to buy SDL for $41 billion. http://articles.latimes.com/2000/jul/11/business/fi-51010. Accessed 18 July 2018

KKR's Acquisition of First Data

41

KKR

KKR is a major global investment firm which manages multiple alternative asset classes which include private equity, energy, infrastructure, real estate, and credit with strategic manager partnerships which manage hedge funds. The company is one of the world's oldest and most experienced private equity firms which specializes in management buyouts. The company was founded in the year 1976. The company focuses on long-term investment approach to its portfolio companies. Its strategy is to work in partnership with management teams for future competitiveness and growth. As of March 31, 2018, the assets under the management of KKR amounted to $176 billion. The company has presence in 20 cities in 14 countries across 4 continents. Approximately 101 portfolio companies in KKR's private equity funds generated over $165 billion in annual revenues as of December 31, 2017. These companies employed a total global workforce of approximately 695,000 as of December 31, 2017. There are 50 million retirees and pensioners with exposure to KKR's investments. KKR had been a leader in the private equity industry with the completion of more than 320 private equity investments in portfolio companies with a total transaction value in excess of $560 billion as of December 31, 2017. KKR earns management, monitoring, transaction, and incentive fees and carries interest for providing investment management, monitoring, and other services to funds, vehicles, CLOs, managed accounts, and portfolio companies. The company generates transaction-specific income from capital market transactions. The company operates business in four segments consisting of private markets, public markets, capital markets, and principal activities. In 2006, Bain Capital, KKR, and Merrill Lynch & Co joined together to pay $21 billion and assume $11.7 billion in debt to acquire hospital operator HCA. The following table provides the financial highlights of KKR (Table 41.1).

B. R. Kumar, *Wealth Creation in the World's Largest Mergers and Acquisitions*, Management for Professionals, https://doi.org/10.1007/978-3-030-02363-8_41

Table 41.1 Financial highlights of KKR

Year	2013	2014	2015	2016	2017
Investment income	8,896,746	6,544,748	6,169,125	762,606	1,838,795
Net income	7,854,228	5,395,020	5,275,032	950,664	2,560,042
Total assets	51,427,201	65,872,745	71,042,339	39,002,897	45,834,719
Total liabilities	4,842,383	14,168,684	21,574,754	21,884,814	25,171,919

Source: Annual Report
The values are given in thousands of dollars

First Data Corp

First Data was founded in Omaha, Nebraska, in 1971. First Data became the first processor of Visa and MasterCard-issued credit cards. First Data was split off from American Express Co. in 1992 as an information processing company which handled billions of credit card and other transactions for third parties. First Data Corporation was spun off from American Express and went public in year 1992. In the year 1995, First Data Corp. merged with First Financial Management Corp. (FFMC), and Western Union became a part of First Data. In 2001, First Data acquired PaySys International and their VisionPLUS payment software system. In 2004, First Data merged with Concord EFS in a deal valued at $6.6 billion. Through this deal, First Data added the STAR Network and PIN-based debit acceptance at more than 1.9 million ATM and retail location. First Data also acquired other companies like GovOne, eONEGlobal, Paymap Inc., and Taxware. In 2006, First Data spun off Western Union into an independent publicly traded company through a tax-free spin-off of 100% of Western Union to First Data shareholders.

First Data Corp. is a leading provider of electronic commerce and payment solutions for businesses worldwide. First Data Corporation is the pivotal center of global electronic commerce. First Data Corp. offers clients the most complete array of integrated solutions in the industry, covering their needs across next-generation commerce technologies, merchant acquiring, issuing, and network solutions. First Data Corporation serves clients in over 100 countries, covering six million business locations and over 4000 financial institutions. First Data is the largest merchant acquirer, issuer processor, and independent network services provider in the world. First Data enables businesses to accept electronic payments and help financial institutions issue credit, debit, and prepaid cards and route secure transactions between them. The company has the largest distribution network in the industry with partnerships from leading financial institutions, direct sales force, and network of distribution partners. In 2017, First Data processed 93 billion transactions globally. In the United States, the company processed $2.1 trillion of payment volume. First Data operates through three segments – Global Business Solutions (GBS), Global Financial Solutions (GFS), and Network Security Solutions (NSS). GBS provides a wide variety of solutions to merchants which include retail point-of-sale merchant acquiring, ecommerce services, as well as next-generation offerings such as mobile payment services and cloud-based Clover point-of-sale operating system which includes marketplace for proprietary and third-party business applications. GFS provides technology solutions for bank and nonbank issuers. These solutions include general-purpose credit, retail private label, commercial card, and loan processing within the United States and international markets, as well as licensed financial software systems. NSS provides a wide range of value added solutions that are sold to clients in GBS and GFS segments. First Data's Star Network provided a nationwide domestic debit acceptance at more than two million retail POS, ATM, and online outlets for nearly a third of all US debit cards. The following table provides the financial highlights of First Data (Table 41.2).

KKR's Buyout of First Data

On April 2, 2007, First Data Corp. announced that it had entered into an agreement to be acquired by an affiliate of Kohlberg Kravis Roberts (KKR) & Co in a transaction valued at $29 billion (Reuters News, 2007). First Data shareholders received $34 in cash for each share of First Data common stock held which represented a premium of approximately 26% over First Data's closing price of $26.90 as on March 30, 2007, and a premium of approximately 34% over the average closing price during the previous 30 trading days (Berman et al., 2007). First Data being a privately owned company was delisted from the New York Stock Exchange on September 24, 2007. This leveraged buyout by KKR was financed with $24 billion in debt. It was the second largest buyout ever. In 2007, KKR and Texas Pacific had an agreement to buy Texas Utility TXU Corp. for $32 billion. In 1988 KKR bought RJR Nabisco for $25.1 billion. The deal had an equity value of $26.4 billion based on 775.1 million shares outstanding. The deal agreement was unanimously approved by the First Data board of directors on the basis of the recommendation of the strategic review committee made up of three independent directors.

The deal included a "go-shop" provision which provided the opportunity to First Data to solicit proposals from other suitors for the next 50 days after the announcement of deal. According to Reuter estimates, at $34 per share, KKR paid 27 times its estimated 2007 earnings of $1.24 per share. On the basis of $26.4 billion equity value, KKR paid approximately 14 times estimated 2007 EBITDA of $1.9 billion. The deal came about 6 months after First Data spun off Western Union.

Citigroup, Credit Suisse, Deutsche Bank, HSBC, Lehman Brothers, Goldman Sachs, and Merrill Lynch provided debt financing for the transaction. These financial institutions also acted as financial advisors to KKR. Simpson Thacher & Bartlett LLP was acting as the legal advisor to KKR. Morgan Stanley & Co served as the

Table 41.2 Financial highlights of First Data

Year	2013	2014	2015	2016	2017
Revenues	10,809	11,152	11,451	11,584	12,052
Net income	−775	−265	−1268	660	1664
Total assets	34,962	34,034	34,362	40,292	48,269
Net cash flow from operations	715	1035	795	2111	2047

Source: Annual Report (2017)

sole financial advisor to First Data. Evercore Group LLC served as financial advisor to the Strategic Review Committee of the First Data board of directors. Sidley Austin LLP acted as legal counsel to First Data.

After the buyout by KKR, First Data's debt swelled to $22 billion by 2012 due to the junk bond-financed deal. The amount of debt was more than double its annual revenue (Grantham, 2012). After KKR's buyout, First Data announced job cuts, and annual expenses were slashed by about $500 million a year. After reporting a $1.5 billion profit in year 2006, First Data made losses amounting to $3.8 billion in year 2008 and $1.1 billion in year 2009. In 2009, KKR cofounder Henry Kravis joined First Data board, and another senior advised of KKR became First Data's chairman. The company moved back its headquarters from Denver back to Atlanta. First Data had to cut more jobs. As a result of restructuring exercise, First Data turned profitable by year 2010.

In 2014, First Data raised a huge $3.5 billion private placement. Approximately $1.2 billion investment was made by KKR and the rest by hedge funds, mutual funds, and other financial institutions. The proceeds were set aside to retire some of the First Data's massive $22 billion in long-term debt which would save around $375 million per year in annual interest payments (Primack, 2014).

First Data was attractive to KKR as the processing company had a good cash flow which was a critical factor for private equity firm to remain in business. First Data's operations underpinned large parts of the US banking system as it processed checks, automated teller machine, debit cards, and credit card transactions.

References

Annual Report (2017). https://investor.firstdata.com/annual-reports-and-proxy-statement

Berman DK, Bauerlein V, Sidel R (2007) KKR to acquire First Data. https://www.wsj.com/articles/SB117549883685956662. Accessed 03 Aug 2018

Grantham R (2012) KKR buyout saddled First Data with massive debt. https://www.ajc.com/business/kkr-buyout-saddled-first-data-with-massive-debt/KumrcBUZpV1VFgqCEu6jxK/. Accessed 03 Aug 2018

Primack D (2014) Why KKR is doubling down on first data. http://fortune.com/2014/06/19/why-kkr-is-doubling-down-on-first-data/. Accessed 03 Aug 2018

Reuters News (2007) First Data agrees to be sold to KKR for $29 bl. https://www.reuters.com/article/us-firstdata-kkr/first-data-agrees-to-be-sold-to-kkr-for-29-bln-idUSN0238467320070402. Accessed 03 Aug 2018

Lucent Technologies Acquisition of Ascend Communications

42

Lucent Technologies

Lucent Technologies was a multinational telecommunications equipment company headquartered in the United States. The company was established in the year 1996 through the divestiture of the former AT&T Technologies business unit of AT&T Corporation. During 2006, Lucent got merged with Alcatel SA of France to form Alcatel–Lucent. The $13.4 billion deal between Alcatel and Lucent Technologies created a French–American maker of telecommunications equipment with revenues of $25 billion (Company Histories, n.d.). The deal was in response to the increased competition that Western telecommunication firms were facing from low-cost manufacturers from Asia. But the merger was a failure due to cultural differences. In 2016, Alcatel–Lucent was absorbed by Nokia. Nokia purchased Alcatel–Lucent basically to penetrate the US market which was one of the world's largest and most important mobile communications markets. The deal was valued at $16.6 billion (Fitchard, 2015).

Through early 2000 Lucent spent $32 billion in stock and cash to acquire or merge with 30 companies. In the year 1997, Lucent acquired Milpitas-based voicemail market leader Octel Communications Corporation for $2.1 billion. In the same year, Lucent acquired Livingston Enterprises Inc., a global provider of equipment used by Internet service providers to connect their subscribers to the Internet for $650 million in stock. In 1999, Lucent Technologies bought the start-up firm Nexabit Networks for about $900 million. Nexabit makes router/switching technology for IP networks to move terabytes of data over a wide area network. In 1999, Lucent Technologies acquired Mosaix Inc. in a stock swap deal valued at about $145 million. The exchange involved conversion of each Mosaix share into 0.1927 a Lucent share. Mosaix was formed due to the 1996 merger between Digital Systems International Inc. and ViewStar Corp, the maker of business processing software.

B. R. Kumar, *Wealth Creation in the World's Largest Mergers and Acquisitions*, Management for Professionals, https://doi.org/10.1007/978-3-030-02363-8_42

Mosaix provides call center software, systems, and services. The acquisition helped Lucent to expand its own CentreVu call center product (Tech Center, 1999). Lucent had acquired more than ten smaller firms to offer broader array of data-based equipment during the period 1998–2000.

In the year 1998, Lucent made a number of acquisitions like ProMinent, Optimay GmbH, Yurie, SDX, MassMedia, LANNET, Quadritek, and Pario Software. ProMinent which was a player in the Gigabit Ethernet networking industry was acquired for $200 million in stock. Optimay GmbH, a German-based software developer for chip set to be used for Global Systems for Mobile Communications cellular phones, was acquired for $65 million. Yurie was a provider of asynchronous transfer mode access technology and equipment for data, voice, and video networking. Yurie was acquired for $ 1 billion. SDX, the provider of business communication systems, was acquired for $200 million. MassMedia was involved in the development of next-generation network interoperability software. LANNET, the Israel-based supplier of Ethernet and ATM switching solutions, was acquired for $117 million. Quadritek, a start-up developer of next-generation Internet Protocol network administration software solutions, was acquired for $50 million. With these acquisitions, Lucent was positioning itself to compete with companies such as Cisco Systems in building multiservice networks which could support voice, video, and data traffic.

In 1999 Lucent acquired WaveAccess which was the developer of high-speed systems for wireless data communications for $54 million. Kenan Systems Corp, a software developer for third-party billing and customer care, was acquired for $1.48 billion in stock. Sybaris, the semiconductor design company, was acquired for $50 million. Lucent Technologies became a leader in both voice and data for service providers with the acquisition of Ascend Communications in the year 1999. Lucent had acquired Ortel Corporation which was the second largest producer of lasers used for video in cable TV networks for approximately $2.95 billion in stock. Lucent Technologies through Ortel supplied interactive television equipment to large cable operators such as AT&T to transform one-way broadcasting systems into interactive two-way communications networks.

In April 2000, Lucent sold its Consumer Products unit to VTech and Consumer Phone Services. In October 2000, Lucent spun off its Business Systems arm into Avaya, Inc., and in June 2002, it spun off its microelectronics division into Agere Systems.

Ascend Communications

Ascend Communications Inc. was engaged in the development, manufacture, and sale of wide area networking solutions for telecommunications. Ascend Communications was established in the year 1988 and had its initial public offering in 1994. Ascend was the second largest independent Internet supplier after Cisco Systems. Ascend Communications designed and manufactured equipment for high-density dial-up installations. In 1997, Ascend Communications acquired Cascade

Communications. Cascade Communications designed and manufactured high-density carrier packet switches which included B-STDX9000 frame relay switch and the CBX500 and GX-550 ATM switches.

In 1998, Ascend Communications Inc. acquired Stratus Computer Inc. in a stock deal valued at $822 million. Ascend exchanged 0.75 Ascend share for each of the 24 million shares of Stratus. The exchange valued Stratus at $33.5 a share. Through Stratus acquisition, Ascend Communications acquired the technology which allowed telephone carriers to offer services such as caller ID and call forwarding over data networks using Internet technology (CNN Money Deals, 1998).

Acquisition of Ascend Communications

In 1999, Lucent Technologies Inc., the topmaker of phone equipment, bought Ascend Communications Inc. for $20.3 billion in stock for expansion into the fast-growing Internet equipment industry. The acquisition created a company which became a provider of complete voice and data systems. The new merged company had critical competitive advantage for attracting telecommunications carriers and large companies (CNET.com, 2002).

Deal Terms

Under the terms of the deal, each share of Ascend stock was converted into 0.825 shares of Lucent stock. The deal valued Ascend at $89 a share based on Lucent's price on announcement period which represented a 19% premium over Ascend's closing price on the day before announcement (Time staff and wire reports, 1999). The deal value was more than double the purchase price paid by Northern Telecom for data player Bay Networks in the year 1998. Northern Telecom had purchased Bay Networks for $7 billion.

Strategic Motives for the Acquisition

Lucent Technologies had undertaken a series of acquisitions to emerge as one of the fastest-growing companies in the telecommunications equipment market industry. Lucent found Ascend's product mix of powerful switches that direct Internet traffic attractive. This acquisition positioned Lucent Technologies to compete with top networking companies like Cisco Systems and Nortel Networks. During the same period, Lucent purchased Kenan Systems a private firm which makes third-party billing and customer care software for $1.5 billion. Lucent focused on multiple acquisitions to complement growth generated by developments from its Bell Laboratories division. The strategy of Lucent was to invest heavily in high-growth segments like software, data networking, microelectronics business, and wireless. The Ascend acquisition gave Lucent an impetus in asynchronous transfer mode or

ATM and remote access technology. Ascend specializes in switches based on frame relay and asynchronous transfer mode (ATM). Ascend is a leader in providing the remote access equipment which providers use to connect dial-up Internet users. The Ascend acquisition catapulted Lucent into direct competition with data market leader Cisco Systems and allowed the firm to offer a wider set of networking equipment to Internet service providers and upstart telecommunications carriers. The acquisition of Ascend enabled Lucent Technologies to add high-end Internet-based switching devices used for upgrading networks of carrier or service provider (Feder, 1999). Approximately 90% of Ascend Communications' $1.5 billion in annual revenues were derived from service providers such as PSINet and UUNet, a division of MCI WorldCom. Ascend became part of a newly formed broadband networks of Lucent Technologies' other data networking, optical networking systems, and communications software group. The union of Ascend Communications made Lucent the top provider of networking gear for a new generation of data networks. In the context of Internet boom, Lucent Technologies was repositioning itself as a business which can serve both voice and data networking markets. The acquisition of Ascend secured skilled workers for Lucent Technologies. The acquisition helped Lucent Technologies to capture a larger share of the world's networking market (Niccolai and Staff Writers, 1999).

Deal Impact on Stock Market

The deal was announced on January 14, 1999. On announcement of the deal, Lucent shares fell $3.63 to close at $104.25 on the New York Stock Exchange. Ascend gained $5.38 to close at $80.31 on NASDAQ.

References

CNET.com (2002) Lucent, Ascend in 20 billion merger. https://www.cnet.com/g00/news/lucent-ascend-in-20-billion-merger/?i10c.encReferrer=aHR0cHM6Ly93d3cuZ29vZ2xlLmFlLw%3D%3D&i10c.ua=1&i10c.dv=14. Accessed 10 Aug 2018

CNN Money Deals (1998) Ascend to acquire Stratus. https://money.cnn.com/1998/08/03/deals/ascend/. Accessed 10 Aug 2018

Company Histories. http://www.company-histories.com/Lucent-Technologies-Inc-Company-History.html. Accessed 10 Aug 2018

Feder B (1999) Finally, Lucent and Ascend Tie the knot for $20 billion. https://www.nytimes.com/1999/01/14/business/finally-lucent-and-ascend-tie-the-knot-for-20-billion.html. Accessed 10 Aug 2018

Fitchard K (2015) What's at stake in the $16.6 billion Nokia-Alcatel-Lucent deal. http://fortune.com/2015/04/16/nokia-alcatel-lucent/. Accessed 10 Aug 2018

Niccolai J, Staff Writers (1999) Lucent completes acquisition of Ascend. https://www.computerworld.com.au/article/45549/lucent_completes_acquisition_ascend/. Accessed 10 Aug 2018

Tech Center (1999) Lucent Tech to acquire Mosaix for about $145 million in stock. https://www.wsj.com/articles/SB923323070363116002. Accessed 10 Aug 2018

Time staff and wire reports (1999) Lucent to buy Ascend in $20.3 billion deal. http://articles.latimes.com/1999/jan/14/business/fi-63310. Accessed 10 Aug 2018

Vivendi–Seagram Deal

43

Vivendi Highlights

Vivendi SA was a French water utility company which transformed itself into a telecommunications and entertainment giant. The company known as CGE was founded as a water supply and waste services business company in 1853 (Vivendi Website, 2018). The company later diversified into businesses such as environmental services, energy transport, construction property, and communication. In 1983, in partnership with Havas, Canal+ was founded. In 1998, the company changed its name to Vivendi. In 1999, Vivendi merged with Pathe in a deal valued at US $2.59 billion. On December 2000, Vivendi Universal was created with the merger of Vivendi, Canal+ television networks, and Seagram's media assets which included Universal Studios. In 2004, 80% of the Vivendi Universal subsidiary was sold to GE, to form NBC Universal, with Vivendi retaining a 20% stake. At the same time, it sold a 50% stake in Canal+ and StudioCanal to the new company. In 2005, Canal+ was merged with TPS which was France's second largest pay-TV provider. Since April 2006, Vivendi in its current form came into existence, after selling 80% stake to GE. The name of the company was changed to Vivendi. In the year 2007, Vivendi merged its game publishing unit with Activision in a $18.8 billion deal to form the merged company, Activision Blizzard. Vivendi sold its stake in NBC Universal on January 25, 2011. During 2011, Vodafone sold its 44% stake in mobile service provider SFR to Vivendi for about $11 billion. During 2013, as a result of its strategic review, it sold the majority of its interest in Activision Blizzard, keeping a 12% stake in the games company. In November 2013, Vivendi also sold its 53% stake in Maroc Telecom to Dubai-based Etisalat for around $4.2 billion. In 2013, Vivendi announced a demerger plan in which Vivendi would be converted into a media group which comprises of Canal+, Universal Music, and GVT. In 2014, Vivendi sold GVT to Telefonica Vivo, which was a subsidiary of Telefonica in Brazil. In the year 2015, Vivendi bought approximately 80% share in Dailymotion. In 2016, Vivendi successfully completed the hostile takeover of Gameloft by acquiring the

B. R. Kumar, *Wealth Creation in the World's Largest Mergers and Acquisitions*, Management for Professionals, https://doi.org/10.1007/978-3-030-02363-8_43

founders' stake in the company. Vivendi acquired Flavorus from SFX Entertainment for $4 million. Vivendi also acquired Paddington and The Copyrights Group.

Vivendi is an integrated content, media, and communications group. The company focuses on the entire media value chain starting from talent discovery to the creation, production, and distribution of content. The Group consists of Universal Music Group, Canal+ group, Havas Group, Gameloft, and Vivendi Village. Universal Music is engaged in recorded music, music publishing, and merchandising. Canal+ is involved in pay-TV in France and other regions of Africa, Poland, Vietnam, and Myanmar. Havas Group is one of the world's largest global communications groups with business units for creativity, media expertise, and healthcare/wellness. Gameloft is a world leader in mobile games with 2.5 million games downloaded per day. Vivendi Village consists of Vivendi Ticketing, MyBestPro for expert counselling, Vivendi Talents, and Olympia Production. The following table provides the financial highlights of Vivendi (Table 43.1).

Seagram Highlights

Seagram Company was a multinational conglomerate headquartered in Montreal, Quebec. In the 1990s it became the largest owner of alcoholic beverage lines. Seagram possessed well-known liquor brands like Chivas Regal, Absolut Vodka, Captain Morgan's Rum, Martell cognac, Glenlivet Scotch whiskies, etc.

Over the years Seagram had grown into a powerful conglomerate being the corporate parent of Hollywood's third largest movie studio, the world's third largest liquor manufacturing and distributing business, and the largest music company in the world. During June 1995, Seagram bought MCA Inc. from Matsushita for $5.7 billion and renamed it as Universal Studios. Seagram sold its 25% stake in DuPont to fund the $5.7 billion acquisition. Seagram had acquired 25% stake in DuPont in the year 1981. Seagram owned the world's largest music company, Universal Music Group, and the largest film and television production company, Universal Studios.

During December 1998, Seagram Co bought PolyGram music company from Dutch electronics giant Philip for $10.4 billion (CNNMoney.News.Companies, 1998). Seagram had also spun off its Tropicana fruit juice business in a $3.5 billion deal (Seagram release: official announcement, 1998). The deal created the world's largest music company. PolyGram was a global entertainment company with annual revenues of over $5.5 billion. It was the leading record company with such pop and classical record labels such as A&M, Decca/London, Def Jam, etc. PolyGram was also the leading producer and distributor of film, television, and video. PolyGram

Table 43.1 Financial highlights in millions of euros

Year	2014	2015	2016	2017
Revenues	10,089	10,762	10,819	12,501
Income from operations	1108	1061	853	1098
EBIT	545	521	887	1018
Total equity	22,988	21,086	19,612	17,886

film's operations include PolyGram Films, PolyGram Television, Propaganda Films, and Working Title Films. Universal Music, formed after the PolyGram purchase, included Island Records and Mercury Records. Seagram's Universal acquired Philips' 75% ownership position in PolyGram through a tender offer for all issued shares for $59 per share in cash or at the shareholders' election, for cash and Seagram common shares. The company integrated PolyGram Film Entertainment into Universal film business. The deal created estimated annual cost savings of $275–$300 million. With the acquisition of PolyGram, Seagram became a global entertainment leader with the largest music company in the world. In 2000, Universal's television holdings were sold off to media entrepreneur Barry Diller, and the rest of the entertainment empire was sold to French conglomerate Vivendi. Seagram's beverage assets were sold to Diageo PLC and Pernod Ricard SA of France (Kapner, 2000).

Merger of Vivendi and Seagram

On June 19, 2000, France-based Vivendi and its television subsidiary Canal+ announced plans of a three-way merger with Canada-based Seagram (CNN Money Deals, 2000). The all-stock deal was valued at $33.7 billion (Came et al., 2003). The new company was named as Vivendi Universal. The merger created an international media and entertainment powerhouse with assets ranging from movies to theme parks and publishing. The deal was announced after more than 2 months of negotiations between Paris-based Vivendi and Seagram, the Canadian entertainment, media, and spirits company.

Terms of Deal

Vivendi paid roughly $51.5 billion for Seagram and the 51% of Vivendi's pay-TV affiliate Canal+ which represented the share Vivendi didn't own (Englisn, 2000). Vivendi offered two of its shares for every share of Canal+ that it does not already own. The deal was valued at $10.9 billion for the 51% stake. The pay-TV company was virtually debt-free. Vivendi paid out $34 billion in stock and assumed $6.6 billion in debt in Seagram. The all-stock deal valued Seagram shares at $77.35 which amounted to a 53% premium over the market price before the deal news came (Independent News Business, 1998). The Bronfman family which owned 24.6% of Seagram acquired roughly 8% of the new company and got five seats on behalf of Seagram on the 18-member board of directors. Philips Electronics, the second largest shareholder in Seagram behind Bronfman family, tendered its 11% stake in Vivendi. Canal+ operated as a joint venture with CNN International in Spain.

Seagram-owned Hollywood's Universal Studios had been the biggest music company in the world. The merger led to the combination of Seagram's film and music segments with Vivendi's cable, satellite, and Internet systems. Vivendi was keen to acquire Seagram's Polygram music unit (Keaten and Paul, 2000). The merger resulted in the combination of Seagram's Universal film and television studios, music group, and theme parks to Vivendi's extensive distribution systems. The distribution systems included France's Canal+ pay-television service as well as the Internet portal Vizzavi which was a gateway for approximately 80 million European subscribers. Seagram was attracted toward Vivendi's expertise in both wireless telephones and Internet. There was immense scope for growth opportunities due to the potential emerging new market for downloading music onto wireless telephones and other media at the time of the deal.

During the period of consolidation, the global music business was expected to increase from $60 billion to $150 billion on account of boom in online digital delivery mechanism. Vivendi had developed the capability to exploit the phenomena. Canal+ had more than 14 million subscribers in 11 countries at the time of the deal. Vivendi had 25% stake in BskyB – which was owned by European satellite television operation. Vizzavi the Internet portal was the joint venture of Vivendi with Vodafone's AirTouch.

The new company Vivendi Universal had a combined annual revenue of approximately $55 billion and EBITDA of $7 billion. It became the number two media and entertainment company after AOL Time Warner merger. The strategy of Vivendi was to deliver content, especially music from Seagram's world leading Universal Music Group across Vivendi's web of telecommunication systems, which included Cegetel which was one of the biggest mobile phone operators in France. The new Vivendi Universal owned businesses which ranged from the Universal film studio and music labels to European pay-TV channels, electronic media, wireless telecommunications, and theme parks. Vivendi was focusing on the development of Vizzavi, a venture with Britain's Vodafone AirTouch to offer Internet access and online content to mobile phone users as one of the outlets for music on the web. Acquisition of Europe's biggest pay-TV company expanded Vizzavi's potential customer base.

Legal Issues with Merger

In 2017, Vivendi settled a 15-year US litigation case against it by an agreement to pay $26.4 million to investors related to accusations of misleading shareholders about its liquidity problems in connection with its merger with Seagram.

Stock Market Reaction

The public announcement of the deal was done on June 19, 2000. On deal announcement Vivendi shares initially declined by 8% to €88.10. The investors might have perceived that the deal was overvalued. In the meantime, Seagram's share price rose by 17%. Canal+ sank more than 10% to €178.60 on announcement of the deal.

On the announcement day, the stock price of Vivendi declined by 2.58%. On +1 day after merger announcement, the stock price of Vivendi declined by 8.66%. Thereafter the stock price increased by 1.53% and 3.75% on +2 day and +3 day after announcement (Table 43.2).

Table 43.2 Announcement returns for Vivendi

Day	Returns (%)
−5	−4.64
−4	4.05
−3	−10.08
−2	−4.88
−1	0.56
0	−2.58
1	−8.66
2	1.53
3	3.75
4	1.29
5	0.00

Table 43.3 Cumulative returns surrounding the merger period

Time window in days	Cumulative returns (%)
−10 to +10	−24.05
−5 to +5	−19.65
−3 to +3	−20.35
−1 to +1	−10.67
−1 to +5	−2.09
−10 to +248	−39.56

Fig. 43.1 Cumulative returns for Vivendi stock during merger announcement period

The cumulative returns for Vivendi were negative in all the time window period of analysis (Table 43.3). The cumulative return for the 254-day period surrounding the merger announcement was approximately 3–9% (Fig. 43.1).

References

Came B, Branswell B, Chisholm P (2003) https://www.thecanadianencyclopedia.ca/en/article/seagram-vivendi-deal/. Accessed 14 Aug 2018

CNN Money Deals (2000) Seagram deal but official. Vivendi, Canal Plus, Seagram boards approve three way, $52 B merger. https://money.cnn.com/2000/06/19/deals/seagram/. Accessed 14 Aug 2018

CNNMoney.News.Companies (1998) Seagram swallows PolyGram. https://money.cnn.com/1998/12/10/companies/seagram/. Accessed 14 Aug 2018

Englisn S (2000) Vivendi buys Seagram in $32 bn deal. https://www.telegraph.co.uk/finance/4455117/Vivendi-buys-Seagram-in-32bn-deal.html. Accessed 14 Aug 2018

Independent News Business (1998) Seagram buys PolyGram from Philips for $10.6 bn. https://www.independent.co.uk/news/business/seagram-buys-polygram-from-philips-for-106bn-1158030.html. Accessed 14 Aug 2018

Kapner S (2000) Diageo and Pernod buy and divide up Seagram beverage assets. https://www.nytimes.com/2000/12/20/business/diageo-and-pernod-buy-and-divide-up-seagram-beverage-assets.html. Accessed 14 Aug 2018

Keaten J, Paul F (2000) Vivendi toasts Seagram. https://money.cnn.com/2000/06/20/worldbiz/vivendi_deal/. Accessed 14 Aug 2018

Seagram release: official announcement (1998) Seagram to acquire Polygram. https://www.universalmusic.com/seagram-release-official-announcement-seagram-to-acquire-polygram/. Accessed 14 Aug 2018

Vivendi Website (2018) Vivendi in brief: http://www.vivendi.com/en/vivendi-en/vivendi-in-brief-2/. Accessed 14 Aug 2018

44 Daimler–Chrysler Merger

Highlights of Daimler

Daimler AG is one of the top automotive companies in the world. The company was founded by Gottilieb Daimler and Carl Benz in the year 1886. The German Daimler Group is the world's biggest manufacturer of commercial vehicles and one of the biggest producers of premium cars. The divisions of Daimler are Mercedes–Benz Cars, Daimler Trucks, Mercedes–Benz Vans, Daimler Buses, and Daimler Financial Services. Daimler Financial Services provides financing, leasing, fleet management, insurance, financial investments, credit cards, and innovative mobility services (Daimler website, 2018).

The Group focusses on innovative and green technologies as well as on safe and superior automobiles. Daimler's vehicles and services are sold in almost all of the countries in the world. The company has production facilities in Europe, North and South America, Asia, and Africa. Mercedes–Benz is one of the world's most valuable premium automotive brands. Its brand portfolio includes Mercedes–AMG, Mercedes–Maybach, and Mercedes me and the brands Smart, EQ, Freightliner, Western Star, BharatBenz, FUSO, Setra, and Thomas Built Buses. Daimler Financial Services brands include Mercedes–Benz Bank, Mercedes–Benz Financial Services, Daimler Truck Financial, moovel, car2go, and mytaxi. The company is listed on the stock exchanges of Frankfurt and Stuttgart. The company employed around 289,300 people in the year 2017. In 2017, the group sold approximately 3.3 million vehicles. The group revenues in the year 2017 amounted to €164.2 billion. The group EBIT amounted to €14.7 billion. The company is a component of the Euro Stoxx 50 stock market index. The following table gives 10 year financial highlights of Dailmer group (Table 44.1).

B. R. Kumar, *Wealth Creation in the World's Largest Mergers and Acquisitions*, Management for Professionals, https://doi.org/10.1007/978-3-030-02363-8_44

Table 44.1 10-year financial highlights

Year	2008	2009	2010	2011	2012	2013	2014	2015	2016	2017
Revenues	98,469	78,924	97,761	106,540	114,297	117,982	129,872	149,467	153,261	164,330
R&D expenses	4442	4181	4849	5634	5644	5489	5680	6564	7572	8711
EBIT	2730	−1513	7274	8755	8820	10,815	10,752	13,186	12,902	14,682
Operating margin (%)	2.8	−1.9	7.4	8.2	7.7	9.2	8.3	8.8	8.4	8.9
Net profit	1414	−2644	4674	6029	6830	8720	7290	8711	8784	10,864
Total assets	132,225	128,821	135,830	148,132	163,062	168,518	189,635	217,166	242,988	255,605
Shareholder equity	32,730	31,827	37,953	41,337	39,330	43,363	44,584	54,624	59,133	65,314

Source: Annual Report (2017)
The values are given in millions of euros

Acquisitions by Daimler AG

In the year 1966, Maybach–Motorenbau GmbH merged with Mercedes–Benz Motorenbau Friedrichshafen GmbH to form Maybach Mercedes–Benz Motorenbau GmbH, under partial ownership by Daimler–Benz. The company was renamed as Motoren- und Turbinen-Union Friedrichshafen GmbH (MTU Friedrichshafen) in 1969. In 1995, MTU Friedrichshafen became a wholly owned subsidiary of Daimler–Benz.

In 1998, the merger of the largest cross-border deal between Daimler and Chrysler Corporation was announced. The merger was aimed to safeguard the long-term competitiveness of both the companies. In 2007 the majority stakes in the Chrysler Group and the associated North American financial services business were sold. Chrysler Group was sold off to Cerberus Capital Management. In October 2007, an extraordinary general meeting approved the change of name from Daimler–Chrysler AG to Daimler AG. During April 2009, Daimler AG also relinquished the 19.9 percent stake which it had initially retained in Chrysler.

In 2000, Daimler–Chrysler acquired Detroit Diesel Corporation. The on-highway division was placed under Daimler Trucks North America. The off-highway division of the target acquired company was combined with MTU Friedrichshafen to form MTU America. In the year 2005, MTU–Friedrichshafen was sold to the Swedish investment firm EQT Partners. Daimler acquired 25 percent stake in Italian motorcycle producer MV Agusta in 2014.

In 2017, Daimler acquired Flinc, a startup which built platform and app for peer-to-peer style carpooling. During March 2018, Daimler paid approximately $85 million to buy the remaining 25 per cent of car sharing company car2Go which it didn't own. The deal valued car2Go approximately at $341 million (Lunden, 2018). Daimler had become a major shareholder in the Chinese company Geely the owner of Volvo cars and Lotus brands. Daimler had been buying stakes in a number of regional app-based car hailing services which were competitors for Uber. For example, Daimler purchased stakes in Chauffeur Prive in Paris.

In 2018, Geely Group, the largest automobile manufacturer in China, took a 9.69% stake in Daimler, making it the company's largest single shareholder.

Highlights of Chrysler Corporation

Chrysler Corporation was founded in the year 1925 by Walter Chrysler. In the year 1928, Chrysler Corporation acquired Fargo Trucks and Dodge Brothers. In the 1970s, Chrysler started an engineering partnership with Mitsubishi Motors and sold Mitsubishi vehicles branded as Dodge and Plymouth in North America. In 1985, Chrysler Mitsubishi partnership was further cemented by establishment of Diamond Star Motors. In 1987, Chrysler acquired American Motors Corporation. Through this acquisition, Chrysler added Jeep brand to its portfolio (Time, 2017). During 1998, Chrysler merged with German automaker Daimler–Benz to form Daimler–Benz AG. In 2007, Chrysler was sold to Cerberus Capital Management and renamed

Chrysler LLC. During 2011, Italian automaker Fiat SpA became Chrysler Group LLC's majority owner, thereby clearing the way for a complete restructuring of Chrysler after it emerged from bankruptcy in 2009. In 2014, Fiat completed its deal to purchase the remaining 41 per cent it did not already own of Chrysler. This transaction completed the $4.35 billion deal (NYTimes, 2014). Fiat acquired the stake from United Automobile Workers union (Krisher et al. 2014).

Daimler–Chrysler Merger

In 1998, German automaker Daimler–Benz purchased Chrysler for $38 billion (CNNMoney.News Deals, 1998). The combined company was named as Daimler–Benz. It was one of the biggest cross-border industrial mergers ever. The merger was called as "Mergers of Equals." The consolidation of two automobile giants resulted in a global automobile company with sales of more than $150 billion, catapulting the combined company as the fifth largest car manufacturer at the time of merger. The deal had expected $8 billion in anticipated cost synergies. For Daimler–Benz, the deal provided a second brand of moderately priced cars and trucks. The merger paved the way for the German auto giant to expand into the United States. For Chrysler the deal meant entry into the European market. The merger brought together the German manufacturer's strong Mercedes brand which was a symbol of high quality and the American carmaker Dodge and Jeep led brands which captured approximately 25 per cent of US market.

At the time of the deal, Chrysler was one of the most profitable auto companies in the world. Revenues were all time high which were driven by strong performance by brands like Jeep Grand Cherokee and Dodge Ram. Chrysler had approximately 23 per cent market share in US industry. A substantial portion of the company's sales came from minivans, trucks, and sport utility vehicles. The company had $7.5 billion in cash on hand. The company was brought back from bankruptcy on several occasions.

Terms of the Deal

Daimler–Benz shareholders received one share of the new company for every share they held. Chrysler shareholders received 0.547 of the new company's shares for every Chrysler share they owned. Based on announcement day stock price, the deal valued Chrysler at $58 a share. Daimler shareholders owned 57% of the company, while Chrysler shareholders owned 43% of the combined company. The merger was expected to result cost savings of $1.4 billion in the first year after merger and $3 billion in savings over the next several years.

The combined company had headquarters in Germany and Michigan. The company was incorporated in Germany and had a traditional German structure with separate supervisory and management boards.

The combined company had $92 billion in market value and estimated $130 billion in annual revenue. The combined company became the fifth largest automaker in the world after Ford Motor Co, General Motors, Toyota Motor Corp, and Volkswagen AG.

Smooth integration was a key challenge to Daimler–Chrysler merger. The two automotive companies were never fully integrated. The potential expected synergies from the deal went unrealized. The merger billed as a "merger of equals" was actually a takeover of Chrysler by Daimler. There were unbridgeable differences in the cultures of the two organizations. The expected synergy in brand architecture and platform synergy required deep integration of Daimler and Chrysler (Herndon, 2017). The envisaged global brand strategy and competitive positioning couldn't be achieved since Daimler and Chrysler engineers failed to design cars using each other's component parts. Daimler–Benz was a specialist producer of premium brands and made few efforts to widen its product range and customer base.

The union of the potential global powerhouse turned out to be a colossal disappointment. Cultural differences were attributed to the failure of the merger. Daimler which was known for luxury brands and affluent customers failed to understand the conscious concerns of the US automakers. The viewpoint that sharing of Mercedes components would undermine its brand made Daimler break its parts sharing agreement with Chrysler at a time when the company was facing auto crisis in the United States. By 2001, Chrysler was losing $3 billion annually, and its market share fell by approximately 40 per cent. Brand and channel conflict erupted. There were failures of product rationalization and supply chain optimization (Watkins, 2007).

By 2001, the value of the combined company dropped to roughly that of only Daimler–Benz before the merger. Chrysler's market share in the United States dropped to 14%. The combined company's failure to adjust to demand for smaller and efficient cars rather than sports utility vehicles and pickup trucks led to its poor performance as the US economy slumped (The Guardian, 2007).

Shareholders of Daimler believed that Chrysler was an affliction. Daimler sold off Chrysler to Cerberus Capital Management in the year 2007 for $7.4 billion. Comparatively the deal value came down from $38 billion in 1998 to $7.4 billion in 2007 for Chrysler Corporation.

Stock Market Reaction to Merger Announcement

The public announcement of the merger was made on May 7, 1998. Chrysler stock price went up, and Daimler–Benz share price went down. On the announcement day, the stock price of Daimler increased by 3.4%. On one day after announcement, the stock price declined by 1.4% (Fig. 44.1).

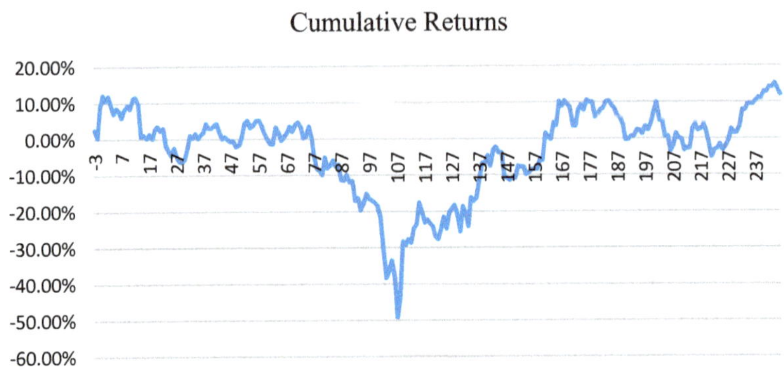

Fig. 44.1 Cumulative returns for Daimler surrounding the merger period

References

Annual Report (2017). https://www.daimler.com/documents/investors/reports/annual-report/daimler/daimler-ir-annual-report-2017.pdf

CNNMoney.News Deals (1998) Daimler Chrysler dawns. https://money.cnn.com/1998/05/07/deals/benz/. Accessed 13 Aug 2018

Daimler website (2018) Daimler at a Glance. https://www.daimler.com/company/at-a-glance.html. Accessed 13 Aug 2018

Herndon M (2017) What really happened to Daimler Chrysler. https://www.mapartners.net/insights/what-really-happened-daimler-chrysler. Accessed 13 Aug 2018

Krisher T, Strumpf D, Writers A (2014) Done deal: Fiat buys Chrysler assets. https://abcnews.go.com/Business/story?id=7804697&page=1. Accessed 13 Aug 2018

Lunden I (2018) Daimler buys remaining 25% stake of car sharing startup Car2Go from EuropCar for $85 M. https://techcrunch.com/2018/03/01/daimler-buys-remaining-25-stake-of-car-sharing-startup-car2go-from-europcar-for-85m/. Accessed 13 Aug 2018

NYTimes (2014) Fiat completes acquisition of Chrysler. https://dealbook.nytimes.com/2014/01/21/fiat-completes-acquisition-of-chrysler/. Accessed 13 Aug 2018

The Guardian (2007) International Edition. From $35 billion to $7.5 billion in nine years. https://www.theguardian.com/business/2007/may/14/motoring.lifeandhealth. Accessed 13 Aug 2018

Time (2017) Top 10 Chrysler moments. Cars, Crisis and Chrysler. Daimler Benz Merger. http://content.time.com/time/specials/packages/article/0,28804,1894731_1894734_1894722,00.html. Accessed 13 Aug 2018

Watkins MD (2007) Why DaimlerChrysler never got into gear, Harv Bus Rev. https://hbr.org/2007/05/why-the-daimlerchrysler-merger. Accessed 13 Aug 2018

Arcelor–Mittal Merger

45

In 1967, the world produced less than 500 million tons of steel. In 2016 the world produced over 1600 million tons. The global growth in steel industry is accounted by the new industrializing nations like Brazil, China, India, Iran, and Mexico. The global steel industry had long fragmented capacity. According to statistics, the top ten auto companies and major buyers of steel control about 95% of the market, while the top three ore companies control 75% of supply. Consolidation in the form of mergers and acquisitions would increase the pricing power for both suppliers and buyers. Capacity fragmentation is such that the top five steel companies control approximately 20% of the business. The major 20 global steel companies have 30% share of the one billion capacity.

Growth of Mittal Steel

Before its merger with Arcelor, Mittal Steel was the fourth largest producer of steel with Indian origin. Mittal Steel was formed in the year 2004 by the merger of two sister companies belonging to the Mittal family – LNM Holdings and ISPAT International. The growth of Mittal steel was centered around mergers and acquisitions. During the period 1985–2005, Mittal Steel acquired many steel making companies like Trinidad, Tobago, Sibalsa, Dosco, Ispat International, Island Steel Company, Unimetal, Alfasid, Iscar, Novahut, Polskie Huty, Balkan Steel, etc. During the above period, Mittal Steel made 19 acquisitions in countries ranging from China to Poland. Through acquisitions, the company made it to the list of Fortune 500 companies. Mittal Steel increased its capacity by ten times on account of these acquisitions. The products of Mittal Steel consisted of semifinished steel, flat products, finished products, wire rod, coated steels, tubes, and pipes. The strategy of Mittal Steel had been to acquire loss making companies owned by formerly public enterprises and then make investments to reduce their production costs and expand capacity.

B. R. Kumar, *Wealth Creation in the World's Largest Mergers and Acquisitions*,
Management for Professionals, https://doi.org/10.1007/978-3-030-02363-8_45

Arcelor Steel

In February 2002, Arcelor Steel was formed due to the merger between France's Usinor, Spain's Aceralia, and Luxembourg's Arbed. The Luxembourg government owned 5.6% of Arcelor. Arcelor products were used in all major steel segments which included automotive, construction, metal processing, primary transformation, household appliances, and packaging. Arcelor Steel had employed approximately 94,000 employees in over 60 countries. At the time of the deal, Arcelor was the world's largest steel manufacturer in terms of sales turnover. The company had a turnover of over euro 30 billion. Arcelor Steel produced long steel products, flat steel products, and inox steel. In the year 2006, Arcelor tool over Dofasco, Canada's largest steel producer for a deal valued at Can $ 5.6 billion. The deal came through after an intense bidding war against German ThyssenKrupp.

Arcelor–Mittal Deal

In January 2006, Lakshmi Mittal the chairman of Mittal Steel announced a hostile bid for Arcelor. After an intense struggle, the two companies merged to become the world's largest steel which controlled 10% of the global steel business. The deal was valued at $38.3 billion.

Arcelor's directors, including Chief Executive Guy Dolle, had opposed the takeover. The French, Luxembourg, and Spanish governments strongly opposed the takeover. The Belgian government, on the other hand, declared its stance as neutral and expressed interest in associating with both companies for future investments in research in Belgian steel plants. Indian government also took the stance that the attempts to block the deal would lead to trade war. Mittal's bid for Arcelor had stirred up passions in Europe, with politicians, ministers, and ordinary citizens joining in. Other steel makers, like Japan's Nippon Steel, have adopted poison pills to thwart hostile takeovers in the future. Goldman Sachs, Credit Suisse, and Citigroup were the advisors for Mittal Steel. The advisors for Arcelor included Merrill Lynch, Morgan Stanley, Deutsche Bank, AG, BNP Paribas SA, and UBS AG. JPMorgan was the advisor for the government of Luxembourg. Lazard was the counsellor for the Belgian government.

The Merger Battle

Defensive Mechanism Against the Deal

In its first step to prevent the deal, Arcelor transferred its subsidiary, Dofasco, into a trust and adopted the poison pill strategy to keep Mittal from buying Arcelor. The adoption of poison pill made it difficult for Mittal Steel to carry out the deal. Mittal met European governments and convinced them that the takeover would not result in any loss of jobs.

Arcelor CEO brought in the Russian Steel major Severstal, as its white knight. On May 26, 2006, Arcelor announced a deal with Severstal that would give it a controlling stake in Russia's largest steelmaker and $1.59 billion in cash in exchange for 32% stake in Arcelor. But shareholders were apprehensive. Arcelor also adopted a mechanism by which over 50% shareholders were required to vote against the deal for it to fail instead of a simple majority (Aiyar, 2006).

Reactions from Mittal Steel

Investment banks advising Mittal Steel activated shareholders across regions to sensitize the deal. Mordashov of Severstal Steel offered to hold only 25% of the Arcelor stock but was unsuccessful. Romain Zaleski, who owned 7.8% of the Arcelor stock, triggered the opposition to the deal with Severstal. Mittal had the support of Jose Aristrain who held 3.6% of shares of Arcelor. The unions too swung behind the deal as Mittal promised no job cuts. Mittal capped his stake under 45% and offered 12 of 18 seats on the board to independent directors, including those from the unions, and also agreed to a lock in on his shares for 5 years. By mid-June, the board of Arcelor was under pressure to consider the deal. Mittal raised his bid once again by 40% over the original offer price and a premium of 80% on the pre-offer price of Arcelor shares.

Severstal increased its valuation of Arcelor. The Arcelor management came under fire as the markets believed that the company had been undervalued. Arcelor presented a strategic plan to investors in a bid to persuade them that the company could generate more value as a stand-alone, than as part of Mittal Steel, and raised its dividend to euro 5 billion. This has provoked the institutional shareholders not to reelect the Arcelor Chairman and Vice Chairman as a protest against them for not being consulted over the anti-takeover defense mechanisms (Mukerjea, 2006a).

On June 25, 2006, the Arcelor board decided to go ahead with the merger with Mittal Steel and scrapped plans for Severstal Steel. The new company was called ArcelorMittal. Arcelor also paid Severstal euro 140 million as fine for the fallout of their talks. Lakshmi Mittal the owner of Mittal Steel became the president, and Joseph Kinsch, formerly, Arcelor chairman, was appointed the chairman of the new company till his retirement. Roland Junck, Arcelor's senior executive vice president, became the CEO of the company. Aditya Mittal became the CFO of the merged entity. ArcelorMittal sold Thuringen long carbon steel plant to Grupo for euro 591 million and Italian long carbon steel production, Travi e Profi lati di Pallanzeno, to Duferco for euro 117 million for regulatory approval from the European Commission (Mukerjea, 2006b).

The combined company was based in Luxembourg and called ArcelorMittal.

Terms of the Deal

According to the terms of the deal, Arcelor investors received 50.5% of ownership, and Mittal Steel investors received 49.5% of ownership of the merged company (ET Bureau, 2016). Arcelor shareholders received 13 Mittal Steel shares plus euro 150.60 in cash for 12 Arcelor shares. After the $33.7 billion deal, approximately 43% of the shares remained with the Mittal Family (Kumar, 2010). The new board had 18 members of which 6 were from Arcelor, 6 from Mittal Steel, 3 from Arcelor shareholders, and 3 representatives of employees. The management board consisted of seven members – four from Arcelor and three from Mittal Steel. Mittal family agreed to a standstill at 45% of share capital and a 5-year lock in period.

Expected Benefits of Merger

The combined ArcelorMittal with production of 110 million tons became three times larger than its nearest rival. The combined ArcelorMittal accounted for 10% of world's steel production. It occupied number one position in North America, South America, Europe, and Africa. The merger was expected to give Arcelor entry into emerging markets and access to raw materials through low-cost operations of Mittal Steel. It also created leadership position for Arcelor in North America. The merger was expected to give leadership position for Mittal Steel in high-end steel segment in Western Europe and access to low-cost manufacturing in Brazil. The merger was beneficial as Mittal got access to Arcelor products like flat products, cold rolling, and stainless steel which Mittal Steel was not producing. Mittal's access to raw materials and commodity steel became value additions at Arcelor plants which resulted in cost savings of $1 billion dollars (Knowledge@Wharton, 2006).

In 2011, ArcelorMittal split of the stainless steel division as a new company named Aperam. In 2012, low demand and excess capacity led 9 of the 25 blast furnaces to become idle. In October 2012, ArcelorMittal permanently shut down two furnaces at Florange, France. By December 2012, ArcelorMittal wrote down the goodwill in its European businesses by approximately $4.3 billion. During September 2014, ArcelorMittal and its partner Gerdau Ameristeel sold of its stake in Gallatin Steel to Nucor Corp for $770 million.

Merger Announcement and Wealth Creation

The public announcement of the hostile bid of Mittal on Arcelor was made on January 27, 2006. Arcelor agreed to the takeover by Mittal Steel on June 25, 2006. The analysis was done from the first hostile bid announcement event to the final acceptance event date. On announcement of the hostile bid, the Arcelor stock price increased by 4.56%, 6.07%, and 4.30%, respectively, on the 3-day window event period (−1 to +1 event period) (Fig. 45.1).

Fig. 45.1 Cumulative returns for Arcelor stock during the takeover period

References

Aiyar S (2006) The art of the deal. Cover story. Arcelor takeover. India Today, pp 36–42, July 10

ET Bureau (2016) Tale of two acquisitions: Mittal Steel's acquisition of Arcelor and Tata Steel's acquisition of Corus. https://economictimes.indiatimes.com/industry/indl-goods/svs/steel/tale-of-two-acquisitions-mittal-steelsacquisition-of-arcelor-and-tata-steels-acquisition-of-corus/articleshow/51624431.cms. Accessed 14 Aug 2018

Knowledge@Wharton (2006) Forging a Steel giant: Mittal's bid for Arcelor. http://knowledge.wharton.upenn.edu/article/forging-a-steel-giant-mittals-bid-for-arcelor/. Accessed 14 Aug 2018

Kumar R (2010) The Mittal Arcelor merger. Mergers and acquisitions, text and cases, 1st edn. Tata McGraw Hill Education, India, p 391–396

Mukerjea DN (2006a) Battleground Arcelor. Business World, pp 31–42, May 15

Mukerjea DN (2006b) Special report. Outmaneuvering Arcelor. Business World, pp 39–40, July 10

MIX
Papier aus verantwortungsvollen Quellen
Paper from responsible sources
FSC® C105338

If you have any concerns about our products,
you can contact us on
ProductSafety@springernature.com

In case Publisher is established outside the EU,
the EU authorized representative is:
Springer Nature Customer Service Center GmbH
Europaplatz 3, 69115 Heidelberg, Germany

Printed by Libri Plureos GmbH
in Hamburg, Germany